*Reef Fishes*
*of the*
*Sea of Cortez*

# Reef Fishes of the Sea of Cortez

## THE ROCKY-SHORE FISHES
## OF THE GULF OF CALIFORNIA

**DONALD A. THOMSON**

*Professor and Curator of Fishes*
*Department of Ecology and Evolutionary Biology*
*The University of Arizona, Tucson*

**LLOYD T. FINDLEY**

*Professor and Curator of Fishes*
*Escuela de Ciencias Marítimas y Alimentarias*
*Instituto Tecnológico y de Estudios Superiores de Monterrey*
*Guaymas, Sonora, México*

**ALEX N. KERSTITCH**

*Research Associate*
*Department of Ecology and Evolutionary Biology*
*The University of Arizona, Tucson*

*Illustrated by*
*ALEX N. KERSTITCH*
*TOR HANSEN*
*CHRIS VAN DYCK*

*A Wiley-Interscience Publication*

JOHN WILEY & SONS, *New York* • *Chichester* • *Brisbane* • *Toronto*

AN INTERNATIONAL
OCEANOGRAPHIC FOUNDATION SELECTION

**Miami, Florida 33149**

*Library of Congress Cataloging in Publication Data*

Thomson, Donald A
  Reef fishes of the Sea of Cortez.

  "A Wiley-Interscience publication."
  Bibliography: p.
  Includes index.
  1. Marine fishes—California, Gulf of.  2. Fishes—
California, Gulf of.  I. Findley, Lloyd T., joint
author.  II. Kerstitch, Alex N., joint author.
III. Title.

QL629.T56     597'.0926'1     78-18835
ISBN 0-471-86162-6

Printed in the United States of America

10 9 8 7 6 5 4 3 2 1

*To all students of Sea of Cortez fishes and to those ichthyologists who have made the study of Gulf of California fishes a part of their lives, especially Boyd W. Walker*

# Foreword

In recent years biologists have been turning their attention increasingly to reef fishes. One reason is the world food problem. Reef fishes represent a resource that, if properly managed, could have a significant impact on local protein supplies in many areas. Another reason is that reef fishes are becoming excellent systems to use in testing the theory of population biology[*]; for example, in the company of some Australian and American colleagues I have been examining some basic ideas on the organization of communities, using butterflyfishes as a test system. On the barrier reefs off northern Queensland censuses of more than 20 species can be made visually merely by swimming for measured distances and counting the individuals seen. I know of no group of animals in a complex terrestrial ecosystem such as a tropical rain-forest that can be counted with so little effort. Indeed, most diurnal reef fishes quickly become accustomed to the presence of human observers and go about their business in the open and in relatively restricted areas. Even the nocturnal reef fauna can be observed by divers with lights. These characteristics make reef fishes excellent subjects for various kinds of behavioral observation and experiment.

The perfection of scuba equipment in the last quarter century has had the interesting effect of opening up what was virtually an alien planet to biologists, for fish ecologists are now busily engaged in investigating the spatial structure of reef-fish populations, the coevolution of reef-fish herbivores and the plants they eat, the interaction between predacious fishes and their prey, and mimicry and other symbiotic relationships among reef fishes. These scientists have the immense advantage of being able to move quietly through three-dimensional space in the vicinity of the animals they are studying, an opportunity only dreamed of by their terrestrial colleagues. They are also able to work in a world of unsurpassed beauty and tranquility—and on some of the most attractive denizens of that world.

Of course, it is not only the professional biologist who is being attracted to reef fishes; they are also objects of interest to growing numbers of sport divers, many of whom, hopefully, will become competent amateur naturalists who will then be in a position to assist professional biologists in much the same way as amateur ornithologists and butterfly collectors do now. But a prerequisite of creating a cadre of knowledgeable amateurs is the availability of well-done manuals to provide sport divers with basic information on the identity, distribution, ecology, and behavior of reef fishes. *Reef Fishes of the Sea of Cortez* is especially valuable in this respect. Not only does it meet the highest professional standards, while being fully understandable to laypersons, it also covers a most critical area. The Gulf of California is a popular one for West Coast divers, and the fishes of its rocky reefs are largely representative of groups that are abundant on coral reefs. Therefore development of

---

[*] See P. R. Ehrlich, "The Population Biology of Coral Reef Fishes," *Annual Review of Ecology and Systematics*, vol. 6, pp. 211–247, 1975.

knowledge of the biology of the fishes of the Sea of Cortez will provide a critical comparison with that of their near relatives in coral habitats.

Finally, of course, this book will be welcomed by professional biologists. It will encourage those of us who do research on the ecology of fishes to do work in the Gulf, for problems of identification will now be minimized. It will also be of great value to all with an interest in Pacific zoogeography, representing as it does a study of a fascinating outlier of the great Indo-Pacific fauna.

PAUL R. EHRLICH

*Stanford, California*
*September 7, 1978*

# *Preface*

Our knowledge of marine reef fishes has expanded greatly in the last two decades, primarily because of the advances made in underwater technology. Foremost was the development of scubadiving which opened the frontiers of the shallow waters of the sea to biologists and a rapidly growing cadre of recreational divers. Subsequent developments, such as motorized submersibles, man-in-the-sea underwater habitats, and underwater television, have lent technological sophistication to underwater investigations. Most research, however, is still being done by the free-swimming diver aided only by scuba or the simple snorkle. Furthermore, the recent wide application of rotenone-based ichthyocides for the scientific collecting of fishes has led to the discovery and description of hundreds of new species, many of which are never or rarely ever seen unless driven from their shelters by this selective fish poison. These advances in technique have resulted in the rapid accumulation of new information on the behavior, ecology, and systematics of reef fishes in the scientific and lay literature. Fishwatching, like birdwatching, is becoming a popular pastime that requires only a dive mask, snorkle, and swim fins and can be enjoyed by young and old.

Fundamental to the enjoyment of fishwatching is the ability to identify the fishes one sees. The proficiency in identification demonstrated by both professional and amateur birdwatchers has not yet been achieved by fishwatchers because of the more difficult access to the world of fishes and the relative paucity of field guides and books on fishes compared with the much greater availability of bird books. In the last decade, however, several excellent fish guides have appeared for the areas most popular and accessible to lay divers and scientists.

In *Reef Fishes of the Sea of Cortez* we present the first comprehensive treatment of the reef- or rocky-shore fish fauna of the Gulf of California. The foundation for this work was cast long ago, beginning with the many nineteenth-century fish-collecting expeditions in the Gulf which resulted in volumes of scientific descriptions of fishes from North American waters. The first popular book to treat of Gulf of California fishes was Lionel A. Walford's *Marine Game Fishes of the Pacific Coast from Alaska to the Equator* (1937), an excellent and still highly useful book (recently reprinted) for anglers and ichthyologists. In the late-1940s Drs. Boyd W. Walker and Kenneth S. Norris and their students from the University of California at Los Angeles began a thorough systematic collection of Gulf of California fishes and prepared a working checklist that has been extremely useful to all serious students of the area. Many of Dr. Walker's graduate students have done research on Gulf fishes, and two in particular, Dr. Richard H. Rosenblatt (Scripps Institution of Oceanography) and Dr. Edmund (Ted) S. Hobson (National Marine Fisheries Service), have made significant contributions to their systematics and ecology.

We began our Gulf of California fish collection in 1963 at the University of Arizona with a few Gulf specimen lots given to us by Dr. Charles H. Lowe, Jr. (University of Arizona), which were originally gifts from Dr. Walker's UCLA Fish Collection. The senior author (D. A. Thomson), assisted by William H. Eger and Alex Kerstitch, began a series of collections and observations of fishes along the Gulf's Sonoran coast. In 1968 Lloyd T. Findley, a former student of Dr. Walker's, joined us as assistant curator of fishes. A long period of extensive systematics collections, their curation and study, occupied the next 10 years. The UA Fish Collection, which has grown to more than 100,000 specimens and is presently curated by D. A. Thomson (curator) and Matthew R. Gilligan (assistant curator), forms the basis for this book.

The need for field guides on Gulf of California fishes became obvious to us in our teaching of courses in ichthyology and marine ecology. After putting together a rough family key we formed a team that included Tor Hansen, a fine young illustrator, Lloyd T. Findley, an exacting fish taxonomist and Sea of Cortez enthusiast, and Alex Kerstitch, an exceptionally talented artist, photographer, and underwater naturalist. We soon realized that our collections, the literature, and the state of the art of the taxonomy of certain groups of Gulf fishes were inadequate to produce a comprehensive book that would include all Gulf of California fishes. We tried to optimize our resources and talents by concentrating on the rocky-shore or reef-fish species.

To many the term "reef" will be interpreted to mean "coral reef." A reef, however, may be any hard structure, parts of which may lie near the surface of the water. Artificial reefs can be constructed by dumping old car bodies, tires, boats, concrete blocks, and so on, into the sea to provide a substrate for the attachment and growth of marine life and the crevices used as shelters by mobile marine animals. The heterogenous surfaces of natural rocky reefs form a firm substrate for the attachment of algae and many sessile invertebrates (e.g., sponges, clams, anemones, hydroids, and barnacles), and the irregularities of rock formations provide holes, crevices, and caves used as refuges by fishes and a wide variety of mobile invertebrates (e.g., crabs, octopuses, and starfish). Structurally, a warmwater rocky-reef community may be almost as complex ecologically as a coral-reef community that includes many species of colorful fishes characteristic of these formations. In the tropical eastern Pacific, in which the Sea of Cortez is situated, coral reefs are sparse, but the hundreds of miles of rocky shorelines and offshore patch reefs are inhabited by a fish fauna similar to that of the coral-rich Caribbean Sea. In fact, tropical eastern Pacific fishes are commonly mistaken for those of the tropical western Atlantic, a forgivable error, considering the scarcity of popular information on the former.

In *Reef Fishes of the Sea of Cortez* we emphasize ecology or natural history as well as taxonomy and highlight the common and more conspicuous reef fishes. We are concerned primarily with fishes that are true residents of reefs and only briefly mention the transients and visitors whose principal habitat is elsewhere (e.g., sandy shores, estuaries, or pelagic zone). Overall, we present information on 271 species of reef residents and supplement it with notes on about 45 species of transients or visitors to reefs. In addition, we comment on several tropical eastern Pacific, Caribbean, and Indo-west Pacific reef fishes closely related to Sea of Cortez fishes to give the reader a better appreciation of the origin and affinities of this fish fauna and to demonstrate to those unfamiliar with tropical reef fishes how similar and how different they are around the world.

D. A. THOMSON
L. T. FINDLEY
A. N. KERSTITCH

*Tucson, Arizona*
*January 1979*

# *Acknowledgments*

We are grateful to our numerous colleagues, students, and friends who have directly and indirectly contributed to the content of this book. We are especially indebted to Boyd W. Walker for his extensive work on Gulf of California fishes, for providing research space and access to his personal library and the UCLA Fish Collection for one of the authors (Findley), and for guiding the development (along with Wayne J. Baldwin) of Findley's taxonomic skills. Dr. Walker's unpublished checklist of Gulf of California fishes served as an invaluable guide to our studies. The cooperation and advice of Edmund (Ted) S. Hobson is greatly appreciated. Dr. Hobson reviewed the manuscript critically and permitted us to use several of his excellent underwater photographs. His ecological research on Gulf fishes added considerable relevant information to the species accounts. The research of Richard H. Rosenblatt and his students has contributed much to the systematics of tropical eastern Pacific fishes and has made our task of compiling taxonomic and zoogeographic information less difficult. We thank Edwin Janss, Jr., for his generosity in permitting us to use some of his superb underwater photographs, John S. Stephens, Jr. (and the University of California Press) for letting us use his illustrations of Gulf chaenopsid blennies, and Gerald R. Allen for sending us a copy of his and Loren P. Woods' manuscript on eastern Pacific *Eupomacentrus*. We also thank the following for contributing photographs or illustrations: James E. Böhlke, John E. McCosker, David G. Lindquist, Norman S. Smith, Charles E. Lehner, Matthew R. Gilligan, Richard M. McCourt, Douglas A. Peacock, Christine Flanagan, and John van Ruth.

For logistic support we thank the University of Arizona Foundation and anonymous donors for funds to illustrate Gulf fishes. We owe special thanks to Jack Abert for his gift of the research vessel *La Sirena* to the University of Arizona and for permission to hire her captain, Felipe Maldonado, who has competently and conscientiously served us on many collecting expeditions in the Sea of Cortez. We greatly appreciate the warm hospitality of Chuck, Gratia, and Mike Duecy, who opened their beach home to us in San Carlos, and acknowledge with thanks the gift of their boat, *Chuparosa Dos,* to the University of Arizona. We are grateful to A. Richard Kassander, Carl N. Hodges, the staff of the Environmental Research Laboratory, and the Universidad de Sonora for use of their facilities at Puerto Peñasco since 1965. We thank Albert R. Mead for his moral support and encouragement over the years and for the many things he and John R. Hendrickson did for the Marine Sciences Program which aided our work on Gulf fishes.

The preparation of the manuscript was furthered by the participation of many people and we sincerely thank them all. Bill Eger helped to establish our Fish Collection and Tor Hansen did many of the earlier illustrations. Bill Reynolds and Yvonne Maluf helped to edit the first complete draft of the manuscript, and Christine Flanagan and Matt Gilligan the final. They and Nancy Moffatt were most help-

# ACKNOWLEDGMENTS

ful in checking various details. The following assisted in the preparation of species accounts: Bill Reynolds (Pomacanthidae), Jeff Leis (Haemulidae and Diodontidae), Dave Lindquist (Chaenopsidae), and Phil Miles (Gobiidae). Noni McKibbin, Nancy Moffatt, Charles Lehner, Matt Gilligan, Rich McCourt, Manuel Molles, and Libby Stull contributed useful information and advice. We were fortunate in obtaining the services of Chris van Dyck who prepared most of the introductory maps and diagrams and illustrated several fishes. The tedious task of typing and retyping the manuscript was borne by several people over the years. We especially thank Kathy Boyer, Erlinda and Virginia Ramirez, Karen Bieber, Verla Goodman, Yvonne Maluf, and Peggy Turk. The final stages of preparation were aided by Peggy Turk, Carrie Franz, Jenean Thomson, and Kathleen Kennedy, who typed the final draft. We also thank Eleanor Shisslak, Roberta Streicher, and the office staff of the Department of Ecology and Evolutionary Biology for their cooperation, Mary Conway and Joan Samuels of John Wiley and Sons, for their patience, and Lupe Hendrickson for correcting our Spanish.

We appreciate the enthusiastic efforts of the many students in the senior author's ichthyology and marine ecology classes for help in collecting, sorting, and identifying fishes.

We especially appreciate their creative efforts in preparing many unpublished research papers on Gulf fishes. Most of the marine sciences students, their spouses and friends, contributed in various ways. We thank Kurt Thomson for his keen eye and angling skill, which resulted in the addition of some uncommon species to our collections, and his sisters Madelon, Lisa, and Erin for help and companionship on field trips. The following people, excluding those already mentioned, are also gratefully acknowledged: R. Brusca, R. Houston, N. Yensen, G. Hansen, M. Helvey, A. Gollub, J. Sheffield, S. Amesbury, D. Lassuy, J. Petti, P. Cook, P. Winkler, E. Synder-Conn, S. Kessler, C. Constant, K. Muench, J. van Ruth, J. Antlfinger, P. Magarelli, D. Scoggin, J. Sotelo, M. Niemi, J. Orzel, S. Jones, L. Doner, T. Miller, C. O'Kelley, T. French, W. Fee, K. Curry, G. Key, M. McCourt, T. Cox, E. Kehl, R. Bock and J. Carreto. We also thank D. Peacock, M. Robinson, M. Stinson, D. Hoese, S. Strand, L. Montgomery, A. Mearns, A. Kubo, C. Niethammer, T. Hinton, J. Foster, S. Applegate, B. Winn, W. Cornell, A. Findley, E. and J. Fisher and many members of the Sea of Cortez Institute of Biological Research.

We are grateful to the people and government of Mexico for the hospitality and cooperation that enabled us to study Gulf fishes and for providing an atmosphere of congeniality, friendship, and goodwill. From the Universidad de Sonora we thank Manuel Puebla, Carlos Peña, Xico Murietta, Agustin Cortés, and Ramon Durazo. From the Escuela de Ciencias Maritimas y Tecnología de Alimentos, I.T.E.S.M., at Guaymas we thank Henry Schafer, Fernando Manrique, Leon Tissot, Karl Heinz Holtschmit, and Ed Pfeiler. We also thank David Moore and Jim Ure of the Peñasco Experimental Unit for their support over the years and Magdalena Mahieux for her skillful interpretation of Spanish during our recent field trips to Mexico.

We are especially indebted to Christine Flanagan, without whose considerable help in editing, proofing galleys, meeting deadlines, and correcting our errors this book would still be unfinished.

## ACKNOWLEDGMENTS

Finally, we owe our deepest gratitude to our loving wives, Jenean Thomson, Sonnie Findley, and Dana Kerstitch, for their companionship and encouragement as well as their patience and understanding during the many working weekends, evenings, and summers spent away from home.

D. A. T.
L. T. F.
A. N. K.

# *Contents*

# Introduction

Millions of years ago the Baja California peninsula was part of what is now the mainland of Mexico. As the continental crust shifted along the San Andreas fault system, Baja California began to separate from the mainland, moving gradually northwestward. In the process a new sea was created—the Sea of Cortez, or Gulf of California.

The official name of the Sea of Cortez is El Golfo de California (the Gulf of California). On sixteenth century maps it appears as Mer de Californie (Sea of California) or Mer Vermeille (Vermillion Sea). In 1540 the Spanish explorer Francisco de Ulloa, who discovered that "les Californies" (the Californias) was not an island, named this sea El Mar de Cortés (the Sea of Cortez) after Hernán Cortés, his leader and the conqueror of Mexico. Today the Gulf of California is popularly referred to as the Sea of Cortez. We use both names interchangeably in this book.

The Gulf of California (Plate 1) has been aptly characterized by Dr. Boyd W. Walker of the University of California as a "caricature of oceanography" because its oceanographic dynamics are dramatically exaggerated.* It has deep basins in its central and lower portions and some of the greatest tides in the world in its upper reaches. It contains about a hundred islands and strong upwelling of cold, nutrient-rich waters are evident along both its coasts. The annual sea surface temperatures in its northernmost portions range from below 50°F (10°C) to more than 90°F (32°C). Because the Gulf acts as a large evaporation basin, its average salinity is higher than that of the Pacific off the Baja California coast. Surrounded by arid deserts, it is buttressed from the cool, moist ocean breezes by high Baja California mountains. The semi-isolation of the Gulf protects it from the swells of the Pacific and makes it appear at times like a large, salty lake, although its tranquility is occasionally disturbed by violent local storms known as "chubascos" and devastating tropical hurricanes.

Rocky shores mark the central and lower Baja coast and occur around nearly all Gulf islands. Hundreds of miles of gently sloping sandy beaches interrupted by short stretches of rocky headlands characterize the mainland. Both coastlines have numerous coves, bays, lagoons, and estuaries bordered by mangrove swamps and salt marshes. The lagoons in the upper Gulf exhibit higher salinities at their heads than at their mouths and thus are considered "negative" estuaries.

These estuarine lagoons, often at the mouths of dried-up river beds, are referred to as "esteros." Estuaries in the lower Gulf are fed by freshwater rivers so that their salinities grade from fresh at their heads to brackish at their mouths, and thus are considered "positive."

* For reviews of the physical oceanography of the Gulf of California see Roden (1964), Parker (1964), Brusca (1973), Thomson et al. (1969), and Hendrickson (1974).

1

## INTRODUCTION

Before the construction of Hoover Dam in 1935 the Colorado River delta was a positive estuarine system. Since that time dams and the agricultural use of water have literally dried up the lower Colorado River which empties into the Gulf. Evaporation has turned the delta into a negative estuarine system, and formerly brackish areas are now hypersaline.

The great diversity of topographic and bathymetric features of the Gulf of California has produced a variety of habitats for fishes and other marine life. The only thorough analysis of the distribution of Gulf of California fishes was done by Walker (1960). Walker recorded 586 species of fishes in the Gulf which he estimated to constitute 85 to 90% of the actual fish fauna. He analyzed the zoogeographic affinities of 526 shallow-water fishes and noted that 73% of the species are Panamic (tropical), 10%, northern (temperate), and 17%, endemic; that is, found only in the Gulf of California. He noted that two-thirds of the species have principal ranges extending beyond the Gulf to the south, most as far as Panama. Thirty-eight species range commonly both north and south and 50 species range only to the north. About half of the northern-ranging species occur as disjuncts in the upper Gulf; that is, they also appear along the Pacific coast but are absent or rare in the lower Gulf. The remaining 92 species, which had not been collected outside the Gulf, he considered endemic.

Using this pattern of species distribution, Walker proposed four faunal areas, each characterized by a distinctive assemblage of shore fishes:

the upper Gulf, which extends north of a line from Bahía San Francisquito past the southern tip of Isla Tiburón; . . . the central Gulf, which includes the short length of shoreline from Bahía Kino to Guaymas on the east side of the Gulf, and the much longer shoreline between Bahía San Francisquito and La Paz; the Cabo San Lucas area, which extends north from the cape to the vicinity of La Paz, and the southeast Gulf, which includes the low, estero-broken shoreline south of Guaymas (Walker, 1960).

Walker characterized the Gulf fish fauna as being "clearly part of the Panamic fauna." Briggs (1974), in the latest treatise on marine zoogeography, places the Gulf of California (with its boundaries at La Paz and Topolobampo) in the warm temperate California region mainly because of its wide thermal regime. Rosenblatt (1974) and Hubbs (1974) take exception to this view because of the high number of tropical species in the Gulf, and we agree with them. Even in the far northern Gulf most of the rocky-shore species have tropical affinities (Thomson and Lehner, 1976).

In the 15 years following Walker's 1960 paper numerous collections of fishes were made in the Gulf of California. The University of Arizona has assembled more than 1000 collections from this region (see Figure 1), and several California institutions, including Scripps Institution of Oceanography and the University of California, Los Angeles, have made extensive collections in the Gulf. These new data essentially support the boundaries of Walker's faunal areas. For rocky-shore fishes we combine Walker's "Cabo San Lucas area and southeast Gulf" into a lower Gulf region. The reef-fish faunas of the Cabo San Lucas-La Paz region and the Topolobampo-Mazatlán region may indeed be distinct enough to justify another subdivision, but reef-fish collections along the predominately sandy shore of the southeastern Gulf are presently inadequate to support another faunal area.

2

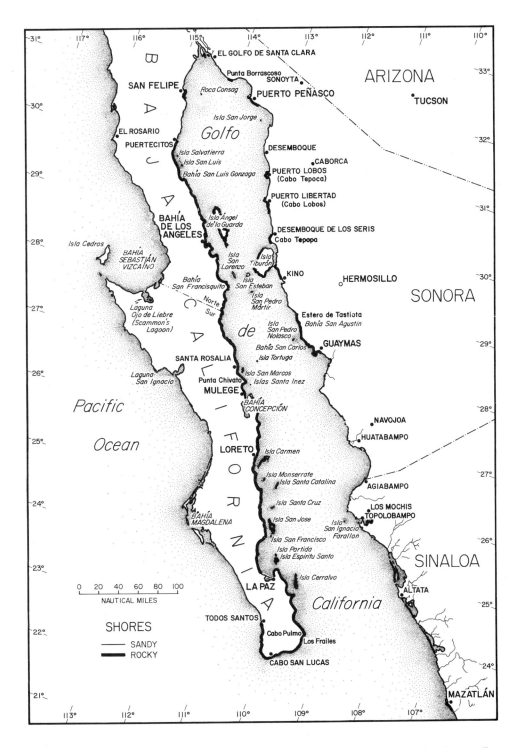

Figure 1    Locality map of the Sea of Cortez (Golfo de California) shows the extent of rocky coastline within the Gulf. Fish collections and observations have been made at all localities given on this map as well as at many sites not labeled.

3

## INTRODUCTION

Including deep-sea and pelagic fishes, the Sea of Cortez supports a rich fish fauna of over 800 species which can be categorized ecologically by its distinctive communities: (1) pelagic (inshore and offshore surface waters), (2) deep-sea (mesopelagic, bathypelagic, and abyssal), (3) offshore shelf (soft bottoms at intermediate depths), (4) sandy shore and estuarine (inshore soft bottoms), and (5) reef (rocky shores and rocky bottoms). In this book we treat only the reef or rocky-shore fishes, a diverse group of species consisting of 39 families and 271 species.

# The Reef-Fish Community

The characterization of a "reef" depends on the perspective of the discipline requiring a definition. Nautically, a reef is an offshore consolidated rock hazard to navigation with a least depth of 10 fathoms (20 m) or less. Geologically, reefs are rigid wave-resistant formations constructed of the calcium carbonate secretions of marine organisms (e.g., coral reefs). Ecologically, reefs are any submerged rocky structures that provide a hard substrate for growth of marine life. We use the ecological definition of a reef that includes all rocky surfaces, such as boulder and consolidated rock beaches, cliff faces, platform benches, and patch and coral reefs.

We consider reef fishes to be those whose life histories are intimately associated with a rocky substrate for the purposes of feeding, shelter, and reproduction. These fishes spend a majority of their time on reefs or along rocky shorelines. Our designation of a reef fish as opposed to a nonreef fish concerns the significance of interaction of that species with a rocky substrate. The selection of fishes to be included in this book was based on what we know of the biology of a species and how often we collected or observed that species over rocky bottoms. Our final decision was made on what we considered to be the principal habitat of the fish. We have been conservative in our categorizations by excluding many fishes that we consider to be visitors or transients rather than residents of the reef (these fishes are discussed in the last chapter). Among them are pelagic and sandy-bottom fishes that frequently occur over reefs (mullets, mojarras, jacks, and needlefishes). Likewise, we have excluded all sharks, rays, and skates, although some (stingrays) are frequently seen over reefs. On the other hand, certain fishes that regularly exploit the reef-sand interface, feeding on sandy-bottom invertebrates while obtaining shelter from the reef (grunts, porgies, and goatfishes), are considered reef residents. In addition, we have included a few species of typical reef-fish families whose habits, though poorly known, indicate at least marginal association with reefs. Using these criteria, we have designated 271 species as reef fishes, almost one-half of all the bony fishes in the Sea of Cortez.

THE REEF-FISH COMMUNITY

## *ROCKY HABITATS*

About one-half of the coastline of the Sea of Cortez is rocky (Plate 1 and Figure 1). Almost all of the Baja California coast of the Sea of Cortez is rocky, whereas the mainland coast of Sonora and Sinaloa has short stretches of rock formations separated by extensive sandy beaches and estuaries. Add to this the rocky shores of about 100 islands and the extensive offshore patch reefs and it becomes clear that reefs are major habitats in the Gulf of California.

The rocky-shore habitat of the Gulf of California is better developed than the offshore patch-reef habitat, which in warm shallow seas (such as the Caribbean) is dominated by coral reefs. Coral reefs are rare in the eastern Pacific; in the Gulf the only one of reasonably large size can be found between Cabo Pulmo and Los Frailes in the cape region. Whether these Cabo Pulmo reefs are "true coral reefs" is controversial for coral grows here on rock dikes of extruded igneous rocks (Squires, 1959). Nevertheless, these reefs support a species-rich coral reef community (Brusca and Thomson, 1975).

The Gulf's northernmost rocky reefs occur at Punta Borrascoso, Sonora, about 35 miles (56 km) southeast of the small fishing village of El Golfo de Santa Clara. A platform reef constructed of volcanic rock, beachrock, and coquina limestone stretches out to a considerable distance offshore (Figure 2). Sport fishermen from Cholla Bay (Puerto Peñasco) fish this series of patch reefs for groupers and other bottom fishes. Extensive platform benches at Puerto Peñasco are formed of coquina limestone running approximately east to west. To the north these reefs terminate at

Figure 2 Aerial view of Punta Borrascoso, Sonora, the northernmost rocky shore in the Gulf of California. The dark patches in the sea are reefs that extend a considerable distance offshore. (Photograph by D. A. Thomson.)

6

Figure 3   Station Beach Reef, Puerto Peñasco, Sonora, a coquina limestone, beach rock reef bench with many large tide pools provides shelter for shore fishes in a region of extreme tides. (Photograph by D. A. Thomson.)

Punta Roca de Toro, known locally as Pelican Point, and to the south at the mouth of Estero Morua, 6 miles (10 km) east of Punta Peñasco. Pelican Point is a granitic outcropping with numerous angular boulders covering parts of the reef. Punta Peñasco is a basaltic rocky point. Black rounded boulders are strewn over the adjacent platform reef. At low tide numerous tide pools are exposed. The largest and deepest pools occur at Station Beach Reef (Figure 3) which is a 6-mile-(10-km)-long reef bench bordered by a coarse sand and shell beach running from Punta Peñasco to Estero Morua. These limestone reefs support a rich flora and fauna in comparison to the platform reef at Punta Borrascoso which is relatively species-poor.

Southeast of Puerto Peñasco a series of subtidal patch reefs extends from the mouth of Estero San Jorge to Isla San Jorge, a precipitous rocky island a few miles offshore populated by a large colony of sea lions. Station Beach Reef is separated by a continuous sandy shoreline from the next rocky outcropping at Puerto Lobos (Cabo Tepoca) about 95 miles (153 km) southeast. The rocky outcropping of Cabo Tepoca consists of a dense basaltic rock known as diabase (Figure 4). The intertidal flora and fauna of these diabase reef benches are not so rich as those of Puerto Peñasco, but many tropical species not found at Puerto Peñasco have the northern limits of their ranges at Puerto Lobos.

South of Puerto Lobos, separated by about 30 miles (48 km) of sandy beach, is the next rocky outcropping at Puerto Libertad (Cabo Lobos). Farther south the mainly rocky shoreline of mixed rock types and boulder-cobble beaches extends down to the northern mouth of the channel (El Infiernillo) between Isla Tiburón and

7

Figure 4 The rocky shore line of Puerto Lobos (Cabo Tepoca), Sonora, consists mainly of a hard basaltic diabase outcropping. (Photograph by D. A. Thomson.)

Figure 5 Tide pools of Punta Robinson at Puerto Libertad (Cabo Lobos), Sonora. Punta Cirio lies on the horizon to the south. (Photograph by L. T. Findley.)

Figure 6 Bahía San Agustin, Sonora. Rocky headlands and cobble beaches extend from south of Estero Tastiota to Guaymas. (Photograph by Alex Kerstitch.)

Figure 7 Playa Algodones, north of Bahía San Carlos, Sonora. Just outside the gentle breakers are numerous shallow patch reefs that support a rich community of fishes. (Photograph by D. A. Thomson.)

Figure 8   Isla San Pedro Nolasco, Sonora. This small offshore island has a steep rocky shoreline and supports a large colony of California sea lions, *Zalophus californianus* (Lesson). (Photograph by Alex Kerstitch.)

the Sonoran mainland (Figure 5). From there sandy shores and esteros prevail to just north of Bahía Kino, where a large rocky headland emerges and marks the boundary between the upper and central Gulf. Entering the central Gulf we find sandy beaches from Bahía Kino to Estero Tastiota. Just below this estero an almost uninterrupted rocky coast extends south to Guaymas (Figure 6).

The greatest diversity of rocky coastlines on the eastern side of the Gulf occurs in the vicinity of Guaymas. There are rocky cliffs, boulder beaches, and fine sand beaches with numerous shallow patch reefs close to shore (Figure 7). Offshore a small island (Isla San Pedro Nolasco) supports the richest assemblage of reef fishes in the area as well as a large colony of sea lions (Figure 8). Below Guaymas (to Mazatlán, where reefs again appear) is a nearly uninterrupted sandy-shore coastline more than 400 miles long (650 km) with numerous positive estuaries and with only a poorly developed rocky shore at Topolobampo. However, the sole island along this coast, Isla San Ignacio Farallon, is similar to Isla San Pedro Nolasco in the composition of its substrate and richness of its fish fauna (Figure 9).

The Baja California coast of the Gulf is a nearly continuous rocky shoreline (with scattered sandy beaches) beginning at Puertecitos and ending far to the south at Cabo San Lucas. North of Puertecitos a poorly developed rocky headland rises at San Felipe and a small rocky island, Roca Consag, lies offshore (Figure 10).

Three large bays are found along the Gulf's Baja coast. The smallest and northernmost is Bahía de Los Angeles, a shallow sandy inlet broken by several rocky bluffs. It is protected from the open Gulf by a chain of about 15 small rocky

Figure 9   Isla San Ignacio Farallon, the only rocky island along the southeastern Gulf coast from Guaymas to Mazatlán, supports a rich reef-fish fauna and a large colony of sea lions. (Photograph courtesy of Matthew Gilligan.)

islands. The large Isla Angel de la Guarda lies offshore (Figure 11). Farther south is Bahía Concepción, an elongated narrow bay more than 30 miles long. The eastern shore consists mainly of sand or pebble beaches. Along the western shore several rocky promontories are interrupted by small sandy coves. The bay is the most protected large body of water in the Sea of Cortez. Because of its poor circulation, summer water temperatures may exceed 95°F (35°C).

The largely rocky coast between Bahía Concepción and Bahía de La Paz is bordered by several small to moderately sized islands. The protected waters near Loreto embody one of the richest habitats for central Gulf reef fishes (see Figure 12).

The largest body of water along the Gulf's Baja coast is Bahía de La Paz, a sweeping, hook-shaped bay. Rocky shores line its southeast tip (Figure 13). Bahía de La Paz marks the transition from the central Gulf to the insular Cape region of the lower Gulf, where the colonization of several Indo-west Pacific shore fishes contributes to its fauna.

Below Bahía de La Paz are broad sandy beaches and rocky headlands. The only coral reef in the Sea of Cortez occurs in this region at Cabo Pulmo and Los Frailes. Although the tide range is not great in the lower Gulf, the rocky tide pools along this coastline rival those of Puerto Peñasco in size and surpass them in richness (Figure 14). At Cabo San Lucas the Gulf and Baja California end abruptly in bold, precipitous rocks that jut out at the tip of the peninsula (Figure 15). Just around these rocks the huge swells of the open Pacific crash on unprotected beaches. Going north

11

Figure 10   Roca Consag (north side). A number of Sea of Cortez reef-fish species find their northern distributional limits at this small precipitous island in the far northern Gulf. The guano-covered slopes attest to a large population of sea birds. (Photograph by L. T. Findley.)

Figure 11   Puerto Refugio, Isla Angel de la Guarda. This protected bay at the north end of the island shelters sea lions and many kinds of sea birds. Several species of central Gulf fishes may be found inhabiting the island's rocky shore. (Photograph courtesy of Doug Peacock.)

Figure 12 A cove at the northern end of Isla Carmen, near Loreto, B.C.S. The calm, clear waters of this region of the central Gulf are ideal for studying reef fishes. (Photograph by L. T. Findley.)

Figure 13 Puerto Ballandra, La Paz region, Baja California Sur. This beautiful shallow bay is typical of the diverse shoreline in the La Paz vicinity. Sandy beaches, mangrove esteros, and rocky shores support a rich mixture of shore fishes. (Photograph by D. A. Thomson.)

13

Figure 14   Tide pools along the rocky coastline near Cabo San Lucas, Baja California Sur. This region just below Puerto Chileno has the most extensive rocky intertidal zone in the lower Gulf. (Photograph by Alex Kerstitch.)

Figure 15   This short stretch of sandy beach at Cabo San Lucas borders the Gulf and Pacific sides of Baja California Sur. (Photograph by Alex Kerstitch.)

along the Pacific coast of Baja California there are long stretches of sandy beaches and rocky bluffs until Bahía Magdalena is reached. It is in this great system of bays and lagoons that the northward distribution of many Sea of Cortez fishes ends.

## REEF-FISH DIVERSITY

To appreciate the diversity of reef-fish species in the Sea of Cortez it is helpful to compare the Gulf of California's fauna with that of similar regions. This is no easy task because there are few comprehensive works on marine-shore fish faunas and fewer still solely on reef fishes. In recent years, however, extensive surveys of marine fishes have resulted in some excellent works on regional fish faunas that include taxonomic groups comparable to those found in the Sea of Cortez. Using the most recent comprehensive books on fishes of Hawaii (Gosline and Brock, 1960), California (Miller and Lea, 1972), the northern Gulf of Mexico (Walls, 1975), and the Bahamas (Böhlke and Chaplin, 1968), we have compared the reef fishes found in these areas with those of the Gulf of California. In Table 1 we have listed the families and numbers of species of reef-associated fishes that occur in these regions. We have also categorized the reef fishes on the basis of the information provided in these works, although sometimes we found that this was not possible because habitat information was often lacking. Nevertheless, we feel that the numbers listed for each region is a reasonable estimate of the diversity of reef-fish species.

It is not surprising that the coral-rich shores of the Bahamas support the greatest number of reef fishes (323 species). Hawaii, with about 306 species, is almost as rich as the Bahamas, but this figure is probably an underestimate because recent collecting and taxonomic changes have increased the total species listed for the Hawaiian Islands from 584 to 681 (Randall, 1976). The northern Gulf of Mexico (161 species) is the most depauperate region of the five for reef fishes probably because of the relative scarcity of reefs in this region of primarily soft bottoms as well as the rigorous warm temperate physical regime. The warm-to-cold temperate Pacific waters off the California coast support an ichthyofauna that is markedly different in composition from that of the subtropical regions. Nevertheless, the Sea of Cortez has more species (but not genera) in common with this coastal region than any of the others primarily because of its geographical proximity rather than habitat or environmental similarities.

Zoogeographically, the reef-fish fauna of the Gulf of California most closely parallels that of the Bahamas (i.e., tropical western Atlantic; e.g., see Rosenblatt, 1967). This is especially evident in the numbers of shared genera in the families Muraenidae (morays), Serranidae (sea basses), Lutjanidae (snappers), Haemulidae (grunts), Pomacentridae (damselfishes), Labridae (wrasses), Blenniidae (combtooth blennies), Clinidae (clinids), Chaenopsidae (tube blennies), Gobiidae (gobies), and Gobiesocidae (clingfishes). Several species found in the Gulf closely match others in the tropical western Atlantic that appear to be nearly identical in morphology, behavior, and ecology. These species are variously termed geminate, sibling, twin, cryptic, or, more simply, species pairs. Most species pairs can be taxonomically separated by minor morphological differences, whereas in others the separation into two species is difficult or questionable. The number of species pairs between the western Atlantic and eastern Pacific may exceed 100, although the eastern Pacific fish fauna is not yet well enough known to present a complete list. Examples of

*Table 1.   Reef-Fish Diversity of the Sea of Cortez Compared with Estimates for Some Other Regions*

| Family | Numbers of Species | | | | |
|---|---|---|---|---|---|
| | Hawaii[1] | California[2] | Sea of Cortez[3] | Northern Gulf of Mexico[4] | Bahamas[5] |
| Xenocongridae (false morays) | 2 | — | — | — | 2 |
| Muraenidae (morays) | 32 | 1 | 16 | 2 | 10 |
| Congridae[6] (garden eels only) | — | — | 3 | — | 1 |
| Ophidiidae (brotulas only) | 4 | 1 | 8 | 2 | 5 |
| Antennariidae (frogfishes) | 7 | 1 | 3 | 4 | 7 |
| Holocentridae (squirrelfishes) | 15 | — | 2 | 3 | 8 |
| Aulostomidae (trumpetfishes) | 1 | — | — | 1 | 1 |
| Fistulariidae (cornetfishes) | 2 | — | 2 | 1 | 1 |
| Syngnathidae[6] (seahorses and pipefishes) | 3 | 2 | 3 | 3 | 5 |
| Scorpaenidae (scorpionfishes and rockfishes) | 7 | 61[7] | 3 | 1 | 5 |
| Caracanthidae (caracanthids) | 2 | — | — | — | — |
| Cottidae (sculpins) | — | 43[7] | — | — | — |
| Agonidae (poachers) | — | 17[7] | — | — | — |
| Liparididae (snailfishes) | — | 6 | — | — | — |
| Serranidae (sea basses) | 10[7] | 12 | 22 | 28 | 29 |
| Grammistidae (soapfishes and allies) | 2 | — | 3 | 1 | 5 |
| Grammidae (basslets) | — | — | — | — | 4 |
| Kuhliidae (aholeholes) | 1 | — | 1 | — | — |
| Priacanthidae (bigeyes) | 4 | 1 | 2 | 2 | 2 |
| Apogonidae (cardinalfishes) | 10 | 1 | 4 | 5 | 18 |
| Branchiostegidae (tilefishes) | 1 | 1 | 3 | 2 | 1 |
| Lutjanidae (snappers) | 9[7] | — | 8 | 13 | 12 |
| Haemulidae (grunts) | — | 2 | 13 | 7 | 12 |
| Sparidae (porgies) | 1 | 1 | 1 | 10[7] | 5[7] |
| Sciaenidae[6] (drums and croakers) | — | — | 1 | 2 | 3 |
| Mullidae (goatfishes) | 10[7] | 1 | 1 | 2 | 2 |
| Pempheridae (sweepers) | — | — | — | — | 2 |
| Kyphosidae (sea chubs) | 2 | 4 | 7 | 1 | 2 |
| Ephippidae (spadefishes) | — | 1 | 2 | 1 | 1 |
| Chaetodontidae (butterflyfishes) | 20 | 2 | 4 | 5 | 5 |
| Pomacanthidae (angelfishes) | 6 | — | 3 | 4 | 6 |
| Embiotocidae (surfperches) | — | 19[7] | — | — | — |
| Pomacentridae (damselfishes) | 12 | 2 | 13 | 5 | 12 |
| Cirrhitidae (hawkfishes) | 5 | — | 3 | — | 1 |
| Labridae (wrasses) | 48 | 3 | 16 | 6 | 15 |
| Scaridae (parrotfishes) | 6 | — | 6 | 5 | 12 |
| Opistognathidae (jawfishes) | — | — | 8 | 3 | 5 |
| Blenniidae (combtooth blennies) | 12 | 3 | 6 | 9 | 8 |
| Tripterygiidae (triplefin blennies) | 1 | — | 6 | — | 5 |
| Clinidae (clinids) | — | 11 | 24 | 3 | 29 |
| Chaenopsidae (tube blennies) | — | 1 | 14 | — | 12 |

*Table 1.*   *(continued)*

| Family | Numbers of Species | | | | |
| --- | --- | --- | --- | --- | --- |
| | Hawaii[1] | California[2] | Sea of Cortez[3] | Northern Gulf of Mexico[4] | Bahamas[5] |
| Misc. Blennioid fishes (coldwater) | — | 23 | — | — | — |
| Callionymidae (dragonets) | 4 | — | — | 1 | 2 |
| Gobiidae (gobies) | 12 | 4 | 28 | 6 | 33 |
| Acanthuridae (surgeonfishes) | 22 | — | 6 | 3 | 3 |
| Gobiesocidae (clingfishes) | — | 7 | 11 | 2 | 7 |
| Balistidae (triggerfishes and filefishes) | 18 | 3 | 5 | 12 | 13 |
| Ostraciontidae (trunkfishes) | 5 | 1 | 2 | 2 | 5 |
| Tetraodontidae (puffers) | 6 | 2 | 5 | 2 | 2 |
| Diodontidae (porcupinefishes) | 4 | 2 | 3 | 2 | 5 |
| Total species | 306 | 239 | 271 | 161 | 323 |
| Total familes | 35 | 31 | 39 | 36 | 43 |

[1] Gosline & Brock, 1960.

[2] Miller & Lea, 1972 (Addendum, 1976).

[3] See Appendix I.

[4] Walls, 1975.

[5] Böhlke & Chaplin, 1968.

[6] Most species in these familes are not reef fishes (sandy bottoms, sea-grass beds, deep sea, or pelagic); only reef species numbers are given.

[7] All species included; no attempt has been made to separate the species ecologically.

species pairs of reef fishes are given in Table 2. Their high number demonstrates the common ancestry of the present fish faunas of the tropical western Atlantic and tropical eastern Pacific oceans which have been separated in the geologically recent past by the Isthmus of Panama (Rosen, 1975). More are found among fishes that may be categorized ecologically as secondary residents to reefs such as the sea basses, snappers, and grunts than among primary residents such as blennies, gobies, and clingfishes (Thomson and Lehner, 1976). Secondary residents are fishes with fairly high mobility, usually indeterminate growth, and long life-spans. Primary residents are less mobile fishes which in their relatively short life-spans approach determinate growth and are more restricted to the reef habitat because of their small size and poor means of dispersal. Their short life spans permit rapid "reshuffling" of their gene pools and result in a greater rate of natural selection for new genotypes (Rosenblatt, 1963). The greater rate of speciation and limited dispersal mechanisms of primary residents make these species useful in zoogeographical studies.

The reef-fish faunas of Hawaii and the Bahamas can be clearly categorized as tropical-insular by using the criteria proposed by Robins (1971). These areas are characterized by clear waters, development of coral reefs, calcium carbonate sediments, and generally low environmental fluctuations (temperature, salinity, turbidity, etc.). The reef-fish faunas of California, the northern Gulf of Mexico, and the Gulf of California can be categorized as primarily continental. Continental faunas experience wide fluctuations in both physical and biological environmental factors. Water is usually more turbid, bottom sediments contain more muds and

17

*Table 2. Examples of Species Pairs of Reef Fishes from the Sea of Cortez and the Bahamas[a]*

| Family | Sea of Cortez Species | Bahaman Species |
|---|---|---|
| Muraenidae | *Gymnothorax castaneus* | *Gymnothorax funebris* |
| Scorpaenidae | *Scorpaena mystes[b]* | *Scorpaena plumieri[b]* |
| Serranidae | *Epinephelus analogus* | *Epinephelus adscenscionis* |
|  | *Paranthias colonus[b]* | *Paranthias furcifer[b]* |
|  | *Mycteroperca jordani* | *Mycteroperca bonaci* |
| Grammistidae | *Rypticus bicolor* | *Rypticus saponaceus* |
|  | *Pseudogramma thaumasium* | *Pseudogramma gregoryi* |
| Lutjanidae | *Lutjanus argentiventris* | *Lutjanus apodus* |
|  | *Lutjanus novemfasciatus* | *Lutjanus cyanopterus* |
| Haemulidae | *Anisotremus interruptus* | *Anisotremus surinamensis* |
|  | *Anisotremus taeniatus* | *Anisotremus virginicus* |
|  | *Haemulon scudderi* | *Haemulon parrai* |
| Mullidae | *Mulloidichthys dentatus* | *Mulloidichthys martinicus* |
| Kyphosidae | *Kyphosus elegans* | *Kyphosus sectatrix* |
|  | *Kyphosus analogus* | *Kyphosus incisor* |
| Ephippidae | *Chaetodipterus zonatus* | *Chaetodipterus faber* |
| Pomacanthidae | *Pomacanthus zonipectus[c]* | *Pomacanthus paru* or *arcuatus[c]* |
|  | *Holacanthus passer[c]* | *Holacanthus ciliaris* or *bermudensis[c]* |
| Pomacentridae | *Abudefduf troschelii* | *Abudefduf saxatilis* |
|  | *Chromis atrilobata* | *Chromis multilineata* |
|  | *Eupomacentrus flavilatus* | *Eupomacentrus variabilis* |
| Blenniidae | *Ophioblennius steindachneri* | *Ophioblennius atlanticus* |
| Clinidae | *Malacoctenus hubbsi* | *Malacoctenus triangulatus* |
| Chaenopsidae | *Emblemaria hypacanthus* | *Emblemaria pandionis* |
| Gobiidae | *Bathygobius ramosus* | *Bathygobius soporator* |

[a] From Jordan, 1908, Ekman, 1953, Springer, 1958, Rosenblatt, 1963, Smith, 1971, and judgment of the authors.
[b] These species are considered conspecific by some authorities.
[c] Juveniles show greater similarity than adults.

silts, and coral reefs are absent or scarce. The upper Gulf of California fits this type quite well, but the faunas of parts of the central and especially the lower Gulf (Cape region) have attributes of an insular type. This great diversity of habitats and environments of the Sea of Cortez has resulted in a richer reef-fish fauna than otherwise might be expected.

## REEF-FISH COMMUNITIES OF THE SEA OF CORTEZ

A community is an association of species inhabiting an area characterized by a particular set of environmental factors. In a broad sense a community consists of all an area's plants, animals, and microorganisms. In a loose sense it is fashionable among ecologists to consider a certain taxonomic group (birds, mollusks, fishes, etc.) as a community (more properly called a taxocene or guild) if its members are similar in ecological requirements. This is done because one would need to be familiar with the biology of many different taxonomic groups to be able to characterize an entire community ecologically.

After analyzing our collections and observations of reef fishes throughout the Sea of Cortez we can recognize distinctive reef-fish communities characteristic of each of the three faunal subdivisions of the Gulf (upper, central, and lower). Next we characterize a typical community for each subdivision by fish-species composition and local physical environmental features.

## Upper Gulf

The physical environment of the upper Gulf is characterized by wide annual ranges in sea-surface temperature (54-91°F or 12-33°C), great tides (to 32 ft or 10 m), turbidity gradients, and gently sloping shorelines. The reef-fish communities of the upper Gulf have relatively few species and show great seasonal population fluctuations. An example of an intertidal (littoral) fish community characteristic of the northern portion of the upper Gulf is shown in Figure 16. The location is Station Beach Reef at Puerto Peñasco, Sonora, where numerous tide pools provide refuge for about 60 species of fishes when at least two-thirds of the rocky shoreline is exposed at low tide. The most abundant species is the Panamic sergeant major (*Abudefduf troschelii*), followed by the Gulf opaleye (*Girella simplicidens*), two clinids (*Paraclinus sini, Malacoctenus gigas*), and the Sonora goby (*Gobiosoma chiquita*). The major piscivorous predator is the spotted sand bass (*Paralabrax maculatofasciatus*), which ranks among the 10 most abundant species in this intertidal community.

The long-term diversity, stability, and other aspects of the ecology of this community have been studied by Thomson and Lehner (1976). It was noted that a few warm-temperate species dominate this community with their numbers and biomass: the Gulf opaleye (*Girella simplicidens*), spotted sand bass (*Paralabrax maculatofasciatus*), rock wrasse (*Halichoeres semicinctus*), sargo (*Anisotremus davidsonii*), and bay blenny (*Hypsoblennius gentilis*). These cold-tolerant species are able to survive the low sea temperatures of winter that periodically cause winterkills of several tropical species in the upper Gulf and parts of the central Gulf. The abundant tropical Panamic sergeant major often suffers catastrophic seasonal declines in its population, although this resilient species rebounds well from winterkills and juveniles are abundant every summer. Other tropical species, which are better cold-adapted than their close relatives in the southern Gulf, are able to survive the harsh, physically unstable environment of the upper Gulf.

## Central Gulf

Below the midriff islands of the Gulf the tides are not so great, the water is clear, and the rocky shoreline is steeper. Summer sea surface temperatures are similar to those of the upper Gulf but winter sea temperatures rarely drop below 60°F (16°C). The rocky coasts of this region (from Kino to Guaymas and Bahía San Francisquito to La Paz) are characterized by a more tropical fish fauna and one more distinctive of the Sea of Cortez as a whole. The reef-fish community illustrated in Figure 17 is one typical of the Guaymas or Loreto areas. The warm-temperate species so common in the upper Gulf are absent or uncommon in the central Gulf. The Panamic

*High tide*

*Low tide*

Figure 16 Rocky-shore fish community in the upper Gulf of California. Station Beach Reef. Puerto Peñasco, Sonora, diagrammatically illustrated at high and low tide, shows the typical fish assemblage that uses this reef in summer (from Thomson and Lehner, 1976). For the key to Figures 16, 17, and 18, see p. 25.

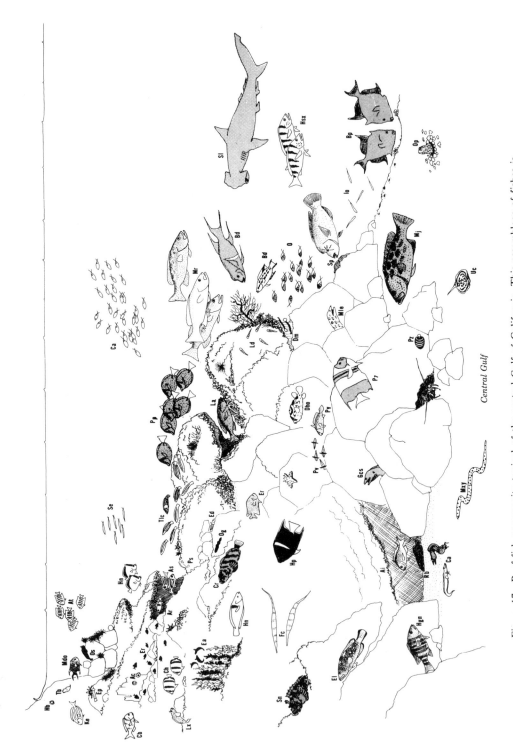

*Central Gulf*

Figure 17  Reef-fish community typical of the central Gulf of California. This assemblage of fishes is characteristic of the Guaymas and Loreto regions. For the key to this figure see p. 25.

22

sergeant major is still quite abundant, but the Cortez damselfish (*Eupomacentrus rectifraenum*), uncommon in the upper Gulf, becomes one of the most conspicuous fishes on the reefs. The dominant piscivorous predator is the leopard cabrilla (*Mycteroperca rosacea*), although this crepuscular (dawn or dusk) predator prefers to feed on flat-iron herring (Hobson, 1968) rather than reef fishes. Angelfishes (*Pomacanthus zonipectus* and *Holacanthus passer*) and butterflyfishes (*Chaetodon humeralis* and *Heniochus nigrirostris*) are frequently encountered on the reefs, and several species of wrasses (*Halichoeres nicholsi, H. dispilus, Bodianus diplotaenia* and *Thalassoma lucasanum*) are more abundant. The large baya grouper (*Mycteroperca jordani*) is perhaps the most important predator on large reef fishes and the spotted sand bass is replaced by the flag cabrilla (*Epinephelus labriformis*) as the main predator on the smaller species. Moray eels (*Gymnothorax castaneus* and *Muraena lentiginosa*), relatively uncommon in the upper Gulf, are the dominant nocturnal predators. The finescale triggerfish (*Balistes polylepis*) is as abundant as it is on the subtidal reefs of the upper Gulf. Large schools of grunts (*Microlepidotus inornatus* and *Haemulon sexfasciatum*) swim lethargically over the reef by day and feed over the adjacent sandy bottoms at night. The huge bumphead parrotfish (*Scarus perrico*) and the yellowtail surgeonfish (*Prionurus punctatus*) are common herbivores, especially along the Baja California side of the Gulf. Overall, about twice as many species of reef fishes inhabit the central Gulf as the upper Gulf. The fishes here are more colorful than the drab cryptic species characteristic of upper-Gulf rocky shores. The northern portion of the central Gulf (Guaymas) has an annual sea temperature range nearly as wide as that of the upper Gulf. Consequently, there is a strong seasonal turnover in relative abundance of certain reef fishes (Molles, 1976). Upwelling of deep cold water along the coasts maintains relatively low sea temperatures (61–64°F or 16–18°C) throughout the winter and early spring in Sonora and late spring and early summer in Baja California Sur.

### Lower Gulf (Cape region)

The lower Gulf extends from La Paz to Cabo San Lucas, Baja California Sur, and from just below Guaymas, Sonora, to Mazatlán, Sinaloa, on the mainland side. Tides are minimal (less than 6 ft or 2 m), and sea-surface temperatures range from about 68°F (20°C) to 86°F (30°C). On the Baja coast the shorelines are steeper and the water, clearer than elsewhere in the Gulf.

Reefs are scarce on the mainland side of the lower Gulf, where the meager reef-fish fauna has not been adequately studied. In contrast, the Baja California coast of the lower Gulf is characterized by a rich reef fauna and the only extensive growths of coral in the Sea of Cortez (see Figure 18). The reef-fish fauna includes several species of Indo-west Pacific origin which have become established in the tropical eastern Pacific (Rosenblatt et al., 1972). These transpacific species include the parrotfishes, *Scarus ghobban* and *S. rubroviolaceous*, the wrasses, *Hemipteronotus pavoninus, H. taeniourus* and *Thalassoma lutescens*, the moorish idol, *Zanclus canescens*, the moray, *Echidna zebra*, and the puffer, *Arothron meleagris*. One notices an increase in this region in the number of more colorful species like the Pacific porkfish, *Anisotremus taeniatus*, the blue-and-gold snapper, *Lutjanus viridis*, the Clarion angelfish, *Holacanthus clarionensis*, and the Pacific boxfish, *Ostracion meleagris*. Some species common in the central Gulf, such as the barberfish, *Henio-*

*Lower Gulf*

Figure 18   Reef-fish community of the lower Gulf of California. This assemblage of fishes is typical of the steep rocky coasts in the vicinity of Cabo San Lucas.

24

*chus nigrirostris,* the Mexican goatfish, *Mulloidichthys dentatus,* the beaubrummel damselfish, *Eupomacentrus flavilatus,* the orangeside triggerfish, *Sufflamen verres,* and the coral hawkfish, *Cirrhitichthys oxycephalus,* have become even more abundant in the lower Gulf. Because of the proximity of deep reefs near shore,

---

KEY TO FIGURES 16, 17, AND 18

Aa, *Antennarius avalonis* (roughjaw frogfish); Ac, *Acanthemblemaria crockeri*; Ad, *Anisotremus davidsonii* (*sargo*); Ah, *Anchoa helleri* (anchovy); Ai, *Anisotremus interruptus* (burrito grunt); Am, *Arothron meleagris* (guineafowl puffer); Ap, *Apogon dovii* (tailspot cardinalfish); Ar, *Apogon retrosella* (barspot cardinalfish); As, *Adioryx suborbitalis* (tinsel squirrelfish); Asa, *Antennarius sanguineus* (sanguine frogfish); Asp, *Alutera scripta* (scrawled filefish); At, *Abudefduf troschelii* (Panamic sergeant major); Ata, *Anisotremus taeniatus* (Panamic porkfish); Atr, *Acanthurus triostegus* (convict tang); Bd, *Bodianus diplotaenia* (Mexican hogfish); Bp, *Balistes polylepis* (finescale triggerfish); C, *Chromis* sp. (blue-and-yellow chromis); Ca, *Chromis atrilobata* (scissortail damselfish); Cae, *Chaenopsis alepidota* (orangethroat pikeblenny); Cb, *Calamus brachysomus* (Pacific porgy); Ch, *Chaetodon humeralis* (threebanded butterflyfish); Co, *Cirrhitichthys oxycephalus* (coral hawkfish); Cp, *Canthigaster punctatissima* (spotted sharpnose puffer); Cr, *Cirrhitus rivulatus* (giant hawkfish); Dho, *Diodon holocanthus* (balloonfish); Dhx, *Diodon hystrix* (spotted porcupinefish); Dm, *Doryrhamphus melanopleura* (fantail pipefish); Ea, *Exerpes asper* (sargassum blenny); Eaf, *Epinephelus afer* (mutton hamlet); Ed, *Elacatinus digueti* (banded cleaner goby); Edr, *Epinephelus dermatolepis* (leather bass); Ef, *Eupomacentrus flavilatus* (beaubrummel); Eh, *Emblemaria hypacanthus* (signal blenny); Ei, *Epinephelus itajara* (jewfish); El, *Epinephelus labriformis* (flag cabrilla); Ep, *Elacatinus puncticulatus* (redhead goby); Epa, *Epinephelus panamensis* (Panama graysby); Er, *Eupomacentrus rectifraenum* (Cortez damselfish); Ez, *Echidna zebra* (zebra moray); Fc, *Fistularia commersonii* (reef cornetfish); Ff, *Forcipiger flavissimus* (longnose butterflyfish); Gc, *Gobiosoma chiquita* (Sonora goby); Gcs, *Gymnothorax castaneus* (Panamic green moray); Gp, *Gobiesox pinniger* (tadpole clingfish); Gs, *Girella simplicidens* (Gulf opaleye); Hb, *Hypsoblennius brevipinnis* (barnaclebill blenny); Hc, *Holacanthus clarionensis* (Clarion angelfish); Hd, *Halichoeres dispilus* (chameleon wrasse); Hg, *Hypsoblennius gentilis* (bay blenny); Hgn, *Hoplopagrus guentheri* (barred pargo); Hi, *Hippocampus ingens* (Pacific seahorse); Hn, *Heniochus nigrirostris* (barberfish); Hnc, *Halichoeres nicholsi* (spinster wrasse); Hp, *Holacanthus passer* (king angelfish); Hpv, *Hemipteronotus pavoninus* (Pacific razorfish); Hr, *Hyporhamphus rosae* (California halfbeak); Hs, *Halichoeres semicinctus* (rock wrasse); Hsx, *Haemulon sexfasciatum* (graybar grunt); Ht, *Hemipteronotus taeniourus* (clown razorfish); Io, *Ioglossus* sp. (hovering goby); Ke, *Kyphosus elegans* (Cortez chub); La, *Lutjanus argentiventris* (yellow snapper); Ld, *Lythrypnus dalli* (bluebanded goby); Lv, *Lutjanus viridis* (blue-and-gold snapper); Lx, *Labrisomus xanti* (largemouth blenny); Mc, *Mugil cephalus* (striped mullet); Md, *Mulloidichthys dentatus* (Mexican goatfish); Mdo, *Microspathodon dorsalis* (giant damselfish); Mg, *Malacoctenus gigas* (Sonora blenny); Mh, *Manta hamiltoni* (Pacific manta); Mj, *Mycteroperca jordani* (Gulf grouper); Mle, *Muraena lentiginosa* (jewel moray); Ml, *Myripristis leiognathos* (Panamic soldierfish); Mr, *Mycteroperca rosacea* (leopard grouper); Mx, *Mycteroperca xenarcha* (broomtail grouper); Mxy, *Myrichthys xystreurys* (tiger snake eel); Nc, *Nexilarius concolor* (dusky sergeant major); O, *Opistognathus* sp. (bluespotted jawfish); Og, *Ogilbia* sp. (brotula); Om, *Ostracion meleagris* (Pacific boxfish); Op, *Opistognathus punctatus* (finespotted jawfish); Os, *Ophioblennius steindachneri* (Panamic fanged blenny); Pa, *Plagiotremus azaleus* (sabertooth blenny); Pc, *Priacanthus cruentatus* (glasseye); Pco, *Paranthias colonus* (Pacific creolefish); Pm, *Paralabrax maculatofasciatus* (spotted sand bass); Pn, *Pseudojulis notospilus* (banded wrasse); Pp, *Prionurus punctatus* (yellowtail surgeonfish); Ps, *Paraclinus sini* (flapscale blenny); Pv, *Pareques viola* (rock croaker); Pz, *Pomacanthus zonipectus* (Cortez angelfish); R, *Remora* sp. (remora); Rb, *Rypticus bicolor* (Cortez soapfish); Se, *Sphyraena ensis* (Mexican barracuda); Sl, *Sphyrna lewini* (scalloped hammerhead); Sm, *Scorpaena mystes* (stone scorpionfish); Sp, *Scarus perrico* (bumphead parrotfish); Sr, *Scarus rubroviolaceus* (bicolor parrotfish); Ss, *Scomberomorus sierra* (sierra mackerel); Sv, *Sufflamen verres* (orangeside triggerfish); Tb, *Tomicodon boehlkei* (Cortez clingfish); Tc, *Taenioconger canabus* (Cape garden eel); Tcr, *Tylosurus crocodilus* (Mexican needlefish); Th, *Tomicodon humeralis* (Sonora clingfish); Tlc, *Thalassoma lucasanum* (Cortez rainbow wrasse); Tlt, *Thalassoma lutescens* (sunset wrasse); Tr, *Trachinotus rhodopus* (gafftopsail pompano); Uc, *Urolophus concentricus* (bullseye stingray); Zc, *Zanclus cornutus* (Moorish idol).

**25**

certain rare deepwater reef fishes readily observed in the Cape region are the scythe-marked butterfly fish, *Chaetodon falcifer,* the longnose hawkfish, *Oxycirrhitus typus* and the colorful sea bass, *Liopropoma* sp.

In the Cape region there are occasional records of fishes whose principal ranges are farther north or south outside the Gulf. From the north are the California opaleye, *Girella nigricans,* and the garibaldi, *Hypsypops rubicundus*; from the south, the whitetail damselfish, *Eupomacentrus leucorus,* and the peculiar rock-skipping clinid, *Mnierpes macrocephalus.*

The relatively short stretch of shoreline from La Paz to Cabo San Lucas harbors the richest reef-fish fauna in the Sea of Cortez and perhaps the entire eastern Pacific. The fauna and flora has an insular character; indeed, the Cape region was an island in the early stages of the formation of the Gulf.

Although the Sea of Cortez ends spectacularly at the Cape at the tip of the Baja California peninsula, the sea is still warm along the Pacific coast to Bahía Magdalena, where the cold waters of the California current provide a barrier to the northern distribution of most tropical fishes.

# How to Use This Book

This book is based primarily on collections and observations of reef fishes we and our students and colleagues at the University of Arizona have made from 1963 to the present. Most of the illustrations and photographs are original and are representations of living and preserved specimens.

The choice of fishes for major species accounts was based on our studies of the reef-fish communities throughout the Sea of Cortez. Those that we encounter frequently on reefs and in our collections are treated more fully in the species accounts. Occasionally less common fishes are highlighted if their appearance or behavior is distinctive (e.g., moorish idol and sabertooth blenny). Other fairly common fishes are treated less thoroughly, usually because we are unfamiliar with their habits or their taxonomic status is unclear (e.g., some triplefin blennies, brotulas, and jawfishes). Whenever possible we highlight what is known about their ecology and behavior, information that is too often lacking in identification-oriented books on fishes.

We do not include keys for identification because we feel that the distinguishing characteristics given and the illustrations are adequate to identify the species. When applicable, we point out notable changes in shape, color pattern, and behavior between juveniles and adults or between males and females.

## EXTERNAL ANATOMY OF A BONY FISH

All the fishes treated in this book are teleosts (tele = end or complete, ost = bone), which are members of the class Osteichthyes (the bony fishes). They represent the most advanced evolutionary forms and constitute about 96% of the almost 19,000 living species of fishes (Nelson, 1976). The teleosts are characterized by a well ossified skeleton, which contrasts with the cartilaginous skeleton of sharks and rays. Typically, they have scales, paired and median fins with fin rays, and a bony gill cover (operculum). Some of these features are lacking in a few teleosts.

To identify a teleostean fish it is necessary to become familiar with its basic external anatomy. Most reef-fish species belong to the order Perciformes (perchlike), the largest and most diverse order of nearly 7000 species. They have many anatomical features in common, though differences in the shape, size, and position of these features as well as the variation in the numbers of their components (e.g., scales, fin rays) are used as diagnostic characters. Figures 19 and 20 present

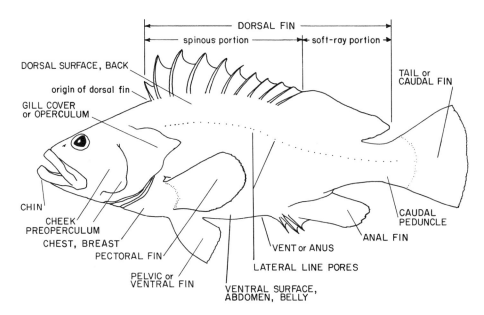

Figure 19    The external anatomy of a typical percoid fish (the flag cabrilla, *Epinephelus labriformis*).

some of the external anatomical features commonly used by ichthyologists to identify teleostean fishes.

The head of a teleost is conspicuous and bony and its prominently placed eyes lack eyelids. The paired nostrils (nares) consist of tubes with incurrent (anterior) and excurrent (posterior) openings that pass water in and out. In a few fishes (e.g., damselfishes) there is only a single opening on each side. In all teleosts the nostrils are essentially blind sacs that do not open into the mouth cavity as ours and nearly all other vertebrates' do. The mouth may be large or small, with or without teeth, but always with at least two bones (premaxillary and maxillary) in the upper jaw and a prominent dentary bone in the lower. In the higher teleosts the upper jaw bones are free from the skull which enables the fish to open its mouth wide to seize and engulf large prey. The gills are protected by a bony cover (operculum) consisting typically of four bones; the preopercle and opercle are most often used in taxonomic descriptions.

The dorsal fin is formed of two portions, an anterior usually with hard sharp spines and a posterior with soft fin rays. Sometimes they are separate, and in lower teleosts (e.g., sardines) there is only a single dorsal fin without spines. The position of the pelvic (ventral) fins varies. In higher teleosts they are generally thoracic or jugular (see Figure 21), but in some teleosts they are greatly reduced or absent. In the perciform fishes the pelvic fins normally have a single spine followed by five or fewer soft fin rays. The pectoral fin lacks spines in most fishes, but the anal fin which is always positioned behind the vent (anus), usually has two to three spines and a variable number of soft fin rays. The caudal fin has 17 or fewer principal soft fin rays and takes various shapes (rounded, forked, truncate, etc.). The caudal fin is lost in some fishes or greatly reduced and confluent with the dorsal and anal fins (e.g., morays).

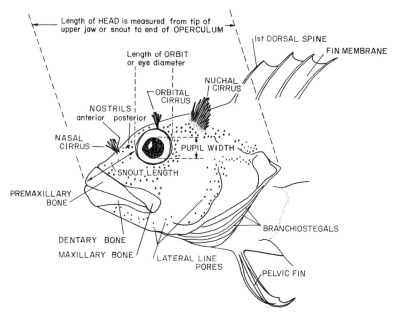

Figure 20   External anatomy of the head of a blennioid fish (largemouth blenny, *Labrisomus xanti*).

Scales (cycloid and/or ctenoid) are present on most fishes but many species lack scales completely or in part. Usually the scales lie in well defined oblique rows, and the number in a particular row is often used as a taxonomic character. The lateral line scales are pored and have small round openings that are part of the lateral line sensory system.

Many fish have various sensory structures on the head and body, such as taste and touch receptors, that are not grossly obvious, and skin growths assume various

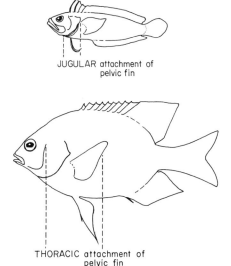

Figure 21   Position of the pelvic fins in higher teleosts (upper fish: flapscale blenny, *Paraclinus sini*; lower fish: beaubrummel, *Eupomacentrus flavilatus*).

29

shapes in the form of barbels, flaps, papillae, and cirri (singular, cirrus). They frequently have sensory or camouflage functions.

Coloration and color patterns may also be used as a means of species identification. Caution must be exercised, however, because some fish not only have the ability to change their color patterns almost instantaneously to blend with the background coloration of their immediate habitats, but, depending on age, sex, and diet, may have several different color patterns.


## TAXONOMIC TECHNIQUES: COUNTS AND MEASUREMENTS

A taxonomist may use whatever is necessary to classify and diagnose fishes. The characters may be morphological, behavioral, physiological, or even biochemical. It is more practical, however, to use the morphological features of the specimen-in-the-hand before searching for the more elusive characteristics of the living fish. Therefore a species description consists of a rather complete list of certain standardized counts and measurements and detailed descriptions of the external and sometimes internal anatomy of preserved specimens. The standards for modern taxonomic methods in ichthyology have been established by Hubbs and Lagler (1947) in their classic book *Fishes of the Great Lakes Region.* Their methods have been adopted in general by most ichthyologists, and we present an abridged version of those techniques that will be useful in identifying reef fishes of the Sea of Cortez.

### Measurements (morphometrics)

For the precision required in taxonomic work all measurements should be point-to-point, straight-line measurements made with needle-pointed calipers or dividers laid against a precise metric rule. Tapes or measuring boards should not be used.

**Body Length.**   The distance from the tip of the snout or upper jaw (with mouth closed) to the farthest tip of the caudal fin (when the fin is pinched together) is known as the *total length* (abbreviated TL) (see Figure 22). This measurement is common in fishery science or is used to express the maximum length that a species attains. *Standard length,* as in taxonomy (abbreviated SL), is the distance from the tip of the snout or upper jaw (with the mouth closed) to the base of the caudal fin (posterior margin of the hypural bone; i.e., the last vertebra, which usually shows a crease in the skin when the caudal fin is bent back and forth). This measurement is required for precise work because caudal fin rays are often damaged or lost.

**Body Depth.**   The greatest vertical dimension of the body from the dorsal to ventral midlines, exclusive of fin-ray structures.

**Head Length.**   The distance from the tip of the snout or upper jaw to the most distant point of the operculum, usually including the membranous opercular flap (see Figure 20).

**Eye Length or Diameter.**   The horizontal distance between the margins of the eyeball. This is essentially the same as the *length of orbit,* which is measured between the bony anterior and posterior orbital rims (see Figure 20).

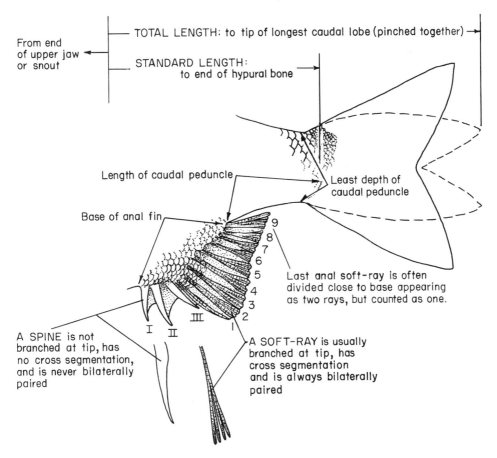

Figure 22   Tail area of the zebraperch, *Hermosilla azurea*, showing body length measurements, fin-ray construction, and caudal peduncle measurements. (modified from Miller and Lea, 1972.)

***Jaw Lengths.***   The *upper jaw length* is the distance between the tip of the pre-maxillary bone and the posterior tip of the maxillary. The *lower jaw* or *mandibular length* is the distance between the tip of the lower jaw to the end of its posteriormost bone (angular).

### Counts (meristics)

By convention, counts and measurements are taken from the left side of a fish's body. Also, specimens should be illustrated or photographed from the left side. This is done because when preserving a large specimen an incision is made on the right side of the abdomen to permit the preservative to enter the body cavity freely.

***Fin-ray Counts.***   Fin-ray counts are preceded by abbreviations for the fins (D, dorsal; A, anal; C, caudal; $P_1$, pectoral; and $P_2$, pelvic). Roman numerals indicate the number of spines and Arabic numerals, the number of soft fin rays; for example, a species with nine dorsal spines and 14 to 16 soft fin rays would be given as D.IX, 14–16. If the spinous and soft-rayed portions of the fin are continuous, the counts are separated by a comma, as shown. If the fin is divided into two parts, a plus sign (+) separates the counts, as in D.IX + 14–16. If only a single fin-ray count is given instead of a range, this count should be interpreted as being usual, with infrequent or no variation.

True spines are hardened, unsegmented, unpaired fin rays that are never branched (Figure 22). They are usually stiff and pungent but rudimentary spines may be flexible and blunt.

Soft-rays are flexible, segmented, bilaterally paired fin rays that are often (but not always) branched at the tips. The last ray of the dorsal and anal fins is sometimes branched at the base and should be counted as one ray.

**Scales.** Scale counts should be made under magnification (hand lens or dissecting microscope) to ensure accuracy. The maximum possible count, including scales greatly reduced in size, is used. Because scale counts are more variable than fin-ray counts, a range as well as the average count is given. The *lateral line scale count* is the number of pored scales in the lateral line. The count begins with the first scale touching the shoulder girdle at the upper end of the gill opening and ends with the last overlying the rear margin of the hypural plate at the caudal-fin base. A *lateral scale count* is made in those fishes that have interrupted, incomplete, or no lateral lines. This is essentially a count of the oblique scale rows along the midside or a count of scales along the lateral scale row that normally would bear a lateral line. The *scales above* or *below* the *lateral line* are counted from the origin of the first dorsal or anal fin and along the oblique scale row to, but not including, the lateral line scale. Precise scale counts below the lateral line are often difficult because the scales at the base of the anal-fin origin are often small, numerous, and irregular. The *predorsal scale count* is the number of scales on the midline from the origin of the first dorsal fin to the occiput (end of head marked by a line separating scaled and scaleless parts of the skin).

**Teeth.** The teeth of the jaws and roof of the mouth may be useful taxonomic characters (Figure 23). In general, five major types of teeth are characterized by size, shape, and function: cardiform, villiform, caniniform, incisiform, and molariform. Cardiform and villiform teeth are similar in that they occur in pads consisting of numerous, fine, closely set, pointed teeth. Cardiform teeth are shorter and may be found in catfishes and a few sea basses (e.g., giant sea bass). Villiform teeth, which are longer and may be likened to intestinal villi, occur, for example, in some scorpionfishes. Caniniform teeth are fanglike, strong, sharply pointed teeth that are used for grasping prey. They may be straight or recurved. Incisiform teeth are chisellike and have sharp cutting edges. They may be saw-edged and separated or fused into a cutting beak (e.g., parrotfishes, puffers) and are often used for scraping. Molariform teeth have flattened broad surfaces and are used for crushing and grinding (e.g., porgies).

The kind, position, and number of tooth rows in the jaws and roof of the mouth may often be used to distinguish closely related species. The primary tooth-bearing bone in the higher teleosts is the *premaxillary.* The *maxillary* bone bears teeth only in some lower teleosts. Median teeth in the roof of the mouth often occur on the vomer, and lateral teeth are found on the paired *palatine* bones flanking it.

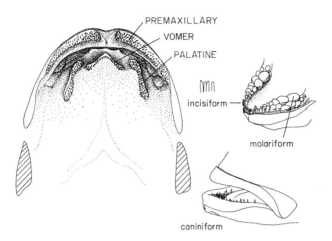

Figure 23   Tooth-bearing bones of the upper jaw and roof of the mouth of the stone scorpionfish, *Scorpaena mystes*, and types of jaw dentition in the Pacific porgy, *Calamus brachysomus* (upper right), and the spotted sand bass, *Paralabrax maculatofasciatus* (lower right).

***Gill rakers.***   Gill rakers are bony rods of various sizes and shapes that function as accessory feeding structures and as protection for the delicate gill filaments (Figure 24). The numbers of gill rakers on the gill arches may be diagnostic in the identification of closely related species. Gill-raker counts are most frequently expressed as the total number of rakers on the outer face of the lower limb of the first arch, starting with the rudimentary rakers at the foremost end and stopping with the one at the angle of the arch. A rudimentary gill raker is an element whose height is less than the width of its base. Sometimes these rudimentary rakers are not included in the count.

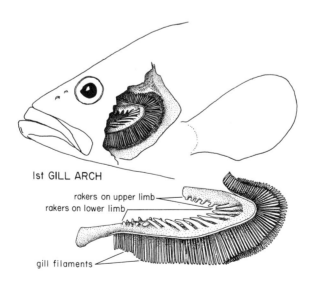

Figure 24   Position (with operculum cut away) and side view of the first gill arch of a sea bass showing the gill rakers. Usually only the gill rakers of the lower limb are employed in species diagnoses.

33

## *SPECIES ACCOUNTS*

The sequence of fishes appearing in this book follows the classification of families of teleostean fishes by Greenwood et al. (1966) with some recent changes found in Norman and Greenwood (1975) and Nelson (1976). A brief discussion of each familiy, which includes references to pertinent literature (mainly on the systematics of tropical eastern Pacific species), precedes treatment of the individual reef-fish species. We also include the number of species worldwide for each family, usually following Nelson (1976). See Appendix I for a checklist of Gulf of California reef fishes treated in the species accounts.

The species-account format is adapted from that used effectively by Böhlke and Chaplin (1968). The English common name of the family is given in the upper right corner, the Spanish common name, in the upper left corner. The scientific name appears in the center.

For the species we use the available English common names assigned by the Committee on Names of Fishes of the American Fisheries Society and the American Society of Ichthyologists and Herpetologists (Bailey et al., 1970). However, because there are few Gulf fishes on this list, we use names from the literature, for example, Walford (1937), Hobson (1968), Shiino (1976) or we propose new names. The generally accepted or most widely used Spanish common name follows the English. When a Spanish common name is unavailable or unsuitable, we translate the English into Spanish or propose a new one.

The scientific name consists of the genus, or generic name, and the species, or specific name, in italics, followed by the author who described the species and the date of publication of the original description. Parentheses around the author and date indicate that the species has been reassigned to a genus other than the one in the original description. The author and date which refer only to the trivial (specific) name of the fish and are always retained (with few exceptions) unless it is found that an earlier published name had been used for that species. In such cases the trivial name, author, and date are changed.

Most of the illustrations are based on preserved specimens, supplemented by color photographs and observations of live fish when available. A few illustrations are taken from published material. Photographs of specimens of live fish are used when judged adequate for species identification. The illustrations were done by Alex Kerstitch, Tor Hansen, Chris van Dyck and Paul Barker. The total length of the illustrated specimen is given, with additional information on maturity and sex, when appropriate, followed by the maximum size (total length and sometimes weight) attained by the species (determined from museum collections and the literature).

The section on Distinguishing Characteristics is intended to be a concise description of the characters that can be used to separate the species from closely related forms, a diagnosis that also includes male-female and adult-juvenile differences, when appropriate. Dorsal and anal fin-ray counts and sometimes other relevant counts are provided. This section, and its illustration or photograph, should be adequate to identify the species.

The Distribution section contains the species geographical range inside and outside the Gulf of California. The within-the-Gulf distribution of reef fishes often includes the northermost and southernmost points at which the species has been collected. Use of the phrase "throughout the Gulf" means that the species is commonly found from San Felipe or Puerto Peñasco to Cabo San Lucas or Mazatlán.

Figure 25    Zoogeographical subdivisions of Gulf of California inshore fishes (based on Walker, 1960).

The relative abundance of the species in the Gulf of California is also included in this section. A species is considered abundant if it is found in large numbers throughout its principal range. A species is considered common if it is taken in most collections and frequently observed. A species is considered uncommon if it is infrequently collected or observed on the reefs. Rare species are those known from only a few specimens.

In Figure 25 we use a modification of the zoogeographical subdivisions of Walker (1960) when relating relative abundance to distribution. The upper Gulf includes the region north of Kino, Sonora, and Punta San Francisquito, Baja California Norte

35

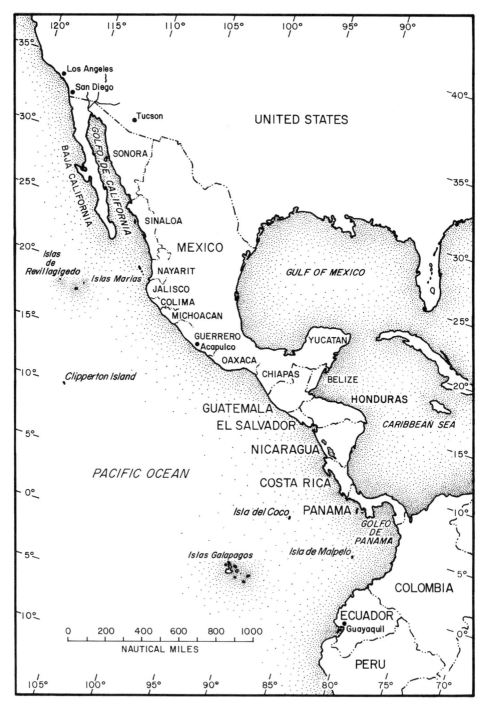

Figure 26  Map including the area of the tropical eastern Pacific (Bahía Magdalena, Baja California Sur, and the Gulf of California to northern Peru) in which the northern and southern distributional limits of most Gulf reef fishes may be found.

36

(B.C.N.). The central Gulf is the region south of these points to Guaymas, Sonora, and La Paz, Baja California Sur (B.C.S.). Our lower Gulf region combines Walker's Cabo San Lucas and southeastern Gulf regions. Because there are no known reefs south of Guaymas until Isla San Ignacio Farallon, mainland distributions in the lower Gulf refer only to this lone island and to Mazatlán, Sinaloa.

Most Sea of Cortez reef fishes have geographical ranges that extend north and south outside the Gulf of California. Figure 26 is a map that covers the area of the tropical eastern Pacific (from Bahía Magdalena and the Gulf of California to northern Peru) in which the northern and southern distributional limits of most Gulf reef fishes may be found. A few species have ranges that extend to the Indo-west Pacific or the tropical western Atlantic. Geographical ranges given for the species are based primarily on published records and Boyd Walker's unpublished checklist. For a few species additional distributional information has been taken from unpublished museum records (mainly our collections and those of the University of California at Los Angeles).

We also indicate whether the species is endemic to the Gulf of California; that is, whether its known distribution is limited to the Gulf (often including Bahía Magdalena and Mazatlán as the extreme northern and southern boundaries of distribution outside the Gulf proper).

The Ecology portion of each species account summarizes the salient features of the known natural history of the species. It may contain information on habitat, depth range, feeding habits, territorial behavior, reproductive habits, physiological tolerances, and other relevant or interesting facts. This information is based on our own observations and research as well as those of University of Arizona students and outside investigators; for example, Dr. Edmund (Ted) S. Hobson has made significant contributions to the knowledge of activity patterns and feeding bahavior of Gulf fishes and his works are frequently cited.

The Related Species account mentions those that are closely related or in some respect similar to the major species treated (usually the same genus). In general, we have less information on these species because of their relative scarcity in collections or their uncertain taxonomic status. When available we add photographs of them. We always provide the species' common and scientific names, its geographical distribution, and its distinguishing characteristics. Brief life history notes are included when knowledge and space permit.

# Family and Species Accounts of Reef Fishes of the Sea of Córtez

Figure 27 The Panamic green moray, *Gymnothorax castaneus*, the largest of the moray eels in the Sea of Cortez. (Photograph courtesy of E. S. Hobson.)

# FAMILY MURAENIDAE
## Moray eels (Morenas)

The morays are specialized eels well adapted to the reef habitat (Figure 27). Their wedgeshaped heads, smooth, scaleless skins, and muscular bodies enable them to squeeze into small rocky crevices in search of crustaceans and small fishes. They lack paired fins, and their fleshy and confluent dorsal, caudal, and anal fins* are often reduced to mere ridges. The gill opening is reduced to an oval slit on each side of the head. Their teeth are usually sharp, needlelike, and depressible. The anterior and often the posterior nostrils are tubed, and the olfactory sense is well developed and essential to their nocturnal food-searching habits. Many morays have bold colorful markings, whereas others are somber in uniform shades of green or brown. Morays pass through a leptocephalous larval stage, a ribbonlike transparent larva characteristic of certain primitive teleosts.

Worldwide, the family includes 12 genera containing about 100 species and is well represented in shallow tropical waters, although some occur in temperate seas and in the deep waters of the continental shelf. Sixteen species in six genera have been collected in the Gulf of California; about the same number may be found in other regions of the tropical eastern Pacific and tropical western Atlantic. The family reaches its highest diversity in the tropical Indo-west Pacific.

*References.* Gosline (1958); McCleneghan (1976); Hildebrand and Barton (1949); McCosker and Rosenblatt (1975); Myers and Wade (1941); Randall and McCosker (1975); Rosenblatt, McCosker, and Rubinoff (1972).

* The fin rays are not usually visible externally; consequently, no counts are given in the species format.

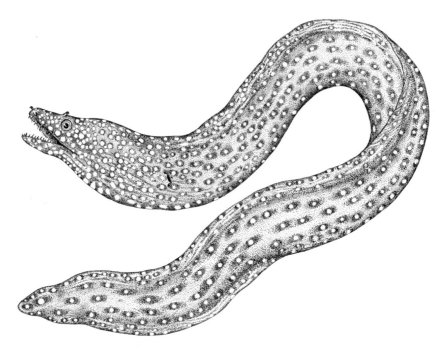

# JEWEL MORAY, morena pinta
## *Muraena lentiginosa* Jenyns, 1843

**Illustrated specimen.** Adult, 17 in. (435 mm), by Tor Hansen; see also Plate 2a; maximum size about 2 ft (0.6 m).

**Distinguishing characteristics.** Adult moray eels in the genus *Muraena* are characterized by tubed anterior and posterior nostrils. The jewel moray can be distinguished from other Gulf morays by its striking color pattern of many light elongated spots ringed by dark brown in chainlike rows over a brown background. The dorsal fin origin is just behind the head, well in advance of the gill opening.

**Distribution.** Distributed throughout the central and lower Gulf, this common moray ranges to Peru and Islas Galápagos.

**Ecology.** Primarily a nocturnal predator, the jewel moray feeds largely on crustaceans and fishes. During the day this eel remains under cover in rocky crevices and will defend its shelter against intruders. Some members of the genus (*M. helena* in the Atlantic) have been reported to be venomous. One of the authors (Kerstitch) was bitten on the finger by a small jewel moray. The bite stung like a bee sting and bled profusely but no other effects were noticed.

**Related species.** Another species of *Muraena*, which ranges from Rocas Alijos, far west of Bahía Magdalena, into the Gulf (Guaymas) and south to Peru and the Islas Galápagos, is the magnificent moray, *M. argus* (Steindachner, 1870). It can be distinguished from *M. lentiginosa* by the conspicuous white margin of the dorsal and anal fins and by numerous small white spots scattered over three rows of large irregular yellow blotches on a dark brown ground color (adults). A third species, the hourglass moray, *M. clepsydra* Gilbert, 1898, ranges mostly outside the Gulf from Costa Rica to Salinas, Ecuador, and the Islas Galápagos, but we collected a small specimen in a tide pool at Cabo San Lucas. *M. clepsydra* has a prominent black spot surrounding the gill opening, lacks white margins on its fins, and has hourglass-shaped light spots on a brown background (juveniles). The adults are speckled with tiny irregular spots on the body and fins.

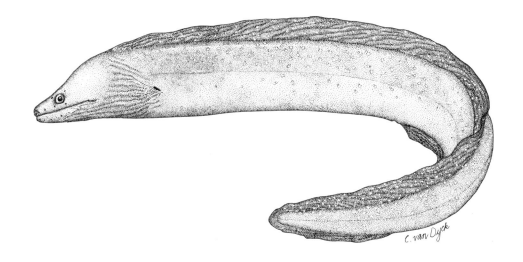

# PANAMIC GREEN MORAY, morena verde
## *Gymnothorax castaneus* (Jordon and Gilbert, 1882)

**Illustrated specimen.** Adult, 38.8 in. (731 mm), by Chris van Dyck; see also Plate 2b and Figure 27; exceeds 4 ft (1.2 m) in length.

**Distinguishing characteristics.** The posterior nostrils of species of the genus *Gymnothorax* lack tubes, a characteristic that serves to distinguish these eels from all Gulf morays except very young individuals of *Muraena*. Body color is greenish brown to chestnut overall but may be darker with a purplish tinge. Often there are small white flecks on the body, mostly on the posterior half and dorsal fin, but they may also be absent. The dorsal fin origin is just behind the head, well in advance of the gill opening. The teeth are caniniform (fanglike or bladelike) and the snout is usually sharply pointed. In ichthyological literature *G. castaneus* has often been confused with similar species in the genus (e.g., *G. dovii*).

**Distribution.** The Panamic green moray is the commonest large moray in the central and lower Gulf. Our northernmost Sonoran record is from Puerto Lobos, although along Baja California, it has been collected as far north as San Felipe. It ranges as far south as Panama and Isla Malpelo, Colombia.

**Ecology.** An opportunistic predator that feeds mainly on fishes and crustaceans, this moray forages occasionally in the daytime as well as by night. It is able to sense wounded or distressed fishes and sometimes will leave its shelter in daylight to attack its prey. Hobson (1968) reported a big green moray seizing a large stone scorpionfish (*Scorpaena mystes*) when the latter, startled by the diver, settled near the eel's lair. We collected a 3½-ft (1.1-m) green moray with a foot-long finescale triggerfish (*Balistes polylepis*) in its stomach, attesting to its voracious appetite.

Divers are cautioned not to tamper with this eel. In fact, spearing any large moray can be quite dangerous. The late Vernon Brock, prominent marine biologist and expert diver, was bitten severely on the elbow by a 7-to-8 ft (2.1-to-2.4 m) moray eel (probably *G. javanicus*) he speared at Johnston Island (central Pacific). The wound put him in a hospital for a month and it was three months before he had any reasonable use of his arm (Randall, 1969). While collecting fishes at Cabo Pulmo, a University of Arizona student was bitten by a 3-ft (1-m) *G. castaneus* as someone handed him a net with the distressed eel thrashing about inside. The moray bit through the net and slashed the student's thigh with its sharp canines. Often a distressed moray will clamp its jaws on any object that approaches its head.

**Related species.** Three other species of *Gymnothorax* are known from the Gulf. The fine-spotted moray, *G. dovii* (Günther, 1870), is similar to *G. castaneus,* but its dark brown to blackish body is profusely covered with small whitish spots. Unlike *G. castaneus,* the spots are usually slightly larger and more numerous. It ranges from the central Gulf (Isla Santa Catalina) to Salinas, Ecuador, and the Islas Galápagos. Another species, the masked moray *G. panamensis* (Steindachner, 1876), is smaller [about 12 in. (305 mm)] and has a shorter snout; it is a uniform light brown without white flecks or spots on the body. A prominent black ring surrounds the eye and pores in prominent white spots show on the upper and lower jaws and snout. Also, unlike the first two species, the dorsal fin origin is above (juveniles) or behind (adults) the gill opening. The teeth are relatively shorter and broader and some of them at the sides of the lower jaw show distinctive recurved tips. *G. panamensis* is widely distributed from the central Gulf (Islas Santa Inés, B.C.S., and

Isla San Pedro Nolasco, Sonora) to the Islas Galápagos and Juan Fernandez Islands off Chile and Easter Island. It has recently been reported from Lord Howe Island far off the eastern coast of Australia (Allen et al., 1976). A fourth species, the shark-tooth moray, *Gymnothorax* (=*Priodonophis*) *equatorialis* (Hildebrand, 1946), ranges throughout the Gulf (off Puerto Peñasco) to Peru. It is a deeper water species, commonly seen in shrimp trawl catches in the central Gulf. It differs from the preceding three species of *Gymnothorax* by having compressed, serrated, sharklike teeth in a single series in each jaw, a character that Hildebrand thought distinctive enough to erect a new genus (*Priodonophis*) for it. The ground color is brown and the body is strikingly covered with many white spots that become much larger and fewer near the greatly compressed and tapering tail. A prominent elongate white spot bordered by black marks the tip of the tail and the eye is ringed in black.

Another species (originally placed in the genus *Gymnothorax*) is the slenderjaw moray, *Enchelycore octaviana* (Myers and Wade, 1941), an uncommon Gulf moray that ranges from the upper Gulf (Isla San Esteban) to Colombia and the Islas Galápagos. This plain grayish brown eel can be easily identified by its curved, slender jaws and numerous fanglike teeth which are shown clearly even when the mouth is completely closed (see Plate 2c).

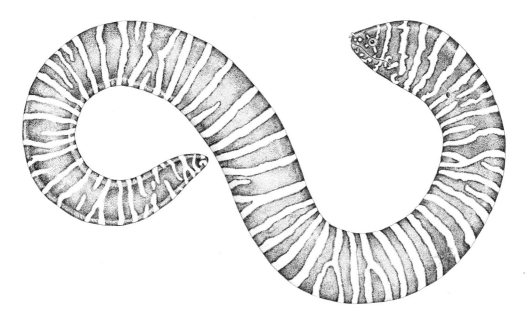

# ZEBRA MORAY, morena cebra
## *Echidna zebra* (Shaw, 1797)

**Illustrated specimen.** Adult, 23.6 in. (600 mm), by Tor Hansen; attains a length of 2½ ft (0.76 m).

**Distinguishing characteristics.** The specialized morays of the genus *Echidna* can be distinguished by their blunt molariform teeth. Other morays have sharply pointed caniniform teeth. The snout is short and blunt and the body is more robust in comparison to most other morays. *E. zebra* is easily recognized by the striking color pattern of narrow whitish bands that encircle the dark reddish brown body.

**Distribution.** This species is widespread in the Indo-west Pacific and has colonized the tropical eastern Pacific, mainly on offshore islands (e.g., Clipperton Island) and coral reef areas (Cabo Pulmo). In our area it ranges from the central Gulf (Isla Carmen) to Panama and the Islas Galápagos.

**Ecology.** Little is known about the habits of this eel. Its rounded molariform teeth suggest that it feeds largely on hard-shelled crustaceans and mollusks. Hobson (1974) found that it feeds primarily on crabs in Hawaii and doubts that heavy-shelled mollusks are eaten. Because of its secretive habits, it is rarely seen, but is occasionally collected at rotenone stations in rocky and coral reef areas.

**Related species.** Two other species of *Echidna* range into the Gulf. The more common palenose moray, *E. nocturna* (Cope, 1872), is darkly colored, lacking the banding of *E. zebra*. Instead, it is sparsely covered with small yellowish spots often slightly ringed with black. The teeth are not so flattened and are slenderer than those of *E. zebra,* suggesting a softer diet. The anterior nostril tubes are pale and the jaw pores are in pale spots. This species ranges from the central Gulf (Islas Santa Inés and Bahía San Agustin) to Peru and the Islas Galápagos. The floral moray, *E. nebulosa* (Ahl, 1789), is a tropical Indo-west Pacific and Hawaiian species that has been collected sporadically in the eastern Pacific from the central Gulf (Bahía Muertos and Bahía San Lucas, B.C.S.) to Panama, including Clipperton Island and Isla del Coco. A color pattern of large, dark, amoeba-shaped blotches with round, light centers distinguishes this small moray (less than 2 ft, or 0.6 m) from the other two Gulf species of *Echidna.*

In contrast to the morays in the genus *Echidna* are the degenerate morays of the genus *Uropterygius,* which have almost completely lost their vertical fins. Only a rudiment of the dorsal-caudal-anal confluent fins appears as a ridge around the tip of the tail. They have small pointed teeth and a single lateral line pore above and before the gill opening (most other morays have two pores). There are three described and at least one undescribed species of *Uropterygius* ranging into the Gulf. The rusty moray, *Uropterygius necturus* (Jordan and Gilbert, 1882) is the most common species of the genus in our collections. It ranges from Bahía Santa Inés, B.C.S., to Isla Gorgona, Colombia, and the Islas Galápagos. The peppered moray, *U. polystictus* Myers and Wade, 1941, ranges from Islas Santa Cruz and Ildefonso in the central Gulf to the Islas Galápagos, although we have not collected it in the Gulf. The tiger reef eel, *U. tigrinus* (Lesson, 1829), is an Indo-Pacific species found primarily in the Hawaiian, Johnston, and Society Islands. It has been collected infrequently in the eastern Pacific from the lower Gulf (Isla Espíritu Santo) to Panama (Gulf of Chiriqui) and the Islas Revillagigedo. A specimen was also collected at Isla Jaltemba, Nayarit, Mexico.

*U. necturus* can be distinguished from *U. polystictus* by the characters in the key supplied by McCosker and Rosenblatt (1975): the head and trunk (tip of jaws to anus) of *U. polystictus* are longer than the tail (anus to end of caudal fin); body color is light with dark mottling; and the posterior nostril is tubular and located in front of the center of the eye. The head and trunk of *U. necturus* are shorter than the tail; body color is dark with rusty mottlings, and the posterior nostril, located behind the center of the eye, has only a raised rim. The posterior nostril of *U. tigrinus* is directly over the eye; its head-trunk length is almost twice as long as the tail, and its body color is light with many distinctive round to oval dark blotches. As one of the largest species of *Uropterygius,* it reaches at least 4 ft (1.2 m) in length.

Related to *Uropterygius,* the smallest species in the Gulf is the hardtail moray, *Anarchias galapagensis* (Seale, 1940). It ranges from the central Gulf (Punta Concepción) to Panama and the Islas Galápagos. Dorsal and anal fins are absent and the tip of the tail is hard and pointed with only a few rudimentary caudal rays. Unlike all other eastern Pacific morays, it has a prominent interorbital pore lying over the eye next to the posterior nostril which it resembles. The body color is uniformly brown or with a yellowish brown "reticulated" pattern. As one of the smallest moray eels, it reaches only about 5 in. (125 mm) in length.

# FAMILY CONGRIDAE
## Conger and garden eels (Anguilas congrio y anguilas jardin)

Conger eels superficially resemble the freshwater anguillid eels that are renowned for making long migrations to the sea to spawn. Conger eels are all marine, lacking scales, and are associated with soft bottoms of sand and mud. They should not be confused with the "conger eel," found in rivers of southeastern United States, which is really an amphibian and not a fish. Of the approximately nine species of congrids in the Gulf (worldwide, 38 genera, 100 spp.) we know of only three that may be found near reefs. They are the specialized garden eels of the subfamily Heterocongrinae which differ from the conger eels by their superior oblique mouths, short snouts, large eyes, well developed lips, reduced or absent pectoral fins, extremely elongate form, and burrowing behavior, all which are adaptations for feeding on zooplankton in the water column (see Rosenblatt, 1967). In the Gulf they may be found in colonies or "gardens" of a few to hundreds of individuals in sandy bottoms near rocky reefs, especially around islands at moderate depths (Figure 28). Watching a colony of garden eels swaying slowly with the current is one of the truly great sights afforded to diving naturalists. For a classic account of the behavior of garden eels see William Beebe's *Zaca Venture* (Beebe, 1938).

*References.* Böhlke (1957b); Cowan and Rosenblatt (1974); Miller (1953); Raju (1974); Rosenblatt (1967).

Figure 28 A colony of garden eels in the lower Gulf of California. This appears to be the recently described *Taenioconger canabus*. (Photograph courtesy of E. S. Hobson.)

# CORTEZ GARDEN EEL, ánguila jardín
## *Taenioconger digueti* Pellegrin, 1923

**Illustrated specimen.** Adult, 16.1 in. (421 mm), by Chris van Dyck; see also Plate 2d; reaches a length of at least 25 in. (630 mm).

**Distinguishing characteristics.** *Taenioconger digueti* has a light brown body with a few irregular light bands encircling the trunk below the lateral line. The corner of the mouth (rictus) is black and the minute pectoral fins are dark brown. Each of the conspicuous lateral line pores is surrounded by pigmentless areas. The numerous rays in dorsal-caudal-anal confluent fins are not readily visible; vertebrae 179 to 191 (av 185); lateral line pores 161 to 187 (av 175).

**Distribution.** Large colonies of garden eels have been observed in the central and lower Gulf, especially near offshore islands. Specimens of the Cortez garden eel have been collected from Guaymas (Bahía Bacochibampo) and a few localities in the central and lower Gulf on the Baja side to Puerto Vallarta (Bahía Banderas). These eels are difficult to collect because of their extreme resistance to rotenone ichthyocides. Consequently, there are too few specimens available to give their complete geographical range. We have seen *Taenioconger* species (probably *digueti*) as far north as Isla San Pedro Martir (see Plate 2d).

**Ecology.** Garden eels are gregarious fishes often found in large colonies in open sandy areas near reefs. They retreat into their burrows when approached by divers but soon reappear, their bent undulating bodies looking like question marks. The late William Beebe of bathyscape fame was perhaps the first to observe what he called a "garden of eels" in the Gulf of California. He wrote, "they resemble iron rods as much as anything, slightly bent . . . sticking up from the sand, but unrodlike, swaying very slightly" (Beebe, 1938). Hobson (1968) gives an account of a then undescribed species of *Taenioconger* (probably *canabus*) in the Cape region of the Gulf (Buena Vista). He states that these eels never leave their burrows, and at night they withdraw completely, covering the burrow openings with sand. They prefer moderate depths (exceeding 4 to 6 m) in areas with strong current and feed on zooplankton drifting by.

**Related species.** A new species, the Cape garden eel, *T. canabus* Cowan and Rosenblatt, 1974, was recently described, mainly from specimens from Isla Ceralbo (see Figure 28). *T. canabus* differs from *T. digueti* by its greater lateral line pore count (181 to 209, av 188), higher vertebral count (186 to 199, av 191), darker chocolate-brown body color, and halos of white pigment rather than pigmentless areas surrounding the anterior lateral line pores. *T. canabus* has a slenderer body and shorter head and trunk.

The only other eastern Pacific species is the peppered garden eel, *Gorgasia punctata* Meek and Hildebrand, 1923, which ranges from Bahía Magdalena to the Cape region (Los Frailes) and south to Panama. It can be readily distinguished from *Taenioconger* spp. by its well developed pectoral fins, greatly reduced caudal rays covered by thick skin, uncoalesced upper lip flanges, and longer jaws. It has numerous dark specks over a light body that form dark areas on the head and anterior trunk region.

# FAMILY OPHIDIIDAE
## Brotulas and cusk eels (Brotulas y congrios)

The ophidiids are eellike fishes with pelvic fins that are inserted under or near the chin (cusk eels) or on the throat (brotulas). The pelvic-fin rays are greatly reduced in number (usually 1 or 2). The Gulf cusk eels (subfamily Ophidiinae) are usually found in deeper water over soft bottoms, but the brotulas (subfamily Brotulinae) are commonly found on shallow reefs (Figure 29). Some brotulas are viviparous (give birth to live young) and all seem to be secretive, nocturnal fishes. Among nine species in four genera of Gulf brotulas, about five of the genus *Ogilbia* are undescribed and are the commonest brotulas on Gulf reefs. Worldwide, there are about 6 genera and about 155 species in the subfamily Brotulinae.

Related to the ophidiids are the pearlfishes of the family Carapidae which are also elongate, eellike fishes. Most, however, are specialized commensals that live within the body cavities of clams, starfishes, sea urchins, sea cucumbers, and sea squirts. At least three species have been collected in the Gulf: *Carapus dubius* (Putnam, 1874), which we have found in pen shells (*Pinna rugosa*) and cockles (*Laevicardium elatum*); *Encheliophis jordani* Heller and Snodgrass, 1903 [= *E. hancocki* (Reid, 1940),] found in the sulfur sea cucumber (*Selenkothuria lubrica*), and *Echiodon exsilium* Rosenblatt, 1961, host, if any, unknown. Because of the specialized habitats of these fishes and sparse information on their ecology and distribution in the Gulf, we do not discuss carapids further in this book. For a recent review of the biology of carapids see Trott (1970).

***References.*** Böhlke (1955a); Cohen (1964); De Roy (1974); Heller and Snodgrass (1903); Hildebrand and Barton (1949); Hubbs (1944); Suarez (1975).

Figure 29   A brotula of the genus *Ogilbia*. Note the jugular position of the pelvic fins. (Photograph by D. A. Thomson.)

# CORALLINE BROTULA, brotula de coral
## *Ogilbia* sp. (undescribed)

**Illustrated specimen.** Adult, 3 in. (74 mm), by Alex Kerstitch; maximum size about the same as that of the illustrated specimen.

**Distinguishing characteristics.** The genus *Ogilbia* belongs to the group of brotulas that have separate caudal fins; that is, not joined and confluent with the dorsal and anal fins as in many other genera (e.g., *Oligopus*). Gulf of California brotulas of the genus *Ogilbia* consist of about five undescribed species and *O. ventralis* (Gill, 1864). Boyd W. Walker of the University of California, Los Angeles, is currently undertaking systematic studies of the genus *Ogilbia*. Because of the uncertain taxonomic relationships in the genus we have not made specific distinctions between the species. The illustrated specimen, one of the common undescribed species of *Ogilbia,* is characterized by its bright reddish orange coloration.

**Distribution.** Species of the genus *Ogilbia* are widely distributed in the tropical eastern Pacific, ranging from Bahía Todos Santos (Ensenada) on the outer coast of Baja California and throughout the Gulf of California to Colombia and the Islas Galápagos. The coralline brotula is a common Gulf species (Puerto Lobos to Cabo San Lucas), but we do not know its distribution outside the Gulf.

**Ecology.** Brotulas of the genus *Ogilbia* are small (to about 4 in., or 100 mm) secretive fishes that are rarely observed underwater but are commonly collected when rotenone ichthyocides are used on shallow reefs. They are all livebearers (viviparous), and frequently a pregnant female when collected will abort her young. Species differences are often based on the distinctive male genitalia (functional copulatory organs). At Puerto Peñasco the common *Ogilbia* collected in tide pools is a yellowish brown species, slightly larger than the corralline brotula (see Figure 29). In captivity this *Ogilbia* is extremely shy and always remains hidden under rocks. It will feed on live adult brine shrimp but unlike other aquarium fishes will rarely leave its shelter to feed except in darkness. Members of this genus are active at night but we know little else about their habits. See Suarez (1975) for an account of the reproductive biology of a western Atlantic species (*O. cayorum*).

**Related species.** In addition to the two species mentioned, there are at least three other undescribed species of *Ogilbia* in the Gulf. The sole described species, *Ogilbia ventralis* (Gill, 1864), ranges from Isla San José around the Cape to Bahía Magdalena and from Puerto Peñasco to Mazatlán.

Another small species collected in shallow and moderate depths is the purple brotula, *Oligopus diagrammus* (Heller and Snodgrass, 1903). This species is similar in appearance to *Ogilbia* but is dark purple to almost black in overall coloration. It also lacks the separate caudal fin of *Ogilbia* (see Figure 30). Instead, the caudal fin is confluent with the dorsal and anal fins, the tail tapering to a point. This species ranges from southern California (San Clemente Island) to the central Gulf (Isla San Pedro Nolasco) and to Panama and the Islas Galápagos.

Another shallow-to-moderate-depths form, rarely collected in the Gulf, is the velvetnose brotula, *Petrotyx hopkinsi* Heller and Snodgrass, 1903. Unlike *Ogilbia,* but similar to *Oligopus,* it has a continuous dorsal-caudal-anal confluent fin. The snout is covered with many tiny folds of skin (papillose) that have

the look of velvet. It is a larger species (about 8 in., or 203 mm) and purple in coloration. Each pelvic fin consists of two rays (united for half their length) rather than a single ray as in *Oligopus* and *Ogilbia.* A few specimens have been collected on the Gulf coast of Baja California as far north as Puerto Refugio, Isla Angel de la Guarda. This brotula also occurs at the Islas Galápagos.

All other Gulf brotulas are deeper water fishes, living over soft bottoms (e.g., *Brotula clarki* Hubbs, 1944).

Figure 30   The purple brotula, *Oligopus diagrammus.* Note that the caudal fin is confluent with the dorsal and anal fins. The separate caudal fin, characteristic of the genus *Ogilbia*, is lacking. (Photograph by Alex Kerstitch.)

# FAMILY ANTENNARIIDAE
## Frogfishes (Peces pescadores)

These are peculiar, lumpy, soft-bodied fishes with loose fitting skin often covered with flaps resembling marine growth. Although excellent camouflage artists, their most specialized feature is their "fishing rod (ilicium) and lure (esca)," which is a highly modified first dorsal spine (see Figure 31). The sedentary frogfish wriggles its lure to entice prey to its cavernous mouth and then quickly engulfs its victim. The pectoral fins are limblike and are used to "walk" slowly along the sea bottom. There is a small gill opening just behind the "elbow" of each pectoral fin.

The sargassum fish (*Histrio histrio*), common in floating sargassum mats in the tropical western Atlantic, does not occur in the eastern Pacific. Although sargassum seaweeds are abundant in the Gulf, they do not form permanent drifting mats. None of the Gulf frogfishes is strongly associated with sargassum. Worldwide, there are nine genera and about 61 species of frogfishes; three species in two genera are present in the Gulf of California.

*References.* Jordan and Starks (1907); Rosenblatt (1963); Schultz (1957).

Figure 31  The roughjaw frogfish, *Antennarius avalonis.* Note the modified first dorsal spine which consists of a "fishing rod (ilicium) and a lure (esca)." (Photograph by Alex Kerstitch.)

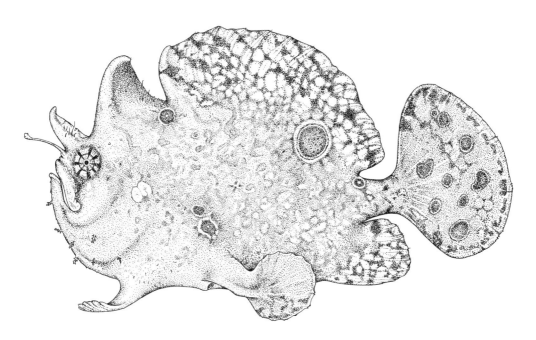

# ROUGHJAW FROGFISH, pez antenado
## *Antennarius avalonis* Jordan and Starks, 1907

**Illustrated specimen.** Juvenile, 3 in. (76 mm), by Tor Hansen; see also Figure 31; our largest specimen (the largest recorded) is 13 in. (330 mm) SL [tail damaged, TL estimated to be 15 in. (381 mm)].

**Distinguishing characteristics.** The roughjaw frogfish may be distinguished from other Gulf frogfishes by its branched pectoral rays (adults), prominent dorsal ringed ocellus, absence of distinct dark spots on the belly (juveniles) and spinule-covered (two-thirds) upper jaw which provides its common name. Color varies from lemon yellow, bright orange, and red to shades of brown and even black. D. III, 12–14; A. 8–9; $P_1$. 12–13.

**Distribution.** The roughjaw frogfish, although uncommon in collections, has been recorded from southern California (Santa Catalina Island) throughout the Gulf (Roca Consag) to Peru.

**Ecology.** Cryptically colored and secretive, juvenile roughjaw frogfish may be found under ledges and in crevices on shallow reefs. The adults inhabit deeper water and are occasionally captured in shrimp trawls, although further studies are needed to determine whether these large individuals represent the same species as the small ones in shallow water. This piscatorial angler attracts smaller fishes by wriggling its wormlike lure at the tip of its thin first dorsal spine. When the prey fish attempts to seize the bait, the frogfish engulfs it by quickly flexing its huge jaws, literally vacuuming the surprised fish into its mouth.

**Related species.** Two other species of frogfish occur in the Gulf. The sanguine frogfish, *Antennarius sanguineus* Gill, 1864, ranges from the central Gulf (Guaymas) to Peru and the Islas Galápagos (Plate 3a). It may be distinguished from *A. avalonis* by its dark, usually unringed ocellus (sometimes the ocellus is absent), 11 to 12 unbranched pectoral fin rays (at all ages), lack of spinules on its upper jaw, and especially by the numerous dark red or brown spots on its belly. The ocellus often has a large clear area surrounding it instead of the narrow ring in *A*.

*avalonis*. The dark spots on the belly are large and evenly spaced (larger specimens of *A. avalonis* have small, irregular dark spots on the belly). This species does not grow so large as *A. avalonis* (maximum size about 3½ in., or 90 mm). A pair of 3-in. (76-mm) *A. sanguineus* successfully spawned a raft of eggs in a small aquarium on the senior author's desk. The floating gelatinous mass, shaped like a canoe, was laid within two hours. Unfortunately the embryos survived only a week.

Another Gulf species, the bandtail frogfish, *Antennatus strigatus* (Gill, 1864), ranges from the central Gulf to Colombia, and the Islas Galápagos. The first dorsal spine in adults typically has a simple slender tentacle at the tip instead of the fleshy bulbous "lure" of Gulf *Antennarius*. However, this character is variable, depending on age (Rosenblatt, 1963), and should not be relied on for species distinctions. The bandtail frogfish can be distinguished best from the other two species by its lack of a dorsal ocellus, only 10 unbranched pectoral rays at all ages, an area between the second and third dorsal spines completely covered by skin denticles (naked patch in both *Antennarius* spp.), and a clear band followed by a dark band around the tail (see Plate 3b).

# FAMILY HOLOCENTRIDAE
## Squirrelfishes (Peces ardilla)

The holocentrids are usually reddish, nocturnal fishes with large eyes, many strong, fine spines, and prickly (ctenoid) scales (Figure 32). They sometimes have seven soft rays in the pelvic fins, a characteristic that distinguishes them from all other spiny-rayed reef fishes in the Gulf. This family is poorly represented in the eastern Pacific. There are only two species in two genera of holocentrids in the Gulf but both are common reef inhabitants in the central and lower regions. By comparison, in the western Atlantic there are seven genera and 11 species, and in Hawaii there are three genera and about 15 species. This family is best represented in coral-reef communities, being especially speciose in the tropical Indo-west Pacific. Worldwide, there are at least nine genera and 70 species.

*References.* Greenfield (1965, 1968, and 1974); Nelson (1955); Woods (1965); Woods and Sonoda (1973).

Figure 32  The tinsel squirrelfish, *Adioryx suborbitalis*. Squirrelfishes hide in caves during the day and swim in the open at night. (Photograph by Alex Kerstitch.)

55

# PANAMIC SOLDIERFISH, soldado
## *Myripristis leiognathos* Valenciennes, 1846

**Photograph.** Adult, by Alex Kerstitch; see also Plate 3c; attains a length of about 7 in. (179 mm).

**Distinguishing characteristics.** Squirrelfishes of the genus *Myripristis* have been referred to as soldierfishes, perhaps because of their schooling formations. Fishes of the subfamily Myripristinae lack the strong preopercular spine characteristic of the subfamily Holocentrinae. There are four species of *Myripristis* in the tropical eastern Pacific (see Greenfield, 1974), but only the widely distributed *M. leiognathos* occurs in the Gulf. It can be distinguished from all other Gulf fishes by its overall bright red coloration, large eyes, and rough (prickly) scales. D. X + I, 14(12–14); A. IV, 12(11–13).

**Distribution.** The Panamic soldierfish ranges widely from Bahía Magdalena to the upper Gulf (Puerto Lobos) and south to Ecuador, including several offshore islands. In the Gulf it is more common in the central and lower regions.

**Ecology.** The Panamic soldierfish is nocturnal, as are all members of the family Holocentridae. This species aggregates in caves or crevices during the day, often sharing its shelter with other nocturnal species such as the barspot cardinalfish, *Apogon retrosella*, and the tinsel squirrelfish, *Adioryx suborbitalis*. At night they swim in open water, often in small aggregations, where they feed mainly on small crustaceans (Hobson, 1965a). When the water is turbid, they may swim in the open during the day but never far from cover.

*M. leiognathos* is found in relatively shallow water from 10 to 50 ft (3 to 15 m). It is little sought after by Mexican fishermen, even though other species of this genus are greatly valued as food in Hawaii and the Indo-west Pacific.

# TINSEL SQUIRRELFISH, candil
## *Adioryx suborbitalis* (Gill, 1864)

**Photograph.** Adult, by Alex Kerstitch; see also Figure 32; grows to about 10 in. (254 mm).

**Distinguishing characteristics.** Until recently this species was placed in the genus *Holocentrus*. It may be easily distinguished from the Panamic soldierfish (*Myripristis leiognathos*) by noting the prominent pre-opercular spine (lacking in *Myripristis*) and less intense red coloration. The body is silvery with a rosy-to-violet tint and has conspicuous markings on the sides except at night when two oblique posteriodorsal dark bars appear along the body. *A. suborbitalis* is the only species of the genus in the Gulf. D. XI + 13–14; A. IV, 9.

**Distribution.** This species ranges from the central Gulf (Bahía San Agustin, Sonora) to Ecuador and out to most of the far offshore islands. It is common along the shallow rocky shores of the central and lower Gulf.

**Ecology.** Squirrelfishes, primarily nocturnal, hide in small caves and crevices during the day. Occasionally they share their refuge with the Panamic soldierfish, although they are more often found apart. Unlike *M. leiognathos*, they do not usually form large aggregations and are often seen near the splash zone in depths of less than 10 ft (3 m), where they dart between large boulders when approached. They feed at night, mostly on small crustaceans, after emerging from their daytime shelters (Hobson, 1965a).

# FAMILY FISTULARIIDAE
## Cornetfishes (Peces corneta)

The cornetfishes are elongated, depressed fishes with a greatly extended tubular snout, a relatively small mouth, and a long thin filament extending from the middle of the caudal fin (see Figure 33). They are closely related to the trumpetfishes (Aulostomidae), which lack the caudal filament. The family contains only four species in one genus but is represented throughout the warm oceans of the world. Two species occur in the Gulf of California. No trumpetfishes have been recorded from the Gulf, but *Aulostomus chinensis*, an Indo-west Pacific migrant, has been recorded in Panama and several oceanic islands in the tropical eastern Pacific (Rosenblatt et al., 1972).

***References.*** Fritzsche (1976b).

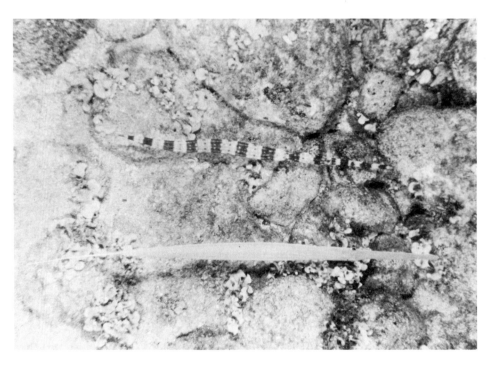

Figure 33  The reef cornetfish, *Fistularia commersonii*, displaying its barred and striped phases. This cornetfish assumes a barred pattern (upper fish) when stationary on the bottom. When swimming, the bars fade and thin blue stripes appear (lower fish). This remarkable photograph was taken at the instant the lower fish began to swim away. (Photograph by Alex Kerstitch.)

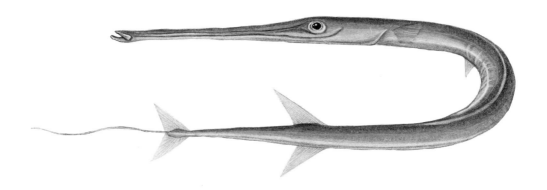

# REEF CORNETFISH, pez corneta
## *Fistularia commersonii* Rüppell, 1835

**Illustrated specimen.** Young adult, 18.3 in. (465 mm), by Alex Kerstitch; see also Figure 33; grows to about 4 ft (1.2 m).

**Distinguishing characteristics.** The systematics of the genus *Fistularia* has been recently clarified by Fritzsche (1976b), who recognizes four extant species, two of which are found in the Gulf. *Fistularia commersonii,* until recently confused with *F. petimba* (a widespread Indo-west Pacific species not found in the eastern Pacific), is the common cornetfish in the Gulf. In life the reef cornetfish usually shows a pair of bluish stripes along the back over an olive-gray background. D. 15–17; A. 14–16; P₁. 13–15.

**Distribution.** This Indo-Pacific cornetfish is widely distributed from the western Indian Ocean to the tropical eastern Pacific, where it ranges from Puerto Lobos, Sonora and Bahía Magdalena, south to Panama and most of the far offshore islands.

**Ecology.** According to observations made by Hobson (1968), the reef cornetfish (discussed as *F. petimba*) is a stalking predator that actively hunts such ecologically diverse species as snake eels, small blennioid fishes, herrings, and halfbeaks. This striped cornetfish can readily assume a mottled or barred color pattern: a striped pattern seems to be more prevalent when swimming; bars or a mottled camouflage pattern sometimes occur when motionless or when feeding (see Figure 33). It does not feed or seek shelter after dark but slowly swims about the reef away from cover.

**Related species.** The only other species in the Gulf is the deepwater cornetfish, *Fistularia corneta* Gilbert and Starks, 1904, which usually occurs at depths greater than 100 ft (30 m). This species is distinguished from *F. commersonii* by higher fin-ray counts (D. 17–20; A. 16–19; P₁. 15–18), a more anterior position of the pelvic fins (insertion is closer to tip of the snout than to the caudal fin base), and wider interorbital space (less than 16 times into the snout length). It ranges from the outer coast of Baja California (Bahía San Hippolito) to Peru and many far offshore islands. In the Gulf it has been collected as far north as Bahía San Luis Gonzaga, B.C.N.

# FAMILY SYNGNATHIDAE
## Pipefishes and seahorses (Peces pipa y caballitos de mar)

These odd-looking fishes have elongated bodies encased in ridged bony plates arranged in concentric rings. Their snouts are tubular and their tiny mouths lack teeth. Fin spines and ventral fins are also lacking. The male has a ventral brood pouch in which to incubate the eggs deposited there by the female. He carries the eggs until they are ready to hatch and then "gives birth" to the young. Syngnathids may be found in a variety of habitats but are usually associated with seaweeds or branches of coral. There are 17 species of syngnathids in the eastern Pacific (Fritzsche, 1976a). Among the five species in four genera of Gulf syngnathids only two pipefishes are commonly encountered on reefs (see Figure 34). The others, including the only eastern Pacific seahorse, *Hippocampus ingens*, are more frequently collected offshore and along sandy shores in bays and estuaries. World-wide, there are 34 genera with 150 species of pipefish and two genera with 25 species of seahorse.

***References.*** Fritzsche (1976a); Ginsburg (1937); Herald (1940, 1953, 1959).

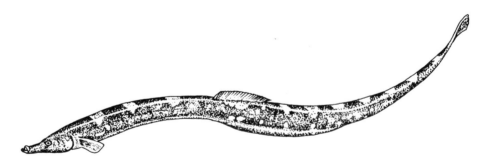

Figure 34  A male snubnose pipefish, *Bryx arctus*. This tiny pipefish ranges throughout the Gulf to northern California. (Illustrated by Tor Hansen.)

# FANTAIL PIPEFISH, pez pipa chica
## *Doryrhamphus melanopleura* (Bleeker, 1858)

**Illustrated specimen.** Adult male, 2.5 in. (63 mm), by Alex Kerstitch; maximum size about 3 in. (76 mm).

**Distinguishing characteristics.** This short-bodied pipefish can be easily recognized by its conspicuous fanlike tail and dark brown to tan coloration. *D. melanopleura* has the lowest number of total body rings (about 35) of all eastern Pacific pipefishes. Other Gulf pipefishes have about 49 to 59 body rings. Herald (1953) recognized several subspecies in the Indo-Pacific. The subspecies in the Gulf, *D. m. melanopleura,* has three longitudinal serrated snout ridges, 18 or 19 trunk rings and 14 to 16 tail rings. The male has an abdominal brood pouch rather than the tail pouch that characterizes all other eastern Pacific syngnathids. D. 23–26; A. 4.

**Distribution.** A widely distributed Indo-Pacific species, the fantail pipefish ranges from the Indian Ocean to the eastern Pacific (from Bahía Magdalena to Ecuador, including Clipperton Island and the Islas Galápagos). It is uncommon in the Gulf, being represented in our collections only from the central and lower regions, but is known to range to Isla Angel de la Guarda in the upper Gulf.

**Ecology.** In the Gulf the fantail pipefish is found under dark ledges and in deep rocky crevices. When under ledges, they are often observed swimming upside down, the dorsal surface showing a lighter color than the belly. Usually occurring in sexual pairs, they rarely swim far from their shelters. Although unaggressive toward other species of fishes, they defend territories from intrusion by their own kind. When alarmed or challenged they spread and display the fanshaped caudal fin.

The number of eggs that a male *D. melanopleura* can incubate at one time depends on the size of the individual. This may be as few as 15 or more than 100 (Herald, 1953).

**Related species.** Four other pipefishes and one seahorse have been recorded from the Gulf. Only one of these, the snubnose pipefish, *Bryx arctus* (Jenkins and Everman, 1889), sometimes occurs along rocky shores (see Figure 34). This small pipefish ranges from northern California to Mazatlán and throughout the Gulf (as far north as Puerto Peñasco). It has only 15 or 16 trunk rings but has 38 to 41 tail rings, 20 to 23 dorsal rays, and a double row of spots along the sides. This pipefish often swims in pairs close to seaweed, sometimes lying on a rocky bottom. Other Gulf pipefishes inhabit sandy or estuarine areas and are rarely found over reefs.

Figure 35  The Pacific seahorse, *Hippocampus ingens*, is the only seahorse in the eastern Pacific. (Photograph courtesy of Dave Lindquist.)

The Pacific seahorse, *Hippocampus ingens* Girard, 1858 (see Figure 35), is frequently collected offshore in the Gulf by shrimp trawlers. The only seahorse in the entire eastern Pacific, it ranges from San Diego, California, to northern Peru and the Islas Galápagos and throughout the Gulf of California. It seems to be associated with beds of sea-whip corals on patch reefs offshore. Large numbers of seahorses were found washed ashore at Puerto Peñasco during the 1971 winterkill (Thomson and Lehner, 1976).

# FAMILY SCORPAENIDAE
## Scorpionfishes and rockfishes (Peces escorpión)

Scorpaenids are mostly sedentary fishes known by their cryptic coloration, excessive spininess, and large heads, mouths, and pectoral fins. The family is characterized by a bony ridge (suborbital stay) that runs below the eye across the cheek. Most species also have numerous backwardly projecting spines on the head and some have venomous fin-spines. This family is particularly well represented in the temperate Californian waters by four genera and a whopping 61 species! Most (57), however, are in a single genus (*Sebastes*), the rockfishes. Worldwide, there are about 60 genera with 330 species but only 15 species in four genera, seven of which are rockfishes (*Sebastes*), are established in the Gulf. We consider only three Gulf scorpaenids in two genera as reef fishes (see Figure 36). The others are offshore, deeper water species or associated with soft bottoms. For discussion of the rockfishes occurring in the Gulf see Chen (1975) and Moser (1972). The related family Cottidae (sculpins), common in cold temperate waters (42 species in California), is completely absent in the Gulf of California.

*References.* Eschmeyer (1965, 1969); Eschmeyer and Randall (1975); Ginsburg (1953); Hubbs (1945); Moser et al. (1977).

Figure 36   The stone scorpionfish, *Scorpaena mystes*. This scorpionfish is well camouflaged by abundant skin flaps that give the fish the appearance of a seaweed encrusted rock. (Photograph by Alex Kerstitch.)

# STONE SCORPIONFISH, lapón
## *Scorpaena mystes* Jordan and Starks, 1895

**Illustrated specimen.** Adult, 7.3 in. (185 mm), by Alex Kerstitch; see also Figure 36; average adult size about 1 ft (0.3 m); grows to about 1½ ft (0.46 m).

**Distinguishing characteristics.** The stone scorpionfish has generally been considered a subspecies of the spotted scorpionfish *Scorpaena plumieri* of the Atlantic and is often referred to as *S. plumieri mystes* (see Eschmeyer, 1969). We use the name *S. mystes* pending a revision of the "catch basket" genus *Scorpaena* (see Eschmeyer and Randall, 1975). This scorpionfish can be readily distinguished from all Gulf rocky-shore fishes by its broad spiny head, distinct pit below the eye, large pectoral fins with thickened rays, and usually abundant skin flaps over the head and body which give it the appearance of a seaweed-encrusted rock. Its overall appearance is drab, with grays, browns, reds, olive greens, and blacks intermixed. The more conspicuous young are banded with dark bars and have a prominent white caudal peduncle. Adults usually have a black to red-orange patch (often with white spots) in the axil of the

pectoral fin which is flashed when swimming away after being disturbed. D. XII, 9-10; A., III, 5-6.

**Distribution.** A common species, *S. mystes*, ranges fromm Bahía Sebastián Vizcaino and throughout the Gulf south to Ecuador, including the Islas Galápagos.

**Ecology.** *Scorpaena mystes* is a shallow-water scorpionfish that occurs commonly on seaweed-covered reefs as well as on open, sandy areas. An opportunistic predator, this cryptic fish lies unseen on the reef top waiting for small fishes to pass by. The combination of cryptic appearance, venomous dorsal spines, and reluctance to move makes this fish a hazard to swimmers. One snorkler, attempting to steady himself in a wave surge, mistook a large scorpionfish for a rock. He nearly leapt out of the water when he felt the painful sting of the venomous dorsal spines. The diver's hand rapidly became swollen and he felt ill for two days before recovering.

**Related species.** The only other member of this family commonly collected on shallow rocky reefs in the Gulf is the rainbow scorpionfish, *Scorpaenodes xyris* (Jordan and Gilbert, 1882), a small (usually about 3 in. or 76 mm), brownish to reddish fish that can be identified by a large, dark lower opercular spot (see Figure 37) and 13 dorsal spines (*S. mystes* usually has 12); *S. xyris* ranges from southern California to Peru and the Islas Galápagos. It is more common in the central and lower Gulf but ranges north to the midriff islands.

Another scorpionfish, rare in the Gulf, is *Scorpaena histrio* Jenyns, 1843. We have collected only one specimen over a rocky bottom at 40 ft (12 m) at Isla San Pedro Nolasco, Son. The range of this species is primarily from Panama to Chile and includes the Islas Galápagos. It differs from *S. mystes* by its lack of a distinct pit under the eye and by having a head less broad than deep (it is as broad as deep in *S. mystes*).

The other Gulf scorpionfishes are known from offshore and deep waters (*Pontinus*, most species of *Sebastes*) or associated with sandy bottoms (*Scorpaena guttata, S. russula,* and *S. sonorae*). However, the sculpin or spotted scorpionfish, *S. guttata* is a common rocky-shore species in California.

Figure 37   The rainbow scorpionfish, *Scorpaenodes xyris.* Note the prominent lower opercular spot which is usually diagnostic for this species. (Photograph by D. A. Thomson.)

Figure 38  A jewfish, *Epinephelus itajara*, being examined by a marine biologist (Dr. Manuel C. Molles) at Cabo San Lucas. This is one of the largest species of grouper. (Photograph by Alex Kerstitch.)

# FAMILY SERRANIDAE
## Sea basses (Cabrillas y meros)

The sea basses are generalized spiny-rayed fishes with few diagnostic characters to distinguish them from the other perciform fishes. Most have large mouths and strong jaw teeth. Many have one or more backward-projecting opercular spines just before the opercular flap. The maxilla of the upper jaw never slips under the cheekbone (Lutjanidae) and grunts (Haemulidae). Many, if not most, seabasses are hermaphroditic. Some have both egg and sperm-producing tissues in their gonads at all ages (synchronous hermaphrodites). Others undergo a sex reversal with age (sequential hermaphrodites).

Sea basses range in size from less than a pound to giants of almost 1000 lb (see Figure 38). All are voracious predators on fishes and crustaceans. Nearly 400 species are in the family worldwide which is well represented in the Sea of Cortez by approximately 33 species in about 11 genera. In contrast, the Hawaiian sea basses number nine genera but only 10 species and all are deep-water forms (Gosline and Brock, 1960), excluding the introduced shallow water *Cephalopholis argus.* In the Bahamas 10 genera and 30 species have been recorded (Böhlke and Chaplin, 1968). Many are twin species closely related to eastern Pacific (including Gulf of California) forms. In California there are seven genera and 12 species (Miller and Lea, 1972), one of which is the introduced striped bass (*Morone saxatilis*) which some ichthyologists place in the Family Percichthyidae (temperate basses) along with other species such as the giant sea bass, *Stereolepis gigas.* Nine of these California sea basses range into the Sea of Cortez.

In the Gulf 22 species occur commonly on reefs; the others are found in deeper water over sandy bottoms.

*References.*   Gosline (1966); Robins and Starck (1961); Rosenblatt and Zahuranec (1967); Smith (1961, 1965, 1971); Smith and Young (1966); Walford (1937).

# BARRED SERRANO, serrano
## *Serranus fasciatus* Jenyns, 1843

**Illustrated specimen.** Adult, 4.4 in. (110 mm), by Alex Kerstitch; see also Plate 4; maximum size about 7 in. (178 mm).

**Distinguishing characteristics.** Species of the genus *Serranus* are small, handsomely colored basses that can in general be recognized by their 10 dorsal spines, seven anal soft-rays, nondepressible teeth, and finely serrated preopercles; *S. fasciatus* has eight to 12 diagonal rows of scales on the cheek, a series of about six pairs of broad dark bars on each side (often coalesced into a broad dark stripe), and about eight single bars below the lateral midline. D. X (rarely IX), 12 (11–13); A. III, 7.

**Distribution.** This species ranges throughout the Gulf (to Roca Consag) but is commonest in the central and lower regions. Outside the Gulf it extends to Peru and the Islas Galápagos.

**Ecology.** *Serranus fasciatus* occurs from shallow water to depths of about 200 ft (61 m) and is usually found near patch reefs on sandy or broken-shell bottoms. It is a solitary diurnal predator and always stays close to the bottom.

It is seen more commonly during the winter when the juveniles, which can tolerate low water temperatures [56°F (9.4°C) under laboratory acclimation], are first noticed. The western Atlantic lantern bass, *Serranus baldwini* Evermann and Marsh, is similar to *S. fasciatus* in morphology, coloration, and fin-ray counts but is much smaller, reaching a length of only 2.5 in. (64 mm).

**Related species.** Two other species of *Serranus* (*S. aequidens* Gilbert, 1890 and *S. huascarii* Steindachner, 1902) occur in the Gulf in deep water over soft bottoms and are not reef fishes.

Two deep-water reef basses of the genus *Liopropoma* occur in the Gulf: the scalyfin basslet, *L. longilepis* Garman, 1889, so named because the soft dorsal and anal fins are densely covered with scales, and the rainbow basslet (undescribed species), known from a few specimens from Baja California, and seen by us at Isla San Pedro Nolasco at depths between 200 and 250 ft (61 to 76 m). Data are presently inadequate to give the distinctions and distributions of these deep-water basses. This genus is under study by R. H. Rosenblatt.

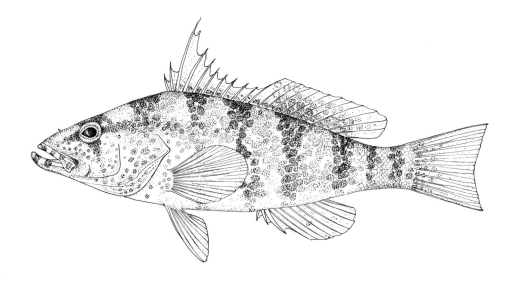

# SPOTTED SAND BASS, cabrilla de roca
## *Paralabrax maculatofasciatus* (Steindachner, 1868)

**Illustrated specimen.** Large juvenile, 5.5 in. (140 mm), by Tor Hansen; attains a length of 22 in. (559 mm).

**Distinguishing characteristics.** The elongated third dorsal spine distinguishes the genus *Paralabrax* from most of the other Gulf basses. Its body and fins are mottled by diffuse black, brown, and orange spots that form six to seven dark bars. A dusky bar extends diagonally downward from the reddish eye (Figure 39) and dark spots occur at the base of the pectoral fin. D. X, 13–14; A. III, 6–8.

**Distribution.** The spotted sand bass ranges from central California to Cabo San Lucas and Mazatlán and throughout the Gulf. It is more common in the upper Gulf, where it ranges to the northernmost Gulf reefs, and less common in the lower Gulf.

**Ecology.** The spotted sand bass prefers low profile reefs next to sandy bottoms. It is commonly found intertidally to depths of about 200 ft (61 m). This bass feeds in the daytime on small fishes and crustaceans and is the most significant predator of juvenile reef fishes at Puerto Peñasco. It has secretive habits, always staying close to the bottom near shelter but roaming widely in search of prey. Although moderately aggressive in captivity, it does not seem to be strongly territorial. Little is known about its breeding habits in the Gulf, but very small juveniles begin to appear intertidally in winter at Puerto Peñasco. Adults and larger juveniles are commonly encountered year-round in the upper Gulf. All species of the genus *Paralabrax* are presumed to be derived from a protogynous ancestor in which the males were sex-reversed females (Smith and Young, 1966).

This eurythermal species tolerates the warmest summer temperatures (greater than 90°F, or 32°C) and survives periodic winterkills of coastal fishes in the northern Gulf. Experimentally, it can tolerate temperatures as low as 45°F (7.5°C), although it ceases feeding at these temperatures (Thomson and Lehner, 1976). The spotted sand bass is the most commonly caught cabrilla in the upper Gulf but has limited commercial or sport value because of its small average size (about 1 lb, or 0.45 kg).

Figure 39 A juvenile spotted sand bass, *Paralabrax maculatofasciatus*. Note the tearshaped pupil of the eye, characteristic of sea basses and other predatory fishes. (Photograph by D. A. Thomson.)

Figure 40 A juvenile goldspotted bass, *Paralabrax auroguttatus*. Juveniles show dark stripes rather than bars and are occasionally seen on shallow reefs. Adults prefer deep patch reefs. (Photograph courtesy of E. S. Hobson.)

**Related species.** At least two other species of *Paralabrax* occur in the Gulf: the goldspotted sand bass, *P. auroguttatus* Walford, 1936, characterized by numerous gold spots over the head, fins, and body, is common at intermediate depths in the central Gulf (Figure 40). This species, known as the "extranjero" (stranger), is often caught by anglers fishing on the bottom at depths of 150 to 250 ft (46 to 76 m). Its third dorsal spine is elongated like that of *P. maculatofasciatus*; a pale streak lies along the lateral line and the lining of its gill cavity is conspicuously orange. It ranges from southern California to the upper Gulf. The other species, *P. loro* Walford, 1936, the parrot sand bass, is a rare lower Gulf form also inhabiting waters of intermediate depth. It can be distinguished from the other two species by a deeper body and a lower number of mid-lateral scales (about 70 in *P. loro*; about 90 in *P. maculatofasciatus* and *P. auroguttatus*). It ranges from Mazatlán to Panama.

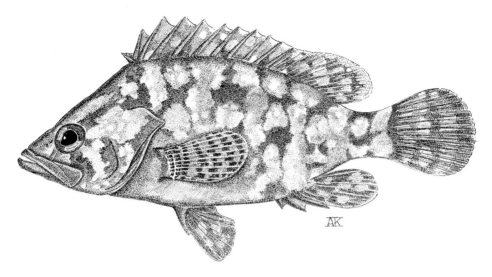

# MUTTON HAMLET, guaseta
## *Epinephelus* (*Alphestes*)\* *afer* Bloch, 1793

**Illustrated specimen.** Young adult, 5.9 in. (150 mm), by Alex Kerstitch; see also Figure 41; reported to reach about 1 ft (305 mm) in length; our largest specimen is 10 in. SL (250 mm).

**Distinguishing characteristics.** Sea basses of the subgenus *Alphestes* can be distinguished by color pattern, head shape (high nape and short snout), and the presence of a strong antrorse spine (point directed downward and forward) at the angle of the preopercle. The spine is inconspicuous, however, often being covered by skin. *E. afer* has a large reddish eye and pink chin. The body is a marbled reddish brown with obscure bars and spots. The seven or eight irregular, transverse dark bars on the pectoral fin are diagnostic for this species (see Related species). D. XI, 18; A. III, 9; P₁. 17.

**Distribution.** The mutton hamlet occurs in the western Atlantic and eastern Pacific where it ranges from the upper Gulf (Isla Angel de la Guarda) south to Peru and the Islas Galápagos. It is more common in the central and lower Gulf than in the upper.

**Ecology.** One of the smaller serranids in the Gulf, this secretive solitary fish is a nocturnal predator, feeding mainly on benthic crustaceans. Inactive during the day, it hides by wedging into crevices or lying among seaweed, and may be easily approached. Sometimes it lies on its side and partly covers itself with sand (Hobson, 1968). Such cryptic behavior and coloration sometimes make this fish difficult to find during the day. In the Caribbean the mutton hamlet is much more common in seagrass beds than on reefs (Randall, 1968).

**Related species.** The Pacific guaseta, *Epinephelus* (*Alphestes*) *multiguttatus* (Günther, 1866), is so closely related to *E. afer* that there has been confusion over the taxonomic status of these and three other nominal species of eastern Pacific *Alphestes*. Smith (1971) clarified much of the problem by placing all of them in the genus *Epinephelus*, relegating *Alphestes* to subgeneric rank and synonymizing *A. galapagensis* Fowler, 1944, *A. fasciatus* Hildebrand, 1946, and *A. immaculatus* Breder, 1936 with *E. afer*. *E. multiguttatus* can be distinguished from *E.*

---

\* The systematics of the American groupers of the genus *Epinephelus* and allied genera have been revised recently by C. L. Smith (1971). Because several name changes have been proposed for these groupers, we include the subgenus (in parentheses) for all species of *Epinephelus*.

Figure 41   A Pacific mutton hamlet, *Epinephelus afer*, showing a typical color pattern for this sedentary/cryptic sea bass. (Photograph by Alex Kerstitch.)

*afer* by its five to six more regularly aligned transverse bars on the pectoral fin. The dark brown spots along the sides also tend to coalesce to form interrupted stripes posteriorly. Fin-ray counts are slightly different: D. XI, 19; A. III, 9; $P_1$. 18. Although Smith (1971) reports that *E. multiguttatus* ranges well into the Gulf, 83 of our 86 Gulf specimens of the subgenus *Alphestes* are *E. afer*. The three *E. multiguttatus* were collected at Mazatlán. Therefore the amended range of *E. multiguttatus* is from Topolobampo, Sinaloa (one specimen at UCLA ), to Panama.

The leather bass, *Epinephelus (Dermatolepis) dermatolepis* Boulenger, 1895, is closely related to the groupers of the subgenus *Alphestes*. Its common name derives from thick, coarse leathery membranes between the fin rays. Along the American mainland it ranges from Bahía Magdalena to Ecuador and the Islas Galápagos (including all the other far offshore islands). In the Gulf it is found primarily in the Cape region but extends into the central Gulf as far north as Isla San Pedro Nolasco (Kerstitch sight record) near deep water. It reaches a length of about 3 ft (1 m).

This is a deep-bodied, compressed species with a steep anterior profile. The small scales with reduced ctenii are embedded in the skin, which is thus smooth to the touch. The adult is often covered with irregular dull white blotches and small dark spots on the grayish background. Solitary individuals show several dark bars with light spots (Figure 42), but this grouper is capable of considerable color changes, depending largely on its association with other species (see Montgomery, 1975). Juveniles are marked with distinct, broad, dark bars on a white background that cover the entire fish including the fins (see Figure 43). The leather bass has specialized habits. Small juveniles have been collected among the spines of the sea urchin *Centrostephanus coronatus*. Older juveniles and adults often form complex feeding associations with grazing fishes, using them as a moving blind as they prey on small benthic fishes disturbed by the grazers (Montgomery, 1975). When feeding solitarily, this grouper is often seen with its body pitched forward in a nearly vertical position cruising over and inspecting boulder surfaces in search of prey (see Plate 7a).

Figure 42   A young adult leather bass, *Epinephelus dermatolepis*. This grouper uses grazing fishes as a blind to attack its prey of smaller fishes. (Photograph courtesy of E. S. Hobson.)

Figure 43   A juvenile leather bass, *Epinephelus dermatolepis*. Strikingly barred juveniles are sometimes seen seeking refuge among the spines of the long-spined, darkly colored sea urchin, *Centrostephanus coronatus* (Verrill). (Photograph by Alex Kerstitch.)

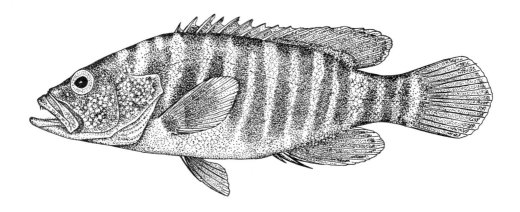

# PANAMA GRAYSBY, enjambre
*Epinephelus* (*Cephalopholis*) *panamensis* (Steindachner, 1876)

**Illustrated specimen.** Young adult, 6.3 in. (160 mm), by Tor Hansen; see also Plate 7b; maximum size attained about 12 in. (305 mm).

**Distinguishing characteristics.** This small sea bass can be distinguished from other Gulf basses by a rounded caudal fin, nine to 10 dark cross bands on the body, and numerous large blue and orange spots on the side of the head. Juveniles are similar to adults in coloration except that the adult has a large dark spot behind the eye. This sea bass has been referred to as *Petrometopon panamensis*. D. IX, 14; A. III, 8.

**Distribution.** The Panama graysby ranges throughout the Gulf (Roca Consag) to Colombia, Isla del Coco, and the Islas Galápagos. It is most common on shallow reefs in the central and lower Gulf.

**Ecology.** The Panama graysby is a secretive and solitary fish found in shallow water to depths of 250 ft (76 m). This bass stays close to the bottom, hiding in crevices, only darting out to seize small fishes and crustaceans. In captivity it will attack and attempt to eat fishes almost its own size. It is frequently collected along rocky shores in the Gulf and may be the most numerous serranid on certain reefs, such as in Bahía Concepción, Baja California Sur.

A species similar to *E. panamensis* occurs in the western Atlantic. The graysby, *E. cruentatus* (Lacépède), is the commonest sea bass in the Bahamas and despite its small size (1 ft) has some importance there as a food fish (Böhlke and Chaplin, 1968). Unlike *E. panamensis*, it is relatively unafraid of divers (Randall, 1968).

75

# GULF CONEY, baqueta
## *Epinephelus* (*Epinephelus*) *acanthistius* (Gilbert, 1892)

**Illustrated specimen.** Adult, 28 in. (710 mm), by Alex Kerstitch; see also Plate 5; attains a length of more than 3 ft (1.0 m).

**Distinguishing characteristics.** This grouper is characterized by a large head and chunky rose-colored body. Depending on age and water depth, the color varies in intensity. The anterior dorsal spines (especially the third and fourth) are elongated and the membranes between them, deeply cleft. A prominent, oblique, black bar (mustache) runs above the upper jaw and the fins are dark distally. Until recently it had been placed in the genus *Cephalopholis*. D. IX, 17; A. III, 9.

**Distribution.** The Gulf coney ranges throughout the Gulf of California to Peru. We have collected it from shrimp trawlers as far north as Puerto Peñasco.

**Ecology.** The Gulf coney, earlier considered a rare species (Meek and Hildebrand, 1925; Walford, 1937), is a common bottom fish throughout the Gulf of California. This moderately deep-water sea bass is found over patch reefs and sandy bottoms close to shore, usually at depths exceeding 150 ft (46 m). We have never observed it while scuba diving on reefs, but it is frequently caught by anglers fishing near the bottom at depths to 300 ft (91 m). Because of its preference for deep water, little is known about the biology of this species. It is sometimes sold as "red snapper" in Puerto Peñasco fish markets.

**Related species.** The snowy grouper, *E.* (*Epinephelus*) *niveatus* (Valenciennes, 1828), appears to be the least common of the Gulf species of *Epinephelus* and is usually collected only in trawls. This is one of the few reef fishes that occurs in both the Pacific and Atlantic. However, it is much more common in the Atlantic, where it ranges from New England to Brazil, and the Gulf of Mexico. In the eastern Pacific it ranges from central California to Bahía San Luis Gonzaga, B.C.N., and south to Panama. The snowy

Figure 44   A juvenile snowy grouper, *Epinephelus niveatus*. This deep-water grouper is often caught in shrimp trawls in the central Gulf. (Photograph by Alex Kerstitch.)

grouper can be recognized by its 11 dorsal spines and several rows of regularly spaced, pearly white spots (which fade with age) on a chocolate-brown body (Figure 44). Juveniles have a large dark saddle on the caudal peduncle. In the western Atlantic this fish ranges from shallow water to depths of 1500 ft (457 m) and the adults assume a coppery golden hue. In the eastern Pacific the deepest it has been collected is 426 ft (130 m).

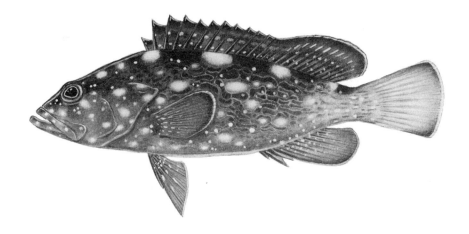

# FLAG CABRILLA, cabrilla piedrera
## *Epinephelus* (*Epinephelus*) *labriformis* (Jenyns, 1843)

**Illustrated specimen.** Young adult, 9 in. (229 mm) by Alex Kerstitch; attains a length of about 20 in. (508 mm).

**Distinguishing characteristics.** *Epinephelus labriformis* is a medium-sized sea bass that can be readily distinguished from other Gulf sea basses by its handsome color pattern: olive-green to reddish brown body, various-sized, irregular white spots scattered over it, and the soft dorsal, anal and caudal fins with red on the dorsal and ventral margins. A distinct black saddle appears on top of the caudal peduncle. The inside of the mouth is red. It has 11 dorsal spines and its rather short pelvic fins do not reach past the vent. D. XI, 16–17; A. III, 8.

**Distribution.** The flag cabrilla ranges from Bahía Magdalena to the upper Gulf (Puerto Lobos) and south to Peru, including all the far offshore islands. It is common in the central and lower Gulf on shallow reefs.

**Ecology.** The flag cabrilla is a solitary predator that seems to feed both day and night, taking mostly smaller fishes by day and crustaceans after dark (Hobson, 1968). A secretive fish, *E. labriformis* darts out from cover to seize its prey but stays close to the rocky bottom. Juveniles appear on the reef from October to December, which indicates that spawning occurs in late summer. Although the adults are most abundant in shallow water, they occur to a depth of at least 100 ft (30 m).

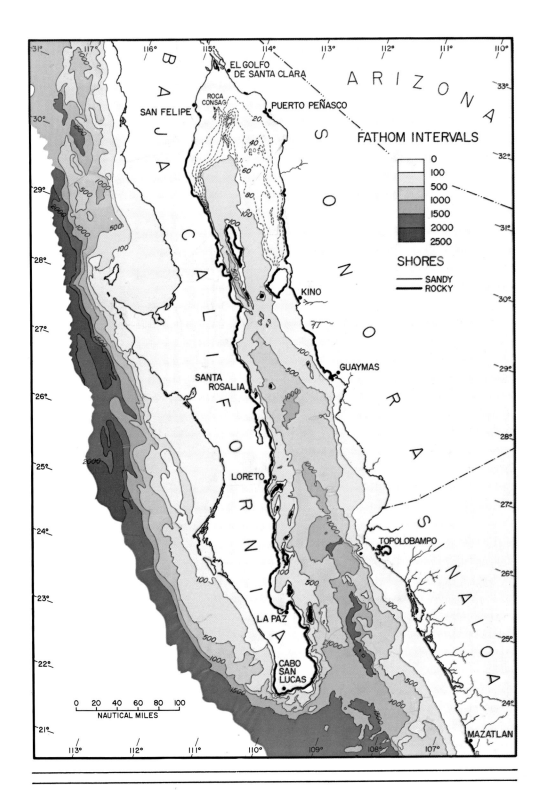

Plate 1   Bathymetric map of the Gulf of California showing locations of rocky and sandy shores within the Gulf (modified from Chart I of Fisher, Rusnak and Shepard, 1964).

Plate 2 Eels (all photographs by Alex Kerstitch): a. Jewel moray (*Muraena lentiginosa*). b. Panamic green moray (*Gymnothorax castaneus*). c. Slenderjaw moray (*Enchelycore octaviana*). d. A garden eel (*Taenioconger* sp.) off Isla San Pedro Martir (probably *T. digueti*).

Plate 3 Secretive fishes (all photographs by Alex Kerstitch): a. Sanguine frogfish (*Antennarius sanguineus*). b. Bandtail frogfish (*Antennatus strigatus*). c. Panamic soldierfish (*Myripristis leiognathos*). d. Barspot cardinalfish (*Apogon retrosella*).

Plate 4 Barred serrano (*Serranus fasciatus*). Illustrated by Alex Kerstitch.

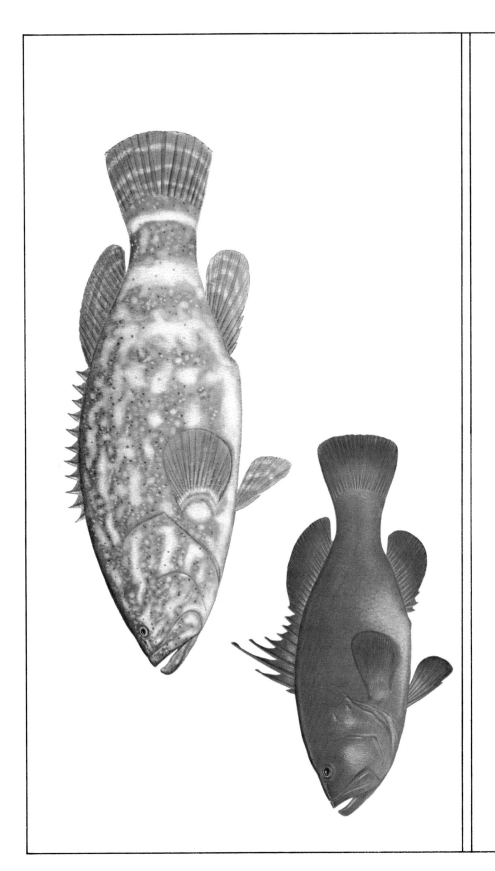

Plate 5  Upper fish, jewfish (*Epinephelus itajara*); lower fish, Gulf coney (*Epinephelus acanthistius*). Illustrated by Alex Kerstitch.

Plate 6 Pacific creolefish (*Paranthias colonus*). Illustrated by Alex Kerstitch.

Plate 7 Sea basses (all photographs by Alex Kerstitch): a. Leather bass (*Epinephelus dermatolepis*), showing pitched-forward posture, in search of prey. b. Panama graysby (*Epinephelus panamensis*). c. Gulf grouper (*Mycteroperca jordani*). d. Leopard grouper (*Mycteroperca rosacea*) showing spotted and golden phases. e. Pacific creolefish (*Paranthias colonus*).

(a)

(b)

(c)

(d)

Plate 8   Snappers (all photographs by Alex Kerstitch except *d*, which is by courtesy of Ed Janss): a. Juvenile barred pargo (*Hoplopagrus guentheri*). b. Adult yellow snapper (*Lutjanus argentiventris*). c. Adult Pacific dog snapper (*Lutjanus novemfasciatus*). d. Blue-and-gold snapper (*Lutjanus viridis*).

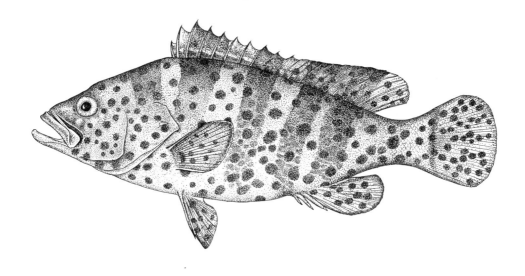

# SPOTTED CABRILLA, cabrilla pinta
## Epinephelus (Epinephelus) analogus Gill, 1864

**Illustrated specimen.** Juvenile, 7.7 in. (195 mm), by Tor Hansen; said to reach a size of 20 lb (9 kg) and about 2½ ft (0.8 m).

**Distinguishing characteristics.** This medium-sized grouper may be distinguished from the other Gulf basses by the following combination of characteristics: 10 dorsal spines, rounded caudal fin, and numerous dark spots and broad dusky bars covering the body. Its overall color is reddish brown with large dark brown spots resembling the color pattern of young jewfish (*E. itajara*). Its western Atlantic twin is the rock hind, *E. adscensionis* (Osbeck), and the name *analogus* (similar) refers to its strong resemblance to this species (Smith, 1971). D. X, 16–18; A. III, 8.

**Distribution.** The spotted cabrilla ranges from southern California and the northernmost rocky reefs of the Gulf to Peru and the Islas Galápagos. The "pinta" is the most abundant small grouper in the upper Gulf.

**Ecology.** Not often found along shore, the preferred habitat of the pinta seems to be offshore patch reefs, where they may be abundant and are commonly caught by anglers. Because adults aggregate on offshore reefs at moderate depths, their ecology has not been studied. The rock hind, in marked contrast, is a shallow-water species (Böhlke and Chaplin, 1968; Randall, 1968).

Spotted cabrillas are voracious predators, feeding largely on crustaceans and fish over rocky and sandy bottoms. In the winter, when Gulf water temperatures are low, these fish move closer to shore in shallower water. There they feed heavily on swarms of "langostina," the "lobster krill" or pelagic red crab (*Pleuroncodes planipes*), which are especially abundant then.

Although it is one of the finest food fishes in the Gulf, the pinta does not rank high with anglers because it is too easy to catch and when hooked does not put up a spectacular fight. Instead, it usually swims to the bottom, often wedging itself in a crevice, making it difficult for the angler to dislodge it. However, Mexican fishermen successfully exploit this species in local hand-line fisheries.

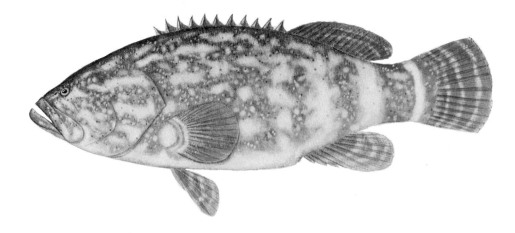

# JEWFISH, cherna, mero

## *Epinephelus* (*Promicrops*) *itajara* (Lichtenstein, 1822)

**Illustrated specimen.** Adult, about 5 ft (1.5 m), by Alex Kerstitch; see also Plate 5 and Figure 38; reported to reach a length of 8 ft (2.4 m) and a weight of more than 700 lb (318 kg).

**Distinguishing characteristics.** Adult jewfish can be recognized by their enormous size and tiny eyes which seem out of proportion to their wide, massive heads. Body coloration varies from greenish or brownish yellow to pale gray, and body and fins are covered with small dark and light spots. The young, which have at least six broad dark bars, resemble the spotted cabrilla, *E. analogus*. Both species have rounded caudal fins and their bodies are barred and spotted; however, the dark spots of *E. analogus* are larger and more uniformly distributed over the body, and there are only four dark body bars. The dark spots of young *E. itajara* are usually found only on the six dark bars. The area between the eyes (interorbital) of *E. itajara* is distinctly flattened or depressed, whereas in *E. analogus* the interorbital space is curved and somewhat elevated. Also *E. itajara* has 11 dorsal spines, whereas *E. analogus* has 10. The common name jewfish is thought to be derived from junefish, the name for this grouper in Panama (Walford, 1937). D. XI, 15–16; A. III, 8.

**Distribution.** The jewfish is found along both coasts of tropical America. In the Atlantic it ranges from Bermuda to Brazil, including the Gulf of Mexico and the Caribbean Sea. In the eastern Pacific it ranges from the central Gulf (Estero Tastiota) to Peru. We have not seen this grouper in the upper Gulf.

**Ecology.** The jewfish is one of the largest groupers known. Because of its size and food value, it is sought as a trophy and for the market. Once relatively common in the Gulf, it is now scarce, especially along coasts accessible to spearfishermen. This sluggish giant shows little fear of man and, unfortunately, can be easily approached and speared by a diver. In the Gulf adults may be found at 15 to 100 ft (5 to 30 m), usually in or around caves, whereas the juveniles inhabit estuaries. Sometimes adult jewfish will defend a territory around their refuge. One of the authors (Kerstitch) was threatened by a large jewfish in a cave. The threat display consisted of an open-jaws approach accompanied by erratic quivering of the body. On another occasion an especially huge jewfish approached him so closely that he had to fend it off by a solid blow on its snout with his fist. The jewfish retreated but circled him curiously

Figure 45   A giant sea bass, *Stereolepis gigas*, at Scripps Aquarium, La Jolla, California. (Photograph by Alex Kerstitch.)

before swimming away. In this instance Mr. Kerstitch interpreted the jewfish's behavior as food seeking rather than territorial attack and he had the eery feeling of being the prey rather than the predator. Jewfish exhibit another type of behavior when they frequent "cleaning stations," where external parasites are removed from fishes by "cleaners." At Shepard's rock, off Cabo San Lucas, a large jewfish was observed being groomed by cleaner gobies, *Elacatinus* sp. Divers were able to approach and "pet" the grouper for nearly 30 minutes, neither causing it to attack nor flee (see Figure 38).

The food habits of the jewfish in the eastern Pacific are not known. In the Atlantic they feed primarily on crustaceans, thought to be a specialization among the predominantly fish-eating groupers (Smith, 1961; Randall, 1967). Randall notes that they feed mainly on lobsters, although he has also found sea turtles and stingrays in their stomachs.

**Related species.**   Although not related to the jewfish, the giant sea bass *Stereolepis gigas*

Ayres, 1859 grows almost as large [world's record is 563 lb (256 kg) and 7 ft 5 in. (2.3 m)] and is included here because of its size (see Figure 45). It can be identified by its numerous, fine, cardiform teeth, but lacks the canine teeth characteristic of other Gulf sea basses and has been placed in the Family Percichthyidae (temperate basses) by some ichthyologists. The adults are dark brown or gray, sometimes showing diffuse dark blotches on their sides. The juveniles are brick red with about six irregular rows of dark spots on the sides. Dorsal and anal fin-ray counts are D. XI + I-II, 9–10; A. III, 8–9. The giant sea bass is a highly valued commercial fish throughout its range from northern California (Humboldt Bay) to Oaxaca, Mexico, and throughout the Gulf of California. It may be found inshore in relatively shallow water but is more common in offshore, deeper waters over patch reefs. A voracious and swift predator, this sea bass preys on various fishes, including mackerels, tunas, sharks, and stingrays, as well as lobsters and crabs.

81

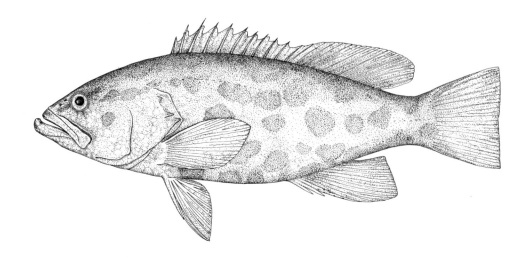

# GULF GROUPER, baya
## *Mycteroperca jordani* (Jenkins and Evermann, 1889)

**Illustrated specimen.** Large juvenile, 17.8 in. (450 mm), by Tor Hansen; see also Plate 7c; reported to grow to about 5 ft (1.5 m) and 200 lb (91 kg).

**Distinguishing characteristics.** The genus *Mycteroperca* is represented in the eastern Pacific by five species of medium-to-large-sized groupers: *M. jordani, M. prionura, M. rosacea, M. xenarcha,* and *M. olfax.* Only *M. olfax* has not been recorded in the Gulf (known from the Islas Galápagos, del Coco and Malpelo, and northern Peru). The genus is characterized by D. X–XI, 15–18, A. III, 10–12, and small embedded scales (90 to 120 rows above lateral line). The largest member of this genus in the Gulf, *M. jordani,* can be distinguished from the other species by its low total number of gill rakers on the first arch (21 to 26). Its color pattern is variable; adults are overall grayish, whereas juveniles have large dusky blotches on a grayish brown ground color with faint streaks radiating from the eye. The fin margins are whitish in both young and adults. D. XI, 15–17; A. III, 10–11.

**Distribution.** The baya grouper is distributed throughout the Gulf and occurs as far north as southern California (La Jolla) but has not been recorded south of Mazatlán. It is the commonest large grouper in the upper and central Gulf.

**Ecology.** Although the Gulf grouper is a common large grouper and is prized by anglers and spearfishermen, little is known about the habits of this giant. Voracious predators, baya groupers have been caught with 2-ft (0.6-m) hammerhead sharks in their stomachs. They roam along the bottom over sand and rocks, moving closer inshore in the evening and early morning. They are often present in underwater caves and large crevices in shallow water where they are vulnerable to spearfishermen.

In summer these fish are usually found in depths below 100 ft (30 m), but by late fall they appear on reefs 15 to 50 ft (4.6 to 9 m) deep, where they stay until early the next summer. These seasonal movements seem to be related to water temperature. In areas in which spearfishing is intense (Guaymas-San Carlos) baya groupers are becoming scarce.

# LEOPARD GROUPER, GOLDEN GROUPER
## cabrilla sardinera, cabrilla calamaria
### *Mycteroperca rosacea* (Streets, 1877)

**Illustrated specimens.** Spotted phase, 14 in. (356 mm), golden phase, 14 in. (355 mm), by Alex Kerstitch; see also Plate 7d and Figure 46; said to reach a length of 3 ft (1 m) and 40 lb (12.2 kg).

**Distinguishing characteristics.** The surest way to identify specimens of *M. rosacea* is to count the total gill rakers on the first arch. It has 38 to 43 (usually 39 to 40), which is more than any other eastern Pacific *Mycteroperca*. Its color pattern is variable. In life the head, body and fins are covered with small reddish brown spots over a greenish to grayish brown background, which give the fish a speckled appearance. There are prominent whitish margins on the soft dorsal, anal, pelvic, and pectoral fins, a character also seen in the Gulf grouper, *M. jordani*. About 1% of the population undergoes a transformation to a completely golden phase, sometimes retaining only a few small patches of dark pigment. D. XI, 17 (16–18); A. III, 10–11.

**Distribution.** Ranging from Bahía Magdalena and throughout the Gulf from the northernmost rocky reefs (Roca Consag) to Puerto Vallarta (Bahía Banderas), the leopard grouper is the most conspicuously abundant rocky-shore grouper in the central and lower regions. In the upper Gulf it is exceeded in abundance among the sea basses only by the spotted sand bass and the spotted cabrilla.

**Ecology.** More is known about the ecology of this serranid than any other Gulf sea bass because of the intensive studies of Hobson (1968) on its predatory behavior. The leopard grouper is essentially a shallow-water, crepuscular predator that aggregates over rocky prominences at midday when it is relatively inactive. Immediately after sunset, however, it begins to feed voraciously on herrings or anchovies, sometimes leaping completely out of the water as feeding intensifies. It seems to prefer to feed on schools of flatiron herring, *Harengula thrissina,* whenever these fish are present. Because of this habit, Mexican fisherman refer to *M. rosacea* as "sardinera." Leopard groupers are rarely found deeper than 150 ft (46 m) and never far from shore.

Figure 46   The spotted phase of the leopard grouper, *Mycteroperca rosacea*. This common grouper is often found in aggregations in midwater over reefs. (Photograph by Alex Kerstitch.)

Some juveniles begin to develop golden pigmentation before they are a foot long and eventually become completely covered with bright yellow-orange pigment. When in the golden phase (see Plate 7d), this strikingly conspicuous fish can be spotted quite easily, even from a boat. The late Ray Cannon (1966) wrote of observing "goldies," as he called them, "herding" schools of forage fish to make them more readily available to the other cabrilla. This suggestion that golden cabrilla act as leaders of the aggregation was not substantiated by Hobson's thorough study, nor have we observed any such behavior. However, the golden phase of this species remains largely unstudied and the ecological significance of its distinctive coloration, if there is any, is unknown.

**Related species.** The broomtail grouper, *M. xenarcha* Jordan, 1888, ranges widely from northern California to Peru and into the central Gulf. It is named "broomtail" because of its jagged ("torn") caudal fin profile. Its color is usually brown to grayish-green with dark, irregular blotches on the sides (see

Figure 47). It is a moderately large grouper (about 100 lb, or 45 kg), and, although widely distributed, it is infrequently encountered along rocky shores in the Gulf, perhaps because of its preference for mangrove estuaries. What was once thought to be the red-spotted phase of *M. xenarcha* has been described as a separate species, *M. prionura* Rosenblatt and Zahuranec, 1967. This species, named the sawtail grouper, is covered with round reddish brown spots that become more numerous and smaller with growth but is never so finely spotted as *M. rosacea* (see Figure 48). It has a sawlike caudal fin profile similar to that of the broomtail grouper and seems to prefer deeper water than the other eastern Pacific *Mycteroperca*. It can be separated from the broomtail and leopard groupers by its total gill-raker count on the first arch: *M. prionura* (34 to 38), *M. xenarcha* (29 to 33), and *M. rosacea* (38 to 43) and their distinctive color patterns. It ranges from the Islas Santa Inés in the Gulf to Bahía Banderas (Puerto Vallarta). The juveniles of both species have normal caudal fin margins.

Figure 47  A juvenile broomtail grouper, *Mycteroperca xenarcha*, in the blotched or pinto color phase. Note the conspicuous black blotch on the dorsal surface of the caudal peduncle. (Photograph by Alex Kerstitch.)

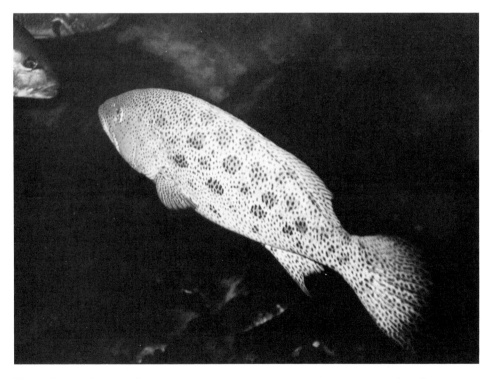

Figure 48  An adult sawtail grouper, *Mycteroperca prionura*. Note the large spots and sawlike margin of the caudal fin that distinguish this species from *M. xenarcha* and *M. rosacea*. (Photograph by Alex Kerstitch, taken at Sea World, San Diego.)

# PACIFIC CREOLEFISH, indio, rabirrubia de lo alto
## *Paranthias colonus* (Valenciennes, 1855)

**Illustrated specimen.** Young adult, 7 in. (178 mm), by Alex Kerstitch; see also Plates 6 and 7e; reaches a length of at least 14 in. (356 mm).

**Distinguishing characteristics.** *Paranthias colonus* and *P. pinguis* Walford, 1936, are considered by Smith (1971) as synonyms of the Atlantic creolefish, *P. furcifer* (Cuvier and Valenciennes, 1828). Although all three nominal forms are similar morphologically, there are significant differences in coloration and body proportions between Atlantic and Pacific *Paranthias*. In the absence of thorough studies of geographical variations Smith (1971) has treated the three forms as a single species. For the same reason we prefer to retain *P. colonus* for the Pacific creolefish, synonymizing it only with *P. pinguis*.

The adult creolefish can be readily distinguished from all Gulf serranids by its overall salmon-red color (darker above, lighter below) and deeply forked, lunate caudal fin. A row of four to five light bluish spots extends from the middorsal region of the back to the caudal peduncle. The young are pinkish-yellow with bright blue dorsal spots. D. IX, 18–20; A. III, 9–10.

**Distribution.** The Pacific creolefish ranges throughout the lower and central Gulf to Peru and most of the far offshore islands. We have observed it as far north as Puerto Lobos in the upper Gulf.

**Ecology.** This creolefish is found typically in small aggregations from the surface to 200 ft (61 m). It feeds at the surface or in midwater and is not so secretive as most serranids. It is not so commonly seen by skin divers as other basses because it frequents the deeper portion of reefs.

**Related species.** The threadfin bass, *Anthias gordensis* Wade, 1946, is numerous in the Cabo San Lucas region at depths of 175 to 250 ft (53 to 76 m). It is a small reddish fish with chainlike yellow stripes along its sides, a yellow forked tail, a rather large eye, and an enlarged second anal spine. Little is known about its distribution, although it has been taken as far north as Santa Catalina Island in southern California (Hobson, 1975).

# FAMILY GRAMMISTIDAE
## Soapfishes and allies (Jaboneros y aliados)

The grammistids are specialized tropical fishes closely related to the serranids. All are small secretive fishes among which the soapfishes are characterized by their toxic skin mucous secretions. They have unusually elongated nasal organs and the upper edge of the opercle is attached to the head by a membrane. Their lower jaw is projecting and they usually have three opercular spines. There are two genera with three species in the Gulf (see Figure 49), two genera with five species in the Bahamas, two genera with two species in Hawaii, but none in California. World-wide, there are at least six genera and 17 species.

**References.**   Böhlke (1960); Gosline (1960); Randall et al. (1971); Schultz et al. (1966); Schultz and Reid (1939).

Figure 49   A juvenile blackfin soapfish, *Rypticus nigripinnis*. The smallest juveniles of this species have broad yellow stripes that later break up into rows of light spots as the fish matures. (Photograph by D. A. Thomson.)

87

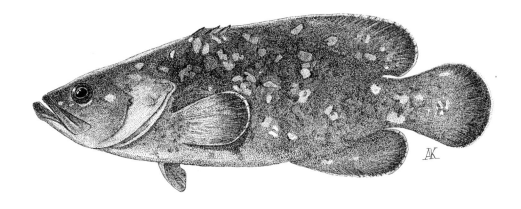

# CORTEZ SOAPFISH, jabonero de Cortés
## *Rypticus bicolor* (Valenciennes, 1846)

**Illustrated specimen.** Adult, 7.1 in. (181 mm), by Alex Kerstitch; reaches a length of about 1 ft (0.3 m).

**Distinguishing characteristics.** Soapfishes are characterized by their skin secretions of mucus which lather like soap when agitated. Soapfishes lack anal spines, have small embedded cycloid scales, and their soft dorsal, caudal, and anal fins are rounded. The Cortez soapfish varies in coloration from a deep chocolate-brown with light tan spots (juveniles) to a pale brown with lighter irregular blotches (adults). A conspicuous white stripe runs between the eyes from the dorsal fin to the tip of the chin. It differs from the blackfin soapfish, *R. nigripinnis,* by having three dorsal spines instead of two and by its projecting lower jaw which, as viewed ventrally, forms a sharp point at the chin. D. III (rarely II), 23–24; A. 14–16.

**Distribution.** Common in the central and lower Gulf, *R. bicolor* ranges from the upper Gulf (where it is rare) to Peru. The Cortez soapfish is the twin species of the commonest and largest soapfish in the tropical western Atlantic, the greater soapfish, *R. saponaceus* (Bloch and Schneider).

**Ecology.** The Cortez soapfish is nocturnal and during the day seeks shelter under ledges or wedges itself tightly into crevices. Normally found in shallow waters, it has been recorded at a depth of 225 ft (69 m). Soapfishes probably have few predators because their toxic secretions can cause hemolysis of the red blood cells. The toxin has been named "grammistin" by Randall et al. (1971), who found that a "taste test" of the skin mucus of six genera of soapfishes was useful in its initial screening.

Both *R. bicolor* and *R. nigripinnis* sometimes exhibit a peculiar behavior during feeding. In approaching small prey fishes, they virtually "stand on their heads," their bodies quivering rapidly and displaying their conspicuous white dorsal stripes. This seems to attract small fishes which are suddenly seized by the soapfishes as they approach.

# BLACKFIN SOAPFISH, negrillo
## *Rypticus nigripinnis* Gill, 1862

**Illustrated specimen.** Juvenile, 3.8 in. (97 mm), by Alex Kerstitch; see also Figure 49; grows to about 8 in. (203 mm).

**Distinguishing characteristics.** This soapfish has numerous small light blotches along the sides in a regular pattern, which give it a spotted or reticulated appearance. Very young *R. nigripinnis* show a broad yellow stripe that runs dorsally from the tip of the chin to the dorsal fin and laterally along the base of the dorsal around the caudal and along the base of the anal fin. As the fish grows this stripe disappears and the small yellowish blotches appear (see Figure 49). This species usually has only two dorsal spines (three in *R. bicolor*) and the tip of the chin appears rounded, not pointed, when viewed ventrally. D. II (rarely I), 24–26; A. 16.

**Distribution.** Not so common as the Cortez soapfish, the blackfin soapfish ranges throughout the Gulf (rare at Puerto Peñasco) to Peru.

**Ecology.** The blackfin soapfish, named because of its darkly pigmented caudal and anal fins, does not grow so large as *R. bicolor*. Little is known about this shy and highly secretive species. Even in aquaria it remains hidden most of the time, whereas *R. bicolor* tames readily and can be fed by hand. One specimen of *R. nigripinnis* lived for three years in captivity, never changing its secretive habits.

**Related species.** The only other grammistid recorded from the Gulf is the blackspot bass, *Pseudogramma thaumasium* (Gilbert, 1900). This species differs from the soapfishes by having three anal spines, a rather long anal fin, and a distinctive black spot on the upper part of the opercle. This smaller uncommon species ranges from the central Gulf (Guaymas) to Panama. Some ichthyologists place this species and its relatives in the family Pseudogrammidae.

# FAMILY KUHLIIDAE
## Aholeholes

These basslike fishes are tropical Indo-Pacific forms that resemble freshwater sunfishes (Centrarchidae) and often migrate into freshwater streams. They have few distinguishing characteristics other than their forked caudal and deeply notched dorsal fins.

The only kuhliid in the eastern Pacific, *Kuhlia taeniura* (Cuvier, 1829), is readily recognizable by its overall silvery body and four oblique dusky bars and center streak on its deeply forked tail. It is collected commonly only in the Cabo San Lucas region of the Gulf but ranges to Colombia and the Islas Galápagos. *K. argae* Jordan and Bollman, 1889, described from eastern Pacific specimens, appears to be conspecific with *K. taeniura* (see Rosenblatt et al., 1972). In Hawaii the kuhliid, *K. sandvicensis,* is called the aholehole. It grows to about 1 ft (0.3 m) in length and is considered a fine food fish. Worldwide, there are three genera with 12 species.

*Reference.* Rosenblatt et al. (1972).

Figure 50  The popeye catalufa, *Pristigenys* (= *Pseudopriacanthus*) *serrula.* Note the large eye of this member of the bigeye family. (Photograph by Alex Kerstitch, taken in Scripps Aquarium, La Jolla, California.)

# FAMILY PRIACANTHIDAE
## Bigeyes (Semáforos)

Large eyes and rough scales are characteristic of this small family of nocturnal reef fishes (Figure 50). The most important diagnostic characteristic of the family is a broad membrane that joins the inner ventral ray to the abdomen. Most bigeyes are deep-water fishes and are rarely seen by the average scuba diver. There are two genera and two species in the Gulf of the three genera and 18 species in the family worldwide.

*References.*  Caldwell (1962); Clark (1936); Hildebrand and Barton (1949); Myers (1958).

# POPEYE CATALUFA, catalufa, ojotón
*Pristigenys* ( = *Pseudopriacanthus*) *serrula* (Gilbert, 1890)

**Illustrated specimen.** From Kumada and Hiyama (1937); see also Figure 50; attains a length of about 13 in. (330 mm).

**Distinguishing characteristics.** A crimson fish with large eyes, the popeye catalufa can be recognized easily by its characteristic color and shape. The squirrelfishes (Holocentridae) and the cardinalfishes (Apogonidae) are the only other rocky-shore species with bright red coloration in the Gulf. *P. serrula* is much more compressed than these fishes and has a larger head and eye but can be separated from similar-appearing fishes by noting the inner ray of the ventral fin which is connected to the abdomen by a broad membrane. D. X, 11; A. III, 10–11.

**Distribution.** Ranging from Monterey Bay, California, to Peru, *P. serrula* is uncommonly collected on rocky reefs in the central and lower Gulf. We have not found it in the upper Gulf.

**Ecology.** The popeye catalufa, like all other members of this small family, is a shy nocturnal fish that prefers the deeper water around islands. It may be found with squirrelfishes and cardinalfishes but tends to range deeper than they do (to 250 ft, or 76 m). Little is known about its ecology because of the depths in which it generally lives. Our largest specimen (nearly 8 in., or 200 mm) was collected at Cabo San Lucas at 110 ft (34 m). We have collected several smaller *P. serrula* (3 to 4 in.) from shrimp trawls in the Guaymas vicinity.

**Related species.** Only one other member of this family occurs in the Gulf. The glasseye, *Priacanthus cruentatus* (Lacépède, 1802), misnamed the glasseye snapper, is a widely distributed species that occurs commonly in the western Atlantic and eastern tropical Pacific, usually near offshore islands (Figure 51). We have collected this species at Isla Jaltemba, Nayarit, and Cabo San Lucas. Its single long spine at the angle of the preopercle distinguishes it from *P. serrula,* which has a serrated preopercle. Although normally overall reddish in coloration, it shows a series of silvery bands and blotches along the back and sides when in stress.

91

Figure 51  The glasseye, *Priacanthus cruentatus*. Note again the large eye of these crimson nocturnal fishes characteristic of the family Priacanthidae. (Photograph by Alex Kerstitch, taken in the Scripps Aquarium, La Jolla, California.)

# FAMILY APOGONIDAE
## Cardinalfishes (Cardenales)

Cardinalfishes are usually small rosy-to-bright-red nocturnal fishes common on shallow tropical reefs. They have a separated dorsal fin and two anal spines rather than the three typical of most percoid fishes (Figure 52). Most are mouth brooders, which incubate the egg mass in the mouth. Although four species of the genus *Apogon* have been recorded from the Gulf, only one species (*A. retrosella*) is common. Worldwide, this fairly large family is represented by 170 species in 20 genera.

***References.*** Böhlke and Randall (1968); Breder (1936); Fraser (1972); Hobson (1969a).

Figure 52  The pink cardinalfish, *Apogon parri* (upper), and the barspot cardinalfish, *Apogon retrosella* (lower). Cardinalfishes have separated dorsal fins, large eyes, and two anal spines. (Photograph by Alex Kerstitch.)

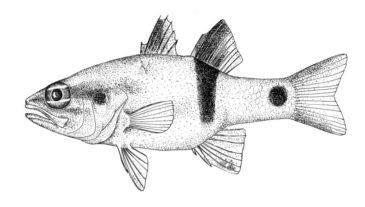

# BARSPOT CARDINALFISH, cardenal
## *Apogon retrosella* (Gill, 1863)

**Illustrated specimen.** Adult, 3.2 in. (80 mm), by Tor Hansen; grows to about 4 in. (102 mm).

**Distinguishing characteristics.** Overall pinkish to brilliant red in coloration, a conspicuous black saddlelike bar under the second dorsal fin, and a large black spot on the caudal peduncle readily distinguish *Apogon retrosella* from all other shallow-water fishes in the Gulf. Although the red coloration sometimes tends to become faint and the black markings suffuse in large adults, the only other overall bright red fish commonly encountered on the reefs is the soldierfish, *Myripristis leiognathos*. The soldierfish lacks black markings and, unlike *A. retrosella,* has strong dorsal, pelvic, and anal spines. Young cardinalfish show a pale-to-rosy-pink color but have the black markings of the adult. The bright scarlet coloration of the adults fades quickly after death and usually completely disappears after preservation. D. VI + I, 10; A. II, 7.

**Distribution.** Commonest of the Gulf cardinalfishes, *A. retrosella* occurs on all rocky reefs from the northern Gulf to Cabo San Lucas and Mazatlán. We have collected it as far south as Puerto Escondido, Oaxaca, and as deep as 200 ft (61 mm) at Cabo San Lucas.

**Ecology.** Essentially a nocturnal species, the barspot cardinalfish seeks shelter under reef ledges in the day and hovers in open water close to shelter at night. At night in Puerto Peñasco it can be easily collected from tide pools with dip nets. This species probably feeds exclusively at night, preying on small crustaceans and fishes. In the Cape region Hobson (1968) observed cardinalfish emerging from their cover after sunset and aggregating in midwater to feed on plankton. Their activity could be directly correlated with available light. On bright moonlit nights they remained rather close to their shelter in relatively tight aggregations, whereas during dark nights they dispersed. Barspot cardinalfishes can be seen in the open during the day in deeper waters.

*A. retrosella,* like most cardinalfishes, is a mouth brooder (see Charney, 1976). At Puerto Peñasco in late September we have collected adults who were carrying bright orange egg masses in their mouths but were unable to determine which sex carries the eggs. The eggs are not loose but are secured by fibrous tissue to form a compact cluster.

**Related species.**    The northern ranges of three other species of *Apogon* extend into the Gulf. The tailspot cardinalfish, *A. dovii* Günther, 1861, extends from Mazatlán to Peru. It is similar to *A. retrosella* in coloration and has a dark caudal spot but lacks the dark saddlelike bar diagnostic of *A. retrosella.* The pink cardinalfish, *A. parri* Breder, 1936, a smaller species known from Isla San Pedro Nolasco and Cabo San Lucas (to 200 ft, or 61 m) to Peru, has no dark caudal spot (see Figure 52). It does possess a shorter dark bar on the body below the second dorsal fin, but unlike *A.*

*retrosella* the dark pigment does not encroach on the usually colorless fin. The plain cardinalfish, *A. atricaudus* Jordan and McGregor, 1898, which occurs in the Islas Revillagigedo, has been collected at Cabo San Lucas. It has a relatively slender body and long caudal peduncle compared with the species already discussed and lacks both body bar and caudal peduncle spot. Small individuals have a prominent dark blotch on the first dorsal fin which becomes less apparent (but still remains) in larger individuals. A record of the Guadalupe cardinalfish, *A. guadalupensis,* from Cabo San Lucas was probably based on misidentification of *A. atricaudus,* which it closely resembles (Hobson, 1969a).

# FAMILY BRANCHIOSTEGIDAE
## Tilefishes (Blanquillos)

A recent revision of the tilefishes (Dooley, 1978) separates the group into two families: Branchiostegidae and Malacanthidae. The branchiostegids (tilefishes) are deep-bodied, robust fishes that inhabit moderately deep water over mud or rubble bottoms (see Figure 53). The malacanthids (blanquillos) are more elongate, fusiform fishes that are generally found in shallow water over sand or rubble bottoms. Unlike the branchiostegids, they construct burrows or mounds. Worldwide, there are three genera and 21 species of tilefishes and two genera and eight species of blanquillos. In the eastern Pacific there are three species of *Caulolatilus* (Branchiostegidae) and one species of *Malacanthus* (Malacanthidae), but only the former range into the Gulf.

***References.*** Dooley (1978).

Figure 53   The Pacific golden-eyed tilefish, *Caulolatilus affinis*. Tilefishes have long dorsal and anal fins. The Gulf species are associated with sand, mud, and rubble bottoms and patch reefs. (Photograph by Alex Kerstitch.)

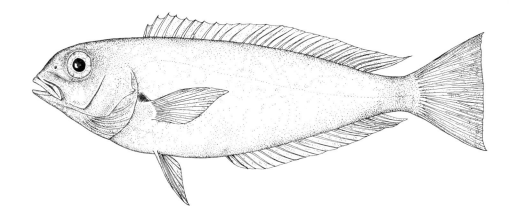

# PACIFIC GOLDEN-EYED TILEFISH, blanquillo
## *Caulolatilus affinis* Gill, 1865

**Illustrated specimen.** Composite from three fish; juveniles, 7.3 to 8.1 in. (185 to 205 mm), by Tor Hansen; see Also Figure 53; largest known specimen, 19.5 in. (495 mm).

**Distinguishing characteristics.** Tilefishes can be easily recognized by their long dorsal and anal fins, each of equal height throughout its length. Overall body coloration of *C. affinis* is olive-green with silvery sides. Freshly caught specimens have lavendar margins around their dorsal scales and a yellow stripe in front of the eye. A conspicuous dark, fleshy patch occurs in the upper axil of the pectoral fin. The tail is slightly forked in adults. D. VIII, 24 (22–25); A. II, 23 (21–24).

**Distribution.** This tilefish occurs throughout the Gulf over rocky and sandy bottoms at moderate depths. It ranges south to Peru.

**Ecology.** The blanquillo lives in water at least 100 to 300 ft (30 to 91 m) deep near patch reefs close to shore. It is an abundant bottom fish and is caught frequently by fishermen in the Guaymas area. We have never collected it in less than 100 ft (30 m) of water.

**Related species.** The ocean whitefish, *Caulolatilus princeps* (Jenyns, 1842), ranges from British Columbia to Peru and throughout the Gulf of California. *C. princeps* has a less abrupt head profile than *C. affinis* and a more deeply forked caudal fin. It lacks the diagnostic markings of *C. affinis* and typically has nine dorsal spines and smaller scales (99–115 pored lateral line scales compared to 80–91 in *C. affinis*). A new species, *C. hubbsi* (Hubbs' tilefish), distinguished by a large mouth and thick fleshy lips, has been recently described by Dooley (1978). It ranges from Islas Santa Inés, B.C.S. and southern California to Peru, including the Islas Galápagos. It occurs sympatrically with *C. affinis* and *C. princeps* but prefers shallower water (58–134 ft or 18–41 m). It is intermediate between these two species in some characters but can be distinguished from *C. affinis* by its higher number of pored lateral line scales (100–110) and lack of markings under the eye and over the pectoral axil, and from *C. princeps* by its nearly truncate (*versus* emarginate) tail and more rounded profile.

# FAMILY LUTJANIDAE
## Snappers (Pargos)

The snappers constitute a large family of warm-water marine fishes prized as food (worldwide, about 23 genera and 230 species). Most are shallow-water reef fishes but several species, especially the juveniles of reef snappers, inhabit mangrove estuaries. Some, such as the commercially exploited red snappers, are deep-water bottom fishes and a few are midwater (Atlantic yellowtail snapper, *Ocyurus chrysurus*). In tropical seas they have a reputation for becoming ciguatoxic (tropical fish poisoning), but fortunately ciguatera has not been found in the Sea of Cortez. In the Gulf there are nine species in three genera: five species are commonly found around shallow reefs, two occur in deeper water, one in midwater, and another is an estuarine species. The snappers are more difficult to classify ecologically than most other Gulf fishes. Their food and habitat requirements are rather generalized, and they roam the shorelines over a variety of bottom types. Their young are found in estuaries and lagoons, around piers in harbors, and in rocky tide pools.

Most snappers can be recognized by their distinctive head profiles. They have moderately long snouts and, compared with basses, rather small mouths (see Figure 54). Their jaws are strong and armed with robust canine teeth in contrast to the weak jaw teeth of the similarly appearing grunts. They can be distinguished from sea basses by noting that the maxilla of the upper jaw slips under the cheek (lachrymal) when the mouth is closed, whereas it does not in sea basses.

***References.*** Breder (1936); Meek and Hildebrand (1925); Walford (1937).

Figure 54 The Pacific dog snapper, *Lutjanus novemfasciatus.* This is the largest of the Gulf snappers. Adults are seen over reefs and juveniles are common in mangrove esteros. (Photograph courtesy of E. S. Hobson.)

# BARRED PARGO, coconaco
## *Hoplopagrus guentheri* Gill, 1862

**Photograph.** Juvenile, 4.7 in. (118 mm) by Alex Kerstitch; see also Plate 8a; grows to about 2½ ft (0.8 m) and 30 lb (13.6 kg).

**Distinguishing characteristics.** This snapper differs from all others by having tubular nostrils that extend beyond its upper lip. The adult is deep-bodied and lacks the typical "snapper profile" characteristic of most shallow-water members of the family. Its coloration varies from greenish brown to dark brown on the back and from dark coppery red to dull maroon on the sides and belly. Eight or nine dark bars appear on the body, but the lower jaw is usually white. The juvenile differs from the adult in that the bars appear paired and a conspicuous dark spot shows below the soft dorsal fin. D. X, 13–14; A. III, 9.

**Distribution.** This snapper occurs from Puerto Peñasco to Panama. It is found commonly on both rocky coasts of the Gulf but is never abundant.

**Ecology.** The barred pargo can be found on most rocky reefs where large boulders form small caves and deep crevices. It is a nocturnal predator that generally spends the day under cover but is occasionally seen outside its shelter, particularly during stormy weather or when underwater visibility is poor. Its diet consists of crustaceans and small schooling fishes (e.g., grunts). Occasionally it will dart out of its refuge during the day to grab small reef fishes (e.g., sergeant majors). Although the barred pargo occurs in depths of more than 90 ft (27 m), it is more common at depths between 10 and 30 ft (3 to 9 m). Juveniles appear from August to October and are relatively common in shallow water on patch reefs around clumps of seaweed. They are often found in the open during the day but they never stray far from shelter.

The adult barred pargo is occasionally seen in dark crevices with several banded cleaner gobies (*Elacatinus digueti*) darting over its surface. However, these small gobies do not remain with it when it leaves the crevice. This pargo's habit of taking shelter in caves when threatened (true for most large snappers) has made it an easy victim of spearfishermen.

# YELLOW SNAPPER, **pargo amarillo**
## *Lutjanus argentiventris* (Peters, 1869)

**Illustrated specimen.** Juvenile, 6.3 in. (161 mm), by Alex Kerstitch; see also Plate 8b; grows to 2 ft (0.6 m) and 20 lb (9 kg).

**Distinguishing characteristics.** The overall yellow color of the tail and lower part of the body distinguishes this snapper from all other Gulf snappers. The adult is generally rose on the fore-half of the body and pale yellow to golden on the rear half. The young have a distinctive sky-blue streak below the eye which breaks into spots as the fish reaches maturity and often disappears entirely with age. Juveniles also have a prominent dark stripe through the eye which becomes obscure in adults. The vomerine teeth in the roof of the mouth form an anchorlike patch with a long backward extension. D. X, 14; A. III, 8.

**Distribution.** The yellow snapper is the commonest snapper in the Gulf, ranging from Puerto Peñasco to Peru and extending north outside the Gulf to Bahía Magdalena.

**Ecology.** Adults are found over rocky bottoms, never far from caves and crevices. Although they are nocturnal feeders, considerable feeding takes place at dusk and dawn. Adults feed on octopuses, small fishes, and crustaceans. Diurnal activity presumably related to courtship is evident during winter months when large adults sometimes mingle and dart in and out of small caves. The young appear in late spring and are often seen in tide pools and estuaries. Large schools of older juveniles are common over reefs during the summer. This euryhaline species sometimes enters freshwater.

Extreme winter temperatures probably limit the abundance of this tropical species in the upper Gulf. During the January 1971 winterkill along the Sonoran coast divers reported languid and emaciated yellow snappers that were so numbed by the cold water that they could be caught by hand.

100

# PACIFIC DOG SNAPPER, **pargo prieto**
## *Lutjanus novemfasciatus* Gill, 1863

**Illustrated specimen.** Juvenile, 5.5 in. (141 mm), by Alex Kerstitch; see also Figure 54 and Plate 8c; largest of the Gulf snappers, it grows to about 100 lb (45 kg).

**Distinguishing characteristics.** This dog snapper is similar in appearance to the yellow snapper (*L. argentiventris*) and the colorado snapper (*L. colorado*). It can be separated from them by a combination of characters used by Walford (1937). The canine teeth of the dog snapper are larger than those of any Pacific coast snapper (largest tooth is longer than the pupil diameter of the eye). The vomerine teeth on the roof of the mouth form a crescentshaped rather than an anchorshaped patch as in the yellow pargo. Both juveniles and adults of the dog snapper usually have nine dusky but well defined bars, although they are sometimes obscure in large adults. Older fish develop considerable reddish coloration, especially along the sides and belly. D X, 14; A. III, 8.

**Distribution.** The Pacific dog snapper ranges throughout the Gulf to Peru. It is more common along the central and lower Gulf coasts than in the upper Gulf.

**Ecology.** This larger snapper prefers rocky habitats. It is a nocturnal predator that hides in caves or crevices by day but adults may occasionally cruise slowly over the reef in the daytime. At night, and especially at dusk, it feeds on crustaceans and small schooling fishes such as croakers, grunts, and wrasses. This snapper occurs most often in depths of 15 to 40 ft (4.6 to 12 m) but is not uncommon at depths greater than 100 ft (30 m). Juveniles aggregate in the protected shallow waters of bays and estuaries and may enter fresh water.

**Related species.** Six other species of snapper occur in the Gulf but none is a common member of the reef communities. The colorado snapper, *Lutjanus colorado* Jordan and Gilbert, 1881, and the blue-and-gold

**101**

Figure 55   An adult spotted rose snapper, *Lutjanus guttatus*. The diagnostic dark spot on the back becomes more diffuse on large adults and can rapidly fade and darken, depending on the behavior of the fish. (Photograph by Alex Kerstitch, taken in Sea World, San Diego, California.)

snapper, *L. viridis* (Valenciennes, 1855) are only occasionally encountered on shallow reefs. The colorado snapper resembles the dog snapper but has more intense red coloration. Its vomerine teeth are also arranged in a crescentshaped patch but its canine teeth are smaller (largest tooth about three-fourths of the pupil diameter of the eye). Its dorsal and anal fins are more angular in profile and the pectoral fin is longer (reaches the anus and beyond in adults). The rear nostril is long and narrow, not round as in the dog snapper (see Walford, 1937). This snapper is uncommon to rare in the Gulf (we have never collected it) but ranges widely outside the Gulf to Panama. *L. viridis* is the most colorful of all the Gulf snappers. It has fine light blue stripes over a golden-to-olive-yellow body (see Plate 8d). In the Gulf it is found only in the Cape region. Outside the Gulf its range extends to Ecuador but is more commonly found around oceanic islands in the tropical eastern Pacific.

The spotted rose snapper, *Lutjanus guttatus* (Steindachner, 1869), and the mullet snapper, *L. aratus* (Günther, 1864), are more strongly associated with sandy bottoms than reefs. *L. guttatus* is a wide-ranging species (throughout the Gulf to Peru). Its coloration varies from pink to yellowish pink with oblique golden-green or brownish stripes. It can be readily distinguished by a large dark spot below the soft dorsal fin. In some individuals, however, the spot is obscure (see Figure 55). The vomerine tooth patch is anchorshaped. This snapper, often collected in trawls, reportedly attains a length of 30 in. (0.8 m); small juveniles occur in the shallow waters of sandy bays. The mullet snapper, *L. aratus,* is not so deep-bodied as most other snappers (Figure 56). It prefers estuarine habitats and ranges from the central Gulf to Ecuador. It has distinctive brown stipes over a yellowish pink body. It is also the only Gulf snapper with 11 dorsal spines (other snappers have 10).

Figure 56 The mullet snapper, *Lutjanus aratus*. Juvenile mullet snappers are commonly found in mangrove esteros in the central Gulf. (Photograph by L. T. Findley.)

The remaining two snappers are deep-water forms. The Pacific red snapper, or huachinango, *L. peru* (Nichols and Murphy, 1922), is an important commercial species wherever it occurs. It is the reddest of all the snappers: its back, head, dorsal, and caudal fins are deep red, its sides are silvery red, and its belly is pure white. This snapper is more fusiform than the others and its head profile is similar to that of *L. aratus*. Its vomerine tooth patch is diamondshaped. Walford had confused it with *L. jordani* (Gilbert). His plate of Jordan's snapper appears to be a photograph of *L. peru,* although he now suggests that it might be an undescribed species (see 1974 reprint of Walford, 1937). The red snapper prefers deep water (300 ft, or 91 m) and is found throughout the Gulf to Peru.

The Pacific rabirubia, *Rabirubia inermis* (Peters, 1869), is a small, open-water form that looks more like a grunt than a snapper. It can be distinguished from the others by its long anal fin with 10 or 11 soft-rays (seven to nine in the others). It reportedly ranges from the lower Gulf to Panama. We have not collected this poorly known species and have not included it in our checklist of reef fishes.

# FAMILY HAEMULIDAE*
## Grunts (Burros)

Grunts are related to the snappers. They are similar in appearance but can be distinguished from them by their lack of canine and vomerine teeth and by presence of a series of chin pits. When collected, these fish grunt audibly—hence their name. Most grunts are small schooling fishes (Figure 57) that swarm over the reef by day and move over sandy shoals to feed at night, primarily on benthic invertebrates such as shrimp, clams, and polychaete worms.

The family has a circumtropical distribution (worldwide, 21 genera and 175 species). In the Gulf 25 species in nine genera have been recorded. There are only 12 species in two genera in the Bahamas and none in Hawaii. We consider 13 species in five genera as Gulf reef fishes and all others as sandy bottom fishes with no close association with rocky bottoms. Though most juveniles of reef grunts are striped, many lose their stripes as adults.

*References.* Breder (1936); Courtenay (1961); Hong (1977); Meek and Hildebrand (1925).

* Other names in use for this family are Pomadasyidae and Pristopomatidae.

Figure 57   A school of graybar grunts, *Haemulon sexfasciatum*. (Photograph courtesy of E. S. Hobson.)

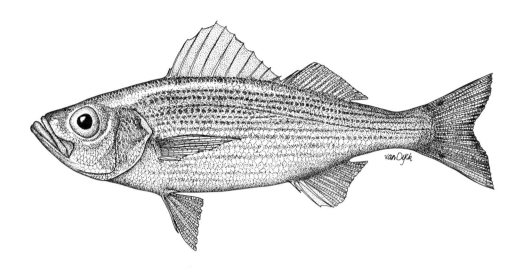

# SALEMA, ojotón
## *Xenistius californiensis* (Steindachner, 1875)

**Illustrated specimen.** Adult, 7.1 in. (180 mm), by Chris van Dyck; attains a length of 10 in. (254 mm).

**Distinguishing characteristics.** The salema, *Xenistius californiensis,* once considered a snapper (family Lutjanidae) and later placed in a distinct family (Xenichthyidae), is now classified as a member of the family Haemulidae. It differs from most grunts by having a completely divided dorsal fin, very large eyes, and long pectoral fins. It has six to eight continuous dark orange-brown stripes over a greenish background along the upper half of the body and looks like a diminutive striped bass, *Morone saxatilis.* D. IX–XI + I–II, 11–14; A. III, 9–12.

**Distribution.** This wide-ranging species is distributed from northern California to Peru and is common throughout the Gulf of California.

**Ecology.** The salema are primarily nocturnal feeders but occasionally forage during the day. In contrast to many other grunts they have oblique mouths and are midwater feeders. Large schools of these fish, often intermixed with schools of other grunts, may be seen milling about piers at night, feeding on the plankton attracted by the pier lights. Young salema are frequently collected in tide pools at Puerto Peñasco. The juveniles are colored much like the adults but lack the dark caudal spot characteristic of the juveniles of several other species of grunt.

**Related species.** The longfin salema, *Xenichthys xanti* Gill, 1863, which ranges from the lower Gulf to Peru, is more elongate than the salema, has a longer anal fin (*Xenichthys,* 16 to 18 soft-rays; *Xenistius,* 9 to 12 soft-rays) and a dark caudal spot (apparent only in the juveniles).

**105**

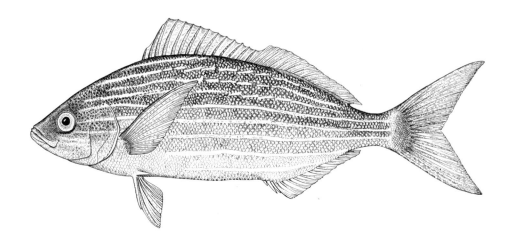

# WAVYLINE GRUNT, rayadillo
## *Microlepidotus inornatus* Gill, 1863

**Illustrated specimen.** Adult, 8 in. (200 mm), by Tor Hansen; grows to about 12 in. (305 mm).

**Distinguishing characteristics.** The wavyline grunt is closely related to species of the genus *Orthopristis,* and perhaps it too, should be assigned to that genus (Boyd W. Walker, personal communication). It differs from species of the genus *Orthopristis,* however, by having 14 dorsal spines instead of the 12 to 13 spines characteristic of that genus. *Microlepidotus inornatus* is a moderate-sized grunt characterized by seven to nine orange-bronze stripes along its body. Above the lateral line some of the stripes are broken up into a wavy pattern. They differ from grunts of the genus *Haemulon* because their soft dorsal and anal fins are mostly devoid of scales. A slight notch occurs between the spinous and soft portions of the dorsal fin. D. XIV, 15; A. III, 12.

**Distribution.** A common central and lower Gulf species, the wavyline grunt ranges from the midriff islands around the Cape to Bahía Magdalena. On the mainland of Mexico it ranges from Puerto Lobos to Manzanillo and possibly farther south.

**Ecology.** Wavyline grunts move in large, densely packed schools that make their way slowly along the edges of reefs and open sandy areas during the day. The schools lie offshore after sunset and form loose aggregations over open sandy areas, where they feed on midwater crustaceans and benthic mollusks (Hobson, 1968). According to Hobson, *M. inornatus* schools are preyed on heavily by larger fishes during twilight hours. Predation reaches a peak 20 minutes after sunset and ceases abruptly just before the grunts move to their offshore feeding grounds.

**Related species.** *M. inornatus* is similar in appearance to the bronzestriped grunt *Orthopristis reddingi* Jordan and Richardson, a sandy-bottom fish not covered in this book. Juveniles of this abundant grunt are occasionally collected in tide pools but can be distinguished from *M. inornatus* by their lower dorsal spine number (12–13).

**106**

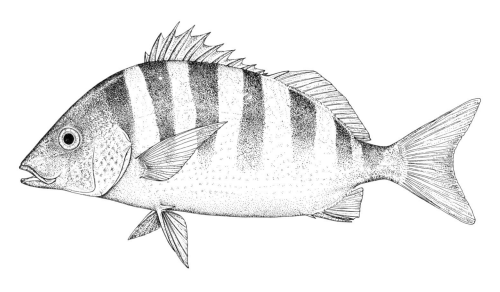

# GRAYBAR GRUNT, burro almejera
## *Haemulon sexfasciatum* Gill, 1863

**Illustrated specimen.** Adult, 8.3 in. (210 mm) by Tor Hansen; see also Figure 57 and Plate 10a; attains a length of about 1.5 ft (0.5 m) but the average adult size is 1 ft (0.3 m).

**Distinguishing characteristics.** The contrasting pattern of six yellow and dark gray bars resembles the pattern of the sergeant major (*Abudefduf troschelii*) and is the only Gulf grunt with this distinctive color pattern. The adults have dark spots on the sides of their heads and the juveniles have dark stripes along the body and a dark caudal spot. Eastern Pacific species of the genus *Haemulon* have densely scaled soft dorsal and anal fins; the scales cover both rays and fin membranes. A recent taxonomic review of the genus in the eastern Pacific was done by Hong (1977). D. XII, 16–17; A. III, 10.

**Distribution.** One of the commonest fishes in the central and lower Gulf, the graybar grunt ranges throughout the Gulf to Panama.

**Ecology.** Schools of graybar grunts are frequently seen around the edges of reefs in the daytime. These diurnal schools disperse at dusk and individual grunts search for food during the night. Most stay on the reef but a few swim over open sandy areas. When feeding, the barred pattern becomes especially intense. The diet of the graybar grunt consists entirely of benthic animals such as lancelets, snake eels, crustaceans, clams, and annelids (Hobson, 1968).

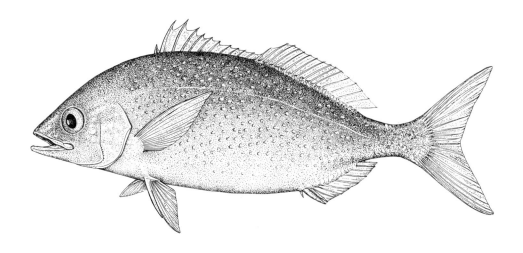

# CORTEZ GRUNT, **burro de Cortés**
## *Haemulon flaviguttatum* Gill, 1863

**Illustrated specimen.** Adult, 8.9 in. (225 mm), by Tor Hansen; grows to about 1 ft (0.3 m).

**Distinguishing characteristics.** A recent review of the genus *Haemulon* (Hong, 1977) synonymized *Lythrulon* and *Orthostoechus* with *Haemulon.* Adult Cortez grunts, formerly known as *Lythrulon flaviguttatum,* have a pearly blue spot on each body scale (giving them a spotted appearance) and a dusky caudal spot. Juveniles have two lateral stripes and a more conspicuous caudal spot than adults. The fins of the juveniles are bright yellow in life. Typically, this species has a total of 27 or 28 gill rakers on the first arch (26–31), more than any other eastern Pacific *Haemulon.* D. XII, 17 (15–18); A. III, 10–11.

**Distribution.** The Cortez grunt ranges throughout the Gulf to the Pacific coast of Baja California (Bahía San Juanico) and south to Panama.

**Ecology.** This small schooling species frequents rocky-sandy shores from Puerto Peñasco to Cabo San Lucas. Schools of *H. flaviguttatum* move offshore at night to feed on midwater and occasionally benthic invertebrates (Hobson, 1968), but like so many other nocturnal predators the Cortez grunt does forage occasionally during daylight.

Cortez grunts form closely knit schools and often mingle with schools of the wavyline grunt, *Microlepidotus inornatus.* In the Cape region both species are preyed on by larger fishes during twilight hours (Hobson, 1968).

**Related species.** The spottail grunt *Haemulon maculicauda* (Gill, 1863), recently known as *Orthostoechus maculicauda,* ranges throughout the Gulf (Rocas Consag) to Ecuador. It is another schooling nocturnal predator that hovers around reefs and piers by day and disperses over sandy bottoms at night (Hobson, 1968). It has pearly scales like *H. flaviguttatum* but they form a striped rather than spotted pattern. Also, its lateral line is exactly concurrent to the scale rows; that is, the scale rows above the lateral line are parallel with the lateral line and not in oblique rows as in *H. flaviguttatum.* It usually has 23 to 26 gill rakers on the first arch (range: 22 to 29). The overall color is dark brown and the pearly scale rows give this fish a wavy-striped appearance. A broad dusky blotch (not a distinct spot) occurs on the tail and caudal base as described by its specific name.

Two other species of the genus *Haemulon* inhabit the Gulf but both are less common than the preceding three species. The mojarra grunt, *Haemulon scudderi* Gill, 1863, ranges from Bahía Magdalena and Guaymas to Ecuador and the Islas Galápagos, and the Latin grunt, *Haemulon steindachneri* (Jordan and Gilbert, 1882), ranges throughout the Gulf to Peru on the Pacific coast and from Panama to Rio de Janeiro on the Atlantic coast. These two species resemble each other superficially but may be distinguished by the following characteristics: *H. scudderi* has a smaller mouth (maxilla does not reach the center of the eye), no dark caudal spot, and 17 to 19 (15–21) gill rakers; *H. steindachneri* has a larger mouth (maxilla reaches to the center of the eye), pearly spots in the center of each scale that look opalescent, a dark caudal spot that persists in the adult, and 23 (19 to 25) gill rakers.

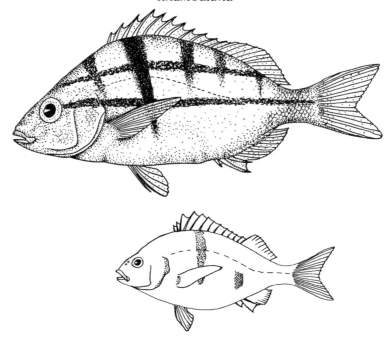

# SARGO, sargo rayado
## *Anisotremus davidsonii* (Steindachner, 1875)

**Illustrated specimen.** Juvenile, 3.6 in. (90 mm), by Tor Hansen; said to reach a length of 23 in. (584 mm) in California waters. A sketch of an adult is shown below juvenile.

**Distinguishing characteristics.** Grunts of the genus *Anisotremus* are larger fishes than the preceding species. The largely naked dorsal and anal fins of *Anisotremus* have only a basal sheath of scales and perhaps a few scales on the membranes between fin rays. Adult sargos can be readily distinguished from all other Gulf grunts by the single broad black bar running from about the fifth to the sixth dorsal spine downward to about the level of the pectoral fin base. This bar appears in specimens about 2 in. (50 mm) long. The overall body color is a pale dusky yellow with a dark bar at the base of the pectoral fin. The young have two to three prominent black stripes (fading with age) and no caudal spot. D. XI–XII, 14–16; A. III, 9–11.

**Distribution.** Common along the kelp beds and fishing piers of southern California and in the upper Gulf, the sargo has a dis-junct distribution. It ranges from Santa Cruz, California, to Bahía Magdalena and throughout the upper and parts of the central Gulf. Gulf sargos were introduced into the Salton Sea, California in 1951 and have become common sport fish there (Walker, 1961).

**Ecology.** *Anisotremus davidsonii* is one of the largest Gulf grunts. In southern California waters it reportedly reaches lengths of almost 2 ft (0.6 m) and weights of 5 to 6 lb (2.3 to 2.7 kg). We have not seen specimens this large in the Gulf of California, in which average adult size seems to be about 12 in. (305 mm). An inshore species frequently encountered on rocky reefs, sargos range to depths of more than 100 ft (30 m) and are occasionally caught over sandy bottoms by shrimp trawlers. Although they are an important sport fish in southern California and the Salton Sea, they are not highly regarded as a game fish in the Gulf. Large schools of juvenile sargos appear in the tide pools at Puerto Peñasco in the spring and summer and it is consistently the most abundant rocky-shore grunt found there.

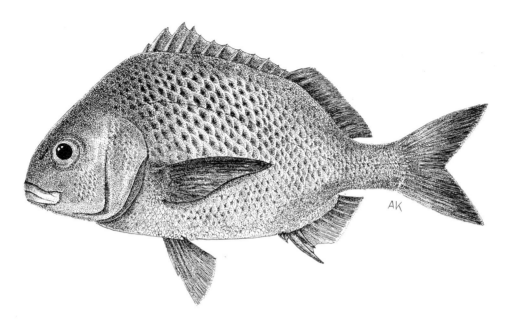

# BURRITO GRUNT, **burrito**
## *Anisotremus interruptus* (Gill, 1863)

**Illustrated specimen.** Young adult, 9.3 in. (250 mm) by Alex Kerstitch; grows to 1½ ft (0.46 m).

**Distinguishing characteristics.** The burrito grunt is a strongly compressed, robust grunt with an abrupt head profile and fleshy lips. In the adult the large conspicuous scales are marked with a dark spot at their anterior margins which grades into a triangularshaped spot on scales below the lateral line. Its overall effect is to outline each scale distinctly in a pattern of oblique stripes. Its color is overall silvery yellowish green, the pectorals are light yellow, and the other fins are a darker greenish brown. The striped young resemble young sargo except that the burrito grunt has two dark stripes, a prominent dark caudal spot, and no bars. D. XII, 16; A. II, 8–9.

**Distribution.** The burrito grunt ranges from Bahía Magdalena and throughout the Gulf to Peru and the Islas Galápagos.

**Ecology.** The burrito grunt is more closely associated with reefs than other Gulf grunts.

Although the young, which appear in late summer, swim in schools, the large adults are often solitary and hide in caves. This grunt is a nocturnal benthic feeder but is more active during the day than other rocky-shore grunts. Its diet consists mainly of benthic invertebrates. At twilight schools of burrito grunts disperse among the rocks rather than over open sand and apparently remain on the reef throughout the night. The schools form again at sunrise but do not stray from the reef (Hobson, 1968).

**Related species.** Three other species of *Anisotremus* occur in the Gulf but only in its extreme southern portions. The colorful Panamic porkfish, *Anisotremus taeniatus* Gill, 1862 (see Plate 10d), appears to be the twin species of the Atlantic porkfish, *A. virginicus* Linnaeus. Adults are readily identified by their coloration: iridescent blue stripes on a golden yellow background with one dark bar running obliquely through the eye and another vertically from the origin of the dorsal fin along the opercle to the pectoral fin base. Their juveniles resemble those of *A. inter-*

*ruptus;* they have dark stripes and a dark caudal spot but may be distinguished by their nine or more oblique scale rows between the first dorsal spine and the lateral line (*A. interruptus* has seven). *A. taeniatus* ranges from the Cape area to Ecuador. The longfin grunt, *Anisotremus caesius* (Jordan and Gilbert, 1881), and the blackbarred grunt, *A. dovii* (Günther, 1864), differ from other Gulf *Anisotremus* by having a scale row running parallel above the lateral line (the same scale row in other *Anisotremus* species is oblique to the lateral line). *A. caesius* has more or less uniform coloration; it lacks bars and its long pectoral fins reach beyond the pelvic-fin tips. *A. dovii* has five distinct black bars and shorter pectoral fins (not reaching pelvic-fin tips). Neither species is well represented in our collections but both are known to range from the southern margins of the Gulf to Panama (*A. caesius*) and Peru (*A. dovii*). Two other *Anisotremus, A. scapularis* (Tschudi) and *A. pacifici* (Günther), occur south of the Gulf of California to Chile and Peru, respectively.

**112**

# FAMILY SPARIDAE
## Porgies (Mojarrones)

The porgies are deep-bodied, long-faced fishes, allied to the grunts, but with heavy molariform teeth in the jaws. They feed on benthic invertebrates, especially shellfish, which they crush with these molars. Like snappers, they range widely and are likely to be found over sandy bottoms near reefs (Figure 58).

Only one species (*Calamus brachysomus*) occurs in the Gulf whereas five species are found in the Caribbean. Worldwide there are 29 genera with about 100 species.

*References.*    Randall and Caldwell (1966).

Figure 58  The Pacific porgy, *Calamus brachysomus*, occurs over Gulf reefs and offshore sandy bottoms. This porgy may assume a barred or blotched color pattern when hiding. The pattern fades when it swims in the open. (Photograph by Alex Kerstitch.)

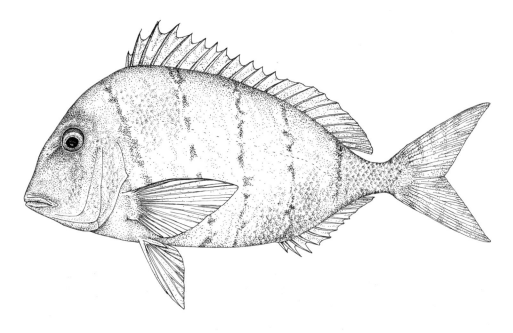

# PACIFIC PORGY, mojarrón
## *Calamus brachysomus* (Lockington, 1880)

**Illustrated specimen.** Young adult, 9.7 in. (245 mm), by Tor Hansen; see also Figure 58; reported to reach a length of 2 ft (0.6 m) and a weight of 5 lb (2.3 kg).

**Distinguishing characteristics.** The Pacific porgy can be distinguished from all other Gulf fishes by the abrupt profile of its head, long broad snout, and greatly compressed body. It is silvery brown marked by irregular brown blotches and five obscure bars on its body, two on its caudal peduncle and a diffuse bar that passes vertically through the eye. Its characteristic profile is sufficient for identification underwater. The juveniles resemble the adults but generally have a more mottled color pattern, although this changes rapidly in both young and adults. D. XII–XIII, 11–13; A. II–III, 9–11.

**Distribution.** A wide-ranging species, *C. brachysomus* is found from Oceanside, California, to Peru and throughout the Gulf of California.

**Ecology.** The Pacific porgy inhabits shallow Gulf shores to a depth of about 225 ft (69 m).

The young are found in very shallow water on reef flats and in sandy bays over mixed sand and rock bottoms. Solitary individuals are most frequently encountered on the reef but occasionally small loose aggregations are seen. Although frequently encountered along most rocky shores, it is not abundant in the Gulf. Its foraging habits are not known, but the heavy molariform teeth and strong jaws suggest that this fish feeds chiefly on mollusks and crustaceans. When feeding, it blows jets of water on the sand to expose burrowing invertebrates.

**Related species.** Of the 13 species of *Calamus* in the world, two are found in the eastern Pacific and 11 in the western Atlantic. *C. taurinus* (Jenyns, 1843), endemic to the Islas Galápagos, was once confused with *C. brachysomus* of the mainland eastern Pacific until the taxonomy of the genus was clarified by Randall and Caldwell (1966). *C. taurinus* differs from *C. brachysomus* by its shorter pectoral fins, less compressed body, and gentler head profile.

114

# FAMILY SCIAENIDAE
## Croakers (Corvinas, roncadores)

The croakers (or drums) are so named because of the sound they make with their resonating swim bladders. This mostly tropical group of fishes inhabits sandy shores and estuaries. Only one species of Sciaenidae of about 30 recorded from the Gulf can be called a reef fish (see Figure 59). Sciaenids are easily distinguished from other perciform fishes by their separated dorsal fins, one or two anal spines, and prominent lateral line that extends onto the caudal fin to its posterior edge instead of ending at base of the tail as it does in most fishes. Sciaenids are also noted for their well developed otoliths (earbones). Worldwide, there are 28 genera with about 160 species.

*References.*   McPhail (1961).

Figure 59   An adult rock croaker, *Pareques viola*, seeking the shelter of a crevice during daylight. Note that its dark coloration blends with the shadow of the refuge. (Photograph courtesy of E. S. Hobson.)

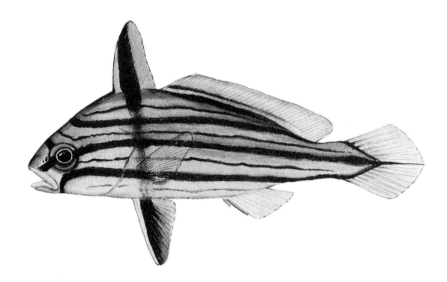

# ROCK CROAKER, gungo
## *Pareques viola* (Gilbert, 1898)

**Illustrated specimen.** Juvenile, 2.1 in. (53 mm), by Alex Kerstitch; see also Figure 59; grows to about 10 in. (254 mm).

**Distinguishing characteristics.** The only rocky-shore croaker in the Gulf, *Pareques viola,* may be distinguished from all other reef fishes by characters diagnostic of many Sciaenids, such as the lateral line extending onto the tail and pores in the chin. Adult rock croakers are a dark chocolate brown, whereas the juveniles show black stripes on a white background. The spinous dorsal fin of the juveniles is a striking feature. The anterior and posterior margins are yellow, as is the eye. A broad dark bar extends from the tip of the dorsal fin across the body to the pelvic fins. This bar disappears in larger juveniles, but the stripes often remain until the fish reaches about 6 in. (150 mm). D. IX–XI + 38–41; A. II, 7–8.

**Distribution.** The rock croaker is distributed widely throughout the Gulf, ranging south to Panama. It is a common but never abundant fish along most rocky shores of the Gulf.

**Ecology.** Small schools of juveniles appear only in the summer, when they may be locally abundant. The adults are secretive nocturnal fish that hide under ledges by day and come out only at night to feed, perhaps exclusively, on crustaceans. During the day the adults sometimes form large inactive aggregations in caves, but little or no feeding occurs (Hobson 1965a, 1968). The colorful juveniles are sought as aquarium specimens, although they are delicate and usually do not prosper in community aquaria.

# FAMILY MULLIDAE
## Goatfishes (Chivos, salmonetes)

Goatfishes, also called surmullets, are characterized by a pair of long slender barbels on the chin (Figure 60). The barbels are usually folded along the jaw when the goatfish is swimming but extend out at right angles to the chin when they are searching for food buried in the sand. They have separated dorsal fins and two anal spines. All are tropical fishes, but they are not particularly well represented in the New World Tropics (worldwide, 6 genera and 55 spp.). Only two forms occur in the Gulf of California and they appear to be sibling species of the two goatfishes in the Bahamas.

***References.*** Rosenblatt and Hoese (1968).

Figure 60 A school of Mexican goatfish, *Mulloidichthys dentatus*, at a cleaning station. Note the vertical posturing and darkening of fish waiting to be cleaned by the barberfish, *Heniochus nigrirostris* (upper center, partly obscured, and lower right). (Photograph courtesy of E. S. Hobson.)

117

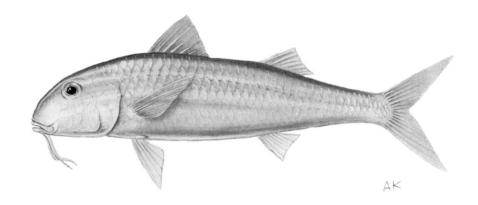

# MEXICAN GOATFISH, salmonete
## *Mulloidichthys dentatus* (Gill, 1863)

**Illustrated specimen.** Adult, 11 in. (279 mm) by Alex Kerstitch; see also Figure 60 and Plate 10c; reaches a length of about 12 in. (305 mm).

**Distinguishing characteristics.** This species, the only rocky-shore goatfish in the Gulf, is characterized by a broad bright yellow stripe running from the eye to the equally bright yellow tail. There is no apparent sexual dimorphism and the juveniles are colored like the adults. D. VII + I, 8; A. I-II, 6.

**Distribution.** The Mexican goatfish ranges from southern California to Peru and the Islas Galápagos. In the Gulf it ranges from Guaymas, where it is uncommon, to Cabo San Lucas, where it reaches its peak abundance. In the Caribbean the yellow goatfish, *Mulloidichthys martinicus* (Cuvier and Valenciennes), appears to be its Atlantic analogue.

**Ecology.** The Mexican goatfish is primarily a nocturnal feeder but it also forages frequently in the daytime, flicking its barbels through the sand in search of small crustaceans, polychaetes, and mollusks. It forms large schools that swim actively over the reef by day, frequenting cleaning stations serviced by the butterflyfish, "el barbero" (*Heniochus nigrirostris*). The goatfish hovers vertically with its head down and long barbels extended, presenting itself to the barberfish. In this posture, some of the goatfish undergo a color change from a pale hue to a dark copper above the central stripe and dark purple below (see Plate 10c). The bright yellow stripe and tail rapidly assume a darker reddish-orange which gives the fish an overall dark appearance and makes it conspicuous among the school. Hobson (1965b) postulated that the dark daytime color change, which also occurs when the fish feed at night, is an adaptation that makes the light-colored parasites more conspicuous to the cleaner.

**Related species.** The only other species collected in the Gulf is the red goatfish, *Pseudupeneus grandisquamis* (Gill), which ranges widely throughout the Gulf to Chile. It is not a reef species in the Gulf; it lives mainly at moderate depths offshore and is frequently collected in shrimp trawls.

**118**

# FAMILY KYPHOSIDAE
## Sea chubs, nibblers, and halfmoons
## (Chopas)

Sea chubs are compressed, ovalshaped, omnivorous fishes with small mouths and fine teeth in their jaws (Figure 61). All feed on benthic algae, plankton, and small invertebrates. Seven species in three subfamilies have been recorded from the Gulf. The sea chubs of the subfamily Girellinae are called nibblers, which refers to their grazing method of feeding, whereas those of the subfamily Kyphosinae are called rudderfishes after their habit of following ships at sea. The Scorpinae, or halfmoons, are named for their lunate tail. Worldwide, there are 15 genera with 31 species.

*References.* Jenkins and Evermann (1889); Lockley (1952); Osburn and Nichols (1916).

Figure 61    A school of Cortez chubs, *Kyphosus elegans*, at Cabo San Lucas. This chub is striped when schooling but darkens and assumes a light-spotted checkered pattern when seeking shelter and at night. (Photograph by Alex Kerstitch.)

119

# GULF OPALEYE, ojo azul
## *Girella simplicidens* Osburn and Nichols, 1916

**Illustrated specimen.** Adult, 10.2 in. (264 mm), by Alex Kerstitch; see also Plate 11; grows to about 1½ ft (0.46 m).

**Distinguishing characteristics.** The opaleyes (subfamily Girellinae) differ from the rest of the kyphosid fishes by their dentition. Their jaw teeth are not fixed but are freely movable and they lack teeth on the vomer. In other respects *Girella* is similar to other members of the family. The adult Gulf opaleye is a dark brownish gray fish with bright blue eyes and three to four white spots along each side of the back. Juveniles are similarly colored. D. XIV, 14; A. III, 12.

**Distribution.** *Girella simplicidens* is endemic to the Gulf of California and is one of the most abundant fishes in the upper part. It ranges throughout the Gulf but is uncommon in the southern region.

**Ecology.** The Gulf opaleye is found in shallow rocky areas of abundant algal growth. A diurnal omnivore, it grazes on algae and preys on invertebrates. Opaleyes roam the reef in large schools and the young frequently aggregate in tide pools. Opaleyes are not territorial but captive individuals are aggressive and social hierarchies are often established in aquaria. The Gulf opaleye is eurythermal, tolerating lower temperatures (46°F or 8°C) than most Gulf fishes as well as high summer temperatures (95°F or 35°C).

**Related species.** The opaleye of the Pacific coast, *Girella nigricans* (Ayres, 1860), ranges from San Francisco to Cabo San Lucas. It is similar in appearance and habits to *G. simplicidens*, differing only slightly in dentition and color pattern. The primary incisors of *G. nigricans* have distinctive trident cusps, which are lacking in *G. simplicidens*. *G. nigricans* has one to two white spots on each side of its back below the dorsal fin, whereas typically *G. simplicidens* has three to four spots. Another species, *G. (Doydixodon) laevifrons* (Tschudi), ranges outside the Gulf from Manzanillo to Chile. Its incisors are bi- or tricuspid like *G. nigricans*.

120

# CORTEZ CHUB, chopa de Cortés
## *Kyphosus elegans* (Peters, 1869)

**Illustrated specimen.** Young adult, 7.4 in. (187 mm), by Alex Kerstitch; see also Plates 10b, 11, and Figure 61; grows to about 15 in. (381 mm).

**Distinguishing characteristics.** In the rudderfishes (subfamily Kyphosinae) the incisors in both jaws are fixed and not freely movable like those of the opaleyes, *Girella* spp. *Kyphosus elegans* may be identified by the fine, brassy pinstripes along its sides, a character that is evident in both juveniles and adults. Small juveniles are dark overall, with elongated pale silvery spots on the sides. The overall color of adults is a drab bluish gray. A broad, silvery, wavy line runs from the maxilla to a point below the pupil of the eye (see Related species to distinguish *K. elegans* from the closely related species *K. analogus*). D. XI, 13; A. III. 12.

**Distribution.** The Cortez chub is common in the Gulf but not especially abundant. It ranges throughout the Gulf to Panama and the Islas Galápagos.

**Ecology.** Little is known about the life history of *K. elegans*. The adults are often observed in small schools along shallow rocky shores and the juveniles are occasionally collected in tide pools. In addition to the pinstripe phase, the juveniles have a spotted nocturnal phase characterized by a series of irregularly shaped silver blotches on ventral sides from the throat to the caudal peduncle. This pattern also rapidly appears when the fish is distressed (see Plate 10d). The Cortez chub has a predominantly herbivorous diet, although it will feed on plankton and benthic invertebrates. The Cortez chub appears to be the twin species of the Bermuda chub, *Kyphosus sectatrix* (Linnaeus), in the Atlantic.

**Related species.** The only other species of *Kyphosus* in the Gulf, the striped sea chub, *K. analogus* (Gill, 1863), is similar in appearance to *K. elegans*. It ranges from Oceanside, Calif. and Bahía Magdalena (see Crooke, 1973) to Panama. Its northern limit in the Gulf appears to be Bahía Topolobampo, Sin. It differs from

*K. elegans* in having smaller scales (about 76 to 80 in an oblique series below the lateral line as compared with about 59 to 61 in *K. elegans*), and 14 dorsal and 13 to 14 anal soft-rays (13 dorsal and 12 anal soft-rays in *K. elegans*). Reportedly, it is a more brightly colored fish when alive than *K. elegans*, although the color patterns are similar. Another kyphosid which is not likely to be confused with either species of *Kyphosus* is the rainbow chub *Sectator ocyurus* (Jordan and Gilbert, 1881). This pelagic species has been recorded off Cabo San Lucas and ranges widely throughout the tropical eastern Pacific to the Society Islands (Randall, 1961). It is a much more elongated fish and has a deeply forked tail. *S. ocyurus* is beautifully colored with bright blue and yellow horizontal bands along the body and yellowish fins. The halfmoon, *Medialuna californiensis* (Steindachner, 1875), has been recorded from the Gulf of California but we have never collected it. It is sometimes referred to the family Scorpididae, but we include it in the subfamily Scorpinae (halfmoons), which is characterized by lack of incisiform teeth. It resembles the opaleye but may be distinguished from *Girella* by the thick sheath of scales covering both its soft dorsal and anal fins. It ranges from northern California, including Isla Guadalupe, to the Baja coast of the lower Gulf. See Fitch and Lavenberg (1975) for information on this species.

# ZEBRAPERCH, chopa bonita
## *Hermosilla azurea* Jenkins and Evermann, 1889

**Illustrated specimen.** Juvenile, 3.9 in. (99 mm), by Chris van Dyck; said to reach about 17 in. (432 mm) in California waters; the Gulf form is slightly smaller.

**Distinguishing characteristics.** Fish of the genus *Hermosilla* can be distinguished from other kyphosids by the lack of scales on the head; this naked area extends beyond the posterior margin of the eyes. The barred pattern, blue opercular spot, and dark patch at the base of the pectoral fin distinguish this species from all other members of the family. Its mouth and dentition are similar to that of the other kyphosids. In juveniles (less than 50 mm) the bars appear initially as silvery extensions of the ventral region, separated by broader brown areas that eventually become the darker bars in the adult. D. XI, 11; A. III, 10.

**Distribution.** The zebraperch ranges to Monterey, California, and throughout the Sea of Cortez; it is most common in the upper and central Gulf.

**Ecology.** The zebraperch is only occasionally encountered by divers in the Gulf and is not often collected. Judging by its mouth and dentition, its diet is partially herbivorous like that of other members of this family. It is a shallow-water schooling fish and an active swimmer, often found schooling with sergeant majors (*Abudefduf troschelii*).

**Related species.** Another species of *Hermosilla, H. robusta* Osburn and Nichols, 1916, has been described from the Gulf. The type specimens collected off Isla Tiburón reportedly differ from *H. azurea* in having a greater body depth, stouter gill rakers, shorter ventral fins, and no bars on the body. The holotype and paratype specimens are 15 and 14 in. long, respectively (381 and 356 mm). It is possible, however, that these are large adults of *H. azurea,* although we have not examined them. The barred pattern of our largest *H. azurea* (9 in. = 229 mm) was quite obscure compared with the juvenile pattern. It seems likely that *H. robusta* is a synonym of *H. azurea.*

# FAMILY EPHIPPIDAE
## Spadefishes (Peluqueros)

Spadefishes are strongly compressed tropical fishes with small mouths (Figure 62). They resemble butterflyfishes (Chaetodontidae) but can be distinguished from them by their separated rather than continuous dorsal fins. The gill membranes are broadly united to the isthmus in spadefishes, whereas in butterflyfishes they are free from the isthmus or narrowly united to it.

Spadefishes feed on sessile invertebrates over rocky and sandy bottoms and the young may be found in brackish water. Worldwide, there are seven genera with 14 species in two subfamilies. Only two species occur in the eastern Pacific.

*References.* Meek and Hildebrand (1928).

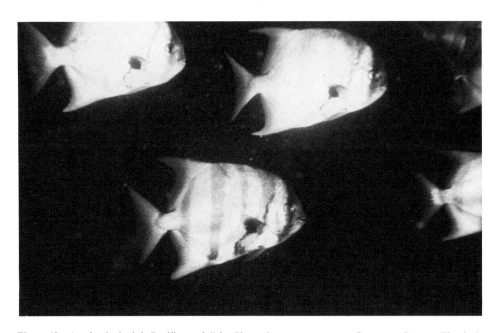

Figure 62   A school of adult Pacific spadefish, *Chaetodipterus zonatus*, at Guaymas, Sonora. The dark bars fade when the fish is over sand or when the water is turbid. The barred pattern is strongest when the fish is over reefs in clear water. (Photograph by Alex Kerstitch.)

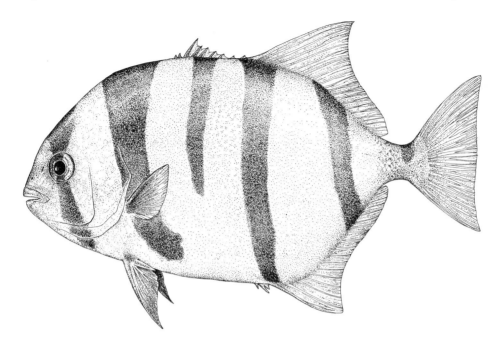

# PACIFIC SPADEFISH, chambo
## *Chaetodipterus zonatus* (Girard, 1858)

**Illustrated specimen.** Large juvenile, 4.7 in. (119 mm), by Tor Hansen; see also Figures 62 and 63; reported to reach a length of 25½ in. (648 mm).

**Distinguishing characteristics.** This is a strongly compressed fish characterized by its six broad dark irregular bars, the first passing through the eye. The bars are more distinct on younger fish and faded on large adults. The smallest juveniles are coppery brown, resembling a blade of brown seaweed, but they show the six bars (see Figure 63). D. VIII + I, 18–23; A. II–III, 16–20.

**Distribution.** The Pacific spadefish is a common wide-ranging species recorded from San Diego to northern Peru and throughout the Gulf.

**Ecology.** The Pacific spadefish is a schooling fish that is uncommon on reefs, and seems to prefer bays with sand or rubble bottoms. Pacific spadefish are caught in trawls and the cryptically colored juveniles are sometimes captured with beach seines. At first glance they resemble seaweed debris, as they lie on their sides among it. Juveniles of the Caribbean spadefish, *C. faber* (Broussonet), the twin species of *C. zonatus*, have a black phase. They look like black gastropods or the black infertile pods of the red mangrove, as they lie on their sides on the sand like drifting trash (Böhlke and Chaplin, 1968).

**Related species.** Only one other spadefish occurs in the eastern Pacific, the Panama spadefish, *Parapsettus panamensis* Steindachner, 1875, a species that is uncommon in the Gulf and ranges from Guaymas to Peru. We have not collected it in the Gulf and suspect that its habitat may be that of sandy bays rather than reefs. It may be distinguished from *C. zonatus* by its short, free dorsal spines, the last of which is the longest (the spines of *C. zonatus* are connected by membranes and the third spine is longest).

125

Figure 63   A small juvenile Pacific spadefish, *Chaetodipterus zonatus*. The very young are coppery-brown, resembling a piece of brown seaweed both in appearance and behavior. (Photograph by Alex Kerstitch.)

# FAMILIES POMACANTHIDAE and CHAETODONTIDAE

## Angelfishes (Peces ángel) and butterflyfishes (Mariposas)

These fishes, until recently considered as two subfamilies (Pomacanthinae and Chaetodontinae) of the family Chaetodontidae, are among the most colorful tropical reef fishes in the world. The name "Chaetodontidae" means "bristletooth," signifying the brushlike teeth in the small mouths of these fishes. The angelfishes (Pomacanthidae) are characterized by a strong conspicuous preopercular spine (see Figure 64), lacking in the butterflyfishes (Chaetodontidae). Young angelfishes, unlike butterflyfishes, differ considerably in color pattern from the adults. Most are grazers and pickers that consume small organisms such as sponges, algae, tunicates, hydroids, coral polyps, and worms, which do not move quickly. This mode of feeding predisposes them to be facultative "cleaners," which pick parasites from other fishes. This behavior has been observed and reported in the young of *Pomacanthus* and *Holacanthus* and in both young and adult butterflyfishes such as *Heniochus nigrirostris,* which maintain cleaning "stations" on the reef.

Three genera with four species of butterflyfishes and two genera with three species of angelfishes occur in the Gulf of California. Sibling species inhabit the Caribbean, which supports six species in three genera of angelfishes and five species in two genera of butterflyfishes. The greatest diversity is found in the Indo-Pacific. The Hawaiian archipelago in the central Pacific has six species in three genera of angelfishes and 20 species in four genera of butterflyfishes. Worldwide, there are seven genera with 30 species of angelfishes and 11 genera with 160 species of butterflyfishes.

*References.* Baldwin (1963); Burgess (1974); Fraser-Brunner (1933); Hubbs and Rechnitzer (1958); Randall and Caldwell (1970).

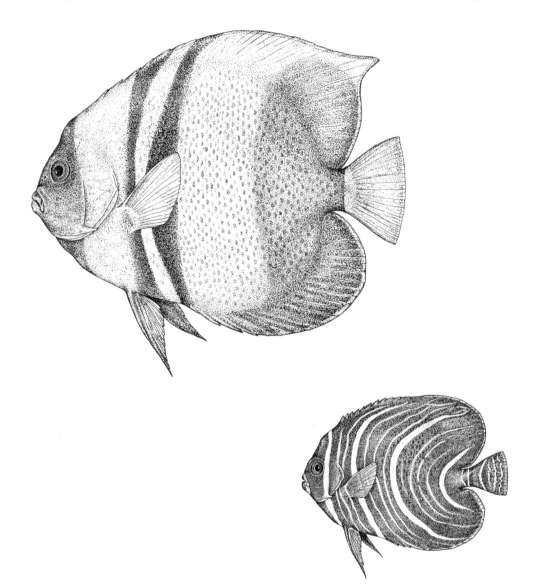

# CORTEZ ANGELFISH, ángel de Cortés
## *Pomacanthus zonipectus* (Gill, 1863)

**Illustrated specimens.** Young adult, 5.9 in. (150 mm) and juvenile, 1.4 in. (35 mm), by Tor Hansen; see also Plates 16a,b, and Figure 64; reaches a length of about 1½ ft (0.46 m); average adult size about 1 ft (0.3 m).

**Distinguishing characteristics.** The Cortez angelfish undergoes a striking color transformation from the juvenile to the adult. The alternating bright yellow and iridescent blue curved bars on a deep blue background, characteristic of the juveniles, is replaced by a more somber brown background with yellow bars in the adult. D. XI, 24–25; A. III, 20–22.

**Distribution.** The Cortez angelfish ranges widely from the northern Gulf (Puerto Peñasco) and north of Bahía Magdalena (Bahía

San Juanico) to Peru. It is a common fish on most shallow reefs in the Gulf.

**Ecology.** This species is a diurnal grazer or substrate feeder. Sponges, the major dietary item of adults, are supplemented by tunicates, algae, bryozoans, hydroids, and eggs (Reynolds and Reynolds, 1977). Juveniles eat a larger proportion of algae and are facultative cleaners. They are also solitary and fiercely territorial (they will attack their own mirror images), whereas adults appear to range widely over the reef and often swim in pairs or loose aggregations. Tiny juveniles may aggregate also, as indicated by our observation of a tight cluster of about 60 half-inch (13-mm) juveniles.

Breeding occurs from midsummer to early fall and juveniles are most abundant from August through November. Offspring of late spawnings may have difficulty surviving low winter temperatures, for they become inactive below 59°F (15°C). Small juveniles collected in winter often appear emaciated, perhaps because of reduced feeding at low temperatures.

**Related species.** *P. zonipectus* is the only member of the genus in the eastern Pacific, but two similar species occur in the Caribbean: the French angelfish, *P. paru* (Bloch), and the gray angelfish, *P. arcuatus* (Linnaeus). The juvenile color patterns of these species are similar, as are their feeding habits (Randall and Hartman, 1968), to those of the Cortez angelfish.

Figure 64   An adult Cortez angelfish, *Pomacanthus zonipectus.* Note the conspicuous preopercular spine which distinguishes angelfishes (Pomacanthidae) from butterflyfishes (Chaetodontidae). (Photograph by Alex Kerstitch.)

129

# KING ANGELFISH, ángel real
## *Holacanthus passer* Valenciennes, 1846

**Illustrated specimen.** Adult, 8.9 in. (224 mm), by Alex Kerstitch; see also Plates 12, 16e, and 16f; grows to about 14 in. (356 mm).

**Distinguishing characteristics.** The adult king angelfish is easily recognized by its dark blue body, bold white bar, and bright orange tail. The juvenile has a series of thin, alternating bluish white and iridescent blue bars interrupted by a broad band of red-orange from behind the eye to near the tip of the pectoral fin. The juvenile color pattern is similar to that of juveniles of the queen angelfish, *H. ciliaris* (Linnaeus), and the blue angelfish, *H. bermudensis* (Jordan and Rutter), in the Caribbean; hence we have named this species "king angelfish." D. XIV, 18–20; A. III, 17–19.

**Distribution.** The king angelfish ranges from the central Gulf to Ecuador and the Islas Galápagos. It is occasionally seen as far north as Puerto Lobos, Sonora.

**Ecology.** Like the Cortez angelfish, the king angelfish is a diurnal grazer on sessile invertebrates and algae but specializes to a larger extent on sponges (Reynolds and Reynolds, 1977). Angelfishes are among the few fishes that eat sponges and may control species diversity by preventing them from monopolizing the reef surface. This species also feeds on plankton (Strand, 1977).

King angelfish are much warier of human approach than Cortez angelfish and seem to prefer clearer water. However, they are often found with the Cortez angelfish, sometimes in mixed aggregations. Reproduction occurs in late summer. Females, which are considerably smaller than males, are territorial and appear to form pair bonds with the males (Strand, 1977). Juveniles appear in fall and winter. Cleaning behavior has been observed in juveniles.

**Related species.** The Clarion angelfish, *Holacanthus clarionensis* Gilbert, 1890, is found in the Cape area (Cabo Pulmo) but is more common at Clarion Island of the Revillagigedo archipelago. The adult is overall bright orange with thin blue bars and olive-brown markings along the posterior trunk and a bright orange caudal fin (see Plate 16c). The juvenile is similar in color to *H. passer* (see Plate 16d).

# THREEBANDED BUTTERFLYFISH, muñeca
## *Chaetodon humeralis* Günther, 1860

**Illustrated specimen.** Adult, 4.6 in. (117 mm), by Alex Kerstitch; see also Plate 13; grows to 10 in. (254 mm).

**Distinguishing characteristics.** This fish has a distinctive color pattern. There are three black bands across the silvery white to yellowish brown body, one of which runs through the eye, and the caudal fin is marked with two additional dark narrow bars. D. XI–XIII, 18–20; A. III, 14–17.

**Distribution.** This species ranges from Bahía Kino to Peru and the Islas Galápagos. It is more commonly found on the mainland coast of the Gulf than on the Baja side. It is the commonest butterflyfish in the tropical eastern Pacific.

**Ecology.** The threebanded butterflyfish is found on shallow patch reefs surrounded by sand or offshore over open sand, where it is occasionally captured in shrimp trawls. It is common at depths from 10 to 40 ft (3 to 12 m) and sometimes ranges to depths below 180 ft (55 m). Over open sand it has been observed to mingle with schools of small spadefish (*Chaetodipterus zonatus*). Rarely solitary, it is usually observed in pairs or small groups. There is no color change between the juvenile and adult stages, although colors are more intense in younger fishes. Young individuals are rarely seen in the central Gulf but are common further south, especially around docks and jetties at Topolobampo.

131

# BARBERFISH, barbero
## *Heniochus nigrirostris* (Gill, 1863)

**Illustrated specimen.** Adult, 5.3 in. (135 mm), by Alex Kerstitch; see also Plate 13 and Figures 60 and 65; grows to about 8 in. (203 mm).

**Distinguishing characteristics.** Color pattern distinguishes this butterflyfish from the three other Gulf chaetodonts. The barberfish has a black raccoonlike mask pattern over the nape and snout and a black band that extends dorsally from the third or fourth dorsal spine diagonally down to the caudal peduncle. Body coloration is pale yellow. Juveniles are similar in color pattern to adults. D. XII, 24–25; A. III, 18–19.

**Distribution.** This species ranges from the central Gulf to Panama, including the Islas del Coco, Malpelo, and Galápagos. It is abundant in the lower Gulf but becomes less common north of Guaymas to Puerto Lobos. We have not observed it at Puerto Peñasco.

**Ecology.** This butterflyfish is best known as a cleaner of other fishes (see Hobson, 1965b). The barberfish aggregates at specific locations on the reef, where it will rid other fish of external parasites (see Figure 65). These cleaning aggregations may involve only a few to many individuals. The diet of this species also includes algae, gastropods, and nonparasitic crustaceans. Like other butterflyfishes, the barberfish is diurnal. At night its color pattern is altered; the dark dorsal band disappears and whitish blotches develop on the body. Mainly a shallow-water species, it prefers depths of 20 to 40 ft (6 to 12 m) but has been recorded at 130 ft (40 m) at Cabo San Lucas.

**Related species.** The scythemarked butterflyfish, *Chaetodon falcifer* Hubbs and Rechnitzer, 1958, is primarily a deep-water species that has been reported from 120 ft (37 m) to

Figure 65   Cleaning by the bar-
berfish, *Heniochus nigrirostris.*
Note the open-mouth posturing
of the host fish (graybar grunt).
(Photograph courtesy of E. S.
Hobson.)

Figure 66   The scythemarked butterflyfish, *Chaetodon falcifer,* the only deep-water chaetodontid in the
Gulf. (Photograph by Alex Kerstitch.)

Figure 67   The longnose butterflyfish, *Forcipiger flavissimus*, in the Gulf is found only in the Cape region. The elongated jaws are specialized for feeding on small invertebrates deep within crevices. (Photograph by Alex Kerstitch.)

below 250 ft (76 m) at Cabo San Lucas. It ranges from southern California (Santa Catalina Island), Isla Guadalupe, Cabo San Lucas and the Islas Galápagos. This yellow butterflyfish resembles the barberfish, *Heniochus nigrirostris,* and is marked with a scytheshaped pattern on its sides (see Figure 66, page 133).

The longnose butterflyfish, *Forcipiger flavissimus* Jordan and McGregor, 1898, is a rare visitor in the lower Gulf and is occasionally collected in the Cabo San Lucas area. This distinctive species, the only Indo-west Pacific chaetodontid in the Gulf, ranges throughout the tropical Pacific. Its long snout, bright yellow color, black mask, and black ocellus on the anal fin margin make it easily recognizable (see Figure 67). This species had been confused with another Indo-west Pacific longnose butterflyfish, *Forcipiger longirostris* (Broussonet) until its taxonomic status was clarified by Randall and Caldwell (1970).

134

# FAMILY POMACENTRIDAE
## Damselfishes (Castañuelas)

The damselfishes are small, usually colorful reef fishes found throughout the subtropical and tropical regions of the world's oceans. They differ from nearly all other marine reef fishes by possession of a single nostril (rarely two) that occurs on each side of the snout; unlike most fishes, which have incurrent and excurrent openings to each nasal organ, this nostril is a blind pouch. The closely related freshwater cichlids (Cichlidae) share this character with the pomacentrids.

Many damselfishes are strongly territorial and solitary, whereas others form loose aggregations in midwater (see Figure 68). During breeding adhesive eggs are attached in clusters to rocky substrates and the nests are vigorously defended. Foraging territories are also maintained by many species. Most damselfishes are omnivores, feeding on benthic algae, crustaceans, plankton, fish eggs, and so on.

There is little variation in general body shape among the nearly 300 species in the family (worldwide, about 23 genera and 275 spp.), although many have juveniles with color patterns that are strikingly different from those of adults. Thirteen species in six genera have been recorded from the Gulf of California, all closely associated with reefs. The systematics of the family is currently under study by Alan R. Emery (Royal Ontario Museum, Toronto) and Gerald R. Allen (Western Australian Museum, Perth).

***References.*** Allen (1976); Heller and Snodgrass (1903); Snodgrass and Heller (1905); Woods and Allen (in press).

Figure 68 A school of scissortail damselfish, *Chromis atrilobata*, at Cabo San Lucas. The bright white spot below the soft-dorsal fin may serve to orient individuals in the school and may be especially effective in dark or turbid water. (Photograph by Alex Kerstitch.)

135

# CORTEZ DAMSELFISH, pez azul de Cortés
## *Eupomacentrus rectifraenum* (Gill, 1863)

**Illustrated specimen.** Juvenile, 2.3 in. (58 mm), by Alex Kerstitch; see also Plates 14 and 17a,b; grows to about 5 in. (127 mm).

**Distinguishing characteristics.** Damselfishes of the genus *Eupomacentrus*\* are characterized by having serrated margins of the preopercle and suborbital. The young of the Cortez damselfish display brilliant purplish blue iridescence; adults lose this iridescence, becoming overall chocolate brown, often with some iridescent blue remaining on the fin margins. D. XII, 15; A. II, 13; $P_1$. 20 (19–21).

**Distribution.** The Cortez damselfish is essentially endemic to the Gulf, ranging from Bahía Magdalena northward to Puertecitos, and from Puerto Peñasco south to Guaymas. It reaches its peak abundance in the central region.

**Ecology.** The adults are strongly territorial and herbivorous. The conspicuous blue juveniles aggregate in shallow water over rocky bottoms. By the time they lose the juvenile

\* Recent systematic studies by Alan R. Emery and Gerald R. Allen may result in the use of the generic name *Stegastes* in place of *Eupomacentrus*.

coloration they will have become relatively solitary and will have established territories around boulders and ledges, which they defend vigorously from competing species, especially *Abudefduf troschelii*, the Panamic sergeant major (Helvey, 1975). They will even attack large fishes and nip at curious divers. Territorial activity is most intense during the breeding season, which begins in late spring and continues throughout the summer. During courtship and egg laying the female assumes a very light tan coloration over the head region to the dorsal fin and has conspicuous yellow lips, whereas the male darkens. The female swims over the rock surface of a shelter, rubbing her ventral surface against it with a wriggling movement as she attaches her eggs. After fertilizing the eggs the male cares for them and defends the nest against predators.

Experimentally, when temperatures approach 54°F (12°C), feeding and territorial behavior cease. In the upper Gulf in winter this species is living at temperatures close to its lower lethal limit (below 54°F), which probably limits its abundance (Thomson and Lehner, 1976).

# BEAUBRUMMEL, pez de dos colores
## *Eupomacentrus flavilatus* (Gill, 1863)

**Illustrated specimen.** Juvenile, 2.3 in. (59 mm), by Alex Kerstitch; see also Plates 14 and 17c,d; reaches a length of about 4 in. (102 mm).

**Distinguishing characteristics.** The juveniles are the most brilliantly colored of the Gulf damselfishes. The dorsal half of the body is light iridescent blue, and the remainder is variably colored, from bright yellow to orange. A prominent dark blue ocellus on the posterior portion of the dorsal fin shows a sky-blue margin. This ocellus and the bicolored pattern disappear with age as the adults assume a light brown body color and yellowish fins. D. XII, 14; A. II, 12; $P_1$. 22 or 23.

**Distribution.** This damselfish is found in the central Gulf and as far as Ecuador, but it is more common along the Gulf's Baja coast than along the mainland. We have not seen it in the upper Gulf north of Bahía Kino.

**Ecology.** Although this colorful species lives mainly at shallow depths between 5 and 30 ft (1.5 to 9 m), it has been observed at depths of 125 ft. (38 m). Like the Cortez damselfish, the beaubrummel is omnivorous, foraging on small invertebrates and benthic algae. It is strongly territorial and quite aggressive toward other fishes as well as its own species. It is more common than the Cortez damselfish in some areas of the lower Gulf but less numerous elsewhere.

The beaubrummel is similar in size, color pattern, and behavior to the west Atlantic beaugregory, *E. leucostictus* (Müller and Troschel), but according to Woods and Allen (in press) it is more closely related to the cocoa damselfish, *E. variabilis* (Castelnau).

**Related species.** Three other species of *Eupomacentrus* have been recorded from the Gulf of California but all are relatively rare: the Acapulco damselfish, *E. acapulcoensis* (Fowler, 1944), the whitetail damselfish, *E. leucorus* (Gilbert, 1892), and the Clarion damselfish, *E. redemptus* (Heller and Snodgrass, 1903).

The juvenile of *E. acapulcoensis* is nearly identical in color pattern to the juvenile of *E. rectifraenum*, which suggests a close relationship. *E. acapulcoensis*, however, has a higher

Figure 69   Adult Acapulco damselfish, *Eupomacentrus acapulcoensis*. Note the marked lightening of the anterior two-thirds of the body of this Isla San Ignacio Farallon fish. (Photograph by Alex Kerstitch.)

Figure 70   A juvenile whitetail damselfish, *Eupomacentrus leucorus*. In this species the color change from juvenile to adult is less striking than in the other members of the genus in the Gulf. Juveniles are more iridescent and the bright greenish back is more intense than in adults. (Photograph by Alex Kerstitch.)

pectoral fin-ray count (21 to 22, rarely 23) than *E. rectifraenum* (19 to 21, rarely 22), which is the only clear difference between juveniles. The adults are more distinct. *E. acapulcoensis* is a larger, slightly more robust fish than *E. rectifraenum*. In the breeding season adult *E. acapulcoensis* may be nearly white on the anterior portion of the body (see Figure 69) and sometimes pale posteriorly, separated by a dark area. A conspicuous white band in the axil of the pectoral fin flashes as the fish moves the fin. Also, most of the scales have noticeable blackish margins. The principal range of *E. acapulcoensis* is from the lower Gulf (Bahía Los Frailes and Isla San Ignacio Farallon) to Peru, but it was recently observed by R. H. Rosenblatt in Bahia Concepción, B.C.S. (personal communication).

The whitetail damselfish, *E. leucorus,* is also similar in general appearance to adult *E. rectifraenum.* We have collected *E. leucorus* from the Cape and Isla San José. This species commonly occurs in the Islas Revillagigedo but also is known from Mazatlán and Isla

Guadalupe. Adults usually have prominent yellowish to whitish margins on the dark pectoral fins and a prominent pale band across the caudal peduncle (see Figure 70). Its overall color is a faded bluish brown with green iridescent scale markings on the head from the dorsal-fin origin to the snout. In the Gulf, at least, this is a deeper-water species and adults are not often encountered in depths of less than 20 ft (6 m). At Cabo San Lucas it is most abundant at 30 to 40 ft (9 to 12 m), but juveniles are found at depths of 10 to 15 ft (3 to 4.6 m). It is closely related to *E. beebei* Nichols, 1924, which occurs mainly at the Islas Galápagos.

We recently collected two specimens of juvenile Clarion damselfish, *E. redemptus,* at Cabo San Lucas. Like *E. leucorus,* this fish usually has a pale caudal peduncle, but its ground color is yellowish (juveniles) and its body scales have prominent dark margins which give it a reticulated appearance (see Figure 71). All previously known specimens came from the Islas Revillagigedo, where this damselfish is common.

Figure 71  Juvenile Clarion damselfish, *Eupomacentrus redemptus.* Note the reticulated pattern on the sides. (Photograph by D. A. Thomson.)

# PANAMIC SERGEANT MAJOR, pintano
## *Abudefduf troschelii* (Gill, 1863)

**Illustrated specimens.** Breeding male (darker fish) and normal adult female, both 7.5 in. (191 mm), by Alex Kerstitch; see also Plate 15 and Figure 72; grows to about 9 in. (229 mm).

**Distinguishing characteristics.** The Panamic sergeant major can be readily identified by the six dark bars on a yellow background that resemble the chevron of an army sergeant major. The only other species with similar coloration is the graybar grunt, *Haemulon sexfasciatum*, which has six to seven dark gray bars on a yellow background. The small mouth, characteristic body shape (similar to freshwater bluegills), and black barred pattern readily distinguish this sergeant major from all other Gulf fishes. D. XIII, 13; A. II, 12.

**Distribution.** One of the commonest of all Gulf fishes, this sergeant major is found throughout the Gulf and from Bahía San Juanico, B.C.S. to northern Peru including the Islas Galápagos.

**Ecology.** Life history studies of the sergeant majors, *Abudefduf saxatilis* (Linnaeus) in Florida and *A. abdominalis* (Quoy and Gai-

mard) in Hawaii, along with our observations on *A. troschelii* in the Gulf, imply that the ecology and behavior of these species are as nearly identical as their morphology. Indeed, for many years *A. troschelii* was considered to be conspecific with *A. saxatilis*. Allen (1976) has shown that *A. troschelii* differs from *A. saxatilis* by a small patch of scales on the outer face of the pectoral axil (scaleless in other sergeant majors).

The Panamic sergeant major in the Gulf of California occurs closely inshore, usually in large aggregations, and the juveniles are common inhabitants of tide pools. This diurnal feeder's diet consists of plankton at the surface or in midwater; it also grazes on benthic invertebrates and algae on the reef. *A. troschelii* starts to breed during early summer in the Gulf and continues throughout the summer until the water cools in the fall. Its breeding behavior appears to be similar to that of the two other sergeant majors mentioned. The male *A. troschelii* assumes a deep metallic blue color when attempting to attract females to the nesting site to lay eggs (see Figure 72). A

Figure 72   A pair of Panamic sergeant majors on a nest. The female (right, partly obscured) is laying eggs. The dark male with conspicuously light lips is waiting to fertilize the eggs stuck to the boulder by the female. (Photograph by D. A. Thomson.)

nest site usually consists of the vertical face of a large angular boulder which is cleaned of algae and other growth by the male. The male becomes very aggressive at this time and drives all other fishes away, permitting only gravid females to approach. The female deposits her eggs as she swims in a circular motion over the rocky substrate. When she leaves, the male fertilizes the eggs by rubbing his genital papilla over them and releasing sperm. The newly hatched young, having a short-lived larval stage, quickly move into rocky intertidal areas where they become conspicuous residents by midsummer. Adult males defend territories only when breeding. Gregarious fish, they swim in loose aggregations in the shallow waters over reefs. In captivity, however, these fish are aggressive when only a few fish are kept together in an aquarium. Aggressive behavior decreases significantly as they become crowded, especially among the small juveniles.

*A. troschelii* is a warmwater, stenothermal species. Its upper lethal temperature is about 97°F (36°C) and its lower lethal temperature is about 52°F (11°C). Our laboratory experi-

ments have shown that this species will cease feeding when temperatures approach 54°F (12°C). In January, 1971 a record cold spell in the upper Gulf reduced sea-surface temperatures at Puerto Peñasco to a low of 48°F (8°C) and caused mortalities in several species of inshore fishes. Many dead and moribund sergeant majors were seen in tide pools on January 8, 1971, when the water temperature was 52°F (11°C). Apparently this winterkill of *A. troschelii* was not catastrophic for the species at Puerto Peñasco because juveniles were again abundant the following summer, although they appeared much later than usual (Thomson and Lehner, 1976).

This versatile fish also appears to be an important cleaner. Large juveniles (second year class) have been observed cleaning schools of striped mullet, halfbeaks, and needlefish in and outside the Gulf. (McCourt and Thomson, ms).

**Related species.** Similar in appearance to *A. troschelii,* the dusky sergeant major, *Nexilarius concolor* (Gill, 1863), which

Figure 73   In the Gulf the dusky sergeant major, *Nexilarius concolor*, is common only in the lower region. This damselfish prefers shorelines with a strong surge zone. (Photograph by Alex Kerstitch.)

we treat as a synonym* of *Abudefduf declivifrons* (Gill, 1863), is commonly found only in the lower Gulf (Cabo San Lucas,

\* The chief character used to separate *concolor* from *declivifrons* (i.e., adnate suborbitals) is inconsistent, showing intermediate conditions among our specimens collected from Cabo San Lucas to Ecuador. D. A. Hensley (Marine Research Laboratory, St. Petersburg, Florida) tentatively considers them as distinct species of the genus *Nexilarius* in his unpublished revision of the Indo-west Pacific species of *Abudefduf*, but he has not tried to solve the species-level problems in *Nexilarius*. We feel that they are conspecific and retain the name *N. concolor* for this damselfish.

Mazatlán) and south along the coast to Peru. We have collected it as far north as Guaymas (single adult) and it has been recorded from Bahía San Francisquito (Gulf coast of B.C.N.) and Bahía Magdalena. This species has six to seven dark brown bars which are less distinct than those of *A. troschelii* and grow obscure with age (see Figure 73). The head profile is much steeper in *N. concolor* and the overall color is a dusky brown to beige in contrast to the metallic greenish blue and yellow of the Panamic sergeant major. The habitat of *N. concolor* is the surf zone of rocky beaches. This species is often more common intertidally than *A. troschelii* in the Cabo San Lucas area.

Plate 9   Yellow snapper (*Lutjanus argentiventris*). Illustrated by Alex Kerstitch.

(a)

(b)

(c)

(d)

Plate 10 Schooling fishes: a. Graybar grunt (*Haemulon sexfasciatum*). Photograph courtesy of Ed. Janss. b. Spotted stress coloration of a juvenile Cortez chub (*Kyphosus elegans*). Photograph courtesy of C. A. Flanagan. c. Mexican goatfish (*Mulloidichthys dentatus*) being cleaned by barberfish (*Heniochus nigrirostris*). Note change in color of fish posing to be cleaned. Photograph courtesy of E. S. Hobson. d. Panamic porkfish (*Anisotremus taeniatus*). Photograph by Alex Kerstitch.

Plate 11   Upper fish, Gulf opaleye (*Girella simplicidens*); lower fish, Cortez chub (*Kyphosus elegans*). Illustrated by Alex Kerstitch.

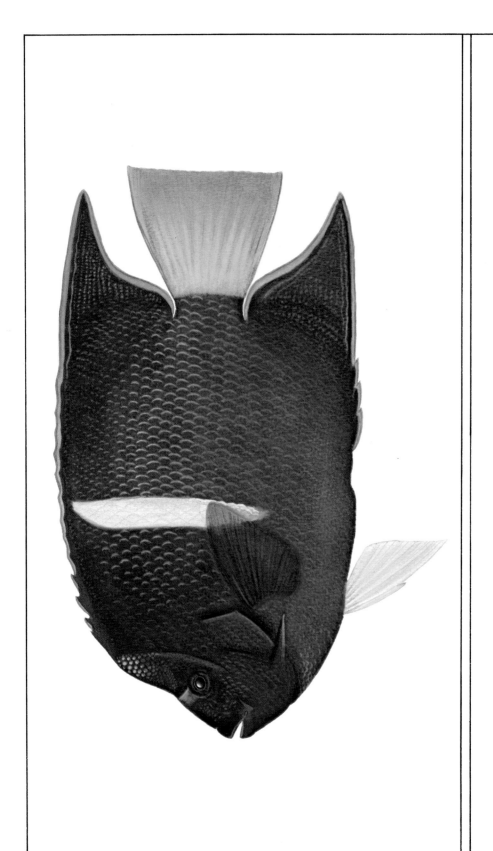

Plate 12   King angelfish (*Holacanthus passer*). Illustrated by Alex Kerstitch.

Plate 13   Sea of Cortez butterflyfishes: upper, barberfish (*Heniochus nigrirostris*); lower, threebanded butterflyfish (*Chaetodon humeralis*). Illustrated by Alex Kerstitch.

Plate 14  Juvenile damselfishes: upper, Cortez damselfish (*Eupomacentrus rectifraenum*); lower, beaubrummel (*Eupomacentrus flavilatus*). Illustrated by Alex Kerstitch.

Plate 15 Panamic sergeant major (*Abudefduf troschelii*): darker fish, territorial male; lighter fish, female with normal coloration. Illustrated by Alex Kerstitch.

Plate 16 Gulf angelfishes [all photographs by Alex Kerstitch except (c), which is by courtesy of Ed. Janss, and (d), which is by courtesy of Matt Gilligan]. a. Adult Cortez angelfish (*Pomacanthus zonipectus*). b. Juvenile Cortez angelfish (*P. zonipectus*). c. Adult Clarion angelfish (*H. clarionensis*). d. Juvenile Clarion angelfish (*H. clarionensis*). e. Adult king angelfish (*Holacanthus passer*). f. Juvenile king angelfish (*H. passer*).

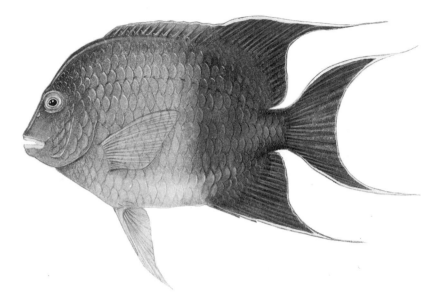

# GIANT DAMSELFISH, castañuela gigante
## *Microspathodon dorsalis* (Gill, 1863)

**Illustrated specimen.** Adult male, 10.2 in. (260 mm) by Alex Kerstitch; see also Plate 17e,f; largest Gulf damselfish; grows to about 12 in. (305 mm).

**Distinguishing characteristics.** Adults are easily distinguished by their size and the trailing edges of their dorsal, anal, and caudal fins. During courtship the head and front half of the body of the adult male are often a silvery white. Other adults may be deep blue or pastel blue overall. Juveniles are iridescent blue and resemble young Cortez damselfish (*E. rectifraenum*) but differ from them by having a few brilliant sky-blue spots along the back and a larger, broader mouth with many closely set, movable teeth. D. XII, 16; A. II, 14.

**Distribution.** The giant damselfish is distributed from the central gulf (Bahía Kino) to Colombia (Isla Malpelo) and the Islas Galápagos.

**Ecology.** The preferred habitat of this common damselfish is among large boulders just beyond the surge zone. These aggressive herbivorous damselfish defend both feeding and breeding territories. Mating generally begins during late April and continues throughout the summer. Courting males have been known to charge large groupers and divers who wander too close to their nests. Large adults (both male and female) develop prominent humps on their foreheads.

**Related species.** The bumphead damselfish, *M. bairdii* (Gill, 1863), is found infrequently in the central and lower Gulf. It ranges south to Ecuador and the Islas Galápagos and Revillagigedo. The adult is similar to the giant damselfish in shape but is dark brown and lacks trailing vertical fins, and has a purplish eye and a more pronounced hump on the forehead. The young resemble the juvenile beaubrummel, *Eupomacentrus flavilatus,* in coloration. Bicolored, they are bright iridescent blue above the lateral line and bright orange below. The garibaldi, *Hypsypops rubicundus* (Girard, 1854), the bright golden orange damselfish common along the southern California coast, has been collected infrequently at Cabo San Lucas (juveniles only) but has not been seen elsewhere in the Gulf. Its principal range is from Bahía Magdalena to Monterey Bay, California.

# SCISSORTAIL DAMSELFISH, castañeta
## *Chromis atrilobata* Gill, 1863

**Photograph.** Adult, about 3 in. (75 mm), by Alex Kerstitch; see also Figure 68; grows to about 5 in. (127 mm).

**Distinguishing characteristics.** This small damselfish is distinguished by a deeply forked tail and a conspicuous white spot on the back below the last dorsal ray. There is no color difference between adults and juveniles. Both are dull grayish brown and have bold black margins on the caudal fin, a light pinkish anal fin, and a dark blotch at the base of the pectoral fin. D. XII, 12; A. II, 12.

**Distribution.** This common species ranges from the upper Gulf (Roca Consag) to northern Peru and the Islas Galápagos.

**Ecology.** Unlike other damselfishes, the castañeta aggregates in large numbers in open water above reefs and feeds on zooplankton. It is not strongly aggressive or territorial as are other Gulf damselfishes. Although it prefers depths of 20 to 65 ft (6 to 20 m), it is occasionally found at depths of 250 ft (76 m). In the darkness of deep water the castañeta becomes almost invisible except for its brilliant postdorsal white spot which gives the illusion of glowing in the dark. This may serve for species recognition or to help keep the aggregation together.

**Related species.** The bicolored blue-and-yellow chromis (*Chromis* sp.) occurs commonly at depths of 60 to 250 ft (18 to 76 m and occasionally shallower) throughout the central and lower Gulf (see plate 17g). They are iridescent blue and bright yellow, although the colors become dull in adults. Another undescribed species of *Chromis*, the silverstripe chromis, is found in deep water (75 to 250 ft; 23 to 76 m) from Guaymas to Cabo San Lucas. The bluish adults have a diagonal silvery stripe along the back paralleling the dorsal-fin base. The juveniles lack yellow pigmentation and are iridescent blue overall (see Plate 17h). This species is more aggressive than the blue-and-yellow chromis and the young resemble the blue young of the Cortez damselfish. The distribution of these *Chromis* spp. outside the Gulf will be included in a revision of this genus in the eastern Pacific by Loren P. Woods and David W. Greenfield.

# FAMILY CIRRHITIDAE
## Hawkfishes (Halcones)

The hawkfishes constitute a small family of sedentary, predatory fishes. Some perch on coral heads or boulders, watching like hawks for their prey (see Figure 74). All hawkfishes have a fringe of cirri on the hind edge of the anterior nostrils, cirri projecting from the membranes near the tips of the dorsal spines, and their lower pectoral fin rays are thickened and unbranched, with deeply incised membranes between the rays. This chiefly Indo-Pacific family has 10 genera and 34 species worldwide. Only one species occurs in the western Atlantic and three genera with three species inhabit the Gulf, although one is a rare deep-water species.

*References.*  Randall (1963a).

Figure 74  The coral hawkfish, *Cirrhitichthys oxycephalus*, is the smallest of the three species of hawkfishes in the Gulf. Note the fringe on the fin membrane near the tips of the anterior dorsal spines, a character diagnostic of this family. (Photograph by Alex Kerstitch.)

145

# GIANT HAWKFISH, chino mero
## *Cirrhitus rivulatus* Valenciennes, 1855

**Illustrated specimen.** Adult, 11.8 in. (300 mm), by Tor Hansen; see also Plates 24c, d; largest hawkfish in the family; grows to at least 20½ in. (520 mm).

**Distinguishing characteristics.** This hawkfish has a massive head and large pectoral fins, the thickened lower rays of which extend beyond the membranes. It has a fringe on the interradial membranes between the dorsal spines. The distinctive color pattern of the giant hawkfish (also called clown hawkfish) consists of markings resembling oriental inscriptions. Edged with sky-blue they are broken into vertical patterns on the olive body and form bands on the head radiating from the eye (see Plate 24c). This color pattern and basslike appearance have given this species its Spanish common name, "chino mero" (Chinese bass). The juvenile color pattern, which is quite different from that of the adult, consists of

several irregularly shaped, broad, dark bars that extend from the tip of the jaw to the tail. The spinous dorsal fin of the juvenile is a bright reddish orange (see Plate 24d). D. X, 11–12; A. III-16.

**Distribution.** Relatively common in the central and lower Gulf but less common in the upper Gulf (to Puerto Lobos), this hawkfish ranges to Colombia and the Islas Galápagos.

**Ecology.** Restricted to shallow depths, the giant hawkfish is found near boulders and fragmented rock, and young adults and juveniles seem to prefer crevices in which wave action is strong. The secretive juveniles are quite shy and are seldom seen in the open. In contrast, the adult is generally inquisitive, readily emerging from hiding to watch divers and often becoming easy prey for spearfishermen. Its diet consists of fish and crustaceans.

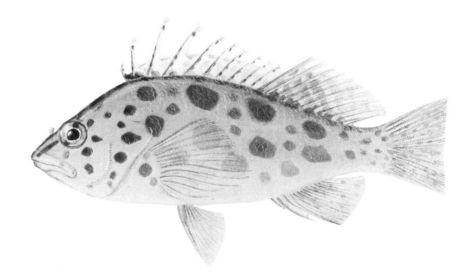

# CORAL HAWKFISH, halcón de coral
## *Cirrhitichthys oxycephalus* (Bleeker, 1855)

**Illustrated specimen.** Adult, 2.3 in. (58 mm), by Alex Kerstitch; see also Plate 24e and Figure 74; one of the smallest hawkfishes; grows to about 3 in. (76 mm).

**Distinguishing characteristics.** Species of the genus *Cirrhitichthys* have large scales on their cheeks (*Cirrhitus* has only small scales) and coarsely serrated preopercular margins. Both juveniles and adults of the coral hawkfish bear small reddish spots on an off-white background, and the first dorsal soft ray is filamentous. D. X, 12; A. III, 6.

**Distribution.** The coral hawkfish, the widest ranging species in the family, occurs throughout the tropical Indo-west and eastern Pacific. In the Gulf it ranges from Isla San Pedro Nolasco and Islas Santa Inés to Cabo San Lucas, being more common in the lower than central Gulf. It ranges south to Colombia, and the Islas Galápagos.

**Ecology.** In the lower Gulf the coral hawkfish is associated with coral heads in which it rests among coral branches. The red spots on the body change color in response to background coloration. They may turn pink, red, or orange if the fish swims to another coral patch of a different color. In the central Gulf, where coral is sparse, this species is found in crevices or among small rocks.

**Related species.** Another Indo-west Pacific species, the longnose hawkfish, *Oxycirrhites typus* Bleeker, 1857, has been collected in deep water at Cabo San Lucas and recently outside Bahía San Carlos, Sonora. Similar in coloration to the coral hawkfish, it has a long pointed snout not unlike that of the longnose butterflyfish, *Forcipiger flavissimus.* In the Cape region the longnose hawkfish is usually associated with yellow-polyped coral at depths around 150 ft (46 m), although we have collected it at about 15 ft (4.6 m). This species has also been collected from deep water in Hawaii (Morris and Morris, 1967) and is probably widely distributed in moderately deep water throughout the tropical Pacific.

# FAMILY LABRIDAE
## Wrasses (Viejas y señoritas)

The wrasses are a diverse family of brilliantly colored fishes, most of which are cigar-shaped. They have protruding canine teeth, large cycloid scales, and only 11 to 12 branched caudal rays. They often swim by paddling with their pectoral fins, appearing to push themselves along, dragging their tails behind them. Some deep-bodied wrasses (*Bodianus, Semicossyphus*) resemble parrotfishes, and one Indo-west Pacific monster (*Cheilinus*) attains a length of 10 ft (3 m). Many have strikingly different color patterns between juveniles and adults, males and females, and some have the ability to change sex, which produces "supermales" with highly conspicuous coloration (protogynous hermaphroditism). The color forms of some wrasses were originally described as distinct species, attesting to the striking color differences among them.

To avoid predators some wrasses (*Halichoeres*) completely bury themselves in the sand at night and when threatened. Others (*Bodianus*) secrete a mucous cocoon that envelops the fish as it sleeps. Some (*Labroides, Thalassoma*) have become specialized as cleaners that service other species by removing their ectoparasites. All wrasses are diurnal (Figure 75) and become inactive at night. In the Gulf seven genera and 16 species have been recorded, but worldwide there are at least 58 genera with more than 400 species in this large circumtropical family.

***References.*** Bussing (1972); Caporiacco (1947); Gilbert (1890); Gomon (1974); Randall (1965); Randall and Böhlke (1965).

Figure 75  A female spinster wrasse, *Halichoeres nicholsi*, following a foraging Mexican goatfish, *Mulloidichthys dentatus*, to feed on organisms driven from the sand by the goatfish. Wrasses are often opportunistic feeders benefiting from disturbances caused by the feeding of other fishes. (Photograph courtesy of E. S. Hobson.)

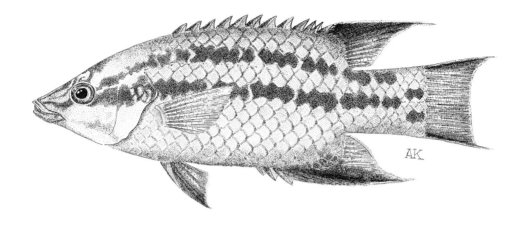

# MEXICAN HOGFISH, vieja
## *Bodianus diplotaenia* (Gill, 1863)

**Illustrated specimen.** Female, 8.9 in. (225 mm), by Alex Kerstitch; see also Plates 21a,b; largest shallow water wrasse in the Gulf; grows to about 2½ ft (0.76 m) and 20 lb (9 kg).

**Distinguishing characteristics.** The juveniles and adult females of this wrasse have a bright to dusky yellow body coloration and two dark interrupted stripes running from the eye to the caudal peduncle. The head and ventral region are occasionally reddish pink. The adult male has a fleshy hump or pad on the forehead, and the tips of all the fins except the pectoral are long and filamentous. The body color is a variable bluish gray and a yellow bar occurs behind the pectoral fin. Very young juveniles under 1 in. (25 mm) are lemon yellow without markings. In deep water adults are predominantly reddish. D. XII, 10–11; A. III, 12–13.

**Distribution.** This predominantly central-Gulf species ranges widely from Isla Guadalupe throughout the Gulf (Roca Consag) to Chile. It has been collected from the Islas del Coco, Malpelo, Revillagigedo, and Galápagos.

**Ecology.** This wrasse is common along both rocky coasts of the central and lower Gulf. Although recorded at depths of more than 250 ft (76 m), adults prefer shallower water 15 to 60 ft (4.6 to 18 m) deep. *Bodianus diplotaenia* and the California sheephead, *Semicossyphus pulcher,* are the largest wrasses in the Gulf, both attaining lengths of more than 2 ft (0.6 m) and weighing more than 20 lb (9 kg). The Mexican hogfish tends to be solitary or forms aggregations of only a few individuals. They feed on crustaceans, mollusks, and small fishes. Opportunistic, it sometimes follows other fish, like large parrotfishes, feeding on scraps torn up from the bottom and on prey driven from shelter by the large grazers. During the night the juvenile sometimes forms a mucous cocoon to cover its body, which presumably protects it from predators (Hobson, 1965a). The California sheephead is the only other Gulf wrasse with this behavioral specialization, an adaptation common to some parrotfishes. The bright yellow juveniles are known to be cleaners, sometimes tending adults of their own

Figure 76    A male California sheephead, *Semicossyphus pulcher*. In the Gulf this wrasse is usually found in deep water (Photograph by Alex Kerstitch.)

as well as other species (Hobson, 1965a). The young begin to appear by late summer when they are often found seeking shelter among branches of yellow-polyped black coral.

**Related species.** The California sheephead, *Semicossyphus pulcher** (Ayres, 1854) occurs uncommonly in the Gulf from the midriff region to the Cape and ranges northward to Monterey, California. The color pattern of the male is distinct: black head, broad crimson band over midbody, black posterior body, and white chin (see Figure 76). The female is a uniform brownish red to rose and the juvenile is rosy red with a single light stripe along the midlateral body to the tail with prominent dark blotches on the soft dorsal and anal fins and the caudal peduncle. This is the only wrasse in the eastern Pacific known to reach a length of 3 ft (1 m) and a weight of 36 lb (16

* Formerly known as *Pimelometopon pulchrum*.

kg) in California waters. We have not seen sheephead approaching this size in the Gulf.

A recently described species related to *Bodianus,* the blackspot wrasse, *Decodon melasma* Gomon, 1974, occurs from the upper Gulf (Isla Tiburón) to Ecuador. This labrid is commonly captured in shrimp trawls, from moderate depths offshore. It differs from *Bodianus* by a lack of scales on the membrane of the soft dorsal fin (Gomon, 1974). It reaches a length of about 8 in. (203 mm) and occurs on patch reefs offshore; we have not collected this wrasse inshore. Its overall coloration is pinkish red above and white below, with three curved yellow stripes on the head and a conspicuous dark spot just above the center of the lateral line (see Plate 22f). This wrasse is a monandric protogynous hermaphrodite; all males appear to be sex-reversed females (Diener, 1977). *D. melasma* is a sibling species of the western Atlantic *D. puellaris* Poey.

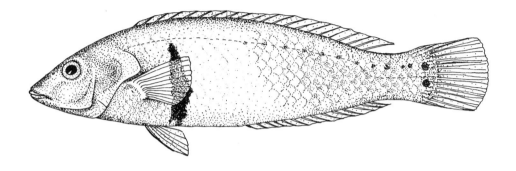

# ROCK WRASSE, señorita piedrera
## *Halichoeres semicinctus* (Ayres, 1859)

**Illustrated specimen.** Adult male, 4.7 in. (145 mm), by Tor Hansen; see also Plate 21f; reaches a length of about 12 in. (305 mm) in the Gulf; reported to grow to 14 in. (356 mm).

**Distinguishing characteristics.** All adults of the genus *Halichoeres* have forward-projecting posterior canine teeth inside the angle of the mouth. The rock wrasse can be distinguished from other Gulf *Halichoeres* by the presence of small predorsal scales extending across the nape of the head. The body color varies from yellowish brown to bronze in the adult and to bright green in the very young (less than 2 in., or 50 mm). The juveniles and young usually have a small dark ocellus on the soft dorsal fin and black flecks on some of the scales on the upper body. The adult males have a prominent dark bar behind the pectoral fin that extends ventrally to the pelvic fin but not above the level of the eye. Adult females retain the black flecks of the juvenile pattern. D. IX, 11–12; A. III, 12.

**Distribution.** The rock wrasse is a northern disjunct species, common both to the upper Gulf and along the southern California coast but uncommon to rare between these regions. It is rare in the lower Gulf and has not been collected south of Mazatlán.

**Ecology.** This species is primarily restricted to shallow rocky reefs and is frequently seen in tide pools and over the reef flat at Puerto Peñasco. Like all the Gulf wrasses of the genus *Halichoeres,* it burrows in the sand at night and is occasionally stranded by a very low tide. It feeds on small crustaceans and gastropods, crushing the larger ones with its well developed pharyngeal teeth. The rock wrasse tolerates colder water than other Gulf wrasses, which perhaps accounts for its success in the northern Gulf where it is the most abundant labrid (Thomson and Lehner, 1976). See Hobson (1976) for notes on cleaning behavior of this wrasse in California waters.

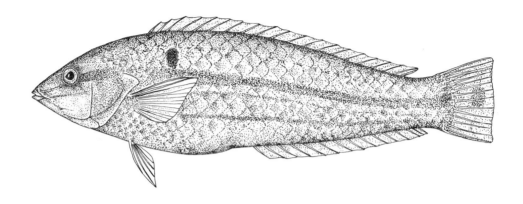

# CHAMELEON WRASSE, señorita camaleón
*Halichoeres dispilus* (Günther, 1864)

**Illustrated specimen.** Young male, 5.1 in. (130 mm), by Tor Hansen; see also Plate 21e; grows to about 8 in. (203 mm).

**Distinguishing characteristics.** This species can be identified by its distinctive color pattern. The head and caudal fin are usually salmon red and the rest of the body is light pink with a prominent round bluish black spot on the lateral line below the fourth and fifth dorsal spines. The young, and occasionally the subadults, have two dark lateral stripes running the length of the body. It can be distinguished from the rock wrasse by a lack of predorsal scales across the nape of the head. D. IX, 11; A. III, 12.

**Distribution.** A widely ranging species, *H. dispilus* is found throughout the Gulf to Peru. One of the commonest Gulf wrasses, it occurs along both coasts from Puerto Peñasco to Cabo San Lucas.

**Ecology.** Rocky shallow reefs, interspaced with sandy patches, seem to be the preferred habitat of *H. dispilus*. Like many labrids, it buries in the sand at night or when disturbed. Occasionally it finds itself stranded on exposed sand bars during periods of extreme low tides. In captivity this wrasse will bury itself in the sand for long periods, often spending more time buried than swimming. This species displays two color patterns that can be altered to match the substrate over which it may be swimming. Normally salmon red in color while over rocky reefs, it may instantly turn pale blue or striped when swimming over sand; hence the name chameleon wrasse (Hobson, 1968). Although normally found in shallow water, it has been captured at 250 ft (76 m). Specimens collected from these depths display marked color variations of deep red and blue.

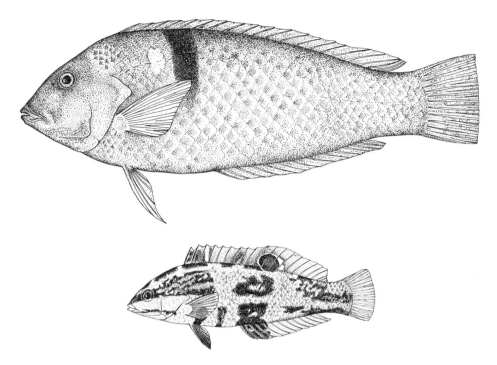

# SPINSTER WRASSE, soltera
## *Halichoeres nicholsi* (Jordan and Gilbert, 1881)

**Illustrated specimens.** Adult male, 8.7 in. (220 mm), and juvenile, 3 in. (75 mm), by Tor Hansen; see also Plates 21c,d, and 22b and Figure 75; largest species of *Halichoeres* in the Gulf; grows to about 15 in. (381 mm).

**Distinguishing characteristics.** The remarkable color transition from juvenile to adult may result in misidentification of this colorful wrasse. Generally the adult male is bluish to green with a diffuse black bar on its side below the fourth to seventh dorsal spines and extending down to the middle of the sides. A prominent yellow blotch touches this cross bar anteriorly (see Plate 21c). All fins except the pectorals are flecked with light blue spots. The female has a more prominent black bar that meets an interrupted black stripe along the midline (see Plate 21d and Figure 75). The young are predominantly pale yellow with irregular dark blotches on their sides. Fins are

clear except for a large dark green ocellus on the soft dorsal fin (see Plate 22b). D. IX, 12; A. III, 11.

**Distribution.** Relatively common throughout the Gulf, the spinster wrasse ranges from Puerto Peñasco to Panama and the Islas Revillgigedo and Galápagos.

**Ecology.** The spinster wrasse prefers depths between 10 and 40 ft (3 to 12 m), although they have been recorded in depths below 175 ft (53 m). The adults are solitary, whereas juveniles, which appear in July to August, are seen in small groups and often mingle with other small labrids. The diet of this wrasse consists of mollusks, brittle stars, sea urchins, and crabs. Occasionally large adults will feed on small blennioid fishes (Hobson, 1968).

This wrasse is difficult to maintain in captivity because it may spend long periods buried in the sand, from which it sometimes emerges weak and emaciated.

153

# WOUNDED WRASSE, señorita herida
## *Halichoeres chierchiae* Caporiacco, 1947

**Illustrated specimen.** Adult male, 6.3 in. (159 mm), by Alex Kerstitch; see also Plates 18 and 22a; grows to about 8 in. (203 mm).

**Distinguishing characteristics.** The adult male's body color is greenish to yellow with a prominent dark green spot margined posteriorly with a red blotch resembling a "spear wound" on and below the seventh to ninth lateral line scales. Dorsal, anal, and caudal fins are salmon red streaked with diagonal light orange stripes (see Plate 18). Females have yellowish bands and an orange tail. Females and juveniles display a black spot between the second and third dorsal spines (see Plate 22a). D. IX, 11; A. II, 12.

**Distribution.** Ranging from Puerto Peñasco (rare) to Acapulco, this wrasse is common in the central and lower Gulf.

**Ecology.** The wounded wrasse prefers shallow rocky reefs with sandy patches, although we have found it as deep as 225 ft (69 m). The adults are solitary diurnal predators, feeding on mollusks, crabs, brittle stars, and sea urchins. Juveniles form small aggregations of three to 15 individuals and occasionally mingle with other species of *Halichoeres*. During the spring juveniles can be seen among sargassum patches in the Guaymas area.

**Related species.** The only other species of *Halichoeres* in the Gulf is the mangrove wrasse, *Halichoeres aestuaricola* Bussing, 1972, which prefers mangrove estuaries, an unusual habitat for a labrid. Our only two specimens of *H. aestuaricola* were collected over a boulder bottom at about 15 ft (4.6 m) in Bahía Bacochibampo, Guaymas.

The mangrove wrasse lacks markings except for a black spot on the upper half of the caudal-fin base. Young (less than 100 mm SL) also have a black spot on the second to fourth dorsal soft-rays. Its anterior lateral line scales have a single pore, whereas *H. nicholsi* and *H. chierchiae* have two to four pores per scale. *H. aestuaricola* ranges from Guaymas to Colombia, including Costa Rica.

# CORTEZ RAINBOW WRASSE, arco iris
## *Thalassoma lucasanum* (Gill, 1863)

**Illustrated specimens.** Rainbow phase (top), 4.2 in. (103 mm); "saddle" phase (bottom), 3.4 in. (86 mm), by Alex Kerstitch; see also Plates 19 and 22c; reaches a length of about 6 in. (152 mm).

**Distinguishing characteristics.** The brilliant yellow and red stripes of the juveniles and adults and the bright yellow band of the purplish blue (secondary) males make *T. lucasanum* the easiest of all Gulf wrasses to identify. Members of the genus *Thalassoma* have eight dorsal spines, whereas all other eastern tropical Pacific labrids have nine or more. D. VIII, 13; A. III, 11.

**Distribution.** A central and lower Gulf species, the rainbow wrasse is common to abundant along the Baja California Sur coast and in the Guaymas region. It ranges north to Puerto Lobos and Bahía San Luis Gonzaga and south to Panama and Islas Malpelo and Galápagos. This tropical species has not been collected by us at Puerto Peñasco.

**Ecology.** Aggregations of *T. lucasanum* can be seen swarming close to rocky substrates feeding on algae, crustaceans, and soft coral. They are ubiquitous on most central Gulf reefs in shallow water close to shore. At night these fish lie wedged in crevices among the rocks, usually at least partly covered with sand (Hobson, 1965a). This is in contrast to the wrasses of the genus *Halichoeres,* which bury themselves completely in sand at night. Although occurring in small aggregations, this species probably has feeding territories and establishes social hierarchies. In captivity they are quite aggressive and peck orders are soon set up in which the largest individual is dominant.

Spawning aggregations and broadcast egg laying have been observed. Normally both sexes exhibit the rainbow color phase in such aggregations. Sex reversal which produces secondary males occurs in some of the females. The secondary males exhibit a "saddle" phase in which they assume a purplish blue body color interrupted by a large conspicuous yellow band behind the head. This "supermale" defends a territory that includes a harem of several females and results in the formation of single sexual pairs during spawning.

Sometimes the young are facultative cleaners, picking parasites off other fishes at cleaning stations (Hobson, 1965a). This behavior is incidental to regular feeding activity, but the young slightly resemble the cleaner specialist *Labroides phthirophagus* Randall from Hawaii.

*T. lucasanum* is a warmwater species that may be excluded from the northern Gulf by low water temperatures. This species becomes very inactive and is not often seen on the reef during winter, even in regions in which it is normally abundant in summer. The record cold wave in the Gulf in January 1971 may

have depressed populations of this wrasse, for it seemed to be scarce in the Guaymas area the following summer.

**Related species.** One other species of *Thalassoma* occurs in the Gulf, the sunset wrasse, *T. lutescens* (Lay and Bennett, 1839). Not so common as *T. lucasanum*, this species is rarely seen in the Guaymas region but is more often found in the La Paz to Cabo San Lucas region (see Plate 22c). This is an Indo-west Pacific wrasse that ranges to Panama and major offshore islands in the tropical eastern Pacific. *T. lutescens* has a greenish blue body with a series of dark vertical marks on the posterior margin of each scale and broad wavy pink lines radiating from the eye. *T. lutescens* is more robust and attains a larger size than *T. lucasanum*.

# BANDED WRASSE, señorita de cintas
## *Pseudojulis notospilus* Günther, 1864

**Illustrated specimen.** Adult, 5.6 in. (141 mm), by Alex Kerstitch; see also Plate 18; grows to about 10 in. (254 mm).

**Distinguishing characteristics.** Species of the genus *Pseudojulis* lack the posterior canines characteristic of *Halichoeres* spp. The banded wrasse has five to eight dark bars on a blue-green to olive body (see Plate 18). These bars run onto the dorsal fin in both juveniles and adults. Juveniles are colored like adults except for a large blue-edged dorsal-fin ocellus that disappears with age. D. IX, 11; A. III, 12.

**Distribution.** Although ranging into the northern Gulf (Puerto Peñasco), this wrasse is common only in the lower Gulf. It ranges from Bahía Magdalena south to Peru and the Islas Galápagos.

**Ecology.** In the Gulf the banded wrasse is uncommon along its rocky coasts but is one of the commonest wrasses south of Mazatlán. Its diet consists of crustaceans, sea urchins, mollusks, and brittle stars. In captivity this wrasse quickly loses its blue-green coloration, and turns dull brown.

**Related species.** At least one other species of *Pseudojulis,* the golden wrasse, *P. melanotis* Gilbert, 1890, occurs in the central and lower Gulf. According to our observations coloration of the juvenile is golden orange and has a prominent dark stripe running from the snout to the caudal peduncle and a thinner dark stripe running below the dorsal fin forward to the head (see Plate 22d). The adult coloration is similar to that of the juvenile but not so brilliant. The Cape wrasse, *P. inornatus* Gilbert, 1890, is known to us only from the original description of a juvenile collected off Cabo San Lucas at a depth of 31 fathoms (57 m). It reportedly differs from *P. melanotis* by having flexible, not pungent, dorsal spines and other poorly defined characters. We do not know the distribution of these two species of *Pseudojulis* outside the Gulf.

# PACIFIC RAZORFISH, viejita
## *Hemipteronotus pavoninus* (Valenciennes, 1839)

**Illustrated specimens.** Adult, 8.8 in. (223 mm), and juvenile, 2.2 in. (55 mm), by Alex Kerstitch; see also Plate 20; grows to about 10 in. (254 mm).

**Distinguishing characteristics.** The distinctive body shape of the adult *H. pavoninus* clearly separates it from other Gulf wrasses. The profile of the head is steep, occasionally almost vertical, and its dorsal surface is a sharp edge; hence the name razorfish. The first two dorsal spines are nearly or completely separated from the rest of the fin. The mature adult body coloration is light blue or gray, with three broad, dark, indistinct cross bars on the sides. The compressed body is speckled with faint dark spots. A prominent black spot edged with blue is located above the lateral line between the pectoral and dorsal fins. Juvenile coloration varies from dark brown overall, to mottled, to banded. The first two spines are filamentous,

separated from the rest of the dorsal fin, and when elevated give the juveniles a "unicorn" appearance. D. II + VII, 12–13; A. III, 12–13.

**Distribution.** This widespread Indo-west Pacific species is well established in the lower Gulf and relatively common at Cabo San Lucas. It has been reported from offshore islands along the Pacific coast to Panama and we have collected it at Guaymas along the mainland coast of the Gulf.

**Ecology.** This bizarre labrid is well adapted to sandy bottoms, where it spends most of its adult life, but it cannot be considered a sandy-shore fish. Adults always seem to occur over open sandy bottom near reefs, although the young rarely stray from the protection of rocks. Tiny juveniles sway back and forth with the waves, resembling debris or pieces of floating algae. The adults are solitary but other individuals are usually nearby. Hovering a few inches above

158

the sand, they adopt an "S" shape when approached and dive head first into the sand at the first sign of danger. Because of their razorlike profiles and compressed bodies, they can swim laterally under the sand when threatened. They prefer fine white sand and shallow water (15 to 40 ft, 4.6 to 12 m) deep, although they have been observed at depths of 80 ft (24 m). When threatened, their filamentous dorsal spines are drawn forward, resembling a sharp lance. This effect is particularly pronounced in juveniles because their dorsal spines are proportionally longer and better developed than those of the adult.

**Related species.** Two other species of *Hemipteronotus* occur in the Gulf. The Cape razorfish *H. mundiceps* (Gill 1863) occurs in the Cabo San Lucas region. The Cape razorfish is a smaller species (to 6 in., or 152 mm) and is common over shallow sandy bottoms where it aggregates in large groups of up to 100 fish. The

adult's body coloration is pale green to blue with three to four blue streaks across the cheek. Each scale is marked with a dark but inconspicuous vertical line. The clown razorfish, *H. taeniourus* (Lacépède, 1802), ranges widely throughout the Indo-west Pacific and extends into the lower and central Gulf to Guaymas and south to Panama. The adult lacks the steep head profile of *H. pavoninus* and is colored dark brown to green with a white area in the center of each scale. A prominent light yellow bar is found at the base of the caudal fin. The juvenile clown razorfish is completely different in color from the adult. The body is maroon or green with four to five dark vertical bands alternating with pearly white spots, and eight to 10 dark streaks radiate from the eye. The first two dorsal spines are elongated and bannerlike (see Plate 22e). Unlike the adult, which lives over patch reefs, the juveniles are found among seaweeds such as *Sargassum* and *Galaxaura.*

# FAMILY SCARIDAE
## Parrotfishes (Peces loro)

Most parrotfishes are large distinctive fishes that can be easily recognized by their fused teeth which resemble a parrot's beak. They are closely associated with reefs on which they graze on algae by scraping and biting off chunks of hard substrate. Parrotfishes are most speciose and abundant in regions in which coral reefs are extensive. Only three genera and six species occur in the Gulf where coral growth is sparse and localized. In the coral reefs of the Bahamas there are three genera and 13 species of scarids. Worldwide, there are about 68 species in two subfamilies. As among the wrasses, however, there are many nominal species because of the problems associated with identifying the several color phases between juveniles and adults and males and females, including changes linked with sex reversals. The males are often gaudily colored like painted clowns, whereas the females are often, but not always, drabber than the males. Large individuals, both male and female, sometimes develop a bulbous, fleshy hump on their heads (Figure 77). Many parrotfishes secrete mucous cocoons in which they sleep at night. These cocoons presumably protect the parrotfishes from nocturnal predators like moray eels, who apparently cannot smell their prey when it is enveloped by this gelatinous covering.

The four eastern Pacific parrotfishes of the genus *Scarus* are distantly related to western Atlantic parrotfishes, which is an exception to the generalization of close relationship between the fish faunas on each side of the Isthmus of Panama (Rosenblatt and Hobson, 1969).

***References.*** Randall (1963b); Rosenblatt and Hobson (1969); Schultz (1958, 1969).

Figure 77   The bumphead parrotfish, *Scarus perrico*, is the largest Gulf parrotfish. (Photograph courtesy of E. S. Hobson.)

# BUMPHEAD PARROTFISH, perico
## *Scarus perrico* Jordan and Gilbert, 1882

**Illustrated specimen.** Adult male, 2 ft (0.6 m), by Alex Kerstitch; see also Plate 23 and Figure 77; grows to about 2½ ft (0.8 m).

**Distinguishing characteristics.** The bumphead parrotfish is the largest of the six species of parrotfishes in the Gulf. It can be distinguished from other Gulf parrotfishes of the genus *Scarus* by its five predorsal scales and five or fewer scales in each row of cheek scales; other *Scarus* spp. have six predorsal scales and six scales in cheek-scale rows. *S. perrico* has a series of dark lines radiating from the eye and its body coloration is light bluish green with darker bluish fins. The heavy tooth plates that form its "beak" are also blue. Large individuals of both sexes have a massive fleshy hump on the head over the eyes which is lacking in the other species. The hump overgrows the predorsal scales so that they, and the rows of cheek scales, are difficult to see in large individuals. D. IX, 10; A. III, 9.

**Distribution.** *Scarus perrico* ranges from the central Gulf (Guaymas) to Peru and the Islas Galápagos; however, we have one sight record from Puerto Lobos (Matt Gilligan). It is more common along the Baja California coast than the mainland coast.

**Ecology.** *Scarus perrico* occurs in small aggregations over reefs in the central and lower Gulf at moderate depths of 10 to 100 ft (3 to 30 m). Although they are not uncommon in the Guaymas vicinity, they are most common along the Baja California coast, especially around islands and in areas with abundant coral growth.

Because parrotfishes seem to be associated with coral reefs, it has been assumed that they feed largely on living coral. There is little evidence to support this contention. The strong beaks of parrotfish are well adapted to scraping a hard substrate and they audibly scrape algae from soft calcareous rocks. They also ingest rock fragments and sand which they use in their pharyngeal mills as an abrasive. The bumphead parrotfish feeds mainly on coralline red algae. However, Hiatt and Strasburg (1960) examined 12 specimens of parrotfishes from the Marshall Islands and found coral polyps in all their samples. In studies of food habits of West Indian reef fishes Randall (1967) discovered

161

only insignificant amounts of coral in the stomachs of 120 specimens of 10 species of parrotfish and never observed parrotfishes feeding on live coral. Rosenblatt and Hobson (1969) noted that Gulf scarids feed by scraping algae from rocks but do not bite off pieces of coral; nor did Hobson (1974) find any evidence that Hawaiian parrotfish feed on living coral. Randall (1974) reached similar conclusions in his recent review.

**Related species.** The following descriptions and ranges of the other Gulf parrotfishes are based mainly on the revision of eastern Pacific parrotfishes by Rosenblatt and Hobson (1969). The bicolor parrotfish, *Scarus rubroviolaceus* Bleeker, 1849, occurs uncommonly in the central Gulf (Loreto area) but it is a common parrotfish in the Cape region. This wide-ranging Indo-Pacific species is known from the Indian Ocean (East Africa) to the eastern Pacific (Panama and the Islas Galápagos) including Isla San Ignacio Farallon off Topolobampo on the mainland side of the Gulf. Male and female *S. rubroviolaceus* are recognized by their two-toned body-color

pattern. In the female the anterior half to one-third is normally maroon to brownish red, whereas the posterior half to two-thirds is lighter maroon to tan (see Figure 78). Green predominates in the male; the upper sides and back are a lighter shade but the anterior portion is usually darker. The caudal peduncle is green and the ventral parts of the body, light blue. Teeth are green in the male and white in the female. In all adults, but especially in large males, the snout is noticeably humped. This species favors areas in which coral is abundant, but like other species of *Scarus* it grazes on algae.

The bluechin parrotfish, *Scarus ghobban* Forskål, 1775, another widely distributed species, ranges from the Indian Ocean and Red Sea, to Panama, the Islas Galápagos, and into the central Gulf. This parrotfish is slenderer than the other scarids and has a conical head. The body color is variable among individuals and between sexes. The commonest coloration in females is light orange-brown with faint blue scales that form vertical bands (see Plate 24b). The males are bluish green over a pink ground color with two horizontal bluish streaks extending posteriorly from the eye, and a

Figure 78   A female bicolor parrotfish, *Scarus rubroviolaceus*. The bicolor pattern is more conspicuous in females than males which often appear predominantly green. (Photograph by Alex Kerstitch.)

Figure 79 The loosetooth parrotfish, *Nicholsina denticulata*. The light blotches on the fish resulted from photographing this secretive fish through a cloud of zooplankton. (Photograph by Alex Kerstitch.)

purplish blue chin. The dorsal and anal fins of the male are a purplish pink broadly edged with blue-green.

The azure parrotfish, *Scarus compressus* (Osburn and Nichols, 1916), is a heavy-bodied parrotfish that resembles *S. perrico* in shape but the tooth plates forming the beak are not so well developed. Large males are bright green with an orange-brown outline around each scale. There are ornate green streaks and lines radiating from the eye. Small females and juvenile males are reddish brown marked by dark streaks along the scale rows. Larger females (18 in., or 450 mm) are light blue to pale blue-gray. The teeth are green in both sexes. This parrotfish ranges from Guaymas and Bahía Concepción in the central Gulf to Cabo San Lucas and the Islas Galápagos.

The loosetooth parrotfish, *Nicholsina denticulata* (Evermann and Radcliffe, 1917), is the smallest eastern Pacific parrotfish (see Figure 79). It can be distinguished from most other Gulf parrotfish (those in the subfamily Scarinae) by teeth that are not completely coalesced into a beak (characteristic of its subfamily *Sparisomatinae*). It also has only one row of cheek scales; the Scarinae have at least two. This scarid resembles a wrasse as much as a parrotfish. Cryptically colored, it is often observed among *Sargassum, Padina,* and other algae and seems to be more common in winter when sea temperatures are low and algae growth is maximal. Although its color is variable, it is usually drab brown like its surroundings. It occurs from Puerto Peñasco throughout the Gulf and from Bahía Magdalena south to Peru and the Islas Galápagos.

Another species of the subfamily Sparisomatinae, the halftooth parrotfish, *Calotomus spinidens* (Quoy and Gaimard, 1824), has been observed by Hobson (Rosenblatt and Hobson, 1969) in Bahía de Palmas, just north of Cabo San Lucas. This species is rare in the eastern Pacific and is considered to be a recent immigrant from the west. It differs from the loosetooth parrotfish by having overlapping teeth with free tips on both jaws and canine teeth in the upper jaw.

Refer to Figure 80 for a summary of the characteristics of the five common Gulf parrotfishes.

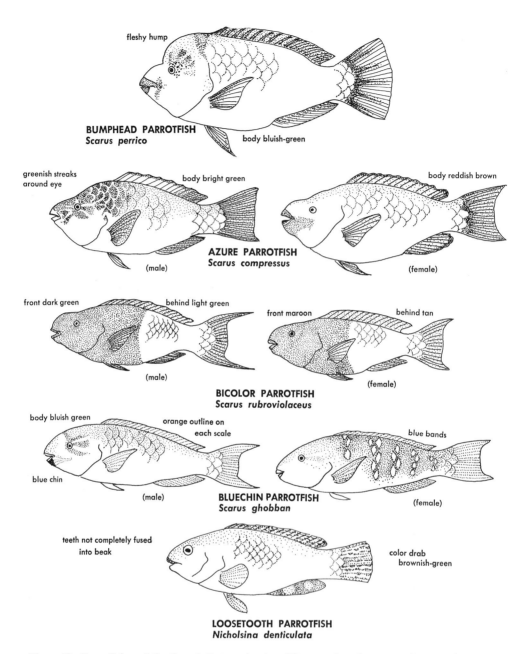

Figure 80   Parrotfishes of the Sea of Cortez, showing differences in color pattern between the sexes. Males and females of the bumphead and loosetooth parrotfishes do not show marked differences in color pattern. (From Thomson and McKibbin, 1976.)

# FAMILY OPISTOGNATHIDAE
## Jawfishes (Bocas grandes)

Jawfishes are curious-looking burrowing fishes with large mouths, big eyes, and elongate flanged maxillary bones (see Figure 81). They construct elaborate burrows in sandy, cobble-strewn bottoms, usually near reefs. They seem to be constantly renovating their burrows by excavating sand and carrying, depositing, and rearranging rocks around the entrances. Most are cryptically colored, but some have brilliant contrasting colors. In the Gulf they range in size from a few inches to nearly 2 ft (0.6 m). They are abundant in certain regions at intermediate depths but are uncommon at less than 20 ft (6 m), for they seem to avoid turbulent areas with much surge.

Two genera and at least eight species of jawfishes, five of which are undescribed, inhabit the Gulf. The behavior and ecology of the Gulf's jawfishes are poorly known. The systematics of the eastern Pacific jawfishes are currently being investigated by Drs. Richard Rosenblatt and Edward Brothers. Worldwide, there are three genera and about 40 species.

*References.* Böhlke (1955b); Fowler (1944); Jenkins and Evermann (1889); Myers (1935).

Figure 81 One of the five undescribed species of jawfish (*Opistognathus* sp.) from the Gulf. (Photograph by D. A. Thomson.)

165

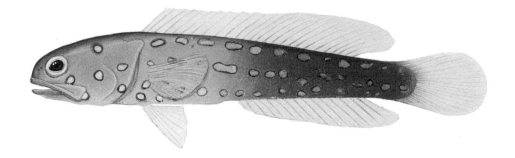

# BLUESPOTTED JAWFISH, **boca grande de manchas azules**
## *Opistognathus* sp. (undescribed)

**Illustrated specimen.** Adult, 2½ in. (66 mm), by Alex Kerstitch; see also Plate 25h; grows to about 4 in. (102 mm).

**Distinguishing characteristics.** This colorful jawfish displays sky-blue spots over its entire body. The overall background color is beige to dull yellowish brown. Juveniles are pale yellow without markings. D. XI, 12–14; A. II, 12–14; $P_1$. 18–19.

**Distribution.** The bluespotted jawfish has been collected from the upper (Isla Angel de la Guarda) and lower Gulf, and a species of similar appearance occurs outside this area (R. H. Rosenblatt, personal communication). We cannot give their complete geographical ranges until these two species are described.

**Ecology.** This colorful jawfish seems to be restricted to offshore islands, where it may occur in large colonies. Like other jawfishes, it constructs deep burrows in coarse sand composed of shell fragments and pebbles, usually near the base of rocky cliffs or near rocky outcroppings offshore. Large colonies of several hundred individuals occur at depths of 60 to 80 ft (18 to 24 m); juveniles are occasionally found in waters as shallow as 15 ft (4.6 m). The burrows are spaced about 3 to 10 ft (1 to 3 m) apart. Each fish constructs a lid over the burrow entrance at dusk and hides in its shelter at night. It rebuilds the opening of its burrow each morning.

Males leave their burrows for courtship display. Hovering 1 to 2 ft (0.3 to 0.6 m) above its hole, a courting male will hang motionless with pelvic and dorsal fins erect. After 2 to 3 sec it will suddenly dive into it with a flashlike whip of its tail. During this display the posterior half of the body becomes dark brown, almost black. The erected pelvic and caudal fins are pale lemon yellow. This display, in which dozens of males are engaged at one time, may continue for several hours.

166

# FINESPOTTED JAWFISH, boca grande manchada
## *Opistognathus punctatus* Peters, 1869

**Photograph.** Young adult, 6.5 in. (165 mm), by Alex Kerstitch; one of the largest Gulf jawfishes; grows to 16 in. (406 mm).

**Distinguishing characteristics.** The fine-spotted jawfish can be distinguished from all other Gulf jawfishes by the profuse, fine dark spots covering the head. Larger dark brown to black spots that cover the body and fins serve to distinguish it further from the other jawfishes, which may have bars, stripes, or mottling along the body but not the evenly spaced dark spotting of *Opistognathus punctatus*. This species has an enlarged maxillary flange that on large individuals is as long as the head. D. XI, 17; A. II, 17.

**Distribution.** The commonest and perhaps the most widespread jawfish in the Gulf, *O. punctatus* ranges throughout the Gulf (Puerto Peñasco) to Bahía Magdalena and south to Panama. In the Gulf juveniles may be found at depths as shallow as 5 ft (1.5 m), although adults are more abundant at 40 to 60 ft (12 to 18 m) and deeper.

**Ecology.** The finespotted jawfish occurs in shallower water than the other Gulf jawfishes and is easier to observe and collect. Like all jawfishes, this species constructs a burrow by digging out sand and pebbles with its large mouth. It is amusing to watch this big-eyed fish rising from its burrow and spitting out a mouthful of sand and rubble. It lines the entrance of the burrow with shells and rocks and spends much time "housekeeping." It defends its shelter against intruders, although one of our aquarium specimens shared its burrow with a moray eel (*Gymnothorax panamensis*), which was unresponsive to the jawfish's threats. This jawfish often returns to its burrow tail first, looking like a movie scene shown in reverse.

All of the jawfishes are predators on small fishes and crustaceans. Their very large mouths

Figure 82 The bullseye jawfish, *Opistognathus scops*, in a threat posture. (Photograph by Alex Kerstitch taken at Sea World, San Diego, California.)

enable them to feed on large food items. The finespotted jawfish appears to be more active at night than in the daytime and may be a nocturnal predator. This species also appears to tolerate extremes in water temperature. We have observed and collected it in the shallow water of Bahía Concepción during the hot summer months when sea temperatures approach 95°F (35°C).

**Related species.** Besides the bluespotted and finespotted jawfishes, six other species have been recorded from the Gulf. Four are undescribed species. The cheekspot jawfish, *Lonchopisthus* sp., is an offshore species commonly collected in shrimp trawls. Its dorsal spines are pungent (not flexible like the spines of *Opistognathus*), its cheeks and opercula are well scaled, and it has a lanceolate tail. Apparently it occurs at intermediate depths throughout the Gulf, but its distribution and ecology remain unknown. The giant jawfish, *Opistognathus rhomaleus* Jordan and Gilbert, 1881, is similar to *O. punctatus* in coloration, having profuse fine spotting over the head and back. *O. rhomaleus,* however, lacks the regular

pattern of larger dark spots on the sides and is distinguished by a more mottled diffuse pattern. Also, its spots on the head are coarse and not so fine as those of *O. punctatus.* Juveniles have six interrupted dark bars on the sides and the operculum shows a dark posterior margin. The maxilla is not so elongated as that of *O. punctatus* and its dorsal soft-rays range from 12 to 14 instead of the 17 characteristic of *O. punctatus.* This jawfish exceeds 20 in. (508 mm) in length and is the largest in the Gulf. It ranges throughout the Gulf to Bahía Magdalena and Islas Revillagigedo and is often caught by anglers and shrimp trawlers. The bullseye jawfish, *O. scops* (Jenkins and Evermann, 1889), lacks the dark spotting characteristic of *O. punctatus* and *O. rhomaleus* but has a prominent ocellated spot on its spinous dorsal fin (see Figure 82). It ranges widely from the central Gulf of California to Panama. The three other undescribed species of *Opistognathus* in the Gulf are smaller than *O. punctatus* and *O. rhomaleus* and have also cryptic coloration. Distinctions of these species are deferred until their descriptions have been published.

# FAMILY BLENNIIDAE
## Combtooth blennies (Trambollitos)

The combtooth blennies can usually be recognized by their steep foreheads, broad lips, big eyes, and prominent head cirri. They lack scales and their teeth resemble those of a comb. The overall peaceful appearance of these small shallow-water bottom fishes belies their aggressive nature. Most are strongly territorial and will defend their homesites against intruders many times their size (see Figure 83).

The combtooth blennies are common inhabitants of rocky intertidal zones throughout the world. Most are grazers, feeding on algae and sessile invertebrates, although in captivity they often become voracious carnivores.

Among the 46 genera and 276 species currently recognized, four genera with six species of Blenniidae have been recorded in the Gulf. These fishes form part of the infraorder Blennioidea, which includes four families, 22 genera and 50 species of blennioid fishes in the Gulf of California. All are associated with reefs and are important components of the rocky-shore communities in the Gulf. Because these blennioid fishes have been largely ignored by Mexican fisherman, few have Spanish vernacular names.

*References.* Kresja (1960); Losey (1968, 1976); Schultz (1942); Smith-Vaniz and Springer (1971); Springer (1962, 1967, 1968); Stephens et al. (1970).

Figure 83 The Pacific fanged blenny, *Ophioblennius steindachneri*, one of the most aggressive Gulf blennies. The large recurved, rear canine teeth of this species are used in territorial defense. (Photograph by D. A. Thomson.)

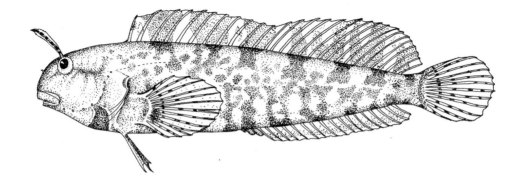

# BAY BLENNY, trambollito de bahia
## *Hypsoblennius gentilis* (Girard, 1854)

**Illustrated specimen.** Adult male, about 3½ in. (89 mm), by Tor Hansen; see also Figure 84a,b, and Plate 25a; grows to about 3½ in. (89 mm); in California, to 5.8 in. (147 mm).

**Distinguishing characteristics.** Species of the genus *Hypsoblennius* can be distinguished from other Gulf blenniids by their relatively small mouths (with the exception of the specialized blenny *Plagiotremus azaleus*). *H. gentilis* shows marked sexual dimorphism. The male has large unbranched orbital cirri, a bright red throat, and an overall darkly pigmented body (see Figure 84a). The latter two characters are most evident during the breeding season. The general coloration of the male usually consists of dark leopardlike spots that cover the head and anterior body and merge posteriorly with diffuse broad bars. Adult males have fleshy pads that cover both anal spines. The female has a smaller head and smaller orbital cirri and lacks large spots but has a more pronounced barred pattern than the male. The female also has a large metallic blue spot that spans the membranes between the first and third dorsal spines (see Figure 84b). D. XI–XIII, 16–18; A. II, 16–19; $P_1$. 11–12; $P_2$. I,3.

**Distribution.** This warm temperate blenny has a disjunct distribution. It ranges from Monterey, California, to Bahía Magdalena on the Pacific coast and from the central (Bahía Santa Inés, B.C.S., and Guaymas) Gulf to the northernmost Gulf reefs. It is the commonest combtooth blenny in the upper Gulf.

**Ecology.** At Puerto Peñasco the bay blenny is a common resident of rocky tide pools. Strongly territorial, this blenny will not hesitate to nip at trespassers, which include human fingers. It feeds mainly on benthic invertebrates and algae. The reproductive behavior of this species has been studied by Losey (1968). As the female approaches the male's territory, the male attempts to attract her into his refuge by a series of "head jerks" and quivering. The female enters the male's refuge tail first and inspects its walls visually and by touching them with her urogenital papilla. The intensity of the male's courting behavior increases significantly and head jerking, quivering, caudal and pectoral fin fanning, and rubbing occur in rapid succession. The female may then deposit her eggs one by one on the wall of the refuge. Each egg is attached to the rock wall by an adhesive

Figure 84   A male (a) and a female (b) bay blenny, *Hypsoblennius gentilis*. Note the prominent, unbranched supraorbital cirri of the male compared with the inconspicuous cirri of the female. The large metallic blue spot between the first and second dorsal spines is characteristic of females (Photographs by D. A. Thomson.)

disc. After the female leaves, the male chews and rubs the eggs, coating them with the sperm ejaculated earlier during courtship.

The bay blenny is a eurythermal species able to tolerate the extreme winter and summer temperatures in the northern Gulf intertidal zone. Hardy in captivity, it quickly tames and has bred in our aquaria. In the upper Gulf this species breeds during late winter and early spring.

**Related species.** The mussel blenny, *H. jenkinsi* (Jordan and Evermann, 1896), also has a disjunct distribution. It ranges from Santa Barbara County, California, to Bahía Magdalena-Todos Santos vicinity (Puerto Marquis). In the Gulf it ranges from Guaymas to Puerto Peñasco and San Felipe. Losey (1968) considers the Gulf *H. jenkinsi* populations distinctive from the California populations because of certain morphological divergences (larger mean size, marked sexual dimorphism in the length of the orbital cirri, more postorbital pores, and shorter lateral lines). *H. jenkinsi* is sometimes found intertidally with *H. gentilis* in the upper Gulf and often shares the same tide pool. However, compared with the bay blenny, it is uncommon in the Gulf. *H. jenkinsi* can be readily distinguished from *H. gentilis* by its branched bushlike orbital cirri (see Plate 25g) and absence of red coloration on the throat.

Another species, the barnaclebill blenny, *H. brevipinnis* (Günther, 1861), subgenus *Blenniolus*, ranges from the central Gulf (Guaymas) to Peru, including the Islas Galápagos and Isla del Coco. This smaller species, which lives in empty barnacle tests, has a shortened body and a dark broad band running the length of the body slightly above the midline. Its outermost orbital cirri are unbranched like *H. gentilis*, but they have one to four shorter cirri at the base, which are lacking in *H. gentilis*. It also has a broad band running diagonally from the eye, and the head of the male is covered with bright red spots (see Plate 25e).

171

# PANAMIC FANGED BLENNY, trambollito negro
## *Ophioblennius steindachneri* Jordan and Evermann, 1898

**Illustrated specimen.** Adult, 6.5 in. (166 mm), by Alex Kerstitch; see also Plate 26 and Figure 83; largest combtooth blenny in the eastern Pacific; grows to about 7 in. (178 mm).

**Distinguishing characteristics.** A formidable pair of large canine teeth far back in the lower jaw give this blenny its name. Its typical color pattern is shown in Plate 26. Red rings the eye and a dark eye spot occurs behind it. D. XI–XIII, 22 (21–23); A. II, 23 (22–24).

**Distribution.** *Ophioblennius steindachneri* ranges from Bahía Sebastián Vizcaino and the upper Gulf (Isla Angel de la Guarda and Puerto Lobos) to Peru and is the most abundant combtooth blenny along rocky coasts in the tropical eastern Pacific. Its Atlantic twin is the redlip blenny, *O. atlanticus* Silvester.

**Ecology.** This large blenny prefers the surge zone of unprotected rocky headlands with steep slopes. It wedges itself in crevices close to shore in shallow water, darting out to defend its territory vigorously against intruders. This blenny is a diurnal feeder that grazes on algae and sessile invertebrates. The comblike teeth are used for feeding and the rear fanglike canines, which are capable of inflicting a puncture wound, are used for territorial defense. *O. steindachneri* has a slender-headed, long-lived pelagic larva with anterior fangs that are lost at metamorphosis. See Nursall (1977) for an account of the territorial behavior of the closely related redlip blenny, *O. atlanticus.*

**Related species.** Another species with rear canines is the smaller notchfin blenny, *Entomacrodus chiostictus* (Jordan and Gilbert, 1883), which ranges from the central Gulf (Punta San Pedro, Sonora) to Colombia, including most of the far-offshore islands. It may be distinguished from *O. steindachneri* by its deeply notched dorsal fin and color pattern of a series of dark vertical lines across the mouth and about six pairs of thick dark body bars over a pale yellowish brown ground color. Much detailed taxonomic and zoogeographic information, as well as an excellent plate of this blenny, is provided by Springer (1967).

172

# SABERTOOTH BLENNY, diente sable
## *Plagiotremus azaleus* (Jordan and Bollman, 1890)

**Illustrated specimen.** Adult, 3.5 in. (89 mm), by Alex Kerstitch; see also Plate 26; grows to about 4 in. (102 mm).

**Distinguishing characteristics.** This specialized blenny can be distinguished by its elongate body, inferior mouth, and coneshaped snout. A clear yellow area between the dark dorsal and midline stripes gives this fish the superficial appearance of a Cortez rainbow wrasse (*Thalassoma lucasanum*). This blenny has a prominent pair of recurved canine teeth in the lower jaw that resembles "saberteeth." Until recently it had been placed in the genus *Runula.* D. VII–IX, 31–35; A. II, 27–30; P$_1$. 12–13.

**Distribution.** The sabertooth blenny ranges throughout the central (Guaymas) and lower Gulf to Peru, including the Islas Galápagos, Revillagigedo, and other far offshore islands (Malpelo, del Coco).

**Ecology.** This specialized blenny feeds on the skin mucus of other fishes and is a mimic of the rainbow wrasse (*T. lucasanum*). Hobson (1968, 1969b) gives a lucid account of the behavior of *P. azaleus*. He reports that these blennies are highly territorial, living in mollusk tubes on the rocks to which they retire at night. In the daytime they often join loose aggregations of the rainbow wrasse, using the cover of these schools to avoid recognition by its victims and to minimize predation on itself. The sabertooth blenny darts upward from these schools, nipping other fishes from behind and below, biting off mucus and perhaps pieces of skin. They often nip the legs of skin divers but the bite feels more like they are nipping at body hairs with their comblike teeth. No divers have reported receiving a puncture wound during such "attacks," although Hobson was bitten on the hand by the canine teeth while handling one of these blennies. It appears likely that the recurved canines are used for territorial defensive purposes rather than feeding.

# FAMILY TRIPTERYGIIDAE
## Triplefin blennies (Tres aletas)

The triplefin or threefin blennies are easily recognized by their dorsal fins which are divided into three distinct sections (Figure 85). The first and second dorsal sections consist only of spines and the third, of soft-rays. Most are small fishes no larger than 3 in. long and are commonly found intertidally, actively scurrying over the surface of boulders. All eastern Pacific triplefins have ctenoid scales, which further distinguish them from the Blenniidae and Chaenopsidae (no scales) and the Clinidae (cycloid scales).

The systematics of this family is under study by Richard H. Rosenblatt (Scripps Institution of Oceanography). Four of the six species in the Gulf are new and there is one new genus.

***References.*** Rosenblatt (1959, 1960).

Figure 85 A male flag triplefin, *Enneanectes* sp. Note the division of the dorsal fin into the three separate portions characteristic of triplefin blennies. (Photograph by Alex Kerstitch.)

# LIZARD TRIPLEFIN, largartija tres aletas
## Undescribed genus and species

**Illustrated specimen.** Adult, 2.5 in. (64 mm), by Alex Kerstitch; see also Plate 26; grows to about 3 in. (76 mm).

**Distinguishing characteristics.** We refer to this largest and most conspicuous of Gulf tripterygiids as the lizard triplefin because its caudal color pattern and display are reminiscent of zebra-tailed lizards (*Callisaurus*). The lizard triplefin has a distinctive "one-step" black mark on the caudal peduncle (the portion above the midline usually extends slightly farther forward than the lower portion). This triplefin has a disconnected lateral line, a longer, slenderer body, and a more attenuate head than other Gulf triplefin blennies. It may be further distinguished by a high number of fin rays in the vertical fins (see Related species), absence of orbital cirri, and small scales (41 to 48 longitudinal rows). The usual color pattern, illustrated in Plate 26, may be obliterated in the almost uniformly black males in breeding coloration. D. III + XVI to XIX + 10–14; A. II, 24–28; $P_1$. 14–15.

**Distribution.** Endemic to the Gulf, the lizard triplefin is known from Cabo San Lucas north to Puertecitos and Roca Consag and from Isla San Jorge south to Isla San Ignacio Farallon.

**Ecology.** The lizard triplefin seems to prefer rocky coastlines with steep slopes and occurs intertidally to at least 125 ft (38 m). It often perches on boulders in shallow water, propped forward on its pectoral and pelvic fins, slowly "wagging" its flaglike tail.

In Guaymas this triplefin breeds in the winter and spring. The following courtship behavior was observed by Matt Gilligan, University of Arizona: the male becomes very dark, almost black overall, which vividly contrasts with the yellowish white caudal fin he flashes to attract nearby females. He will dart back and forth over his territory, pausing momentarily to wag his tail. When the female approaches, the dorsal, anal, and caudal fins of the male quiver rapidly. He then swims alongside the female, nudging her side with his. The female rubs her abdomen along the rock surface with a slow, sinuous motion. On occasion she shakes violently, presumably depositing eggs. The male then swims rapidly past the female laterally, presumably releasing milt in the vicinity of egg deposition.

175

**Related species.** At least five other species in two additional genera of triplefin blennies occur in the Gulf of California. Three have been placed in the genus *Enneanectes* by Rosenblatt (1959). Members of this genus also have a disconnected lateral line. The Gulf *Enneanectes* spp. may be distinguished from the lizard triplefin by the following combination of characters: small, broad, flaplike orbital cirri, fewer rays in the vertical fins (second dorsal spines 10 to 13; anal soft-rays, 15 to 20), larger scales (29 to 32 longitudinal rows), presence of a small patch of ctenoid scales on the operculum, and a generally more robust body, broader head (with short spines on the top), and blunter snout.

The delicate triplefin, *Enneanectes sexmaculatus* (Fowler, 1944), is the smallest (to about 1 in.) and most delicate appearing Gulf species of this genus (Figure 86). It can be distinguished from the other two *Enneanectes* by the larger scales in the first scale row above the pored lateral line than in the row above it and by an enlarged scale that covers the upper two-thirds of the pectoral axil. The body is crossed by five or six dark bars (including the solid dark bar on the caudal peduncle). The pectoral fin has more, thinner, and more distinctive bars, and a dark spot is usually evident on its lower base. It ranges from the central Gulf (Isla Tortuga and Bahía San Agustin, Sonora) to Panama.

The other two Gulf species of *Enneanectes* (both undescribed) are larger (one exceeds 2 in., or 51 mm) than *E. sexmaculatus*, they lack the enlarged axillary scale, and the first two scale rows above the pored lateral line are equal in size. They have four or five dark bars on the body, and the scales of the lighter interspaces are outlined in dark pigment. Both show considerable red coloration, especially on the head, and particularly on breeding males. The larger, more common species (flag triplefin) has horizontal brown lines that parallel the scale rows on the lower sides of the body, usually 16 pectoral and 18 anal soft-rays, and a somewhat narrower head and smaller eye (see Plate 25c and Figure 85). It ranges from Isla Guadalupe and Bahía Sebastián Vizcaino on the outer coast of Baja California to Cabo San Lucas and north to Isla Angel de la Guarda (Puerto Refugio) and Isla Tiburon south to Guaymas. Generally a shallow-water species, we have collected it at 180 ft (55 m) at Cabo San Lucas.

The remaining species of *Enneanectes* (network triplefin) is slightly smaller. It has a slightly wider head and larger eye and, as a rule, 15 pectoral and 17 anal soft-rays. A brown network outlines the scales on the lower sides, but the horizontal brown lines of the flag triplefin are lacking. It is a more southerly species that ranges from Isla San Ignacio Farallon and Mazatlán to Puerto Escondido, Oaxaca.

The remaining genus of triplefin blennies in the Gulf, *Axoclinus,* can be distinguished from the other Gulf tripterygiid genera by its continuous lateral line. Also, the dorsal soft-rays are never branched (some are branched at the tip in the other two genera), and the scales are smaller and more numerous (in 30 to 37

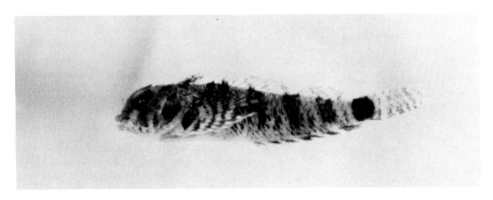

Figure 86   The delicate triplefin. *Enneanectes sexmaculatus*, is the smallest Gulf triplefin. (Photograph courtesy of Matt Gilligan.)

longitudinal rows) than in *Enneanectes*. Two species of *Axoclinus* occur in the Gulf. The carmine triplefin, *Axoclinus carminalis* (Jordan and Gilbert, 1882), is the smaller (to about $1\frac{1}{2}$ in., or 32 mm) and more colorful of the two, with much carmine-red pigment on the lower parts of the head, body, and pectoral, pelvic, and anal fins (especially intense in breeding males). Three wide, irregular reddish brown bars on the sides of the body are followed by a fourth darker (red or black) bar on the caudal peduncle. In some specimens the entire caudal peduncle and fin are solid black. Also, the dark body bars sometimes enclose light spots and are often connected across the light interspaces by a thin dark line along the midside. A minute, rodlike cirrus is present on the upper margin of the eye. The species is known from Bahía Magdalena, south to Bahía Tangola-Tangola, Oaxaca, and north to the southern end of Isla Tiburón, but we have not collected it in the other midriff islands.

The other Gulf species of *Axoclinus* (Cortez triplefin) is undescribed and endemic to the Gulf, being known from Cabo San Lucas north to Roca Consag and from Puerto Peñasco (where we have taken it only once in many years of collecting) south to Guaymas (Plate 25b). It is a larger (to slightly more than $1\frac{3}{4}$ in., or 45 mm), darker species than *A. carminalis*, with red coloration occurring only on the throat and belly of breeding males. It can be further distinguished from *A. carminalis* by the absence of orbital cirri and by five (rather than four) irregular dark bars (darkest at the midside) that slope abruptly backward below the midside (especially posteriorly). The Cortez triplefin is the most abundant triplefin in the Gulf of California and is especially common intertidally.

# FAMILY CLINIDAE
## Clinid blennies (Trambollos)

The clinids form the largest and most diverse group of blennioid fishes in the Gulf. Most differ from the combtooth blennies by having well developed scales and conical jaw teeth and from the triplefins by having cycloid rather than ctenoid scales.

The Gulf clinids are all rather cryptically colored, secretive fishes that stay close to shelter. The largest species (*Labrisomus xanti*) reaches about 7 in. in length (see Figure 87) and the smallest (usually placed in this family), *Stathmonotus sinuscalifornici*, is a tiny, scaleless, eellike fish. Here we have not included *Heterostichous rostratus,* a very large California kelpfish, as a Gulf species though it has been reported to occur as far south as Cabo San Lucas.

Some Gulf clinids are livebearers (starksiin blennies), whereas the others are egg layers. All are bottom dwellers except the sargassum blenny, *Exerpes asper,* which is a "midwater" swimmer that hides in floating sargassum weed.

There are 24 species in nine genera of clinids in the Gulf. Worldwide, there are 30 genera with about 135 species.

***References.*** Böhlke (1953); Hubbs (1952, 1953, 1954); Rosenblatt and Parr (1967, 1969); Rosenblatt and Taylor (1971); Springer (1955, 1958, 1959); Stephens and Springer (1973).

Figure 87   The largest clinid in the Gulf, a male largemouth blenny, *Labrisomus xanti.* Note the conical teeth and prominent head cirri (nasal, orbital, or nuchal) that characterize most of the Gulf's clinids. (Photograph courtesy of Norm Smith.)

# FLAPSCALE BLENNY, trambollo chico
## *Paraclinus sini* Hubbs, 1952

**Illustrated specimen.** Adult male, 2.1 in. (52 mm), by Tor Hansen; one of the smallest Gulf clinids; illustrated specimen about maximum size.

**Distinguishing characteristics.** Clinids of the genus *Paraclinus* are small, sedentary bottom fishes that are often abundant but rarely seen because of their small size, cryptic coloration, and secretive habits. *Paraclinus sini* is easily distinguished from all other eastern Pacific species of *Paraclinus* by its small, membranous, flaplike projections on the posterior margin of its scales (except lateral line scales). The color pattern is highly variable. Some specimens are nearly all white; others are pinkish, orangish, or dark brown and resemble sargassum weed. Many individuals are strongly barred. When preserved in formalin, this species turns deep red. D. XXVIII–XXX; A. II, 16–20.

**Distribution.** One of the most abundant clinids in the Gulf, *P. sini* ranges from the Gulf's northernmost rocky reefs (Punta Borrascoso) to San José del Cabo in the Cape region. Outside the Gulf it extends from Bahía Magdalena north to Scammon's Lagoon.

**Ecology.** The most abundant clinid intertidally at Puerto Peñasco, the flapscale blenny can be readily found among clumps of sargassum in mid- to low tide pools. It is rarely seen swimming because it prefers to creep along the bottom on its pelvic and pectoral fins. *P. sini* defends its territory by threat displays consisting of fully opening its oblique, angular-shaped mouth and gaping at the intruder. Sexual dimorphism and dichromatism are present in this species. The male has a longer upper jaw than the female; the maxilla extends below the middle of the eye in the female and beyond the eye in the male. Females appear to be more strongly barred and more cryptically colored than the males.

**Related species.** Four other species of *Paraclinus* have been collected in the Gulf, among which the Mexican blenny, *P. mexicanus* (Gilbert, 1904), is most widespread. It ranges from Punta Concepción, Baja California, and Guaymas to Ecuador and can be distinguished from *P. sini* by its lack of flaplike projections on its scales and because it turns blackish in formalin. Its last dorsal element is a soft-ray and not a spine as in other Gulf species of *Paraclinus* (except *P. altivelis*). The highfin blenny, *P. altivelis* (Lockington, 1881), is a moderate-depth species (25 to 100 ft, or 7.6 to 30 m), which has been collected from only a few locales in the Gulf (Islas Santa Inés, Ildefonso, Carmen, and Punta Mangles, Baja California). It is characterized by its long first dorsal spine (length equal to predorsal distance). The pink blenny, *P. beebei* Hubbs, 1952, and the longjaw blenny, *P. tanygnathus* Rosenblatt and Parr, 1969, range outside the Gulf but have been collected at Mazatlán and below La Paz. *P. beebei* can be distinguished by broad scaleless areas behind the nape and on the pectoral fin bases. Other *Paraclinus* have at least some scales in these regions. *P. tanygnathus*, like *P. sini* and *P. beebei*, has a spine as its last dorsal fin ray and can be distinguished from the former by a lack of flaps on its scales and from the latter by having a single row of scales on the pectoral base. See Rosenblatt and Parr (1969) for complete taxonomic diagnoses, descriptions, and ranges of these Pacific species of *Paraclinus*.

179

# SONORA BLENNY, trambollo de Sonora
## *Malacoctenus gigas* Springer, 1959

**Photograph.** Adult male (upper fish) and female (lower fish), by Alex Kerstitch; largest species in genus, grows to about 5 in. (127 mm).

**Distinguishing characteristics.** Closely related to clinids of the genus *Labrisomus*, fishes of the genus *Malacoctenus* differ in their smaller adult size and smaller mouths. *M. gigas* may be distinguished from other Gulf *Malacoctenus* by its large number of total dorsal elements (usually 33 or more) and its greater nuchal cirri interspace (interspace contained once or less in a single nuchal cirrus base). Most likely to be confused with *M. hubbsi,* it differs from this species in size and coloration (see *M. hubbsi* account). D. XIX–XXIII, 12–14; A. II, 20–24, $P_1$. 13–15.

**Distribution.** Endemic to the Gulf of California, *M. gigas* ranges from the northernmost reefs (Punta Borrascoso) to Guaymas and Isla Espirito Santo, but it is relatively uncommon in the southern portion of its range.

**Ecology.** The Sonora blenny is the commonest medium-sized clinid in the northern Gulf; only the smaller flapscale blenny is more numerous. The Sonora blenny is an active clinid that swims freely over the reef floor, feeding on amphipods and other small crustaceans, and seeks shelter in seaweed when disturbed. It is tolerant of seawater temperatures as low as 50°F (10°C) and is adapted to the thermally rigorous intertidal zone of the northern Gulf.

Adult *M. gigas* are sexually dichromatic, which is especially evident during the spring breeding season. The dorsal, anal, and caudal fins appear dusky in the male but are distinctly spotted in the female. The sides of the male between the broad irregularly shaped bars become bright golden orange flecked with blue spots; the female has brown reticulations on a lighter background.

# REDSIDE BLENNY, **trambollo rojo**
## *Malacoctenus hubbsi* Springer, 1959

**Photograph.** Adult male (upper fish) and female (lower fish), by Alex Kerstitch; see also Plate 25f; grows to about 3½ in. (89 mm).

**Distinguishing characteristics.** The redside blenny resembles the Sonora blenny, *M. gigas,* but is smaller and has a finer appearance. The male shows a pinkish to deep red splash along its sides. Its total dorsal elements are usually less than 33 and the interspace between nuchal cirri is contained more than once in a single nuchal cirrus base. *M. hubbsi* also has a more pointed snout than *M. gigas,* and a small, dark spot occurs at the base of each pelvic fin in adults. Juveniles and adult females have a series of brownish, interrupted stripes along the lower body below the lateral line in contrast to the reticulated pattern of light and dark spots in *M. gigas.* D. XIX–XXI, 9–13; A. II, 18–23, $P_1$. 13–15.

**Distribution.** The redside blenny ranges throughout the Gulf from Roca Consag to the Cape and Acapulco and north to Bahía Sebastián Vizcaino on the Pacific coast of Baja California. Springer (1958) recognizes a southern subspecies, *M. hubbsi polyporosus,* that occurs just north of Mazatlán and south to Acapulco and the Islas Tres Marias.

**Ecology.** The redside blenny is an aggressive and common fish along shallow rocky shores in the central Gulf, where it is the most numerous clinid. It ranges to at least 25 ft (7.6 m) in depth but appears to be most numerous at depths of 3 to 6 ft (1 to 2 m). *M. hubbsi* preys on a variety of small invertebrates, especially small shrimp. It defends its territory vigorously against its own as well as other species by presenting its side to the intruder and sometimes swimming in a circular motion. The males, which have bright red sides, will often fight if their territories are too close to one another. During territorial disputes the color is intensified and as a rule the fish with the brightest coloration will be dominant. Female *M. hubbsi* have about half as many eggs (more than 2000) as the larger *M. gigas* (up to 5000), but the average egg size of *M. hubbsi* is larger (Y. Maluf, personal communication). These two species have overlapping distributions, but *M. gigas* is dominant in the upper Gulf and *M. hubbsi,* in the central Gulf.

**Related species.** Two other species of *Malacoctenus* are common in the Gulf but neither is so abundant as *M. gigas* or *M. hubbsi.* The throatspotted blenny, *M. tetranemus* (Cope, 1877), ranges throughout the Gulf from Puerto Peñasco (rare), to Cabo San Lucas and Mazatlán, and to Peru and the Islas Galápagos. It can be readily identified by its shorter, blunter head and the profuse dark spots that cover the lateral and ventral surfaces of the fish uniformly, especially on the throat. The margarita blenny, *M. margaritae* (Fowler, 1944), occurs in the central Gulf (Bahía San Agustin) to Panama. In comparison to other Gulf *Malacoctenus* it is a rather delicate species

of subdued greenish yellow color with a yellowish tail (see Plate 25d). Some specimens have three distinct dark spots running below the soft dorsal fin to the notch between the soft and spinous dorsal fins. The typical number of pectoral rays is 15 in this species, compared with 14 in other Pacific *Malacoctenus* species.

Three other species of *Malacoctenus* are rare in the Gulf and have been collected only in the Cabo San Lucas and Mazatlán regions. They have their principal ranges (broadly defined here) outside the Gulf: the glossy blenny, *M. zonifer* (Jordan and Gilbert, 1882), common at Mazatlán, ranges to Ecuador; the fishgod blenny, *M. ebisui* Springer, 1959, ranges to Panama; and the Zaca blenny, *M. zacae* Springer, 1959, ranges from both coasts in the Cabo San Lucas area to Acapulco. These three species are part of a closely related group. For their identification and the details of their complex geographic distributions see Springer's monograph (1958).

# LARGEMOUTH BLENNY, chalapo
## *Labrisomus xanti* Gill, 1860

**Photograph.** Adult male (upper fish) and adult female (lower fish), by Alex Kerstitch; see also Figure 86; largest species of *Labrisomus*; grows to 7 in. (178 mm).

**Distinguishing characteristics.** Species of the genus *Labrisomus* differ from their close relatives in the genus *Malacoctenus* by their larger mouths and wider interspace between the nuchal cirri (base of single cirrus contains less than three times the interspace). *L. xanti*, like most of the clinids, has more dorsal spines (17 to 19) than dorsal soft-rays (10 to 12). The males have larger heads than the females and their throat and head regions assume a bright red coloration during the spring breeding season. D. XVII–XIX, 10–12; A. II, 17–19.

**Distribution.** The commonest *Labrisomus* throughout the Gulf, *L. xanti* also ranges from Bahía Sebastián Vizcaino to Bahía Tenacatita, Jalisco.

**Ecology.** The largemouth blenny is a shallow-water diurnal predator that feeds mostly on benthic crustaceans. Strongly territorial, *L. xanti* dominates the smaller Sonora blenny, *Malacoctenus gigas,* in aquarium hierarchies.

On the reef both species coexist by partitioning space and food needs (Hansen, 1974). The more sedentary *L. xanti* seeks shelter in crevices and feeds on crabs, whereas the more mobile *M. gigas* seeks shelter among seaweed and feeds on amphipods.

**Related species.** Two other more southerly species of *Labrisomus* range into the Gulf: the porehead blenny, *L. multiporosus* Hubbs, 1953, and the green blenny, *L. striatus* Hubbs, 1953. *L. multiporosus,* which occurs widely from Bahía Sebastián Vizcaino and the upper Gulf, south to Peru and the Islas Galápagos, is difficult to distinguish from *L. xanti.* It has a greater number of lateral line pores on the head and palatine teeth, which *L. xanti* lacks. General body shape and color patterns are similar. *L. striatus* ranges from the central Gulf (Guaymas area and Bahía Santa Inés) to Acapulco and can be readily distinguished from the other two *Labrisomus* species by its low number of lateral line scales (fewer than 45; 64 to 69 in *L. xanti* and *L. multiporosus*), dark stripes on the body, and overall bright greenish coloration.

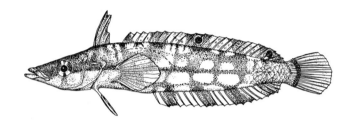

# SARGASSUM BLENNY, sargacero
## *Exerpes asper* (Jenkins and Evermann, 1889)

**Illustrated specimen.** 1.5 in. (39 mm), by Tor Hansen; grows to at least 2½ in. (64 mm).

**Distinguishing characteristics.** This distinctive clinid has a pikelike mouth and two distinct, well separated dorsal fins; it also lacks cirri. Its usual brown color mimics sargassum seaweed, and its lower sides are covered with large silvery patches. Two blue ocelli are present on the second dorsal fin. D. III–IV + XXIV–XXV; A. II, 17–20.

**Distribution.** *Exerpes asper* occurs in the upper and central Gulf and from Bahía Magdalena and Laguna San Ignacio to Scammon's Lagoon. It is common wherever sargassum or eelgrass is abundant.

**Ecology.** This cryptically colored clinid is strongly associated with sargassum seaweed (*Sargassum*) or eelgrass (*Zostera*) and is frequently found among floating sargassum mats.

Young juveniles occur in small schools but as they grow become more solitary and aggressive towards members of their species. When startled or distressed, they tend to curl their tails inward and hide rather than swim away; they appear to depend on their cryptic coloration and form to escape predation.

**Related species.** Although not closely related to *E. asper,* another atypical blennioid fish, usually placed in the family Clinidae (but of uncertain taxonomic affinity), is the worm blenny, *Stathmonotus sinuscalifornici* (Chabanaud, 1942). This small eellike blenny (seldom more than 2½ in., or 64 mm) ranges from Puerto Lobos, Sonora, to Cabo San Lucas. This species lacks scales but has a lateral line. Its variable color ranges from all white to a dark olive-green to black. Rarely seen, this blenny is occasionally collected in rotenone stations along rocky shores. A closely related species, *S. lugubris* Böhlke, 1953, is found in southern Mexico but we have not collected it in the Gulf.

**184**

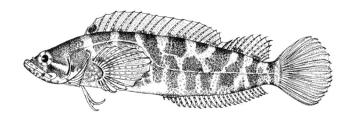

# REDRUMP BLENNY, trambollo de nalga roja
## *Xenomedea rhodopyga* Rosenblatt and Taylor, 1971

**Illustrated specimen.** Adult, about 2 in. (50 mm), by Tor Hansen; grows to about 2½ in. (64 mm).

**Distinguishing characteristics.** The eastern Pacific clinids of the tribe Starksiini have recently been revised by Rosenblatt and Taylor (1971). The result has been the recognition of a new genus and ten species (*Xenomedea rhodopyga* and nine species of *Starksia*). Probably closely related to and similar in appearance and habits to the genus *Paraclinus,* the starksiin fishes differ by their ovoviviparous method of reproduction. The first anal spine of the males is free from the rest of the fin and is usually united with an extended genital papilla to form a functional penis. *Xenomedea* and *Starksia* are the only genera placed in the tribe Starksiini. *X. rhodopyga* can be distinguished from the other Gulf starksiin clinids by a prominent dark spot between the first and second or third spines of the spinous dorsal and rosy red flanks above and anterior to the anus. The ripe adult male has fleshy folds around the genital papilla and anal fin base, whereas the female has a black ridge running along either side of the anterior anal fin base. D. XX–XXIII, 8–11; A. II, 18–22.

**Distribution.** This small clinid is a Gulf endemic that ranges from Roca Consag to Cabo San Lucas. *X. rhodopyga* is the most commonly collected starksiin clinid in the Gulf.

**Ecology.** A small cryptically colored fish, *X. rhodopyga* has been collected at depths of 2 to 100 ft (0.6 to 30 m). In contrast to the flap-scale blenny, *Paraclinus sini, X. rhodopyga* is uncommon intertidally but becomes more common in the sublittoral zone at depths greater than 25 ft (7.6 m). It prefers a rocky bottom with abundant algal growth. This species, like all the starksiin clinids, is a livebearer, but information on its reproductive cycle is incomplete. Based on collections made by Scripps Institution of Oceanography in the central and lower Gulf, it appears that breeding occurs in the spring.

185

**Related species.** Four species of the genus *Starksia* have been collected in the Gulf. The phallic blenny, *S. spinipenis* (Al-Uthman, 1960), ranges from Roca Consag to Acapulco and is the commonest *Starksia* in the Gulf. It can be distinguished from the other Gulf *Starksia* by the combination of color pattern (irregular bars on upper sides), short nasal cirri (length less than ½ of eye diameter; ½–2 diameters in *S. hoesei*), and absence of light lines paralleling scale rows on posterior body (*S. grammilaga*).

The fugitive blenny, *S. cremnobates* (Gilbert, 1890), has been collected only at moderate depths (21 to 33 fathoms, or 38 to 60 m) at two localities near offshore islands in the central Gulf. The scales in the straight portion of the lateral line are not tubed like those of the other starksiins and have only simple pores. It lacks body markings.

The hose blenny, *S. hoesei,* and the pinstriped blenny, *S. grammilaga,* are both newly described species (Rosenblatt and Taylor, 1971) that are rare in the Gulf and are not discussed here. A discussion and a key to all the eastern Pacific starksiin clinids is available in Rosenblatt and Taylor (1971).

Clinids of the tribes Mnierpini and Cryptotremini have been recorded in the Gulf. The foureye rockskipper, *Mnierpes macrocephalus* (Günther, 1861), has been collected by us at Cabo San Lucas. Its large protruding eyes (see Figure 88) have a diagnostic, vertical fleshy bar through the pupil. This clinid ranges to Colombia and is a common intertidal fish along the rocky coasts of Costa Rica and Panama. See Graham and Rosenblatt (1970) for an account of vision in this species.

The hidden blenny, *Cryptotrema seftoni* Hubbs, 1954, is said to inhabit rocky bottoms at depths of 14 to 20 fathoms (26 to 37 m). The type specimens were collected by dredging at these depths at the north end of Isla Angel de la Guarda. We have not collected this species; see Hubbs (1954) for a description.

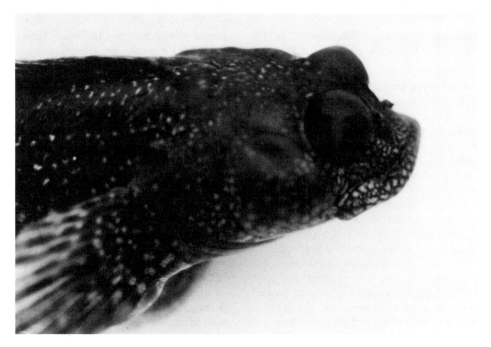

Figure 88   The foureye rockskipper, *Mnierpes macrocephalus.* This clinid is adapted for living out of water for short periods. (Photograph courtesy of Charles Lehner.)

# FAMILY CHAENOPSIDAE
## Tube blennies (Trambollos alargados)

The tube blennies are small, elongate fishes that lack scales, have only a vestigial lateral line and live in various tubes salvaged from deceased invertebrates. They have well developed head cirri like most other blennioid fishes and conical teeth like the clinids. Some ichthyologists include the Chaenopsidae (tube blennies) in the family Clinidae; here we consider the tube blennies as a separate family, following the revision of that group by John S. Stephens, Jr.

Tube blennies engage in an elaborate courtship in which males attract females by a rhythmic jerking in and out of their tubes (see Figure 89). The females lay their eggs in these tubes and the males guard them, a behavior shared by some other blennioids. There are six genera and 14 species of tube blennies in the Gulf (see Figure 90). All are strongly associated with reefs except the pikeblennies which occupy worm tubes in sandy bottoms near reefs. This tropical family (11 genera and about 40 species) is one of two found only in the Americas (the other is Dactyloscopidae, the sand stargazers).

*References.*   Böhlke (1957a); Lindquist (1975); Robins et al. (1959); Rosenblatt and McCosker (1978); Stephens (1963); Stephens et al. (1966).

Figure 89   A courting male signal blenny, *Emblemaria hypacanthus* (a), display his saillike dorsal fin and dark coloration in an attempt to attract a female. Females (b) are more cryptically colored and are usually found in the open. (Photograph of male by Alex Kerstitch; female by D. A. Thomson.)

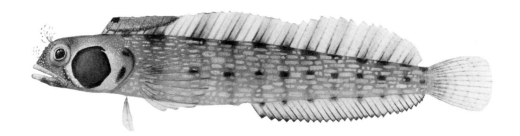

# BROWNCHEEK BLENNY, carillo moreno
*Acanthemblemaria crockeri* Beebe and Tee-Van, 1938

**Illustrated specimen.** Male, 1.6 in. (41 mm), by Alex Kerstitch; see also Plates 27 and 28c; grows to 2 in. (51 mm).

**Distinguishing characteristics.** The genus *Acanthemblemaria* is characterized by well developed spines on the frontal bones at the top of the head. *A. crockeri* can be readily distinguished from all other Gulf chaenopsids by the prominent brown cheek spot outlined in black. This spot is present in juveniles, females, and males. There is a marked sexual dichromatism in the color patterns of this species. The female has a prominent barred pattern along the sides of her body, whereas the male, lacking these bars, is an overall tan, covered rather uniformly with elongate small white spots. A red-spotted phase of *A. crockeri* occurs in the Cabo San Lucas region. D. XXIII–XXVII, 12–15; A. II, 24–28.

**Distribution.** This species is endemic to the Gulf of California and is the commonest chaenopsid in the central and lower regions. It ranges from Puertecitos (Baja California) and Puerto Lobos (Sonora) to Cabo San Lucas and Isla San Ignacio Farallon.

**Ecology.** The browncheek blenny commonly inhabits polychaete worm tubes in the encrusting coral *Porites californica* but utilizes a variety of worm or mollusk tubes in rocky areas. This active blenny is frequently observed in shallow rocky areas, swimming in the open and feeding on plankton, benthic invertebrates, or fishes. Less secretive than most other members of this family, *A. crockeri* will readily leave its tube to feed or to drive away intruders. Both males and females reside in tubes. The males are dominant, however, and will readily fight for the possession of a refuge. We have observed fights between males in an aquarium that lasted as long as 10 minutes and included considerable jaw wrestling and nipping.

Reproductive behavior occurs during the spring when males attract females by displaying a rhythmic up and down jerking movement while erecting their vertical fins and turning very dark. When the female approaches the male's shelter with intentions of entering, the male leaves the tube and the female enters head first. The male then backs into the tube and spawning ensues as the male ejaculates his sperm, swaying to and fro, with his head usually

**188**

extending from the tube. After depositing the adhesive eggs on the tube walls, the female departs, leaving the male to care for the eggs until they hatch. The behavior and ecology of this species have been studied by Lindquist (1975).

**Related species.** Two other species of *Acanthemblemaria* occur in the Gulf. *A. macrospilus* Brock, 1940 (Plate 28a) ranges from Isla Santa Catalina, and Isla San Ignacio Farallon, to Costa Rica and Islas Revillagigedo and del Coco. Known as the barnacle blenny, it can be distinguished from *A. crockeri* by the crimson red coloration of the anterior one-third of the dorsal fin of both sexes. Courting males have dark blue heads. Females have yellow throats and pale heads with a brown marking behind the eye. The clubhead blenny, *A.*

*balanorum* Brock, 1940, ranges from Cabo San Lucas and Isla San Ignacio Farallon to Panama and differs from other *Acanthemblemaria* by its large, blunt, clublike cranial spines, a robust red head, and a series of diamondlike dark spots along the midline. *Ekemblemaria,* a chaenopsid genus intermediate to *Acanthemblemaria* and *Protemblemaria,* is represented in the tropical eastern Pacific by one species, the reefsand blenny, *E. myersi* Stephens, 1963 (Plate 28d). This species ranges from the central Gulf (Bahía Santa Inés) to Ecuador. It has a single pair of beige, branched orbital cirri, no true frontal spines, as in *Acanthemblemaria,* and a dark brown cheek spot outlined with white. It is the chaenopsid species most likely encountered in low-profile rocky areas with much surrounding sandy bottom.

# SIGNAL BLENNY, trambollito señal
## *Emblemaria hypacanthus* (Jenkins and Evermann, 1889)

**Illustrated specimen.** Adult male, 1.7 in. (43 mm), by Alex Kerstitch; see also Plate 27 and Figure 89; grows to about 2 in. (51 mm).

**Distinguishing characteristics.** The most spectacular of the Gulf tube blennies, the male *Emblemaria hypacanthus* can be distinguished from most Gulf blennioid fishes by its prominent saillike dorsal fin (see Figure 89a). The genus is characterized by two parallel bony ridges on the snout and a single pair of orbital cirri. *Emblemaria* lacks small spines on the frontal bones; the pelvic fins are longer than the pectoral fins and there is a single row of palatine teeth. In *E. hypacanthus* the male, although variable, is usually deep brown to tan with dark barlike markings along the body. The orbital cirri of mature males is reddish, tipped with black. The female is colored more cryptically; live specimens have a contrasting black and white pattern with a series of dark patches along the midline and a reticulated pattern of irregular but well defined white patches outlined in black along the sides below the midline. The anal and dorsal fins are irregularly streaked and spotted with black (see Figure 89b). D. XX–XXII, 13–16; A. II, 22–25.

**Distribution.** Endemic to the Gulf of California, *E. hypacanthus* ranges from Puerto Peñasco to Cabo San Lucas and is the commonest chaenopsid in the upper Gulf.

**Ecology.** Male signal blennies are usually found in burrowing mussel holes in limestone or in gastropod tubes but will occupy any suitable hard-walled tubular hole. The females generally remain in the open but will also seek shelter in tubes. The male is highly territorial and will vigorously drive other small fishes from the vicinity of its shelter. In captivity males will engage in prolonged combat that often results in jaw wrestling until the victor drives the other away. The fighting is largely ritualistic, for serious wounds are rarely incurred. Flaring his branchiostegal rays and unfurling his saillike dorsal fin, the male jerks in and out of his tube as a signal threat to the intruder. A similar signal display is used by the male to initiate courtship; it differs in that the male becomes very dark and its jerking movements occur in rapid succession as it tries to attract the female. If the male is successful, the female will enter his shelter with him and spawning will proceed.

The female leaves after depositing a few eggs which adhere to the bottom and sides of the tube. The male protects the eggs while continuing his display to attract other gravid females. Courtship behavior of the signal blenny has been reported by Kerstitch (1971). The congeneric and similarly behaving *E. pandionis* (Evermann and Marsh) of the Atlantic has been studied by Wickler (1964).

*E. hypacanthus* is common, although never abundant, on shallow reef platforms. In the central and lower Gulf it is more often found in open sandy areas near rocks, a habitat preferred by the pike blenny, *Chaenopsis alepidota.*

**Related species.** The only other known *Emblemaria* in the Gulf is the elusive blenny, *E. walkeri* Stephens, 1963, a rare, apparently Gulf endemic that occurs from south of San Felipe to Cabo Pulmo (see Plate 28f). We have collected it at Isla San Pedro Nolasco.

Stephens (1963) notes that it differs from *E. hypacanthus* by the ventral expansion of its suborbital bone.

Formerly in *Emblemaria* is the warthead blenny, *Protemblemaria bicirris* (Hildebrand, 1946). This genus can be distinguished from *Emblemaria* by the two pairs of orbital cirri, shorter pelvic fins, and fused nasal bones and the low dorsal fin of the male. *P. bicirris* ranges throughout the Gulf (Roca Consag) to Bahía Magdalena on the Pacific coast. Another species, the plume blenny, *P. lucasana* Stephens, 1963, which occurs in the lower and central Gulf (Isla Espiritu Santo, Cabo San Lucas, Isla San Pedro Nolasco), differs from *P. bicirris* in that the anterior orbital cirri are twice as long as the posterior cirri in *P. lucasana*. The top of the head of the male *P. lucasana* is covered with long cirruslike flaps (see Plate 28e), whereas in *P. bicirris* it is covered with fleshy wartlike knobs in both sexes.

191

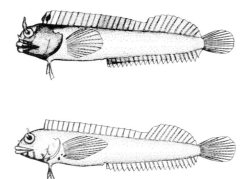

# ANGEL BLENNY, trambollito ángel
## *Coralliozetus angelica* (Böhlke and Mead, 1957)

**Illustrated specimens.** Male (upper fish) and female (lower fish) from Stephens (1963); see also Plate 28g; grows to about 1½ in. (38 mm).

**Distinguishing characteristics.** The tube blennies of the genus *Coralliozetus* are all small fishes (1½ in. or less) with blunt snouts, a reduced number of dorsal and anal fin rays, simple, unbranched orbital cirri, and marked sexual dimorphism. There are six species in the genus—one from the Atlantic and five from the eastern Pacific. Species of *Coralliozetus* are difficult to identify because of their small size and the extreme differences between the sexes. *C. angelica* is the most distinctive of the four Gulf species. Both males and females have robust bodies and large heads. The nuptial body coloration of the male is striking. Its face and throat are red, its cheeks, brown, and the orbital cirri, green. The spinous dorsal fin is low in both sexes. The smaller females are cryptically colored with no body markings except a series of prominent dark bars in the throat, opercular, and pectoral fin base regions. D. XVIII–XX, 11; A. II, 19–21.

**Distribution.** Common in the central and lower Gulf, *C. angelica* ranges from north of Bahía San Agustin (Morro Colorado) to Costa Rica.

**Ecology.** The habitat of *C. angelica* may be characterized as a high-relief rocky substrate, such as steep granitic cliffs in relatively unprotected areas (Lindquist, 1975). This robust little blenny lives in empty barnacle tests (*Balanus*) in the wave-wash zone in which currents and waves are strong. Their shelters may be completely exposed to air between waves. Only the males occupy them. The cryptic females live in the crevices between barnacles. *C. angelica* lives higher in the surge zone than any other chaenopsid and its robust shortened body appears to be an ecological specialization particularly adaptive to this high-relief barnacle habitat.

**Related species.** The three other species of *Coralliozetus* in the Gulf have slenderer bodies and a less specialized habitat than *C. angelica.* The first two have elevated spinous dorsal fins in contrast to the low dorsal profile of *C. angelica.* The scarletfin blenny, *C. micropes* (Beebe and Tee-Van, 1938) is even more common in our collections than *C. angelica.* This species ranges into the upper Gulf to Isla San Jorge and south to Cabo San Lucas and Bahía Magdalena on the outer coast of Baja California. The male *C. micropes* has a high saillike dorsal fin not unlike that of the signal blenny, *E. hypacanthus* (see Plate 28h). It can be distinguished from *Emblemaria* chiefly by its lower dorsal and anal fin-ray counts (D. XIX–XXI, 11–13; A. II, 21–24), blunter snout, shorter pelvic fins, and smaller size. The female has bold body markings, unlike the nearly colorless females of the other *Coralliozetus* spp. She has about 10 dark brown bars along the dorsal base and up to 15 small dark spots on the body midline. Her head is well marked with dark brown bars and, although lacking the high dorsal sail of the male, her anterior dorsal fin may be slightly elevated. *C. micropes* prefers the calmer waters of protected embayments and occupies various refuges from barnacle tests (*Tetraclita*) to mollusk tubes in rocky areas of high-relief. The spikefin blenny, *C. rosenblatti* Stephens, 1963, although rare in our collections, ranges from the outer coast of Baja Calif. (Bahía Magdalena) to Isla Angel de la Guarda and Guaymas. The males of *C. rosenblatti* are quite distinct because of their greatly elongated third dorsal spine which gives their anterior dorsal a spikelike appearance (Figure 90). Its orbital cirri are short and flat and a flaglike flap occurs on the edge of the first dorsal spine, as in *C. micropes.* In both sexes there are 12 brown spots along the anal-fin base. Females have a low dorsal fin with a notch in the fin outline behind the third spine and several distinct lines of small brown spots below the jaws. The barcheek blenny, *C. boehlkei* Stephens, 1963, is similar to *C. rosenblatti* but their ranges do not overlap. In the Gulf *C. boehlkei* occurs only at Mazatlán and ranges south to Costa Rica and Isla del Coco. The dorsal fin of both sexes is uniformly low. The color pattern is similar to that of *C. rosenblatti.* Males can be separated by the low dorsal profile of *C. boehlkei.* Females can be separated by the complete lack of dorsal markings on *C. boehlkei.*

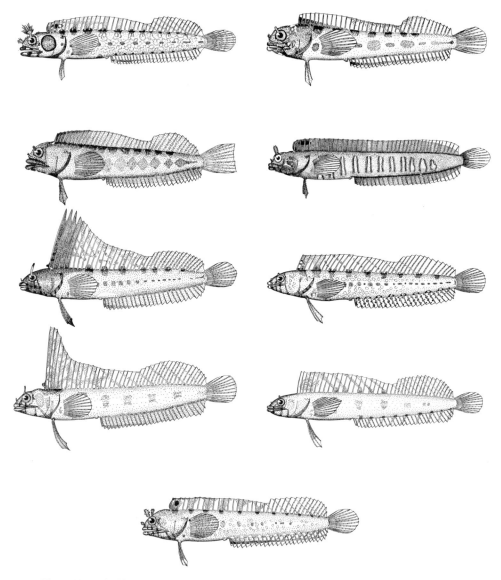

Figure 90    Tube blennies (family Chaenopsidae) of the Sea of Cortez (from Stephens, 1963).

1—*Acanthemblemaria crockeri* ♂        2—*Acanthemblemaria macrospilus* ♂
3—*Acanthemblemaria balanorum* ♂       4—*Ekemblemaria myersi* ♂
5—*Emblemaria hypacanthus* ♂           6—*Emblemaria hypacanthus* ♀
7—*Emblemaria walkeri* ♂               8—*Emblemaria walkeri* ♀
9—*Protemblemaria bicirrus* ♂

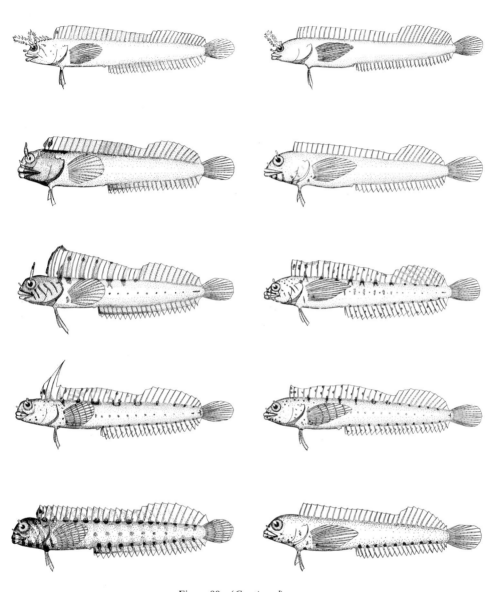

Figure 90 (*Continued*)

10—*Protemblemaria lucasanum* ♂     11—*Protemblemaria lucasanum* ♀
12—*Coralliozetus angelica* ♂        13—*Coralliozetus angelica* ♀
14—*Coralliozetus micropes* ♂        15—*Coralliozetus micropes* ♀
16—*Coralliozetus rosenblatti* ♂     17—*Coralliozetus rosenblatti* ♀
18—*Coralliozetus boehlkei* ♂        19—*Coralliozetus boehlkei* ♀

# ORANGETHROAT PIKEBLENNY, trambollito lucio
## *Chaenopsis alepidota* (Gilbert, 1890)

**Illustrated specimen.** Adult male, 3.8 in. (97 mm), by Alex Kerstitch; grows to about 6 in. (152 mm).

**Distinguishing characteristics.** The pikeblennies (genus *Chaenopsis*) can be separated from the other Gulf chaenopsids by their elongate bodies and pikelike mouths. They lack both orbital and nasal cirri. Male *C. alepidota* in nuptial coloration have orange throats, and bold dark markings on the head. Males have higher dorsal fins than the females. Böhlke (1957a) recognized a subspecies (*C. a. californiensis*) in California. D.XVIII–XX, 34–36, A. II, 34–37; $P_1$. 12–13.

**Distribution.** *Chaenopsis a. alepidota* is endemic to the Gulf of California. It ranges from Isla San Jorge, Sonora, to Cabo San Lucas and is especially common in the Guaymas and La Paz regions.

**Ecology.** This pikeblenny lives in parchment worm tubes in sandy shell-fragment bottoms near patch reefs to a depth of at least 75 ft (23 m). They feed mainly on free-swimming crustaceans. They hover over the bottom with the body bent into an S-shape and maintain this position through rapid beating of their pectoral fins.

Males are territorial and defend their tubes vigorously. During courtship males will assume the S-shaped posture and jerk in and out of these shelters. When threatened, they open their enormous mouths to display two eyelike dark spots. Their branchiostegal rays flare out like the red gular pouch of some lizards.

**Related species.** The only other species of *Chaenopsis* in the Gulf is the Cortez pike blenny, *C. coheni* Böhlke, 1957, which ranges from Isla Angel de la Guarda to Isla Santa Cruz, B.C.S. It has only 28 to 30 segmented dorsal rays and lacks vomerine teeth. It is a relatively uncommon species and we have not collected it in the Gulf.

# FAMILY GOBIIDAE
## Gobies (Gobios)

The gobies are probably the most speciose group of fishes in the world. With approximately 2000 species (Birdsong, 1975), they are rivaled only by the great freshwater family Cyprinidae (minnows and their kin). Their small size, along with their physiological and ecological versatility, has enabled them to exploit varied aquatic habitats and has resulted in a great diversity of species. They include forms resistant to high temperatures and salinities and oxygen-poor waters. They range from deep water to high tide pools and from ocean reefs to hypersaline lagoons, brackish estuaries, and freshwater streams. They include the smallest of all vertebrates (the dwarf pigmy goby, *Pandaka pygmaea,* of the Philippine Islands). Although many species are adapted to life in temperate waters, most are found in the tropics. Their greatest diversity is shown on Indo-west Pacific coral reefs.

Although most gobies are marine, free-living bottom dwellers, there are some midwater-swimming and substrate-burrowing species. Some have intimate living associations with various invertebrates, such as burrowing shrimps and large sponges, and a few make their living by cleaning external parasites from other fishes.

Figure 91  A male secret goby, *Pycnomma semisquamatum.* This species shows the overall shape typical of gobies, but unlike most gobies it has separate rather than united pelvic fins. (Photograph by Alex Kerstitch.)

197

Most gobies can be recognized by their united pelvic fins which form a cone or cuplike sucking disc. Some species however, have lost this union secondarily and, like most fishes, have their pelvic fins separate (Figure 91). In this character these gobies resemble their generally more primitive relatives in the family Eleotridae (sleepers), which are mainly freshwater and estuarine forms. Few diagnostic external characters are present for this largest of fish families. Gobies range from drably colored, cryptic species to brilliantly colored exhibitionists. Some have scales, others have not. Most have a separated dorsal fin with a variable number of flexible spines in the first portion. In the rocky-shore species treated here six or seven spines in the first dorsal fin are typical, whereas the soft-bottom species have four or five. (Note that it is standard practice in goby systematics to count the first element of the second dorsal and anal fins as a soft-ray even though it is a flexible spine; also, the last soft-ray of these fins is usually branched from its base and is counted as one ray even though it may appear as two). All gobiids lack a lateral line on the side of the body. Instead, the lateral line system is confined to the head in a series of mucus canals or tubes (usually with pores). Most have rows of sensory papillae (epipores) on the head, some have barbels, but almost none has the head cirri characteristic of most blennies (with which gobies are frequently confused by beginning ichthyologists). Despite wide morphological variations, nearly all have the typical "goby" appearance that is difficult to characterize.

Gulf gobies include at least 50 species distributed in 22 genera. These numbers are not so firm as those of other groups, for gobies are the most speciose and among the poorest known of Gulf fishes. Of this total we have categorized 28 species in 14 genera as reef or rocky-shore inhabitants. The others live in estuaries, along sandy shores, and over offshore soft bottoms.

*References.*  Barlow (1961a, 1961b, 1963); Birdsong (1975); Böhlke and Robins (1960, 1968); Chen and Ebeling (1971); Eckert (1974); Findley (1975); Ginsburg (1938a, 1938b, 1939, 1947); Hoese (1971, 1976); Miles (1974); Milfer (1973); Wiley (1976).

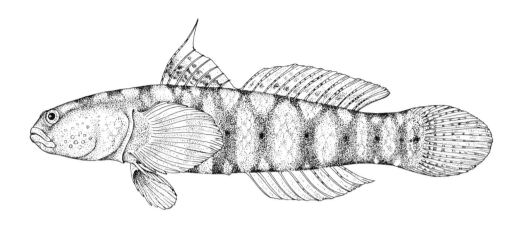

# SONORA GOBY, gobio chiquito
## *Gobiosoma chiquita* (Jenkins and Evermann, 1889)

**Illustrated specimen.** Adult male, 2.2 in. (56 mm), by Tor Hansen; grows to about 2½ in. (64 mm).

**Distinguishing characteristics.** Compared with their brightly colored close relatives in the genus *Elacatinus,* Gulf gobies in the genus *Gobiosoma* are rather drably colored fishes. Seven spines occur in the first dorsal fin and the pelvic fins are united into a conelike sucking disc. *G. chiquita* can be distinguished from other Gulf species of *Gobiosoma* by its many weakly ctenoid scales, which extend forward on the midside from the base of the caudal fin to the pectoral-fin axil. The head, predorsal area, breast, and belly are naked and head barbels are absent. In mature males the first one or two dorsal spines may elongate into short filaments during the spring and summer breeding season. The background color of *G. chiquita* is greenish brown to tan, often with green and yellow overtones. A series of seven to nine diffuse dark bands (often hourglass-shaped) usually occurs on the head and body; the center of each band is marked with a dark spot. In mature females the breast may be covered by a yellow triangular patch. D. VII + 11 (rarely 10 or 12); A. 10 (rarely 9 or 11); $P_1$. 18–21 (usually 19 or 20).

**Distribution.** A Gulf endemic, the Sonora goby is known from Los Frailes, B.C.S., to San Felipe, B.C.N., and from Guaymas to Punta Borrascoso, Sonora.

**Ecology.** *Gobiosoma chiquita* is the commonest intertidal goby in the upper and central Gulf. Its ecology and behavior have been studied by Miles (1974). Especially abundant at Puerto Peñasco, it is frequently seen in sandy-bottom rocky tidepools throughout the intertidal zone. It also occurs less frequently subtidally to depths of about 30 ft (9 m). A diurnal species, the Sonora goby preys on small crustaceans and occasionally on small snails and polychaete worms. During the day it spends most of its time foraging for prey on sandy bottoms and in algal turfs of tide pools, never far from the shelter of a ledge or boulder. The male is highly territorial during most of the year, defending his refuge and the surrounding area from intrusion by other adults. He tends to be darker in color than the female and, when fully mature, is more than half again as large. Following courtship and spawning, the male guards the eggs that adhere to the sides of the refuge until hatching.

**Related species.** According to Hoese (1971), nine species of *Gobiosoma* inhabit the eastern

**199**

Pacific, five of which occur in the Gulf of California. Among these five, four are often associated with rocky habitats (*G. etheostoma* (Jordan and Starks, 1885), the most extensively scaled species, is known only from sandy bottoms in mainland estuaries). The paradox goby, *G. paradoxum* (Günther, 1861), may be distinguished from other Gulf species of *Gobiosoma* by extent of scalation. The caudal peduncle is completely scaled; scales extend forward as a wedge from about the midpoint of the second dorsal- and anal-fin bases and reach an apex (which varies) somewhere below the origin of the second dorsal fin and the fifth dorsal spine. The rest of the body and head is naked except for a small patch of scales (which may be absent) behind the pectoral-fin axil. Barbels are absent. Mature males typically have an elongated first dorsal spine. *G. paradoxum* is rare in the Gulf but ranges from Guaymas to Guayaquil, Ecuador. It is also found on soft bottoms in mangrove estuaries.

As the specific name implies, *Gobiosoma nudum* (Meek and Hildebrand, 1928), the knobchin goby, is either completely or almost devoid of scales. Sometimes a few scales (1 to 4) occur behind the pectoral-fin axil and two tiny ctenoid scales appear at the caudal-fin base. This goby has two small fleshy knobs under the chin and a small median fleshy protuberance at the tip of the snout. There is also a tiny barbel on the preorbital rim below each anterior nostril. This small species of *Gobiosoma* reaches a length of about 1 in. (25 mm) in the Gulf. The knobchin goby ranges from south of Bahía Magdalena (Punta Marquis) to Cabo Pulmo, B.C.S., and from Mazatlán to Colombia.

*Gobiosoma nudum* appears to be the only Pacific goby to have completely crossed the Panama Canal into western Atlantic waters (Rubinoff and Rubinoff, 1969), but despite numerous recent collections in this region of the Atlantic it has not been found again (McCosker and Dawson, 1975).

Closely related to *G. nudum* is the patchscale goby, *Gobiosoma* sp., an undescribed species treated by Hoese (1971) (see Figure 92). Small barbels and "knobs" are present in the same positions as in *G. nudum,* but the patchscale lacks the small fleshy protuberance on the snout tip. Scalation is variable but is always less

Figure 92    The patchscale goby, *Gobiosoma* sp. Note the several wavy, dark bars on the translucent body. (Photograph by D. A. Thomson.)

than in *G. chiquita* and *G. paradoxum* and more than in *G. nudum*. The side of the caudal peduncle has at least a small patch of scales; another small patch lies behind the pectoral-fin axil. The patchscale goby can be distinguished from all other Gulf species of *Gobiosoma* by a lateral canal segment (with a pore at each end of the short tube) above the operculum. This segment appears as a groove in individuals smaller than about 15 mm SL. Body coloration in live specimens is typically dusky translucent; seven to 10 distinct, reticulated, slightly wavy dark bands are each bisected vertically by a narrow light interspace and usually with a series of short black dashes along the midside. The patchscale goby is known from the outer coast of Baja California (Laguna Guerrero Negro to Bahía Magdalena) and the Gulf (Roca Consag to Bahía de los Angeles and Punta Borrascoso to Mazatlán). It ranges south to Nayarit along the mainland coast of Mexico.

At Puerto Peñasco this goby is a common inhabitant of rocky tide pools in the lower intertidal zone, where it coexists with the more numerous *G. chiquita.*

# REDHEAD GOBY, **gobio de cabeza roja**
## *Elacatinus puncticulatus* (Ginsburg, 1938)

**Illustrated specimen.**  Adult female, 1.2 in. (31 ˙mm), by Alex Kerstitch; see also Plate 29; grows to about 1¾ in. (44 mm).

**Distinguishing characteristics.**  Species of the American genus *Elacatinus** are noted for their bright color patterns (neon gobies) and many specialize in cleaning host fishes of external parasites. All have seven spines in the first dorsal fin and completely united pelvic fins. The redhead goby can be readily identified by the diagnostic color pattern shown in Plate 29. D. VII + 12 (rarely 11 or 13); A. 11 (rarely 10); $P_1$. 20–23 (usually 21 or 22).

**Distribution.**  The redhead goby ranges from the upper Gulf (Isla Angel de la Guarda) to

* These gobies have been classified by Böhlke and Robins (1968) in the subgenera *Elacatinus* and *Tigrigobius* of the expanded genus *Gobiosoma*. Here, however, we follow Hoese (1971) by placing them in the genus *Elacatinus*.

Ecuador. In the Gulf it is more common in the central and lower regions.

**Ecology.**  This is a shallow-water goby that prefers depths of about 5 to 20 ft (1.5 to 6 m). It is frequently found living with the club urchin (*Eucidaris thouarsii*) in holes in the reef. The redhead goby is territorial and highly aggressive, and fights between adults sometimes end only after a "jaw wrestling" bout. During courtship males attract females to their shelters by approaching them, then quivering and, turning sharply, swimming back to their shelters. If interested, the female follows and spawning ensues. Males become very dark, almost black overall, during courtship.

This species occasionally removes parasites from other fishes, but it is not an obligate cleaner like many other species in the genus (e.g., see Böhlke and McCosker, 1973; Colin, 1975).

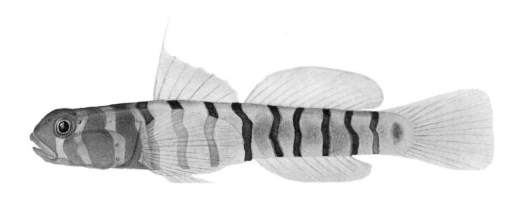

# BANDED CLEANER GOBY, gobio barbero
## *Elacatinus digueti* (Pellegrin, 1901)

**Illustrated specimen.** Adult male, 1.1 in. (29 mm), by Alex Kerstitch; see also Plate 29; grows only to about 1¼ in. (32 mm).

**Distinguishing characteristics.** This small, colorful, completely scaleless goby has a bright orangish-red depressed head crossed by three or four wide light bands. The yellowish translucent compressed body is marked by narrow, conspicuous, wavy dark bands which give it a "honey bee" appearance. Alternating interspaces between bands show dusky patches of deep subdermal pigment. The first dorsal spine of both sexes is elongated. *Gobiosoma brocki*, described by Ginsburg (1938a) from the Gulf of California, appears to be a synonym of *E. digueti*. D. VII + 11; A. 9–10; $P_1$. 19 (rarely 18 or 20).

**Distribution.** This goby ranges from the lower portion of the upper Gulf (Isla Angel de la Guarda) to Colombia [Böhlke and Robins (1968) as *G. brocki*], but southern populations may represent undescribed species. It is common in the central and lower Gulf along rocky shores with steep slopes.

**Ecology.** Being one of the few Gulf fishes that specializes in cleaning host fishes of external parasites, this goby lives in rocky crevices frequented by large predatory fishes such as moray eels and groupers. At these "cleaning stations" it is commonly seen darting over the surface of a large fish searching for edible parasites (probably mainly gnathiid isopods). The host fish postures to elicit cleaning by the goby, which when finished darts back into a crevice to await the next client. Banded cleaner gobies are sometimes indiscriminate in their cleaning activity and will swarm over a scuba diver's fins or other large surfaces looking for parasites, often nipping at body hairs in the process. In aquaria we have occasionally observed other fishes attempting to prey on this cleaner. In one instance a bluespotted jawfish (*Opistognathus* sp.) seized an *E. digueti* but immediately rejected it by convulsively flexing its jaws. On another occasion a frogfish (*Antennarius* sp.), after swallowing a banded cleaner goby, tried without success to regurgitate it by violent, convulsive coughing. The frogfish survived, suggesting that, although this goby (which can secrete considerable body mucus) may be distasteful, it is not poisonous. Similar observations of attempted predation on related gobies in the Caribbean have been made by Smith and Tyler (1972) and Colin (1973).

**Related species.** Another species, *Elacatinus* sp., the widebanded cleaner goby, occurs in the Gulf and is often collected on the same reef as *E. digueti* but is usually found deeper. Although having similar overall coloration, this species displays a different pattern of banding on the body than *E. digueti*. The wider, more evenly spaced, nonwavy dark bands are separated by light interspaces which are about equal in width to the bands, and there is no deep pigment as in *E. digueti* (see Plate 30a). We have collected it at Isla San Pedro Nolasco, Sonora, Isla Santa Catalina, B.C.S., and south to Cabo San Lucas and Bahía Banderas (Puerto Vallarta), Jalisco. Eastern Pacific species of *Elacatinus*, including about three or four undescribed species that occur south of the Gulf, are currently under study by D. F. Hoese of the Australian Museum, Sydney, Australia.

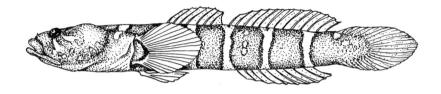

# SLOW GOBY, gobio lento
## *Aruma histrio* (Jordan, 1884)

**Illustrated specimen.** Adult male, 2.5 in. (64 mm), by Tor Hansen; the illustrated specimen is the maximum size attained by the species.

**Distinguishing characteristics.** In typical goby fashion the pelvic fins of this goby are completely united to form a cup-shaped sucking disc. The head is depressed and adults show puffy cheeks when viewed from the top or bottom. Scales are completely lacking, the tongue is bilobed, and a prominent dark, crescentic bar occurs on the outer base of the pectoral fin. The light to dark brown body is crossed by seven or eight irregular, dark-edged, cream-colored bands, but the variation in banding is considerable; posterior bands are often obscure and sometimes broken into faint irregular spots. There is also considerable geographic variation in several meristic and morphometric features (see Hoese, 1976). D. VII + 12–13 (rarely 11); A. 10–13; $P_1$. 17–20 (rarely 16).

**Distribution.** This common goby, which is endemic to the Gulf of California, ranges from Los Frailes, B.C.S., north to San Felipe, B.C.N., and from Puerto Peñasco south to Isla San Ignacio Farallon, Sinaloa.

**Ecology.** The slow goby is a secretive species that hides under rocks and in reef crevices. When undisturbed, it remains motionless or creeps slowly over the substrate. Abundant in tide pools, it is a low intertidal and shallow subtidal species but has been collected at depths of about 45 ft (14 m). Spawning occurs in the spring and at that time the larvae can be seen in dense schools around sargassum seaweed. Metamorphosis into adults occurs at about 15 to 18 mm SL. Males are about 20% larger than females, and individuals from northern Gulf populations are commonly larger than those from southern areas (Hoese, 1976).

**Related species.** *Aruma* is related to the genus *Gobulus,* of which two species are known from the Gulf of California: the crescent goby, *G. crescentalis* (Gilbert, 1892), and the sandtop goby, *G. hancocki* Ginsburg, 1938. Both species are similar to *Aruma histrio* in having seven spines in the first dorsal fin, scaleless bodies, and depressed heads, but both are easily distinguished from it and other related gobies by the uniquely reversed color combination of a cream-colored dorsal and a light brown ventral surface (see Plate 30b). Both species also, have an abbreviated, incompletely united pelvic disc usually with a posterior indentation (i.e., only a short membrane connects the shorter innermost pelvic soft-rays). The anterior membrane (frenum) basally connecting the short outer pelvic spines, and which is well developed in most gobies, is reduced to a weak fold of skin or is completely absent. Both species have a dark crescentic bar at the caudal-fin base and can secrete much mucus from the skin. These gobies live in rock crevices or sand burrows (grooves) under boulders. As they protrude their heads from under a rock they create a small sand trough in which they lie, probably awaiting small crustacean prey to pass by. The sand-colored dorsal surface is thus camouflaged.

*Gobulus crescentalis* is a larger (to 2.4 in. or 61 mm), more robust-bodied species than the slenderer and delicate-appearing *G. hancocki*

(to 1 in. or 25 mm). In *G. hancocki* the sharply demarcated, unmarked pale dorsal surface covers only the upper third of the head and body, whereas in *G. crescentalis* the occasionally mottled dorsal surface covers the upper half to two-thirds, with an often more irregular, less sharply defined border.

*Gobulus hancocki* ranges from Bahía San Agustin, Sonora, to Panama and from Bahía Concepción, B.C.S., to near Cabo San Lucas. *G. crescentalis* is known from the outer coast of Baja California (Laguna Ojo de Liebre and Bahía Magdalena). Within the Gulf, it ranges from Los Frailes, B.C.S., north to Okie's Landing (north of Bahía San Luis Gonzaga), B.C.N., and from Puerto Peñasco south to Guaymas. Both species are relatively uncommon gobies usually found subtidally in sand-surrounded reef or cobble bottoms at depths of about 5 to 60 ft (1.5 to 18 m).

Plate 17 Gulf damselfishes (all photographed by Alex Kerstitch). a. Adult Cortez damselfish (*Eupomacentrus rectifraenum*). b. Juvenile Cortez damselfish (*E. rectifraenum*). c. Adult beaubrummel (*E. flavilatus*). d. Juvenile beaubrummel (*E. flavilatus*). e. Adult giant damselfish (*Microspathodon dorsalis*). f. Juvenile giant damselfish (*M. dorsalis*). g. Juvenile blue-and-yellow chromis (*Chromis* sp.). h. Juvenile silverstreak chromis (*Chromis* sp.).

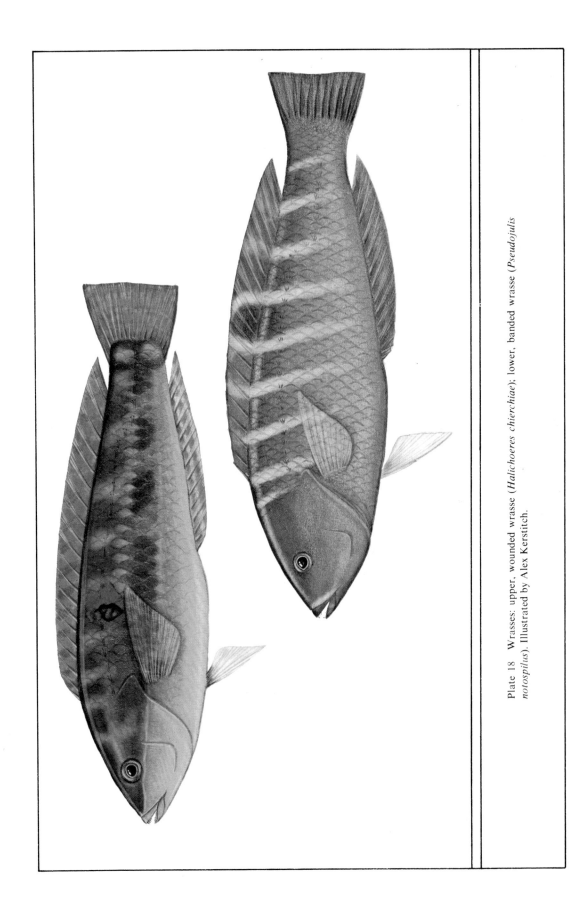

Plate 18 Wrasses: upper, wounded wrasse (*Halichoeres chierchiae*); lower, banded wrasse (*Pseudojulis notospilus*). Illustrated by Alex Kerstitch.

Plate 19 Cortez rainbow wrasse (*Thalassoma lucasanum*): upper, female; lower, secondary male. Illustrated by Alex Kerstitch.

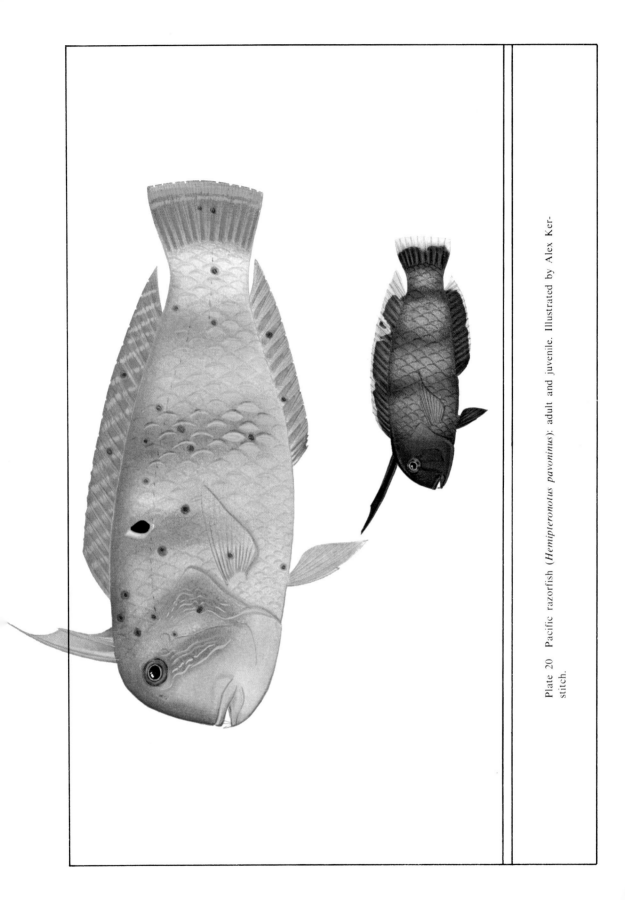

Plate 20 Pacific razorfish (*Hemipteronotus pavoninus*): adult and juvenile. Illustrated by Alex Kerstitch.

Plate 21    Wrasses (all photographs by Alex Kerstitch except *b*, which is by courtesy of Robert Ames, Steinhart Aquarium): a. Male Mexican hogfish (*Bodianus diplotaenia*). b. Female Mexican hogfish (*B. diplotaenia*). c. Male spinster wrasse (*Halichoeres nicholsi*). d. Female spinster wrasse (*H. nicholsi*). e. Male chameleon wrasse (*H. dispilus*). f. Male rock wrasse (*H. semicinctus*).

(c)

(a)

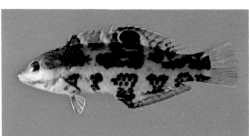

(b)

(f)

(d)

(e)

Plate 22  Wrasses (all photographs by Alex Kerstitch): a. Juvenile wounded wrasse (*Halichoeres chierchiae*). b. Juvenile spinster wrasse (*H. nicholsi*). c. Adult sunset wrasse (*Thalassoma lutescens*) in the midst of an aggregation of Cortez rainbow wrasses (*T. lucasanum*). d. Juvenile golden wrasse (*Pseudojulis melanotis*). e. Juvenile pearlscale razorfish (*Hemipteronotus taeniourus*). f. Adult blackspot wrasse (*Decodon melasma*).

Plate 23   Bumphead parrotfish (*Scarus perrico*). Illustrated by Alex Kerstitch.

Plate 24 Parrotfishes and hawkfishes (all photographs by Alex Kerstitch except *a*, which is by courtesy of E. S. Hobson): a. Male bluechin parrotfish (*Scarus ghobban*). b. Female bluechin parrotfish (*Scarus ghobban*). c. Adult giant hawkfish (*Cirrhitus rivulatus*). d. Juvenile giant hawkfish (*Cirrhitus rivulatus*). e. Adult coral hawkfish (*Cirrhitichthys oxycephalus*).

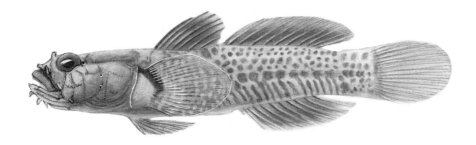

# PANTHER GOBY, gobio pantera
## *Barbulifer pantherinus* (Pellegrin, 1901)

**Illustrated specimen.** Adult 1.4 in. (34.7 mm SL), by Steven P. Gigliotti, from Böhlke and Robins (1968, Figure 16); grows to about 2 in. (51 mm).

**Distinguishing characteristics.** The generic name of this species, *Barbulifer,* is derived from their distinctive head barbels. The panther goby has six to 12 small barbels (all shorter than pupil diameter) on the ventral surface of the head. On close examination they appear as a low fringe between the chin and throat. Also, two small barbels occur behind the upper lip below the eye and nostrils. The pelvic fins are broadly united into a ventral sucking disc, and there are seven spines in the first dorsal fin. Several rows of yellowish to orange-brown, irregularly spaced spots of varying sizes on the body resemble panther markings which often coalesce into short bars, especially ventrally. As in *Aruma histrio,* a prominent dark bar occurs on the outer base of the pectoral fin; scales are absent and the tongue is bilobed. D. VII + 11 (rarely 10 or 12); A. 10 (rarely 9); $P_1$. 17–20 (usually 19).

**Distribution.** The panther goby is known from Isla Angel de la Guarda south along the Baja coast to Cabo San Lucas, and from Puerto Lobos south to Guaymas, Sonora. It is endemic to the Gulf of California.

**Ecology.** This is another secretive goby, often abundant in areas in which rocks range from cobbles to boulders. We have collected numerous individuals in boulder areas that support dense algal growth. Although it is occasionally collected in low tide pools, the panther goby is essentially a shallow subtidal species but occurs to depths of at least 65 ft (20 m).

**Related species.** Two undescribed species of *Barbulifer* are currently being studied by D. F. Hoese. One rare species, the largespotted goby, apparently differs in having far fewer and larger spots than *B. pantherinus*. The other species, the saddlebanded goby (from southern Baja California to Guerrero), has five wide, V-shaped, dark-edged, grayish brown bands on a whitish translucent body, a wide dark bar across the top of the head, a thin dark oblique bar behind the eye and two large barbels below

207

it (both about equal to eye diameter). Several slender barbels (all equal to or greater than eye diameter) occur on the ventral surface.

Although more closely related to the genus *Gobiosoma,* the silt goby, *Enypnias seminudus* (Günther, 1861), is included here because it has barbels somewhat like those of *Barbulifer.* In this goby a single pair of slender barbels (longer than pupil diameter) occurs below the chin, and another pair of much shorter barbels is found on the snout tip between the anterior nostrils. There is also a short but prominent barbel on the preorbital rim below the anterior nostril. Unlike *Barbulifer,* the body of *E. seminudus* is covered with about 40 to 60 rows of small embedded cycloid scales that extend forward almost to the pectoral-fin axil. A few weakly ctenoid scales may occur on the caudal peduncle. There are seven spines in the first dorsal fin and 13 to 16 rays in the second. The pelvic fins are united into a sucking disc. The coloration of preserved specimens is brownish, and about five wide but usually incomplete diffuse body bars give this goby a "mottled" appearance. Large males are usually darker than females, being more or less uniformly brown and often having a series of short dark dashes along the midside. A thin, frequently incomplete, dark bar occurs on the outer base of the upper pectoral rays but is not so well developed as that seen in *Barbulifer pantherinus* or *Aruma histrio.*

We have collected the silt goby at Bahía de Topolobampo, Sinaloa, in a shallow subtidal boulder area surrounded by much silt and organic debris. It is also known from Mazatlán and Panama. A closely related species, *E. aceras* Ginsburg, 1939, occurs on the Pacific coast of Central America and in the Panama Canal.

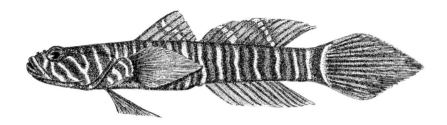

# SPLITBANDED GOBY, gobio blanco y negro
## *Gymneleotris seminudus* (Günther, 1864)

**Illustrated specimen.** Adult female, 1.5 in. (38 mm), by Alex Kerstitch; grows to about 2 in. (51 mm).

**Distinguishing characteristics.** Unlike some of its relatives (e.g., *Gobulus, Aruma*), the ventral fins of this strikingly marked goby are separate and not conspicuously joined by membranes as in most gobies. There are seven spines in the first dorsal fin, the head is depressed, and numerous bands occur over the head and body. The adult body coloration consists of 12 or 13 light to dark brown bands with pale interspaces. The bands are darkest on their outside edges with a lighter central portion. Juveniles have only about six wide body bands. The bands and interspaces increase in number because of a horizontal "splitting" of each band as the fish grows. As the specific name (*seminudus*) implies, this goby is partly naked; cycloid scales

cover only the posterior three-fourths of the body, becoming reduced and embedded anteriorly. Three small pores with fleshy tabs and short rows of tiny sensory papillae occur on each side of the top of the head. D. VII + 11 (rarely 10); A. 10 (rarely 9); $P_1$. 18–19 (rarely 20).

**Distribution.** A Panamic species with a wide range, *G. seminudus* is known from the central and lower Gulf, the outer coast of Baja California Sur (in Bahía Magdalena) and south to Ecuador. In the Gulf it ranges as far north as Bahía Santa Inés, B.C.S., and Bahía San Agustin, Sonora.

**Ecology.** As with other secretive gobies, the ecology of the splitbanded goby is poorly known. It seems to prefer areas of reef rubble and cobble well covered by algae and is occasionally seen by divers during ichythyocide collections when driven from under the rocks and crevices in which it hides. This species of goby ranges in depth from 3 to 75 ft (1 to 23 m) but is usually found at depths of 15 to 30 ft (4.6 to 9 m).

**Related species.** The secret goby, *Pycnomma semisquamatum* Rutter, 1904 (see Figure 91), is another Gulf rocky-shore goby with separate pelvic fins and seven flexible spines in the first dorsal fin (often the first two are elongated in adult males). This robust-bodied goby (to 2½ in., or 63 mm), like *G. seminudus*, is only partly scaled, but the large posterior scales are ctenoid rather than cycloid. Anteriorly, scales become smaller and have fewer or no ctenii. There are four enlarged ctenoid scales at the caudal-fin base. As in *Gymneleotris*, three small pores occur on each side of the top of the head but there are no fleshy tabs. There is a single interorbital

pore between the posterior edges of the eyes which *Gymneleotris* lacks. The sides of juveniles often show six faint hourglass-shaped dark bands on a light background, the darkest pigmentation appearing as spots along the midside. *P. semisquamatum*, however, is never so distinctly banded as *Gymneleotris seminudus* or *Chriolepis zebra*. Adult coloration varies from light brown to almost black; the unpaired fins are the darkest. Where it is not masked by overall darkening, a straight wide dark bar is usually present at the caudal-fin base. The secret goby is known only from the Gulf of California from Bahía de La Paz, B.C.S., north to Isla Angel de la Guarda. We have collected it at Islas San Pedro Martir and San Pedro Nolasco toward the mainland side of the Gulf. This secretive species hides in crevices and under rocks well covered with seaweed at depths of about 6 to 60 ft (2 to 18 m).

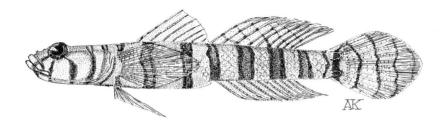

# GECKO GOBY, gobio salamanquesa
## *Chriolepis zebra* Ginsburg, 1938

**Illustrated specimen.** Adult female, 1.7 in. (43 mm), by Alex Kerstitch; grows to 1¾ in. (44 mm).

**Distinguishing characteristics.** As in *Gymneleotris* and *Pycnomma,* the pelvic fins of *Chriolepis* are separate and seven spines occur in the first dorsal fin. Because the color pattern and slow movements of *Chriolepis zebra* remind us of the western banded gecko, a Sonoran Desert lizard, we are calling it the gecko goby. The white to tan body is encircled by six light to dark brown bands, each of which is edged with dark brown pigment, and a thin, dark band is usually present on the caudal peduncle. Other dark bands, bars, and vertical lines on the head and dorsal and caudal fins are as illustrated. The eyes protrude above the depressed head. *C. zebra* is only partly scaled. Posterior scales are ctenoid (as in *Pycnomma*

*semisquamatum*) rather than cycloid (as in *Gymneleotris seminudus*), whereas anterior scales are cycloid and embedded in the skin. Four enlarged ctenoid scales occur at the caudal-fin base. The two outermost, which are the largest, bear greatly enlarged ctenii. Unlike *Gymneleotris* and *Pycnomma,* head pores are absent in *Chriolepis,* but short rows of sensory papillae (epipores) are present. D. VII + 10 (rarely 11); A. 10 (rarely 9); $P_1$. 17–19.

**Distribution.** The gecko goby is known only from the Gulf of California from Cabo San Lucas and Isla San Ignacio Farallon north to Isla Angel de la Guarda and near Morro Colorado (north of Bahía San Agustin), Sonora.

**Ecology.** The gecko goby is found in subtidal reefs, particularly where broken rocks form rubble areas that contain many small caves and crevices and where there is white coralline sand in the rock interspaces. We have observed solitary gecko gobies resting motionless or creeping about very slowly on a small apron of white sand concealed under an overhanging rock or ledge. The gecko goby and its close relatives (*Gymneleotris* and *Pycnomma*) are seldom seen except during ichthyocide collections when they are driven from hiding. Even then they are difficult to collect because of their resistance to rotenone. Most common in the 15-to-70-ft (4.6-to-23-m) depth range, *C. zebra* has occasionally been collected in waters as shallow as 5 ft (1.5 m) and sometimes as deep as 105 ft (32 m).

**Related species.** The genus *Chriolepis* is the most speciose within the group of seven dorsal-spined, separate pelvic-finned gobies. Besides *C. zebra*, which is the commonest in collections, at least eight other species (five undescribed) inhabit the tropical eastern Pacific. The rubble goby, *C. minutillus* Gilbert, 1892, is a smaller (to 1¼ in., or 32 mm) but more robust species with a rounded head and caudal fin. It is easily distinguished from *C. zebra* by having only a few (2 to 13) weakly

ctenoid, embedded scales on the side of the caudal peduncle. Four enlarged ctenoid scales occur at the caudal-fin base as in *C. zebra*. Individuals vary in coloration from pale to dark. Dark individuals often show a series of thin, irregular, broken vertical light lines on the body. The rubble goby is sexually dimorphic in that courting and spawning males often have a greatly elongated (filamentous) first dorsal spine (up to twice as long as the male shown in Plate 30c), a low gular flap on the underside of the head, and overall darker coloration than the pale spawning females. *C. minutillus* is rare in ichthyological collections (only 19 specimens known) undoubtedly because of its small size and the depth and nature of its habitat [patches of reef rubble surrounded by sand or broken shells in depths of about 40 to 150 ft (12 to 46 m)]. The rubble goby has been collected only in the Gulf of California, mainly at islands on the Baja California side from Isla Espíritu Santo north to Isla Angel de la Guarda. We have also taken it at Isla San Pedro Martir. Three other species (undescribed) of *Chriolepis* occur in the central and lower Gulf and are being described by L. T. Findley.

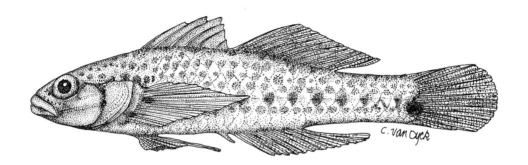

# REDLIGHT GOBY, gobio semáforo
## *Coryphopterus urospilus* Ginsburg, 1938

**Illustrated specimen.** Adult male, 1.8 in. (46 mm), by Chris van Dyck; grows to about 2½ in. (64 mm).

**Distinguishing characteristics.** This common goby has six spines in the first dorsal fin, completely united pelvic fins, and a well scaled body. The specific name (*urospilus*) refers to a prominent dark spot on the lower caudal-fin base. Five horizontal rows of closely spaced red-orange spots occur on the sides of the whitish translucent body, the lower two rows being most prominent and appearing as stripes on the operculum and cheek. Two red-orange spots occur on the outer pectoral-fin base and a short dark horizontal bar appears on the inner base. The bases of the dorsal and caudal fins often show a number of small red-orange spots, whereas the anal and pelvic fins are usually dusky. Four subdermal dark dashes lie along the midventral line from the anterior anal-fin base to the caudal peduncle and six or seven dark spots show at the middorsal line below the dorsal fins. D. VI + 10 (rarely 9); A. 10 (rarely 9); $P_1$. 19–21 (usually 20).

**Distribution.** The redlight goby is one of the most widely distributed species of reef-associated gobies in the tropical eastern Pacific. It is known from Bahía Magdalena and from the northernmost island (Roca Consag) in the Gulf, south to Colombia; it also occurs at most of the far offshore islands such as the Revillagigedos and Galápagos.

**Ecology.** The redlight goby, one of the most numerous gobies in the Gulf, is frequently seen by observant scuba divers near the bases of rocky reefs where the rocks adjoin patches of sand. This is the commonest goby inhabiting this reef-sand interface. It probably forages over sand for small crustaceans and utilizes the reef for safety, for it will quickly dart into a crevice when approached. When over sand, the profuse dark spots on the translucent body resemble sand grains and presumably provide good camouflage. A subtidal species, this goby has been taken occasionally in large tide pools (Colombia). We have collected it at a depth of 125 ft (38 m) at Cabo San Lucas.

213

**Related species.** Although at least nine species of *Coryphopterus* occur in the western Atlantic (Böhlke and Robins, 1960, 1962), only two are known in the eastern Pacific. Besides *C. urospilus,* only the quite different and larger blackeye goby, *C. nicholsii* (Bean), is present on the rocky coast from British Columbia south to the outer coast of Baja California Norte; it does not, however, range into the Gulf of California.

Although not closely related to *Coryphopterus,* the Cortez hovering goby, *Ioglossus* sp., is introduced here because it is another reef-sand interface goby. *Ioglossus* is represented in the tropical eastern Pacific by one or two undescribed species (under study by R. H. Rosenblatt) known from a few specimens collected at islands on the Baja California Sur side of the central and lower Gulf and from Guaymas, Sonora (we have sighted it as far north as Bahía San Agustin). Six curved spines constitute the first dorsal fin; the long pelvic fins are separate and the caudal fin is long and tapering (lanceolate). Our specimens (Guaymas) of this large, distinctive, and strikingly beautiful goby have an elongated, compressed, pale body with lavender overtones and long-based orange to lavender unpaired fins. The entire top of the caudal fin has a bluish white streak. The Cortez hovering goby lives in burrows constructed in sand-shell bottoms, invariably near the base of a reef (see Figure 93). From a distance individuals can be seen hovering in midwater a few inches to a foot or so above their burrows, feeding on planktonic organisms in the water column. They are wary fishes and will quickly dart into their burrows when approached. Two species of *Ioglossus* are known from the tropical western Atlantic (Randall, 1968b).

Figure 93   The Cortez hovering goby, *Ioglossus* sp. This slender goby lives in burrows in sandy-cobbled bottoms near reefs. (Photograph by Alex Kerstitch.)

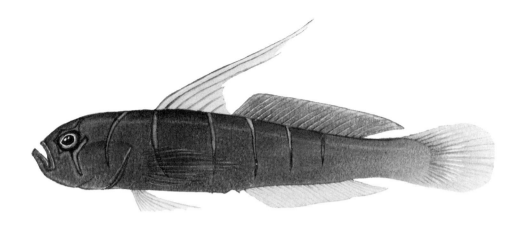

# BLUEBANDED GOBY, gobio bonito
## *Lythrypnus dalli* (Gilbert, 1890)

**Illustrated specimen.** Adult male, 1.2 in. (31 mm), by Alex Kerstitch; see also Plate 29; grows to about 2¼ in. (57 mm).

**Distinguishing characteristics.** It would be difficult to mistake this brightly colored goby for any other Gulf fish. The body is coral red crossed with five to nine narrow blue bands. The head is high and compressed and the pelvic fins are completely united. The first three to four spines of the six-spined first dorsal fin are filamentous, their tips thickened. Small ctenoid scales cover the entire body (except the nape). The systematics and life history of this species in California have been studied recently by Eckert (1974) and Wiley (1976). D. VI + 16–19; A. 12–15; $P_1$. 17–20.

**Distribution.** The bluebanded goby ranges from Morro Bay, California, to the Gulf of California. It is found from Puerto Peñasco, Sonora, to Isla San Ignacio Farallon, Sinaloa, and from Roca Consag to Cabo San Lucas, B.C.S. It is more abundant in the central and lower regions.

**Ecology.** In southern California waters the bluebanded goby prefers subtidal rock surfaces covered by algal mats and encrusting organisms (Eckert, 1974), but along the outer northern coast of Baja California (Punta Banda) it prefers largely bare and exposed rock reefs (Wiley, 1976). *L. dalli* feeds mainly on small crustaceans, such as copepods, ostracods, and amphipods. It is a short-lived species that breeds in the spring and early summer in its first year and only a few individuals survive to the second (Wiley, 1976).

In the Gulf this goby inhabits a broad, vertical zone along steep, rocky slopes. It is known intertidally (rarely) to depths exceeding 250 ft (76 m) (Cabo San Lucas). It is often found in the open near crevices and overhanging ledges, often with the purple sea urchin, *Echinometra vanbrundti*. As might be expected from its geographical and depth ranges, this goby prefers cold water. In summer it is found in deeper water (below 180 ft or 55 m), whereas in winter it is common throughout its depth range. It is an aggressive, territoral goby, and courtship behavior has been observed in captivity. The male initiates courtship with short staccato dashes toward the female (chasing), followed by nudging or nipping that persists until she follows him into his refuge for spawning. The eggs are tended and guarded by the male until they hatch.

**Related species.** There are at least two other species of *Lythrypnus* in the Gulf. The gorgeous goby, *L. pulchellus* Ginsburg, 1938, ranges from Bahía Magdalena to Puerto Vallarta (Bahía Banderas). In the Gulf it has been collected at Puerto Libertad, Sonora (the only known record from the mainland side), and from Cabo San Lucas (to depths of 225 ft or 69 m) north to Isla Angel de la Guarda. *L. pulchellus* can be easily distinguished from *L. dalli* by its greater number of blue bands (13 or more versus no more than nine in *L. dalli*). Background coloration of *L. pulchellus* is pale reddish pink. It is closely related to the larger zebra goby, *L. zebra* (Gilbert, 1890), mainly a California species, which has not been recorded from the Gulf of California. Ginsburg (1938b) and Eckert (1974) separate *L. zebra* from *L. pulchellus* by subtle but consistent color pattern differences in banding and spotting. Another species of *Lythrypnus* has been collected from deep water (70 fathoms or 128 m) in the central Gulf and is being studied by D. F. Hoese.

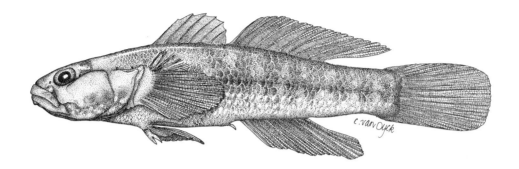

# PANAMIC FRILLFIN, mapo
## *Bathygobius ramosus* Ginsburg, 1947

**Illustrated specimen.** Adult male, 4.3 in. (108 mm), by Chris van Dyck; grows to about 4½ in. (114 mm).

**Distinguishing characteristics.** This is the largest, most robust-bodied, rocky-shore goby in the Gulf of California. It has six spines in the first dorsal fin, pelvic fins that are completely united into a strong sucking disc, and large ctenoid scales over the entire body, including belly, chest, and nape. The head is naked. It is easily distinguished from all other Gulf gobies by noting the upper five pectoral-fin rays that are almost completely free from connecting membranes; thus its "frillfin" appearance. The second and third rays (from the top) usually fork two or three times. Coloration varies from light to dark but is usually overall drab olive-green to brown with a series of dark spots (often diffuse and irregular) along the midside. These spots may extend upward as a series of dark bars that form saddles on the upper half of the body. Often there is a dark spot behind the eye. D. VI + 9–10; A. 9–10; $P_1$. 17–21 (19–21, usually 20, in Gulf populations).

**Distribution.** The genus *Bathygobius* is circumtropical in distribution and contains a number of poorly defined species. *B. ramosus* ranges from Bahía Magdalena and the Gulf of California to northern Peru and is the most abundant rocky intertidal goby in the tropical eastern Pacific. In the Gulf it has been found as far north as San Felipe, B.C.N., and Puerto Peñasco, Sonora, but is common only in the lower portion (Cape region and Mazatlán). Its occurrence in the central and upper Gulf is sporadic.

**Ecology.** The Panamic frillfin prefers to inhabit high, sandy-bottom tide pools along rocky coasts. The Gulf, especially the upper portion, appears to be marginally suitable for this species. Small individuals are sometimes common at Puerto Peñasco but then disappear or become rare (Miles, 1974). It appears that winter low sea temperatures in the northern Gulf prevent *B. ramosus* from becoming established (Thomson and Lehner, 1976).

**Related species.** Ginsburg (1947) recognized four species (and a number of subspecies) of

*Bathygobius* in the tropical eastern Pacific, distinguishing them mainly by differences in numbers of scales and pectoral rays and certain proportional measurements. The widespread *B. ramosus,* however, (with its four nominal subspecies), is the only member of that genus in the Gulf. The other eastern Pacific species are *B. arundelii* (Garman) from Clipperton Island, *B. lineatus* (Jenyns), with two nominal subspecies, from the Islas Galápagos and Isla Lobos de Afuera, Peru, and *B. andrei* (Sauvage), with two nominal subspecies, from Costa Rica to Ecuador (see Brittan, 1966, for a brief comparison and photographs of *B. andrei* and *B. ramosus* from Costa Rica). *B. ramosus* is similar to the Atlantic *B. soporator* (Valenciennes) with which it was often confused in the earlier literature. These two species occur on opposite sides of the Isthmus of Panama. Under certain conditions in captivity they will spawn and produce hybrids, but *B. ramosus* and the closely related *B. andrei* (which sometimes occurs with *B. ramosus* in the same Pacific tide pools) will not interbreed. Evidently behavioral reproductive isolating mechanisms have completely evolved between the coexisting (sympatric) species of *Bathygobius* but only partly between the geographically isolated (allopatric) species (Rubinoff and Rubinoff, 1971).

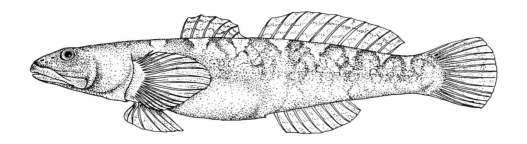

# SHORTJAW MUDSUCKER, chupalodo chico
## *Gillichthys seta* (Ginsburg, 1938)

**Illustrated specimen.** Adult, 2.6 in. (65 mm), by Tor Hansen; grows to about 3½ in. (89 mm).

**Distinguishing characteristics.** The only two species in the genus *Gillichthys* have elongated upper jaws (maxillae), completely united pelvic fins, usually six (sometimes five) spines in the first dorsal fin, and many rows of small scales that cover the body (weakly ctenoid in juveniles, cycloid and embedded in adults). The shortjaw mudsucker, *G. seta,* can be distinguished from other Gulf rocky-shore gobies by its elongated upper jaw which reaches to the preopercle in adults (below the eye in juveniles). The common name "shortjaw mudsucker" is proposed to distinguish adult *G. seta* from adult *G. mirabilis,* the longjaw mudsucker; its extremely elongated upper jaw reaches well beyond the preopercle (and sometimes as far as the pectoral fin base in large individuals). Adult *G. seta,* however, are similar to subadult *G. mirabilis* but have a more depressed head and slightly more pointed snout; they can be separated only by subtle morphological differences (see Barlow, 1961a): the tiny uppermost pectoral ray of *G. seta* is usually partly free (one-quarter to one-half its length) from its connecting membrane, whereas in *G. mirabilis* all pectoral rays are completely bound by membranes; *G. mirabilis* has an inconspicuous narrow strip of scales on the midline of the nape (in front of the dorsal fin) that is usually absent in *G. seta* (this can be determined by scraping with a needle). The sensory papillae on the head are small, crowded, and more numerous in *G. mirabilis,* compared with *G. seta,* in which they are large, distinct, and fewer (see Barlow, 1961a, Figure 1).

Background coloration of *G. seta* is light brown on the sides, and yellowish on the belly. Often patches of darker brown pigment on the sides alternate with patches of pale yellow. Sometimes there are about six irregular, diffuse blackish dorsal saddles. D. V–VI + 10–11; A. 9–11; $P_1$. 20–23.

219

**Distribution.** Endemic to the Gulf, the shortjaw mudsucker ranges from the northernmost rocky reefs (Punta Borrascoso) to Guaymas, Sonora, and from San Felipe to Punta San Francisquito, B.C.N. It is a common and often abundant high intertidal goby along the rocky shores of the upper Gulf.

**Ecology.** The geographically restricted and smaller *G. seta* probably evolved from the widely distributed and larger *G. mirabilis* by adapting to a unique habitat with a vigorous physical regime. Both species, though ecologically separated, are found in the upper Gulf region. *G. mirabilis* is a burrow dweller in intertidal soft bottoms (usually mud flats) in coastal sloughs, lagoons, and estuaries (esteros). *G. seta* is associated with rocky habitats and is usually found high in the intertidal zone in small tide pools and their associated small seepage streams. In the spring, however, juveniles of both species are sometimes found together in ecological transition areas such as rocky outcrops or channels near the mouths of esteros.

Barlow (1961a) hypothesized that *G. seta* is a "neotenic" form that evolved from a *G. mirabilis*-like goby in this physically rigorous high intertidal habitat. Chromosomal analyses support Barlow's contention (Chen and Ebeling, 1971). These two gobies are physiologically as well as morphologically similar (Barlow, 1961b). In times of environmental stress both physiologically tolerant (temperature, salinity, $O_2$) species of *Gillichthys* can breathe air (Barlow, 1961b; Todd and Ebeling, 1966).

*G. seta* feeds on small crabs, amphipods, and polychaete worms and seems to prefer tide pools with bottoms of finer (siltier) sands than do other Gulf rocky intertidal gobies (Miles, 1974).

**Related species.** The other *Gillichthys* in the Gulf is the previously discussed larger (6 in., or 152 mm, in the Gulf; 8 in., or 203 mm, in California) longjaw mudsucker, *G. mirabilis* Cooper, 1864, which occurs in coastal slough, lagoon, and estuarine habitats. It ranges from north of San Francisco, California (Tomales Bay), to Bahía Magdalena. Disjunct populations occur in the Gulf from Mulege, B.C.S., and Bahía Agiabampo, Sonora-Sinaloa, north to the Colorado River delta at the head of the Gulf. It has also been introduced into the inland Salton Sea, California (Walker, 1961), but that population now shows a number of aberrant characters (see Barlow, 1963).

# FAMILY ACANTHURIDAE
## Surgeonfishes (Peces cirujanos)

The surgeonfishes are all strongly compressed reef fishes with small mouths (Figure 94). They are easily recognized by their bony knobs or the forward-directed retractible spines on their caudal peduncles (except the moorish idol). These sharp caudal peduncle spines can be extended like the blade of a switchblade knife and can inflict deep slash wounds on potential predators. Sometimes the spines are fixed and immovable.

Surgeonfishes are among the most efficient herbivorous fishes on the reef, for many are well adapted for grazing on algae covering rocks. In certain areas their flesh is poisonous (ciguatera) to humans when eaten. They are suspected of being intermediary links in the transfer of ciguatera toxins through the marine food chain.

Only three genera and six species of surgeonfishes are present in the Gulf. This family is depauperate in the western Atlantic and eastern Pacific but fairly speciose in the Indo-Pacific (Hawaii has four genera and 22 species of surgeonfish). Worldwide, 7 genera and 77 species are currently recognized. In the Gulf they are common only in its lower portion from La Paz to Cabo San Lucas, although one species (*Prionurus punctatus*) ranges as far north as Puerto Lobos, Sonora. The ornate moorish idol (*Zanclus canescens*) has recently been placed in this family, although it lacks caudal peduncle knobs or spines.

*References.* Barlow (1974); Randall (1955, 1956, 1960); Winterbottom (1971).

Figure 94  A school of convict tangs, *Acanthurus triostegus*. In the Gulf this surgeonfish is found only in the lower region. (Photograph courtesy of Ed Janss.)

221

# YELLOWTAIL SURGEONFISH, cochinito
## *Prionurus punctatus* Gill, 1862

**Illustrated specimen.** Juvenile, 5.7 in. 145 mm, by Alex Kerstitch; see also Plate 31; grows to about 2 ft (0.6 m).

**Distinguishing characteristics.** The yellowtail surgeonfish can be distinguished from other Gulf surgeonfishes by its three stout whitish knobs on the caudal peduncle and bright yellow caudal fin. Its strongly compressed body is covered with round blackish spots on a gray background. Juveniles have two color phases: one brilliant yellow overall and the other colored like the adult. Males and females are colored alike. D. VII or VIII, 25; A. III, 23.

**Distribution.** This species ranges from the upper Gulf (Puerto Lobos) as far south as El Salvador and the Islas Revillagigedo. It is more common along the rocky shores of Baja California in the central and lower Gulf than in Sonora.

**Ecology.** This large species is the only common Gulf surgeonfish. Like other surgeonfishes, *P. punctatus* is a schooling fish with diurnal habits. Because of its herbivorous diet, this fish usually hovers over shallow rocky reefs at depths between 20 and 40 ft (6 to 12 m) and is seldom seen at depths greater than 100 ft (30 m). Juveniles in the yellow color phase appear similar to the Indo-west Pacific yellow tang, *Zebrasoma flavescens* Bennett. In captivity one small yellow juvenile reverted to the spotted phase one week after it was collected.

**Related species.** Four species of *Acanthurus*, all widely distributed in the Indo-west Pacific, have been collected in the Cape region of the lower Gulf. *A. triostegus* (Linnaeus, 1758) ranges from Bahía Los Frailes to Panama and the far-offshore islands in the tropical eastern Pacific (see Figure 94). Called the convict tang,

*A. triostegus* can be easily distinguished from all Gulf surgeonfishes by its color pattern of about six thin dark bars over a creamy yellowish background. A subspecies, the manini, *A. t. sandvicensis* Streets, is the most abundant surgeonfish in the Hawaiian Islands. The purple surgeonfish, *A. xanthopterus* Valenciennes, 1835, ranges widely from the lower Gulf to South Africa, including the Islas Galápagos. This surgeonfish is colored a uniform dark purplish gray but can be identified by the broad yellowish border along the edge of the pectoral fins. The goldrimmed surgeonfish,

*A. glaucopareius* Cuvier, 1829, has been seen occasionally in the Cape region. This species, whose pectorals are uniformly colored, can be recognized by bands of bright yellow along the bases of the dorsal and anal fins on an overall bluish-black body. The achilles tang, *Acanthurus achilles* Shaw, 1803, has been sighted in the Cabo San Lucas region (Kerstitch). This strikingly colored tang has a large, red-orange, tearshaped spot covering its caudal peduncle spine. It is an Indo-west Pacific species found in Hawaii but has not been previously recorded in the eastern Pacific.

# MOORISH IDOL, **idolo moro**
## *Zanclus canescens* (Linnaeus, 1758)

**Photograph.** Adult, by Alex Kerstitch; grows to about 9 in. (229 mm).

**Distinguishing characteristics.** This ornate Indo-west Pacific fish can be distinguished from any other Gulf reef fish by its characteristic shape and color pattern. The eyes and protruding snout are elaborately lined with black and brown. Adding to its elegant shape, the tip of its dorsal fin extends into a long filament. *Z. canescens* resembles butterflyfishes in body shape and color pattern, but the structure of its mouth and head is more like that exhibited by the surgeonfishes. D. VII, 39–42; A. III, 31–33.

**Distribution.** Within the Gulf and eastern Pacific, the moorish idol ranges from La Paz to Cabo San Lucas and from Isla San Ignacio Farallon to Panama, including all the far-offshore islands. It is widely distributed throughout the tropical Indo-west Pacific and is one of the commonest reef fishes in Hawaii.

**Ecology.** The moorish idol is a coral reef fish found at depths of 5 to 40 ft (1.5 to 12 m) in the Gulf. It usually appears in groups of two or three individuals and is rarely observed alone. At Cabo San Lucas it often accompanies the barberfish which aggregates at cleaning stations (see *Heniochus nigrirostris* account). The moorish idol, however, does not join the barberfish in its cleaning activities.

This species is a popular aquarium fish because of its elegant beauty, but the adults are difficult to maintain in captivity. Juveniles are rarely seen in the Gulf or elsewhere. They differ from the adult by having a spine at the corner of the mouth. The original description of *Z. canescens* by Linnaeus was based on a juvenile specimen. Linnaeus also named and described the adult (*Z. cornutus*), believing it to be another species (see Strasburg, 1962).

# FAMILY GOBIESOCIDAE
## Clingfishes (Chupapiedras)

Most clingfishes are small specialized fishes well adapted to living in the intertidal zones of rocky shores. Their pelvic fins are modified into a strong sucking disc which they use to attach to cobbles and boulders or to cling to steep cliff faces in areas with strong wave surge. The ventral surface of the discs have flattened adhesive papillae, the numbers and patterns of which are useful generic and often specific characters (Figure 95). The four pelvic rays form the lateral edge of the disc and the last ray is attached by a membrane to the lower portion of the pectoral-fin base. They have a single dorsal fin, lack scales and fin spines, and secrete copious amounts of mucus. Their usually broad depressed heads and tapering bodies give them a tadpolelike appearance. Some are especially resistant to dessication and, if kept moist, are able to survive several days out of water. The gobiesocids should not be confused with the gobies (family Gobiidae), most of which also have united pelvic fins but are not related to clingfishes.

About 100 species in 33 genera make up the family, which is distributed widely in tropical and temperate waters. Four genera and 11 species have been recorded from the Gulf of California.

*References.* Briggs (1955, 1960, 1969); Briggs and Miller (1960); Critchlow (1972); Eger (1971); Gollub (1974).

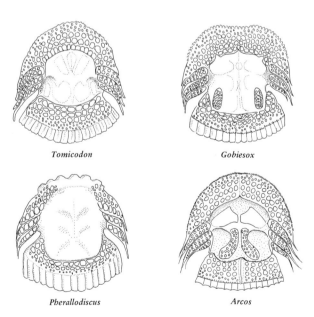

Figure 95   Pelvic disc diagrams of the four genera of Gulf clingfishes. The pattern of flattened papillae on the ventral surface of the disc is diagnostic for each genus. (Redrawn from Briggs, 1955.)

225

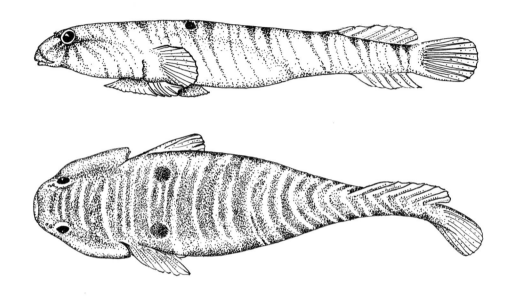

# SONORA CLINGFISH, chupapiedra de Sonora
## *Tomicodon humeralis* (Gilbert, 1890)

**Illustrated specimens.** Adult, 1.8 in. (45 mm) (dorsal view), and adult, 2.4 in. (60 mm) (lateral view), by Tor Hansen; grows to about $3\frac{1}{4}$ in. (83 mm).

**Distinguishing characteristics.** The Sonora clingfish can be distinguished from other Gulf species of *Tomicodon* by its distinctive color pattern of light diagonal stripes, especially apparent along the posterior sides, and 17 to 19 pectoral-fin rays. A pair of dark dorsal spots lie behind the head. D. 8 (8–9); A. 7 (6–7); $P_1$. 18 (17–19); caudal 9–10.

**Distribution.** A Gulf of California endemic, *T. humeralis* is the commonest clingfish in the upper Gulf. Its Sonoran range extends from Punta Borrascoso to Guaymas, and in Baja California it is found from San Felipe to Cabo San Lucas.

**Ecology.** *T. humeralis* is the commonest clingfish on the Puerto Peñasco intertidal reefs. Mainly restricted here to the upper and midintertidal zone, this clingfish may be found attached to the undersides of rocks in little or no standing water. According to Eger (1971), this species is highly resistant to exposure and temperature extremes. Experimentally, it can survive more than two days out of water (if kept moist) and can tolerate water temperatures ranging from 43 to 98°F (6 to 37°C). *T. humeralis* also respires aerially by taking in bubbles of air and holding them under its gill covers. The skin secretes a copious amount of mucus which protects it from dessication.

Breeding activity begins in late spring or early summer. The male, considerably larger than the female, guards the nest of adhesive eggs which are stuck tightly to the undersides of large boulders. Several females may spawn with a single male and assist him in guarding the nest and in secreting mucus over the eggs during low tide.

The Sonora clingfish is a diurnal predator that feeds mainly on barnacles, limpets, and small crustaceans. This clingfish exhibits a tidal activity rhythm; it is active during daylight high tides and inactive during all low tides (Gollub, 1974).

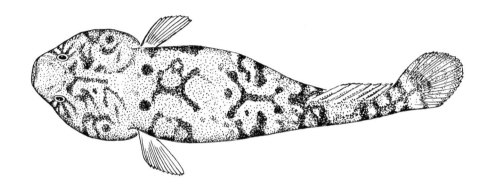

# CORTEZ CLINGFISH, chupapiedra de Cortés
## *Tomicodon boehlkei* Briggs, 1955

**Illustrated specimen.** Adult, 2.5 in. (63 mm), by Tor Hansen; the illustrated specimen is about the maximum size attained by the species.

**Distinguishing characteristics.** *Tomicodon boehlkei* can be distinguished from the similar Sonora clingfish, *T. humeralis,* by color pattern and fin-ray counts. *T. boehlkei* lacks the distinctive diagonal striping of *T. humeralis*; instead it has elongated blackish markings along its posterior sides. Its back is often covered with reddish saddles and fine black vermiculations. A pair of dark dorsal spots lies behind the head but they are smaller than those of *T. humeralis*. *T. boehlkei* usually has more pectoral rays, and fewer dorsal and caudal rays than *T. humeralis*. D. 7 (6–8); A. 6–7; $P_1$. 20 (19–22); caudal 8–9.

**Distribution.** A Gulf endemic, the Cortez clingfish is the widest ranging species of *Tomicodon* in the Gulf. It is found from Puerto Peñasco to Isla San Ignacio Farallon and Cabo San Lucas, and is the commonest clingfish in the central Gulf.

**Ecology.** Unlike *T. humeralis,* this species seems to prefer large boulders and vertical rocky outcroppings to which it clings near the surface of the water. It is more active than *T. humeralis* and may be seen darting quickly along rock surfaces in the wave-wash zone. Its intertidal range is broader than that of *T. humeralis*; it is commonly found subtidally, whereas *T. humeralis* is rarely found below the midintertidal zone. We have never collected *T. boehlkei* on the platform reefs at Puerto Peñasco and Briggs (1955) reports only two specimens from Punta Peñasco. However, it can be found at Isla San Jorge about 20 miles (32 km) southeast of Puerto Peñasco, where the intertidal zone is more steeply sloped than the nearby mainland areas.

Physiologically, *T. boehlkei* is significantly less tolerant to extremes of various environmental factors than *T. humeralis* (see Eger, 1971). Little is known about the ecology of *T. boehlkei* other than the studies by Critchlow (1972) on resource utilization by this species.

**Related species.** Three other species of the genus *Tomicodon* occur in the Gulf. The zebra clingfish, *T. zebra* (Jordan and Gilbert, 1882), which ranges from Guaymas to Oaxaca, Mexico, is closely related to *T. boehlkei*. It may be separated from this species by noting the large dermal flap on the margin of the anterior nostril, the height of which is about equal to the distance between the anterior and posterior nostrils (the dermal flap of *T. boehlkei* is quite small—only slightly greater in height than its nostril diameter). Also, the anus of *T. zebra* is closer to the rear margin of the disc than to the anal fin origin (the anus is closer to the anal fin origin than to the disc in other Gulf *Tomicodon*). As in *T. boehlkei* and *T. humeralis*, *T. zebra* has a pair of dark dorsal spots. The blackstripe clingfish, *T. myersi* Briggs, 1955, recorded from Guaymas to Isla Gorgona, Colombia, is a small (about 28 mm SL = 1.1 in.) rare clingfish that lacks the pair of dorsal spots; the dorsal fin, however, has a heavy black stripe. The caudal fin exhibits dark dorsal and ventral margins. It can best be distinguished from other Gulf species of *Tomicodon* by the elongate papillae (twice as long as the others) of the innermost row of the anterior portion of the disc. This species is usually found in the wave-wash zone of exposed rocky points. The rosy clingfish, *T. eos* (Jordan and Gilbert, 1882), ranges from Guaymas to Oaxaca, Mexico. It is the only Gulf-occurring species of *Tomicodon* that has equal numbers of incisors in the front of both jaws (all others have more incisors in the front of the upper jaw) and usually more pectoral fin rays (21 to 23) than the others. It is a relatively robust species with as large a dermal flap at the margin of the anterior nostril as *T. zebra*. In life this species is colored a bright rosy red. Briggs (1955) recognized two subspecies, *T. eos eos* and *T. eos rhadinus*; only the former ranges into the Gulf (from Guaymas to Jalisco).

Critchlow (1972) notes that both *T. myersi* and *T. eos* coexist as obligate associates of the pocket-forming sea urchin *Echinometra vanbrundti* Agassiz. *T. eos* is a highly aggressive species that drives away all conspecifics and certain congeners (*T. boehlkei* and *T. zebra*) from its sea urchin territory but tolerates *T. myersi*. Critchlow speculates that the smaller size, lack of intraspecific aggression, and cryptic behavior patterns of *T. myersi* enable this species to coexist with the larger, more aggressive *T. eos*.

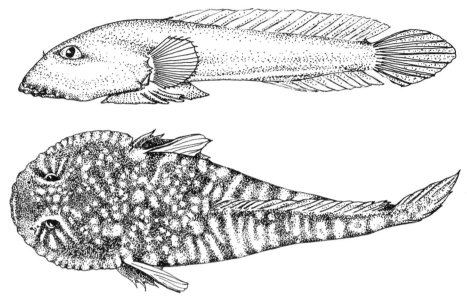

# TADPOLE CLINGFISH, pez renacuajo
## *Gobiesox pinniger* Gilbert, 1890

**Illustrated specimens.** Adult, 2.6 in. (65 mm) (dorsal view), and adult, 3.7 in. (93 mm) (lateral view), by Tor Hansen; maximum size to about 4 in. (102 mm).

**Distinguishing characteristics.** Clingfishes of the genus *Gobiesox* may be recognized by their broad, depressed heads and large discs with a characteristic pattern of flattened papillae on the ventral surface (see Figure 95). *G. pinniger* may be readily distinguished from other Gulf clingfishes by its long dorsal fin (16 to 19 rays) and lobelike papillae on the head and upper lip margin. Also, the anus is positioned about midway between the rear margin of the disc and the origin of the anal fin (the anus is closer to the anal fin in other Gulf *Gobiesox* except *G. adustus,* in which it is closer to the disc). A conspicuous dark stripe usually passes through the eye onto the snout and sometimes a black bar extends vertically from the eye. In life this species often appears very black dorsally, although preserved specimens are often pale. D. 18 (16–19); A. 10 (10–11); P$_1$. 23 (22–23).

**Distribution.** *G. pinniger* is endemic to the Gulf of California; it ranges throughout the Gulf from Roca Consag to Cabo San Lucas and from Puerto Peñasco to Guaymas. It is a common midintertidal to subtidal clingfish in the upper and central Gulf but becomes less abundant farther south.

**Ecology.** Perhaps the most adaptable clingfish in the Gulf, *G. pinniger* occupies a great number of habitats but seems to prefer a cobble beach rather than a flat reef platform (as does *Tomicodon humeralis*) or rock walls (as does *T. boehlkei*). It overlaps with *T. humeralis* in the midintertidal zone but lacks this species' tolerance to dessication and temperature extremes to compete successfully with this species in the upper intertidal zone. We have observed *G. pinniger* feeding on the eggs and young of *T. humeralis,* which may contribute considerably to the skewed distribution of *T. humeralis* toward the upper intertidal zone.

**Related species.** Three smaller species of *Gobiesox* occur in the Gulf. The smoothlip clingfish, *Gobiesox schultzi* Briggs, 1951, common in the Guaymas area, ranges from Isla Tiburón throughout the central Gulf and south to Isla Ceralvo. It can be distinguished from other Gulf species of *Gobiesox* by its smooth upper-lip margin which lacks lobes or papillae. In life *G. schultzi* has a light rose-colored body covered with small dark spots. The Panamic clingfish, *Gobiesox adustus* Jordan and Gilbert, 1882, is present north of Bahía San Agustin (Morro Colorado) to Ecuador and has the greatest range of any Pacific species of *Gobiesox*, although it is rare in our reef collections. This species, like *G. pinniger,* has well developed fleshy lobes (papillae) on the upper lip but a much shorter dorsal fin (11 rays). The dorsal and lateral surfaces are covered with closely set dark spots interrupted by five to six light irregular bars posteriorly. The bearded clingfish, *Gobiesox papillifer* Gilbert, 1890, like *G. adustus,* is uncommon in our reef collections. It ranges from San Pedro, California (only one specimen), to Isla Tiburón and south to Panama. This light-colored, sand-loving species has many more papillae on the head than any other Gulf clingfish. Usually there are three small papillae at the center of the upper lip and numerous papillae on the head, some forming fingerlike projections. Briggs (1955) recognized two subspecies, *G. papillifer papillifer* (northern) and *G. papillifer microspilus* (Panama).

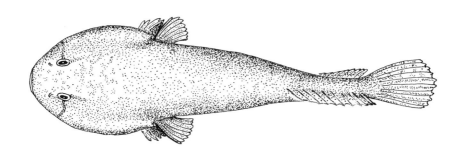

# FRAILDISC CLINGFISH, pez discofrágil
## *Pherallodiscus funebris* Gilbert, 1890

**Illustrated specimen.** Adult, 3.4 in. (85 mm), by Tor Hansen; grows to about 4 in. (102 mm).

**Distinguishing characteristics.** A distinctive disc pattern (no papillae on the midanterior margin of the disc) and a patch of conical teeth at the front of the upper jaw separate this species from all other Gulf clingfishes. *Pherallodiscus funebris* superficially resembles *Gobiesox pinniger* but has a shorter dorsal fin (10 to 11 rays) and overall dark brown coloration without a distinctive pattern. D. 11 (10–11); A. 7 (7–8); $P_1$. 19 (17–20).

**Distribution.** The fraildisc clingfish is endemic to the Gulf of California; it ranges from Puerto Peñasco and San Felipe to Guaymas and La Paz.

**Ecology.** Limited to the upper and midintertidal zones of rocky beaches, this clingfish seems to prefer a pebble-gravel beach, where it lives under small boulders. It is the hardiest of all Gulf clingfishes but is paradoxically uncommon at Puerto Peñasco and Puerto Lobos, where the tides are extreme and where *Tomicodon humeralis* is the dominant clingfish. Experimentally, an individual survived four days out of water in a moist chamber (Eger, 1971). Its rate of water loss, less than that of *T. humeralis*, may be due to a thicker epidermis and larger, better developed mucous glands.

**Related species.** The rockwall clingfish, *Arcos erythrops* (Jordan and Gilbert, 1882), also the only member of the genus in the Gulf, is distributed from Guaymas to Oaxaca, and along the central and lower Gulf coast of Baja California. It can be distinguished from all Gulf clingfishes by a pair of arcshaped pads of papillae in the midposterior region of the disc (see Figure 95). Also, *A. erythrops* has a wide, depressed head and a large disc in proportion to its slender, tapering body, an adaptation to living on vertical rock walls in heavy surge zones. In life it has three to four dark bands on a reddish background. The bands fade after death.

# FAMILY BALISTIDAE
## Triggerfishes and filefishes (Peces puerco)

Balistids are a group of rather bizarre-looking fishes belonging to a highly specialized order noted for its unique defensive adaptations. Included with the triggerfishes in the family Balistidae are the filefishes (Monocanthidae and Aluteridae) which differ in minor characters. Filefishes normally have two dorsal spines; triggerfishes have three. They all have a first dorsal spine that locks when erect but can be released by a trigger mechanism formed by the second spine. This enables these fishes, when threatened, to wedge themselves tightly into crevices, thus making it difficult for a predator to get them out.

Their skin is covered with large platelike scales (triggerfishes) or small, rough-textured scales that feel velvety to the touch (filefishes). Their jaw teeth resemble humanoid incisors and their strong jaws and teeth are capable of crushing mollusks and sea urchins. Many are fearless carnivores and virtually no prey is safe from their attack. Triggerfishes are one of the few fishes that will prey on large, spiny sea urchins, venomous fireworms, and even the exceptionally spiny and venomous crown-of-thorns starfish (*Acanthaster*).

The body shape of balistids is characteristic throughout the group and their pelvic fins have been reduced to rudiments. They have often been considered poisonous to

Figure 96   A school of finescale triggerfish, *Balistes polylepis*. This triggerfish is abundant in the upper and central Gulf. (Photograph by Alex Kerstitch.)

232

eat, but this reputation is largely undeserved for their flesh is quite palatable. In regions in which ciguatera (tropical fish poisoning) occurs, however, they have been known to concentrate this toxin in their flesh like many other species of reef fishes. Fortunately, ciguatera is extremely rare in the eastern Pacific and one can eat Gulf triggerfishes or filefishes without fear of being poisoned.

At least five genera and five species of balistids occur in the Gulf (Figure 96), although occasional records of more southern species may be expected. Worldwide, there are more than 120 species in about 19 genera.

*References.* Berry and Baldwin (1966); Berry and Vogele (1961); Randall (1964) Winterbottom (1974).

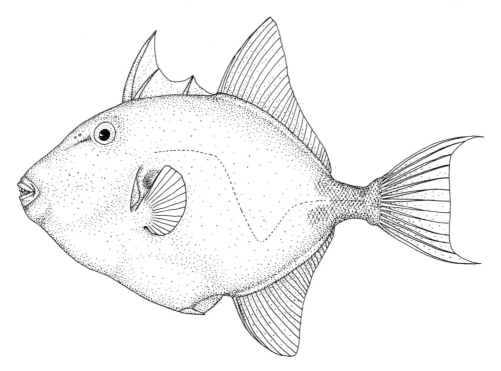

# FINESCALE TRIGGERFISH, cochi
*Balistes polylepis* Steindachner, 1876

**Illustrated specimen.** Juvenile, 6.7 in. (170 mm), by Tor Hansen; see also Figure 96; grows to 2½ ft (0.76 m).

**Distinguising characteristics.** This moderately deep-bodied triggerfish can be distinguished from other eastern Pacific triggerfishes by its deeply notched teeth and the absence of longitudinal ridges on the posterior part of the body. Fine scales and a drab pattern also distinguish this species from other Gulf triggerfish. Body coloration is variable from olive-brown to gray to light blue-gray. D. III + 26–28; A. 24–26; $P_1$. 13–15.

**Distribution.** Wide-ranging from northern California to Chile, the finescale triggerfish occurs abundantly in the upper and central Gulf but becomes less common in the lower. It is the only abundant triggerfish in the Gulf.

**Ecology.** This ubiquitous species occurs over rocky and sandy bottoms, inshore and offshore. Adults tend to stay close to the protection of reefs but juveniles roam over open sand, hiding in broken shells and among debris. Aggregations of adults occur over rocky areas during the day but disperse at night; individuals hide by wedging themselves in crevices. They graze on rock surfaces and crunch mollusks, sea urchins, and crustaceans with their strong jaws and teeth. In sandy areas triggerfish feed on polychaete worms and other burrowers by "blowing" a jet of water through their mouths to uncover their prey (Hobson, 1965a). One of the most versatile predators of the reef community, they feed on a wide variety of animals, including some venomous species that other predators avoid.

In July and August large aggregations mingle close to the bottom, hovering near guarded nests. The eggs are laid in clusters at the bottom of shallow depressions ringed by small rocks. These nests are guarded by females (Strand, 1977). If the female is disturbed and leaves the nest, swarms of other triggerfish will converge over it and eat the eggs.

# ORANGESIDE TRIGGERFISH, cochino
## *Sufflamen verres* (Gilbert and Starks, 1904)

**Illustrated specimen.** Young male, 5.6 in. (142 mm), by Alex Kerstitch; see also Plate 31; grows to about 15 in. (380 mm).

**Distinguishing characteristics.** A distinctive adult coloration distinguishes this species from all other Gulf triggerfishes. The brownish gray body has a large, distinct orange side blotch that extends from the caudal peduncle to the base of the pectoral fins and a line that runs from the posterior angle of the lips to below the gill slit. Females are less brightly hued. The smallest juveniles (12 mm) are dark on the upper body and light on the lower. Spots appear along the base of the dorsal fin and elongate into an irregular series of broken lines in juveniles up to 75 mm (see Berry and Baldwin, 1966). Larger juveniles are often light tan on the top with dark sides but can change color rapidly. D. III + 30–33, A. 27–30; $P_1$. 14–15.

**Distribution.** This triggerfish is known from Cedros Island, Baja California, to Salinas, Ecuador. In the Gulf it is found primarily in the Cape region, although it has been observed as far north as Isla San Pedro Martir. It is found along all the far-offshore eastern tropical Pacific islands.

**Ecology.** Unlike the finescale triggerfish, *B. polylepis,* this species tends to be less gregarious and rarely aggregates in large numbers. It feeds on a wide variety of animals such as crustaceans, sea urchins, mollusks, and worms. Like *B. polylepis,* it may seek food buried in the sand by blowing jets of water and exposing its prey. At night it will find shelter among rocks by wedging itself into small crevices (Hobson, 1965a). At Guaymas it seems to prefer deeper water (50 to 100 ft, or 15 to 30 m), but in the lower Gulf it is abundant at depths of 10 to 50 ft (3 to 15 m).

**Related species.** The blunthead triggerfish, *Pseudobalistes naufragium* (Jordan and Starks, 1895), which occurs uncommonly in the Gulf (see Figure 97), ranges from Guaymas to Ecuador. The largest of the Gulf triggerfishes, it can be distinguished from the other two species by its lack of scales around the snout. Its coloration varies from light bluish gray to brownish gray with four or five dark bars on its sides. This tropical species has been collected as far north as Bahía San Quintin on the outer coast of Baja California.

The scrawled filefish, *Alutera scripta* (Osbeck, 1765), is occasionally encountered in the central and lower Gulf. *A. scripta* is distributed throughout the world in tropical seas but is uncommon in the Gulf. The body coloration of this large filefish (to 3 ft, or 1 m) varies from light bluish gray to olive-brown, with bright blue-green scrawled markings and spots

on its sides, to a solid dark brown (see Plate 30e).

The vagabond filefish, *Cantherines dumerilii* (Hollard, 1854), was collected recently at Los Frailes by Linn Montgomery (the specimen is in the UCLA Fish Collection). This Indo-west Pacific filefish is the widest ranging species in the genus (from Africa to the eastern Pacific, including Japan, Hawaii, and Islas Revill-agigedo). It can be identified by its two pair of prominent forward-curving spines on the caudal peduncle. In life it is grayish brown with a slight yellowish cast ventrally and about 12 faint vertical dark brown bands (Randall, 1964).

Figure 97   The blunthead triggerfish, *Pseudobalistes naufragium*. This robust triggerfish is uncommon in the Gulf but well known farther south. (Photograph by Alex Kerstitch.)

# FAMILY OSTRACIONTIDAE
## Trunkfishes (Peces cofre)

The trunkfishes, often mistaken for puffers, are literally encased in a hard dermal carapace not unlike the shell of a turtle. Only the fins, mouth, and eyes are movable as these curious little fishes scull over the reef propelled by their pectoral fins and fleshy tail (see Figure 98). Some have sharp spines which give these slow-moving fishes additional protection from predation. As an added defense, trunkfishes have evolved a toxic mucous secretion of the skin that is released only under duress. All trunkfishes are believed to produce this toxic stress secretion, but that of the smooth-carapace boxfishes is the most potent (Thomson, 1968).

Only two species of trunkfish occur in the Gulf and one is a wide-ranging pelagic species that is rarely seen. The other is a wide-ranging Indo-Pacific species that is uncommonly seen in the Cabo San Lucas area. Worldwide, there are about 24 species in 12 genera.

*References.* Boylan and Scheuer (1967); Brock (1956); Fraser-Brunner (1935, 1940); Halstead (1970); Randall (1972); Thomson (1964, 1968, 1969).

Figure 98   A female Pacific boxfish, *Ostracion meleagris*. (Photograph by D. A. Thomson of the Hawaiian subspecies *O. m. camurum.*)

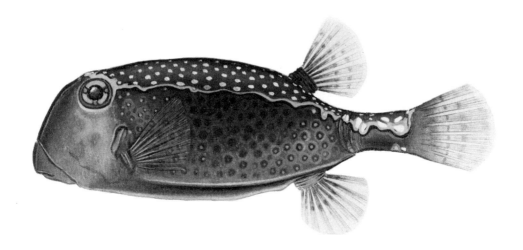

# PACIFIC BOXFISH, pez caja
## *Ostracion meleagris* Shaw, 1796

**Illustrated specimen.** Adult male, 6.4 in. (161 mm), by Alex Kerstitch; see also Plate 32 and Figure 98; grows to about 7 in. (179 mm).

**Distinguishing characteristics.** The Pacific boxfish shows such striking sexual dimorphism that the male (above) had been described as a distinct species. Females and juveniles are uniformly dark bluish brown, covered with white spots (Figure 98). Randall (1972) recognizes a Hawaiian subspecies (*O. m. camurum*). D. 9; A. 9.

**Distribution.** This Indo-west Pacific species ranges widely from East Africa to Panama. In the Gulf we have collected it only at Cabo San Lucas.

**Ecology.** The Pacific boxfish is usually the dominant *Ostracion* species wherever it occurs. It grazes on algae and sessile invertebrates in quiet shallow waters over reefs. It is a slow-swimming, nonaggressive fish that probably

has few enemies because of its ability to secrete a toxin from its skin glands, called "ostracitoxin" (Thomson, 1964), which is poisonous to fishes and other gill-breathing animals. This toxin is a choline chloride ester of a fatty acid (Boylan and Scheuer, 1967); the biological nature of the toxic secretions of the Hawaiian subspecies has been studied by Thomson (1969).

**Related species.** The only other trunkfish recorded from the eastern Pacific is the spiny boxfish, *Lactoria diaphanus* (Bloch and Schneider, 1801), an Indo-west Pacific pelagic species occasionally found in the Cabo San Lucas area (with one record from San Felipe) and from Santa Barbara, California, to the Islas Galápagos. This pale brown boxfish has a "horn" over each eye, a single dorsal spine, small paired spines on the dorsal and ventral ridges of the carapace, and a long tail.

# FAMILY TETRAODONTIDAE
## Puffers (Tamborines, botetes)

When seen swimming over the reef, puffers resemble trunkfishes superficially (see Figure 99), but when collected and handled they may blow themselves up like balloons; this characteristic makes it difficult to mistake them for any other fish. Their skins are covered with tiny prickles that give them little protection, but they, too, have a highly toxic mucous secretion called tetrodotoxin that protects them from predators. This toxin is chemically unrelated to the trunkfish secretion (ostracitoxin) and is one of the most poisonous substances known. Puffer flesh, however, is a gourmet's delight and is widely eaten in Japan, where only specially licensed "fugu" cooks are permitted to prepare them for human consumption (tetrodotoxin is concentrated in the skin, viscera and gonads). Despite such precautions puffer poisoning is the number one cause of food poisoning in Japan (Halstead, 1967).

The puffers (like the trunkfishes) lack pelvic fins and have strong beaklike teeth that are even more formidable than those of the triggerfishes. Consequently puffers enjoy a wide variety in their diets and are also known to prey on the crown-of-thorns starfish.

There are four genera and 9 species of puffer in the Gulf but only about half can be categorized as reef fishes. Some puffers of the genus *Sphoeroides* commonly range over reefs and along sandy shores. The two species of *Sphoeroides* most frequently found along rocky shores are treated here as reef fishes. The family as a whole is large, with 10 genera and about 131 species.

**References.** Breder (1936); Eger (1963); Fraser-Brunner (1943); Goe and Halstead (1953); Halstead (1967, 1970); Morrow (1957); Smith (1886); Winterbottom (1974); Woods and Schultz (1966).

Figure 99  A guineafowl puffer, *Arothron meleagris*. This white-spotted puffer may be mistaken for a female Pacific boxfish (*Ostracion meleagris*) and vice versa. (Photograph courtesy of Ed Janss.)

# GUINEAFOWL PUFFER, botete negro
# GOLDEN PUFFER, botete de oro
*Arothron meleagris* (Bloch and Schneider, 1801)

**Illustrated specimens.** Spotted phase, 6.9 in. (175 mm), golden phase, 7.8 in. (198 mm), by Alex Kerstitch; see also Figure 99 and Plates 30d and 32; reaches a length of about 12 in. (305 mm).

**Distinguishing characteristics.** The largest of the rocky shore puffers, *A. meleagris,* can be readily distinguished by its numerous white spots which are spaced uniformly over its entire body, including the bases of its fins. Its deep purplish-black background coloration provides a strongly contrasting pattern of black and white. This puffer's body is covered with soft short spines which are erected when it inflates. *A. meleagris* also has a golden phase. D. 11–12; A. 12.

**Distribution.** The guineafowl puffer ranges throughout the tropical Pacific. In the eastern

Pacific it is found from Guaymas to Ecuador, including all of the far-offshore islands (Revillagigedos, Galápagos, etc.).

**Ecology.** Like nearly all members of this family, guineafowl puffers contain the potent poison tetrodotoxin, which is especially concentrated in the liver, gonads, and skin. The skin mucus contains copious amounts of tetrodotoxin that evidently protect this species from predation. The striking black and white color pattern may serve as a warning to potential predators. The ecological significance of the golden phase is not known, but symbolically the golden puffer has become an award for aspiring University of Arizona ichthyologists (see Thomson and Flanagan, 1977).

The guineafowl puffer is a diurnal feeder that grazes on turf-covered rocks. Its food habits in the Gulf have not been studied, but in the Marshall Islands Hiatt and Strasburg (1960) reported that *A. meleagris* fed almost entirely on live coral, cropping the stony tips with its strong beaklike incisors. In Hawaii Hobson (1974) also reported that this puffer feeds on encrusting coral and tunicates. In the Gulf it is commonest in areas in which coral occurs, although we have no evidence that it is feeding on it.

**Related species.** The Hawaiian "makimaki" puffer, *Arothron hispidus* (Linnaeus, 1758), has been recorded in the Cabo San Lucas region (Rosenblatt et al., 1972). This puffer, perhaps a recent immigrant to the eastern Pacific, ranges throughout the Indo-west Pacific to Panama and most offshore islands. *A. hispidus* is more cryptically colored than *A. meleagris*. Its body is olive-gray, often with white spotting on the back. There are black circles around the pectoral base and longitudinal dark lines on the abdomen (Gosline and Brock, 1960). Its highly poisonous flesh justifies the Hawaiian name "makimaki," which in translation is "deadly death."

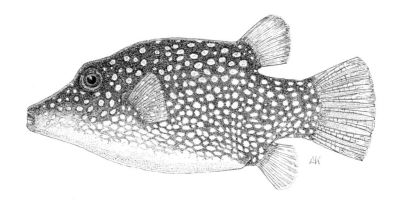

# SPOTTED SHARPNOSE PUFFER, **botete bonito**
## *Canthigaster punctatissima* (Günther, 1870)

**Illustrated specimen.** Adult, 2.8 in. (70 mm), by Alex Kerstitch; see also Plate 30f; grows to about 3½ in. (89 mm).

**Distinguishing characteristics.** This small colorful puffer differs from all the other Gulf puffers by the sharp ridge on its back in front of the dorsal fin. A long pointed snout, small gill openings, and a broad caudal peduncle make this fish easy to recognize on the reef. Its body is covered with white or bluish white spots against a dark reddish-brown ground color. Unlike the guineafowl puffer, whose ground color uniformly covers its entire body, its ventral surface is pale. Puffers of the genera *Arothron* and *Canthigaster* have only a single nostril opening on each side of the snout. D. 9–10; A. 9.

**Distribution.** This puffer ranges from the central Gulf (Guaymas) to Panama and the Islas Galápagos. It is commonest on the Baja California side of the central and lower Gulf, especially in areas of abundant coral growth.

**Ecology.** An active little puffer, *C. punctatissima* is often observed in the open but close to its shelter. It is a slow swimmer, like all the puffers, and may be caught easily with a hand net. Seemingly easy prey for larger fish, this puffer is protected by its extremely toxic skin secretions. Its color pattern of white spots on a dark background is similar to that of the guineafowl puffer, *Arothron meleagris,* and the Pacific boxfish, *Ostracion meleagris,* both of which have toxic skin secretions. Sharpnose puffers do not inflate so readily as other puffers and cannot achieve the degree or duration of inflation characteristic of the other tetraodontid puffers.

Nothing is known of its food habits, but a very similar Hawaiian species, *C. jactator* (Jenkins), feeds mainly on coralline algae and various benthic invertebrates (Hobson, 1974).

# BULLSEYE PUFFER, **botete diana**
## *Sphoeroides annulatus* (Jenyns, 1843)

**Illustrated specimen.** Young adult, 8 in. (205 mm) by Paul Barker; see also Figure 117; grows to about 15 in. (380 mm).

**Distinguishing characteristics.** Puffers of the genus *Sphoeroides* are elongate, relatively smooth-skinned puffers capable of considerable inflation. Like most fishes but unlike puffers of the genera *Arothron* and *Canthigaster,* their nostrils have two distinct openings on each side. The bullseye puffer is so named because of the pattern of contrasting concentric rings on its back that resemble a "bullseye," although it may be obscure in large adults. Its back and sides are uniformly covered with small dark brown spots over a light brown ground color. Its fins and belly are without spots. Separation of *S. annulatus* from the five other *Sphoeroides* spp. in the Gulf is difficult because at least two undescribed *Sphoeroides* in that group closely resemble *S. annulatus.* The systematics of this genus in the eastern Pacific is being studied by

Boyd Walker and Wayne Baldwin. D. 7–9; A. 6–9.

**Distribution.** The bullseye puffer is the most abundant and widespread puffer in the Gulf of California. It ranges from San Diego to Peru, including the Islas Galápagos, and occurs throughout the Gulf of California.

**Ecology.** The bullseye puffer could be classified as a sandy-shore–estuarine species because it is most abundant over sandy bottoms. However, it is also commonly encountered over reefs and along rock-sand interfaces. We suspect that its impact on the reef community is considerable compared with other sandy-shore transient fishes. At night it burrows in the sandy pockets along rocky shores (see Figure 117) and by day it forages along the reef and surrounding sand flats. This versatile, highly mobile puffer ranges widely along all coasts of the Gulf but is usually found in shallow water close to shore.

It has few predators, presumably because of its highly poisonous skin secretions (tetrodotoxin) and its ability to inflate when threatened. Although it may be palatable we do not recommend this or any puffer as human food because the potent toxin in the skin, viscera, and gonads may contaminate the flesh while the fish is being cleaned for cooking.

**Related species.** Only one other species of *Sphoeroides* occurs frequently enough over reefs to be included here. The lobeskin puffer, *S. lobatus* (Steindachner, 1870), is a rather distinctive puffer that has scattered triangular flaps of skin along the sides and abundant, short, and prominent spines covering the body. Sometimes there is a series of obscure dark bars along the sides. Uncommon in the Gulf, it ranges from Bahía San Luis Gonzaga to Peru and the Islas Galápagos. It is also known from Bahía Magdalena.

There is another very common (undescribed) species of *Sphoeroides* in the Gulf that resembles *S. annulatus*. It is a sandy-shore species that ranges farther offshore than the bullseye puffer. Although not a reef fish, we mention it here because it is frequently collected inshore and may be confused with juveniles of the bullseye puffer. It lacks the clear bullseye pattern on the back, having instead dark saddles over a grayish ground color. There are small whitish spots over the back and sides but no dark spots along the sides. The posterior half of its caudal fin is more darkly pigmented than that of *S. annulatus*. It completely lacks skin spinules (prickles).

# FAMILY DIODONTIDAE
## Porcupinefishes (Peces erizos)

The porcupinefishes are not only more adept than puffers at inflating but are covered with long, sharp spines that give them added protection (see Figure 100). They also may have a toxic skin secretion but are less poisonous than puffers. They have strong jaw teeth, fused to form a solid beak, but the beak is not separated in the middle as it is in the puffers. They can deliver a crunching bite, as painfully demonstrated by a woman who naively stuck her thumb in the mouth of a large *Diodon hystrix* and lost a fingernail!

The porcupinefishes range widely throughout the world's tropical seas. Their young are pelagic, and juveniles and adults may be found over sandy and rocky bottoms. We include them here as reef fishes because they appear to feed more consistently on reef invertebrates and are frequently encountered by divers. Their carcasses are inflated, dried, and sold as curios, but we frown on this tasteless attempt to make these unique fishes appear ludicrous.

In the Gulf there are two genera and four species of porcupinefishes, two of which appear to be cosmopolitan in tropical seas. Worldwide, there are five genera and about 15 species.

*References.* Fraser-Brunner (1943); Leis (in press).

Figure 100   A balloonfish, *Diodon holocanthus*. (Photograph courtesy of Robert Ames, Steinhart Aquarium.)

245

# BALLOONFISH, pez erizo
## *Diodon holocanthus* Linnaeus, 1758

**Illustrated specimen.** Juvenile, 110 mm SL (4.3 in.), by Paul Barker; see also Fig. 100; grows to about 1½ ft (0.46 m).

**Distinguishing characteristics.** This species and *Diodon hystrix* are the only two Gulf porcupinefishes with long, movable, erectile spines. *D. holocanthus* usually has longer spines on the forehead than behind the pectoral fin, whereas the reverse is true of *D. hystrix*. *D. holocanthus* has a broad dark brown bar over the forehead and through the eyes and usually four dark saddles over the back. The body is sparsely covered with dark brown spots over a lemon-brown ground color. The fins lack spots. The body and fins of *D. hystrix* is profusely covered with small dark-brown spots and lacks dorsal bars. D. 13–14; A. 13–14.

**Distribution.** Circumtropical in distribution, the balloonfish is common in both the Pacific and Atlantic. In the Gulf it is frequently encountered in the central and lower regions but is uncommon in the upper Gulf.

**Ecology.** Common on shallow reefs in the Gulf, the slow-moving balloonfish is often collected by skindivers. It readily inflates with water or air when distressed and erects its long spines. Although this species has toxic skin secretions, it is only weakly toxic in comparison to the puffers with smoother skin.

**Related species.** The larger (to 3 ft, or 1 m) spotted porcupinefish, *Diodon hystrix* Linnaeus, 1758, is also distributed throughout the tropics and is common in the lower Gulf. It can be distinguished from *D. holocanthus* by its shorter spines, overall dark spotting (including the fins), and lack of bars on the head. It cannot inflate as fully as *D. holocanthus*. A pelagic species of *Diodon* has recently been described by Leis (in press). It has been collected in Gulf offshore waters and resembles *D. hystrix* but does not grow so large.

The Pacific burrfish, *Chilomycterus affinis* Günther, 1870, which ranges widely throughout the tropical Pacific, is found from southern California to the Islas Galápagos but is rarely encountered in the Gulf (Guaymas). This species has short immovable three-based spines in contrast to the longer movable two-based spines of *Diodon*. It resembles *D. hystrix* in coloration.

246

# Nonresident
# Reef Fishes

Many fishes frequently encountered on reefs or along rocky shores are not residents of these areas and have not been included in our checklist of reef fishes. These fishes are regarded as transients and visitors. Most are pelagic or midwater schooling fishes that range widely in search of food. Others are benthic fishes that normally inhabit sandy shores, estuaries, or offshore soft bottoms. Because divers and anglers often meet nonresident fishes in rocky areas, we mention some of the common transients and visitors to Sea of Cortez reefs. Most of them can be identified by using the *Gulf of California Fishwatcher's Guide* (Thomson and McKibbin, 1976). Additional information and illustrations may be found in Hobson (1968), Walford (1937), Kato et al. (1967), and the references listed at the end of this section.

## SHARKS AND RAYS

Sharks are infrequent visitors to reefs in the Sea of Cortez. Although about 38 species of sharks have been reported from the Gulf, most are found in deeper water over soft bottoms or swimming near the surface in open water. Divers only rarely see sharks on shallow reefs and are more likely to find them in or near deep water at offshore islands. The most commonly encountered sharks on shallow reefs are the horn sharks, *Heterodontus mexicanus* Taylor and Castro-Aguirre and *H. francisi* (Girard). The former hides under boulders at the base of the reef in the daytime and forages over it at night. Another frequently observed shark is the scalloped hammerhead, *Sphyrna lewini* (Griffith and Smith), which is often seen in small aggregations (usually two to five, occasionally more than 30) sometimes close to shore (Figure 101). This species, which reaches a length of 12 ft (3.7 m), is potentially dangerous and on occasion has displayed its threat posture to scuba divers who have approached them too closely. The most abundant requiem shark in the Gulf is the Pacific sharpnose shark, *Rhizoprionodon longurio* (Jordan and Gilbert); however, this small species (to 4 ft) is usually found offshore over soft bottoms and rarely frequents rocky shores. Another requiem shark, the blacktip shark, *Carcharhinus limbatus* (Valenciennes), is an occasional visitor to reefs, especially in the lower Gulf, where a commercial fishery exists for it.

In contrast to the relative scarcity of sharks on Gulf reefs, various species of ray may be quite abundant. Among the stingrays, the round stingray, *Urolophus halleri* Cooper, is frequently seen on reefs in the upper Gulf. This usually sandy-bottom

Figure 101   Two large scalloped hammerheads, *Sphyrna lewini,* cruising in the deep murky waters of a Sonoran reef. (Photograph courtesy of John van Ruth.)

species occurs abundantly in some regions and often visits reefs adjacent to sandy areas. The closely related stingray, *Urolophus concentricus* (Osburn and Nichols), is commonly found on rocky bottoms in the central and lower Gulf (Figure 102). There is some question whether this species and another stingray, *Urolophus maculatus* (Garman), are conspecific with *U. halleri,* for they differ essentially only in color pat-

Figure 102   A bullseye stingray, *Urolophus concentricus,* swimming over a rocky bottom near Guaymas. (Photograph by Alex Kerstitch.)

tern. The larger longtail diamond stingray, *Dasyatis* sp., is seen occasionally on patch reefs. Torpedo or electric rays, *Narcine entemedor* Jordan and Starks, and *Diplobatis ommata* (Jordan and Gilbert), sometimes lie partly buried on sandy bottoms near reefs. These fishes can deliver a painful electric shock and divers obviously should never spear them.

The bat ray, *Myliobatis californica* Gill, and the spotted eagle ray, *Aetobatus narinari* (Euphrasen), may be met in large aggregations along the perimeter of patch reefs. The huge Pacific manta ray, *Manta hamiltoni* (Newman), which attains a width of 25 ft (7.7 m) and a weight of almost 2 tons, is often sighted "basking" over shallow reefs near shore. This manta, a spectacular jumper, leaps high out of the water and lands flat on its belly with a thunderous "smack," which is audible from a great distance. The much smaller (width about 4 ft) smoothtail mobula, *Mobula lucasana* Beebe and Tee-Van, gathers in large schools near reefs (Figure 103). Both mantas are primarily plankton feeders and their occurrence near reefs may be fortuitous or for the purpose of being cleaned of ectoparasites by certain reef fishes.

Figure 103   A school of smoothtail mobulas, *Mobula lucasana,* a smaller species of manta ray, swimming over a reef. (Photograph courtesy of E. S. Hobson.)

The shovelnose guitarfish, *Rhinobatos productus* Ayres, and the banded guitarfish, *Zapteryx exasperata* (Jordan and Gilbert), often move to reefs to feed over the sandy patches, especially at night.

## PELAGIC SCHOOLING FISHES

A great variety of schooling fishes from small planktivorous species (e.g., anchovies and herrings) to large predators (e.g., jacks and mackerels) are often observed along

Figure 104   A large school of machete, *Elops affinis*. These crepuscular predators feed on herrings and other small fishes that aggregate close to shore. (Photograph courtesy of E. S. Hobson.)

Figure 105   The flatiron herring, *Harengula thrissina*, schooling close to shore. This herring is the preferred prey of the sardinera, or leopard grouper (*Mycteroperca rosacea*). (Photograph courtesy of E. S. Hobson.)

rocky shores and over patch reefs. The machete, *Elops affinis* Regan, is a crepuscular (twilight) predator of smaller fishes, especially herrings (Figure 104). Schools of machete generally aggregate off rocky points and along beaches. The commonest herrings seen over reefs are the Pacific thread herring, *Opisthonema libertate* (Günther), and the flatiron herring, *Harengula thrissina* (Jordan and Gilbert). The thread herring is more commonly found in the upper Gulf and the flatiron herring is more abundant in the central and lower Gulf, where it is preyed on by the machete, the leopard grouper (*Mycteroperca rosacea*) and by many other fishes (Figure 105). The thread herring grows to about 10 in. (254 mm) and occasionally preys on smaller fishes. Dense schools of anchovies are often driven close to shore by large predatory fishes, such as the mackerels (Figure 106). These small, tightly schooling planktivorous fishes sometimes form a solid band along a beach as they attempt to escape their predators.

Schools of young-of-the-year Gulf grunion, *Leuresthes sardina* (Jenkins and Evermann), often approach rocky shores. The adults spawn on central and upper Gulf beaches during winter and spring (January to May) and then move offshore. The young stay close to shore along sandy beaches and in esteros and are often seen over reefs. Halfbeaks (*Hyporhamphus*) and needlefishes (*Strongylura, Tylosurus*) are larger predatory fishes that are frequent visitors to reefs. Halfbeaks feed mainly on fish larvae and zooplankton and are preyed on by larger pelagic predators (e.g., sailfish and dolphinfish). Needlefishes feed mainly on small schooling fishes (e.g., herrings, anchovies, and mullets) and only rarely on resident reef fishes (Figure 107). These fishes probably follow their prey to rocky shores; some, however, come to be cleaned of ectoparasites (Figure 108) by the Panamic sergeant major (*Abudefduf troschelii*).

In the Gulf, barracudas (*Sphyraena* spp.) are not the important predators of reef fishes that they are on the coral reefs of the tropical western Atlantic. They are open-water predators, and large schools of adults occur only infrequently near reefs (Figure 109), but small schools of juveniles are common.

Figure 106    A school of anchovies seeking refuge on a Sonoran reef. (Photograph by D. A. Thomson.)

Figure 107  A school of needlefish (family Belonidae) swimming near the surface. (Photograph by Alex Kerstitch.)

Figure 108  A school of halfbeaks (*Hyporhamphus* sp.) being cleaned by the Panamic sergeant major (*Abudefduf troschelii*). (Photograph courtesy of Rick McCourt.)

252

Mullets are widespread inshore fishes in all tropical seas. Most mullets feed on detritus and algae in muddy or sandy bottoms. They are usually abundant in estuaries and sandy bays but are frequent transients over rocky bottoms, where they may seek shelter from predators or aggregate to be cleaned of ectoparasites by certain reef fishes. The striped mullet, *Mugil cephalus* Linnaeus, a circumtropical species in warm seas, occurs throughout the Gulf, frequently over rocky bottoms. The mullet *Chaenomugil proboscideus* (Günther) grazes on algae attached to rocks by scraping with its many small crowbar-shaped teeth. This mullet is common in the lower Gulf and may be categorized as a true reef resident when more is learned about its ecology.

The mojarras (Gerreidae) are compressed, silvery schooling fishes with strongly protrusible mouths. They are primarily sandy-bottom fishes but are commonly found

Figure 109   A school of adult barracuda, *Sphyraena* sp. Juveniles are more commonly seen on Gulf reefs than adults. (Photograph courtesy of Ed Janss.)

over rocky bottoms that have numerous sandy patches. Mojarras feed on invertebrates in the sand in which some bury themselves completely when threatened.

Jacks are fast-swimming, predatory fishes that frequently follow their usual prey of smaller schooling fishes over the reefs. Some may prey on reef fishes and others will feed on benthic invertebrates in the sandy patches near rocks. The largest of the jacks found near reefs in the Gulf are the yellowtail, *Seriola lalandi* Cuvier, and the almaco amberjack, *Seriola rivoliana* Cuvier. The yellowtail (to 5 ft and 80 lb) is an important sportfish sought by anglers trolling off rocky points during the winter. The larger and more robust amberjack is more common in the lower Gulf, where it is also esteemed as a sportfish (Figure 110). Several species of the genus *Caranx* occur over rocky bot-

Figure 110  An adult almaco amberjack, *Seriola rivoliana*. (Photograph by Alex Kerstitch, taken at Sea World, San Diego.)

Figure 111  Jacks of the genus *Caranx*. These swift-swimming fishes are frequent visitors to central and lower Gulf reefs. (Photograph courtesy of E. S. Hobson.)

toms (Figure 111), among which the large crevalle jack, *Caranx hippos* Linnaeus, is occasionally observed along the margins of reefs (Figure 112). The yellow jack, *Gnathanodon speciosus* (Forskål), which is characterized by a strongly protrusible mouth, feeds on benthic invertebrates and small fishes over rocky and sandy bottoms. The juveniles of this jack are colored bright yellow with black bars and have "piloting" habits; that is, they seek protection from predators by swimming alongside larger fishes. The Mexican lookdown, *Selene brevoorti* (Gill), is a frequent visitor to lower Gulf reefs to which it may come to be cleaned by barberfish (Figure 113).

Figure 112   A large jack crevalle, *Caranx hippos*. (Photograph by Alex Kerstitch, taken at Sea World, San Diego.)

Figure 113   A school of Mexican lookdowns, *Selene brevoorti*, being cleaned by barberfish, *Heniochus nigrirostris*. (Photograph courtesy of E. S. Hobson.)

255

The gafftopsail pompano, *Trachinotus rhodopus* Gill, may be the commonest reef jack. This colorful, distinctive fish often occurs in huge schools and can be observed feeding on zooplankton near the surface. Other pompanos of the genus *Trachinotus* are infrequent visitors to the reefs.

Occasionally the large and spectacular roosterfish, *Nematistius pectoralis* Gill, can be seen over sandy bottoms around reefs (Figure 114).

Mackerels and tunas swim close to the reefs in pursuit of schools of prey fish. The sierra mackerel, *Scomberomorus sierra* Jordan and Starks, may be the most abundant predator on small schooling fishes in the Sea of Cortez (see Figure 115). Ranging throughout the Gulf, the mackerel is commonly seen over reefs when schools

Figure 114   An adult roosterfish, *Nematistius pectoralis.* (Photograph courtesy of E. S. Hobson.)

Figure 115   The sierra mackerel, *Scomberomorus sierra,* is abundant in the Sea of Cortez and occurs frequently inshore. (Photograph courtesy of E. S. Hobson.)

of its forage fishes (anchovies and herrings) seek refuge inshore. Tunas are mostly open-ocean fishes, but the black skipjack, *Euthynnus lineatus* Kishinouye, often appears close to offshore reefs and islands.

Billfishes (sailfish and marlins) are occasionally found inshore in the Gulf, but they prefer deep open water and seem to avoid the shallows.

## BENTHIC SANDY-BOTTOM FISHES

These are usually solitary nonschooling fishes that use the sandy bottoms near and within reefs for refuge and feeding.

The snake eels constitute a group of burrowing eels commonly represented on reefs by the spotted tiger snake eel, *Myrichthys xystrurus* Jordan and Gilbert (formerly *M. tigrinus*) which can be seen at times in daylight searching for prey under rocks and in crevices over rocky bottoms. When inactive, it buries itself completely in the sand.

Gulf lizardfishes are rarely found in shallow water. They occur over shell and cobble bottoms at moderate depths, usually below 60 ft (18 m), on patch reefs (Figure 116). Outside the Gulf *Synodus* spp. are more commonly present in shallow water.

Figure 116   A lizardfish (*Synodus* sp.) poking its head above the sand in search of prey. (Photograph courtesy of E. S. Hobson.)

The midshipman, *Porichthys notatus* (Girard), an offshore, soft-bottom fish characterized by rows of photophores along its body, swims onto the reef to spawn. Eggs are attached to the undersides of rocks in shallow water.

Flounders and soles are occasionally found on the sandy patches of reefs. These fishes prefer fine-grained sandy and muddy bottoms. They burrow in the sediment for protection and most can camouflage themselves by rapidly changing color. Juveniles

257

of the Cortez halibut, *Paralichthys aestuarius* Gilbert and Scofield, can be collected by seining sandy beaches near reefs, as can the juveniles of the ocellated turbot, *Pleuronichthys ocellatus* Starks and Thompson. None of the Gulf flatfishes, however, seems to have any predilection for rocky bottoms.

Many species of the predominantly rocky-bottom grunts prefer soft bottoms. Juveniles of the common bronze striped grunt, *Orthopristis reddingi* Jordan and Richardson, are frequent transients over rocky bottoms, but species of the genera *Haemulopsis* and *Pomadasys* show only weak associations with reefs and are rarely seen there.

The large family of drums and croakers consists almost exclusively of soft-bottom fishes. Occasionally corvinas (*Cynoscion* spp.) are caught over rocky bottoms and the giant totoaba, *Cynoscion macdonaldi* Gilbert, has been seen on reefs by scuba divers. (This species is now considerably less abundant and has been placed on the endangered species list.)

The sand stargazers are small burrowing fishes found along sandy beaches. The redsaddled sand stargazer, *Dactyloscopus pectoralis* Gill, is a common fish of the sandy bottoms of rocky tide pools but other Gulf sand stargazers are less frequently collected in rocky areas.

About one-half of the Gulf species of the large family Gobiidae (gobies) inhabit soft bottoms. Some are exclusively estuarine: for example, the Guaymas goby, *Quietula guaymasiae* (Jenkins and Evermann) and the longtail goby, *Gobionellus sagittula* (Günther) are rarely found in rocky areas. Others live in deeper water over soft bottoms (*Bollmania* spp.). Few of the sandy- or muddy-bottom gobies ever occur on reefs.

Puffers of the genus *Sphoeroides* are primarily shallow, sandy-bottom fishes (see Figure 117). The bullseye puffer (*S. annulatus*), however, is so abundant in rocky areas that we have included it as a reef fish.

***References.*** The following taxonomic works are useful in identifying some Sea of Cortez nonresident reef fishes: Sharks (Kato et al., 1967); rays (Miller and Lea, 1972); mullets (Ebeling, 1957, 1961); jacks, mackerels and tunas (Walford, 1937); snake eels (McCosker, 1977); croakers (McPhail, 1958); sand stargazers (Dawson, 1975, 1976).

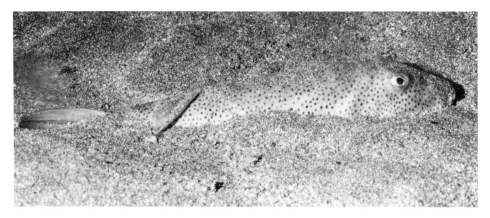

Figure 117  A bullseye puffer, *Sphoeroides annulatus,* seeking refuge in the sand at night. (Photograph courtesy of Ed Janss.)

# Reef Fishes of the Sea of Cortez

## SPECIES CHECKLIST

Listed species of reef fishes are based largely on an unpublished checklist of all Gulf of California fishes by Boyd W. Walker, University of California, Los Angeles, and our records. A species has been included even if only a single record exists of its occurrence in the Gulf. Within each taxonomic group the species are listed alphabetically by genus and species. Subspecies have not been included. Higher taxonomic categories basically follow the provisional classification of teleostean fishes proposed by Greenwood, Rosen, Weitzmann, and Myers (1966), with some changes and additions as found in Nelson (1976) and/or Greenwood (1975).

Phylum Chordata
  Subphylum Vertebrata (Craniata)
    Superclass Gnathostomata
      Class Osteichthyes (Teleostomi, "Pisces")
        Subclass Actinopterygii
          Infraclass Neopterygii
            Division Teleostei
              Cohort Taeniopaedia
                Superorder Elopomorpha
                  Order Anguilliformes
                    Suborder Anguilloidei
                      Family Muraenidae
                        Subfamily Muraeninae
                          *Echidna nebulosa* (Ahl, 1789)
                          *Echidna nocturna* (Cope, 1872)
                          *Echidna zebra* (Shaw, 1797)
                          *Enchelycore octaviana* (Myers and Wade, 1941)
                          *Gymnothorax castaneus* (Jordan and Gilbert, 1882)
                          *Gymnothorax equatorialis* (Hildebrand, 1946)
                          *Gymnothorax dovii* (Günther, 1870)
                          *Gymnothorax panamensis* (Steindachner, 1876)

*Muraena argus* (Steindachner, 1870)
*Muraena clepsydra* Gilbert, 1898
*Muraena lentiginosa* Jenyns, 1843
Subfamily Uropterygiinae
*Anarchias galapagensis* (Seale, 1940)
*Uropterygius necturus* (Jordan and Gilbert, 1882)
*Uropterygius polystictus* Myers and Wade, 1941
*Uropterygius tigrinus* (Lesson, 1829)
*Uropterygius* sp. (one undescribed species)[1]
Family Congridae
Subfamily Heterocongrinae
*Gorgasia punctata* Meek and Hildebrand, 1923
*Taenioconger canabus* Cowan and Rosenblatt, 1974
*Taenioconger digueti* Pellegrin, 1923
Cohort Euteleostei
Superorder Paracanthopterygii
Order Gadiformes
Suborder Ophidioidei
Family Ophidiidae
Subfamily Brotulinae
*Ogilbia ventralis* (Gill, 1864)
*Ogilbia* spp. (about five undescribed species)[2]
*Oligopus diagrammus* (Heller and Snodgrass, 1903)
*Petrotyx hopkinsi* Heller and Snodgrass, 1903
Order Lophiiformes (Pediculati)
Suborder Antennarioidei
Family Antennariidae
Subfamily Antennariinae
*Antennarius avalonis* Jordan and Starks, 1907
*Antennarius sanguineus* Gill, 1864
*Antennatus strigatus* (Gill, 1864)
Superorder Acanthopterygii
Order Beryciformes
Suborder Berycoidei
Family Holocentridae
Subfamily Holocentrinae
*Adioryx suborbitalis* (Gill, 1864)
Subfamily Myripristinae
*Myripristis leiognathos* Valenciennes, 1846
Order Gasterosteiformes (Syngnathiformes)
Suborder Aulostomoidei
Superfamily Aulostomoidae
Family Fistulariidae
*Fistularia commersonii* Rüppell, 1835
*Fistularia corneta* Gilbert and Starks, 1904
Suborder Syngnathoidei
Family Syngnathidae
Subfamily Snygnathinae

      *Bryx arctus* (Jenkins and Evermann, 1889)
      *Doryrhamphus melanopleura* (Bleeker, 1858)
    Subfamily Hippocampinae
      *Hippocampus ingens* Girard, 1858
Order Scorpaeniformes
 Suborder Scorpaenoidei
  Family Scorpaenidae
   Subfamily Scorpaeninae
     *Scorpaena histrio* Jenyns, 1843
     *Scorpaena mystes* Jordan and Starks, 1895
     *Scorpaenodes xyris* (Jordan and Gilbert, 1882)
Order Perciformes
 Suborder Percoidei
 Superfamily Percoidae
  Family Serranidae (including Percichthyidae)
    *Anthias gordensis* Wade, 1946
    *Epinephelus acanthistius* (Gilbert, 1892)
    *Epinephelus afer* Bloch, 1793
    *Epinephelus analogus* Gill, 1864
    *Epinephelus dermatolepis* Boulenger, 1895
    *Epinephelus itajara* (Lichtenstein, 1822)
    *Epinephelus labriformis* (Jenyns, 1843)
    *Epinephelus multiguttatus* (Günther, 1866)
    *Epinephelus niveatus* (Valenciennes, 1828)
    *Epinephelus panamensis* (Steindachner, 1876)
    *Liopropoma longilepis* Garman, 1889
    *Liopropoma* sp. (one undescribed species)[1]
    *Mycteroperca jordani* (Jenkins and Evermann, 1889)
    *Mycteroperca prionura* Rosenblatt and Zahuranec, 1967
    *Mycteroperca rosacea* (Streets, 1877)
    *Mycteroperca xenarcha* Jordan, 1888
    *Paralabrax auroguttatus* Walford, 1936
    *Paralabrax loro* Walford, 1936
    *Paralabrax maculatofasciatus* (Steindachner, 1868)
    *Paranthias colonus* (Valenciennes, 1855)
    *Serranus fasciatus* Jenyns, 1843
    *Stereolepis gigas* Ayres, 1859
  Family Grammistidae (including Pseudogrammidae)
    *Rypticus bicolor* (Valenciennes, 1846)
    *Rypticus nigripinnis* Gill, 1862
    *Pseudogramma thaumasium* (Gilbert, 1900)
  Family Kuhliidae
    *Kuhlia taeniura* (Cuvier, 1829)
  Family Priacanthidae
    *Priacanthus cruentatus* (Lacépède, 1802)
    *Pristigenys* (= *Pseudopriacanthus*) *serrula* (Gilbert, 1890)
  Family Apogonidae
    *Apogon atricaudus* Jordan and McGregor, 1898

*Apogon dovii* Günther, 1861
*Apogon parri* Breder, 1936
*Apogon retrosella* (Gill, 1863)
Family Branchiostegidae
   *Caulolatilus affinis* Gill, 1865
   *Caulolatilus hubbsi* Dooley, 1978
   *Caulolatilus princeps* (Jenyns, 1843)
Family Lutjanidae
   *Hoplopagrus guentheri* Gill, 1862
   *Lutjanus aratus* (Günther, 1864)
   *Lutjanus argentiventris* (Peters, 1869)
   *Lutjanus colorado* Jordan and Gilbert, 1881
   *Lutjanus guttatus* (Steindachner, 1869)
   *Lutjanus novemfasciatus* Gill, 1863
   *Lutjanus peru* (Nichols and Murphy, 1922)
   *Lutjanus viridis* (Valenciennes, 1855)
Family Haemulidae (Pomadasyidae, Pristipomatidae)
   *Anisotremus caesius* (Jordan and Gilbert, 1881)
   *Anisotremus davidsonii* (Steindachner, 1875)
   *Anisotremus dovii* (Günther, 1864)
   *Anisotremus interruptus* (Gill, 1863)
   *Anisotremus taeniatus* Gill, 1862
   *Haemulon flaviguttatum* Gill, 1863
   *Haemulon maculicauda* (Gill, 1863)
   *Haemulon scudderi* Gill, 1863
   *Haemulon sexfasciatum* Gill, 1863
   *Haemulon steindachneri* (Jordan and Gilbert, 1882)
   *Microlepidotus inornatus* Gill, 1863
   *Xenichthys xanti* Gill, 1863
   *Xenistius californiensis* (Steindachner, 1875)
Family Sparidae
   *Calamus brachysomus* (Lockington, 1880)
Family Sciaenidae
   *Pareques viola* (Gilbert, 1898)
Family Mullidae
   *Mulloidichthys dentatus* (Gill, 1863)
Family Kyphosidae
 Subfamily Kyphosinae
   *Hermosilla azurea* Jenkins and Evermann, 1889
   *Kyphosus analogus* (Gill, 1863)
   *Kyphosus elegans* (Peters, 1869)
   *Sector ocyurus* (Jordan and Gilbert, 1881)
 Subfamily Girellinae
   *Girella nigricans* (Ayres, 1860)
   *Girella simplicidens* Osburn and Nichols, 1916
 Subfamily Scorpinae
   *Medialuna californiensis* (Steindachner, 1875)
Family Ephippidae

Subfamily Ephippinae
 *Chaetodipterus zonatus* (Girard, 1858)
 *Parapsettus panamensis* Steindachner, 1875
Family Chaetodontidae
 *Chaetodon falcifer* Hubbs and Rechnitzer, 1958
 *Chaetodon humeralis* Günther, 1860
 *Forcipiger flavissimus* Jordan and McGregor, 1898
 *Heniochus nigrirostris* (Gill, 1863)
Family Pomacanthidae
 *Holacanthus clarionensis* Gilbert, 1890
 *Holacanthus passer* Valenciennes, 1846
 *Pomacanthus zonipectus* (Gill, 1863)
Superfamily Pomacentroidae
 Family Pomacentridae
 Subfamily Pomacentrinae
 Tribe Pomacentrini
  *Eupomacentrus acapulcoensis* (Fowler, 1944)
  *Eupomacentrus flavilatus* (Gill, 1863)
  *Eupomacentrus leucorus* (Gilbert, 1892)
  *Eupomacentrus rectifraenum* (Gill, 1863)
  *Eupomacentrus redemptus* (Heller and Snodgrass, 1903)
 Tribe Abudefdufini
  *Abudefduf troschelii* (Gill, 1863)
  *Hypsypops rubicundus* (Girard, 1854)
  *Microspathodon bairdii* (Gill, 1863)
  *Microspathodon dorsalis* (Gill, 1863)
  *Nexilarius concolor* (Gill, 1863)
 Subfamily Chrominae
 *Chromis atrilobata* Gill, 1863
 *Chromis* spp. (two undescribed species)[3]
Superfamily Cirrhitoidae
 Family Cirrhitidae
 *Cirrhitichthys oxycephalus* (Bleeker, 1855)
 *Cirrhitus rivulatus* Valenciennes, 1855
 *Oxycirrhites typus* Bleeker, 1857
Suborder Labroidei
 Family Labridae
 *Bodianus diplotaenia* (Gill, 1863)
 *Decodon melasma* Gomon, 1974
 *Halichoeres aestuaricola* Bussing, 1972
 *Halichoeres chierchiae* Caporiacco, 1947
 *Halichoeres dispilus* (Günther, 1864)
 *Halichoeres nicholsi* (Jordan and Gilbert, 1881)
 *Halichoeres semicinctus* (Ayres, 1859)
 *Hemipteronotus mundiceps* (Gill, 1863)
 *Hemipteronotus pavoninus* (Valenciennes, 1839)
 *Hemipteronotus taeniourus* (Lacépède, 1802)
 *Semicossyphus* ( = *Pimelometopon*) *pulcher* (Ayres, 1854)

*Pseudojulis inornatus* Gilbert, 1890
*Pseudojulis melanotis* Gilbert, 1890
*Pseudojulis notospilus* Günther, 1864
*Thalassoma lucasanum* (Gill, 1863)
*Thalassoma lutescens* (Lay and Bennett, 1839)
Family Scaridae
Subfamily Scarinae
*Scarus compressus* (Osburn and Nichols, 1916)
*Scarus ghobban* Forskål, 1775
*Scarus perrico* Jordan and Gilbert, 1882
*Scarus rubroviolaceus* Bleeker, 1849
Subfamily Sparisomatinae
*Calotomus spinidens* (Quoy and Gaimard, 1824)
*Nicholsina denticulata* (Evermann and Radcliffe, 1917)
Suborder Blennioidei
Infraorder Trachinoidea
Family Opistognathidae
*Lonchopisthus* sp. (one undescribed species)[4]
*Opistognathus punctatus* Peters, 1869
*Opistognathus rhomaleus* Jordan and Gilbert, 1881
*Opistognathus scops* (Jenkins and Evermann, 1889)
*Opistognathus* spp. (four undescribed species)[4]
Infraorder Blennioidea
Family Blenniidae
Subfamily Blenniinae
Tribe Blenniini
*Hypsoblennius brevipinnis* (Günther, 1861)
*Hypsoblennius gentilis* (Girard, 1854)
*Hypsoblennius jenkinsi* (Jordan and Evermann, 1896)
Tribe Salariini
*Entomacrodus chiostictus* (Jordan and Gilbert, 1883)
*Ophioblennius steindachneri* Jordan and Evermann, 1898
Subfamily Nemophidinae
Tribe Nemophidini
*Plagiotremus azaleus* (Jordan and Bollman, 1890)
Family Tripterygiidae
*Axoclinus carminalis* (Jordan and Gilbert, 1882)
*Axoclinus* sp. (one undescribed species)[1]
*Enneanectes sexmaculatus* (Fowler, 1944)
*Enneanectes* spp. (two undescribed species)[1]
Genus and species (one undescribed genus and species)[1]
Family Clinidae
Subfamily Labrisominae
Tribe Labrisomini
*Labrisomus multiporosus* Hubbs, 1953
*Labrisomus striatus* Hubbs, 1953
*Labrisomus xanti* Gill, 1860
*Malacoctenus ebisui* Springer, 1959

*Malacoctenus gigas* Springer, 1959
*Malacoctenus hubbsi* Springer, 1959
*Malacoctenus margaritae* (Fowler, 1944)
*Malacoctenus tetranemus* (Cope, 1877)
*Malacoctenus zacae* Springer, 1959
*Malacoctenus zonifer* (Jordan and Gilbert, 1882)
Tribe Paraclinini
*Exerpes asper* (Jenkins and Evermann, 1889)
*Paraclinus altivelis* (Lockington, 1881)
*Paraclinus beebei* Hubbs, 1952
*Paraclinus mexicanus* (Gilbert, 1904)
*Paraclinus sini* Hubbs, 1952
*Paraclinus tanygnathus* Rosenblatt and Parr, 1969
Tribe Starksiini
*Starksia cremnobates* (Gilbert, 1890)
*Starksia grammilaga* Rosenblatt and Taylor, 1971
*Starksia hoesei* Rosenblatt and Taylor, 1971
*Starksia spinipenis* (Al-Uthman, 1960)
*Xenomedea rhodopyga* Rosenblatt and Taylor, 1971
Tribe Mnierpini
*Mnierpes macrocephalus* (Günther, 1861)
Tribe Cryptotremini
*Cryptotrema seftoni* Hubbs, 1954
*Incertae sedis*
*Stathmonotus sinuscalifornici* (Chabanaud, 1942)
Family Chaenopsidae
*Acanthemblemaria balanorum* Brock, 1940
*Acanthemblemaria crockeri* Beebe and Tee-Van, 1938
*Acanthemblemaria macrospilus* Brock, 1940
*Chaenopsis alepidota* (Gilbert, 1890)
*Chaenopsis coheni* Böhlke, 1957
*Coralliozetus angelica* (Böhlke and Mead, 1957)
*Coralliozetus boehlkei* Stephens, 1963
*Coralliozetus micropes* (Beebe and Tee-Van, 1938)
*Coralliozetus rosenblatti* Stephens, 1963
*Ekemblemaria myersi* Stephens, 1963
*Emblemaria hypacanthus* (Jenkins and Evermann, 1889)
*Emblemaria walkeri* Stephens, 1963
*Protemblemaria bicirris* (Hildebrand, 1946)
*Protemblemaria lucasana* Stephens, 1963
Suborder Gobioidei
Family Gobiidae
*Aruma histrio* (Jordan, 1884)
*Bathygobius ramosus* Ginsburg, 1947
*Barbulifer pantherinus* (Pellegrin, 1901)
*Barbulifer* spp. (two undescribed species)[5]
*Chriolepis minutillus* Gilbert, 1892
*Chriolepis zebra* Ginsburg, 1938

*Chriolepis* spp. (three undescribed species)[6]
*Coryphopterus urospilus* Ginsburg, 1938
*Elacatinus digueti* (Pellegrin, 1901)
*Elacatinus puncticulatus* (Ginsburg, 1938)
*Elacatinus* sp. (one undescribed species)[5]
*Enypnias seminudus* (Günther, 1861)
*Gillichthys seta* (Ginsburg, 1938)
*Gobiosoma chiquita* (Jenkins and Evermann, 1889)
*Gobiosoma nudum* (Meek and Hildebrand, 1928)
*Gobiosoma paradoxum* (Günther, 1861)
*Gobiosoma* sp. (one undescribed species)[5]
*Gobulus crescentalis* (Gilbert, 1892)
*Gobulus hancocki* Ginsburg, 1938
*Gymneleotris seminudus* (Günther, 1864)
*Ioglossus* sp. (one undescribed species)[1]
*Lythrypnus dalli* (Gilbert, 1890)
*Lythrypnus pulchellus* Ginsburg, 1938
*Lythrypnus* sp. (one undescribed species)[5]
*Pycnomma semisquamatum* Rutter, 1904
Suborder Acanthuroidei
Family Acanthuridae
Subfamily Acanthurinae
Tribe Acanthurini
*Acanthurus achilles* Shaw, 1803
*Acanthurus glaucopareius* Cuvier, 1829
*Acanthurus triostegus* (Linnaeus, 1758)
*Acanthurus xanthopterus* Valenciennes, 1835
Tribe Prionurini
*Prionurus punctatus* Gill, 1862
Subfamily Zanclinae
*Zanclus canescens* (Linnaeus, 1758)
Order Gobiesociformes (Xenopterygii)
Suborder Gobiesocoidei
Family Gobiesocidae
*Arcos erythrops* (Jordan and Gilbert, 1882)
*Gobiesox adustus* Jordan and Gilbert, 1882
*Gobiesox papillifer* Gilbert, 1890
*Gobiesox pinniger* Gilbert, 1890
*Gobiesox schultzi* Briggs, 1951
*Pherallodiscus funebris* (Gilbert, 1890)
*Tomicodon boehlkei* Briggs, 1955
*Tomicodon eos* (Jordan and Gilbert, 1882)
*Tomicodon humeralis* (Gilbert, 1890)
*Tomicodon myersi* Briggs, 1955
*Tomicodon zebra* (Jordan and Gilbert, 1882)
Order Tetraodontiformes (Plectognathi)
Suborder Balistoidei

Superfamily Balistoidae
Family Balistidae
Subfamily Balistinae
*Balistes polylepis* Steindachner, 1876
*Pseudobalistes naufragium* (Jordan and Starks, 1895)
*Sufflamen verres* (Gilbert and Starks, 1904)
Subfamily Monacanthinae
*Alutera scripta* (Osbeck, 1765)
*Cantherhines dumerilii* (Hollard, 1854)
Superfamily Ostraciontoidae
Family Ostraciontidae
Subfamily Ostraciontinae
*Lactoria diaphanus* (Bloch and Schneider, 1801)
*Ostracion meleagris* Shaw, 1796
Suborder Tetraodontoidei
Superfamily Tetraodontoidae
Family Tetraodontidae
Subfamily Tetraodontinae
*Arothron hispidus* (Linnaeus, 1758)
*Arothron meleagris* (Bloch and Schneider, 1801)
*Sphoeroides annulatus* (Jenyns, 1843)
*Sphoeroides lobatus* (Steindachner, 1870)
Subfamily Canthigasterinae
*Canthigaster punctatissima* (Günther, 1870)
Family Diodontidae
*Chilomycterus affinis* Günther, 1870
*Diodon holocanthus* Linnaeus, 1758
*Diodon hystrix* Linnaeus, 1758

Taxa noted by superscript numbers in the checklist are under study by the following:

1   Richard H. Rosenblatt, Scripps Institution of Oceanography, University of California at San Diego, La Jolla.
2   Boyd W. Walker, University of California, Los Angeles.
3   Loren P. Woods, Field Museum of Natural History, Chicago, and David W. Greenfield, Northern Illinois University, DeKalb.
4   Richard H. Rosenblatt, Scripps Institution of Oceanography, University of California at San Diego, La Jolla, and Edward B. Brothers, Cornell University, Ithaca, New York.
5   Douglass F. Hoese, The Australian Museum, Sydney.
6   Lloyd T. Findley, University of Arizona, Tucson.

## APPENDIX  II

# *Localities of Reef Fishes Illustrated*

## FIGURES

269

Figure 57   Graybar grunt (*Haemulon sexfasciatum*); Gulf of California.

Figure 58   Pacific porgy (*Calamus brachysomus*); Bahía San Carlos, Sonora.

Figure 59   Rock croaker (*Pareques viola*); Gulf of California.

Figure 60   Mexican goatfish (*Mulloidichthys dentatus*); Gulf of California.

Figure 61   Cortez chub (*Kyphosus elegans*); Cabo San Lucas.

Figure 62   Pacific spadefish (*Chaetodipterus zonatus*); Bahía San Carlos, Sonora.

Figure 63   Pacific spadefish (*Chaetodipterus zonatus*); Puerto Peñasco.

Figure 64   Cortez angelfish (*Pomacanthus zonipectus*); Bahía San Carlos, Sonora.

Figure 65   Barberfish (*Heniochus nigrirostris*); Gulf of California.

Figure 66   Scythmarked butterflyfish (*Chaetodon falcifer*); Cabo San Lucas.

Figure 67   Longnose butterflyfish (*Forcipiger flavissimus*); Cabo San Lucas.

Figure 68   Scissortail damselfish (*Chromis atrilobata*); Cabo San Lucas.

Figure 69   Acapulco damselfish (*Eupomacentrus acapulcoensis*); Isla San Ignacio Farallon.

Figure 70   Whitetail damselfish (*Eupomacentrus leucorus*); Cabo San Lucas.

Figure 71   Clarion damselfish (*Eupomacentrus redemptus*); Cabo San Lucas.

Figure 72   Panamic sergeant major (*Abudefduf troschelii*); Bahía San Carlos, Sonora.

Figure 73   Dusky sergeant major (*Nexillarius concolor*); Manzanillo, Colima.

Figure 74   Coral hawkfish (*Cirrhitichthys oxycephalus*); Isla San Pedro Nolasco.

Figure 75   Spinster wrasse (*Halichoeres nicholsi*); Mexican goatfish (*Mulloidichthys dentatus*); Gulf of California.

Figure 76   California sheephead (*Semicossyphus pulcher*); Cabo San Lucas.

Figure 77   Bumphead parrotfish (*Scarus perrico*); Gulf of California.

Figure 78   Bicolor parrotfish (*Scarus rubroviolaceus*); Isla San Ignacio Farallon.

Figure 79   Loosetooth parrotfish (*Nicholsina denticulata*); Isla San Pedro Nolasco.

Figure 81   A jawfish (*Opistognathus* sp.); Guaymas.

Figure 82   Bullseye jawfish (*Opistognathus scops*); Sea World, San Diego, California.

Figure 83   Pacific fanged blenny (*Ophioblennius steindachneri*); Guaymas.

Figure 84   Bay blenny (*Hypsoblennius gentilis*); Puerto Peñasco.

Figure 85   Flag triplefin (*Enneanectes* sp.); Guaymas.

Figure 86   Delicate triplefin (*Enneanectes sexmaculatus*); Mazatlán.

Figure 87   Largemouth blenny (*Labrisomus xanti*); Bahía San Carlos, Sonora.

Figure 88   Foureye rockskipper (*Mnierpes macrocephalus*); Costa Rica.

Figure 89   Signal blenny (*Emblemaria hypacanthus*); male—Guaymas, female—Puerto Peñasco.

Figure 91   Male secret goby (*Pycnomma semisquamatum*); Isla San Pedro Nolasco.

Figure 92   Patchscale goby (*Gobiosoma* sp.); Puerto Peñasco.

Figure 93   Cortez hovering goby (*Ioglossus* sp.); Guaymas.

Figure 94   Convict tangs (*Acanthurus triostegus*); tropical eastern Pacific.

Figure 96   Finescale triggerfish (*Balistes polylepis*); Bahía San Carlos, Sonora.

Figure 97   Blunthead triggerfish (*Pseudobalistes naufragium*); Isla San Ignacio Farallon.

Figure 98   Pacific boxfish (*Ostracion meleagris*); Oahu, Hawaii.

Figure 99   Guineafowl puffer (*Arothron meleagris*); tropical eastern Pacific.

Figure 100   Balloonfish, *Diodon holocanthus*; Bahía San Carlos, Sonora.

Figure 101   Scalloped hammerhead (*Sphyrna lewini*); Sonora.

Figure 102   Bullseye stingray (*Urolophus concentricus*); Guaymas.

Figure 103   Smoothtail mobula (*Mobula lucasana*); Gulf of California.

Figure 104   Machete (*Elops affinis*); Gulf of California.

Figure 105   Flatiron herring (*Harengula thrissina*); Gulf of California.

Plate 25  Jawfish and blennies. Photographs (a), (b), (c), (f), and (h) by Alex Kerstitch, (g) by D. A. Thomson, and (e) by courtesy of Dave Lindquist: a. Male bay blenny (*Hypsoblennius gentilis*). b. Adult Cortez triplefin (*Axoclinus* sp.). c. Male (lower fish) and female (upper fish) flag triplefin (*Enneanectes* sp.). d. Adult margarita blenny (*Malacoctenus margaritae*). e. Male barnaclebill blenny (*Hypsoblennius brevipinnis*). f. Adult male redside blenny (*Malacoctenus hubbsi*). g. Male mussel blenny (*Hypsoblennius jenkinsi*). h. Bluespotted jawfish (*Opisthognathus* sp.).

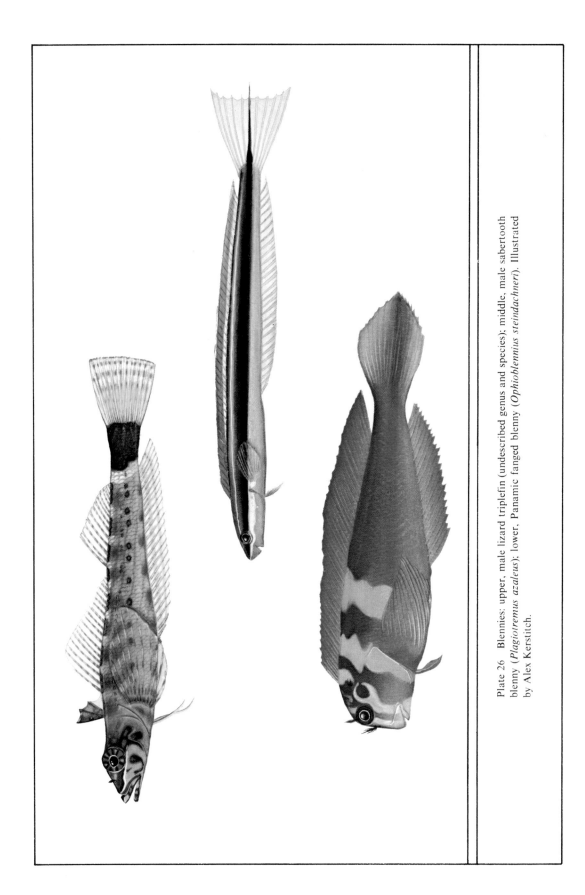

Plate 26 Blennies: upper, male lizard triplefin (undescribed genus and species); middle, male sabertooth blenny (*Plagiotremus azaleus*); lower, Panamic fanged blenny (*Ophioblennius steindachneri*). Illustrated by Alex Kerstitch.

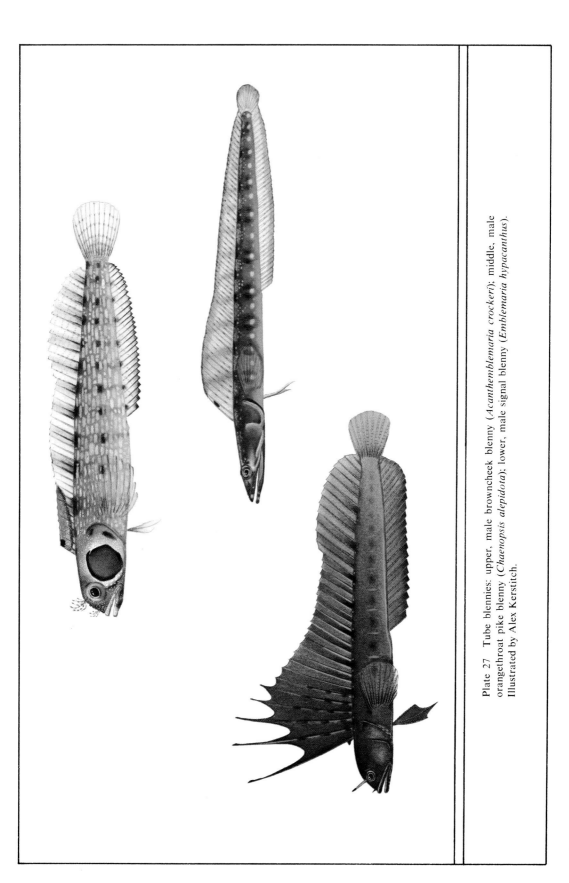

Plate 27   Tube blennies: upper, male browncheek blenny (*Acanthemblemaria crockeri*); middle, male orangethroat pike blenny (*Chaenopsis alepidota*); lower, male signal blenny (*Emblemaria hypacanthus*). Illustrated by Alex Kerstitch.

Plate 28   Tube blennies (photographs *a, b,* and *d* by courtesy of Dave Lindquist, *c* by D. A. Thomson, and *e, f, g,* and *h* by Alex Kerstitch): a. Male barnacle blenny (*Acanthemblemaria macrospilus*). b. Male clubhead blenny (*Acanthemblemaria balanorum*). c. Male browncheeck blenny (*Acanthemblemaria crockeri*). d. Reefsand blenny (*Ekemblemaria myersi*). e. Plume blenny (*Protemblemaria lucasanum*). f. Female elusive blenny (*Emblemaria walkeri*). g. Male angel blenny (*Coralliozetus angelica*). h. Male scarletfin blenny (*Coralliozetus micropes*).

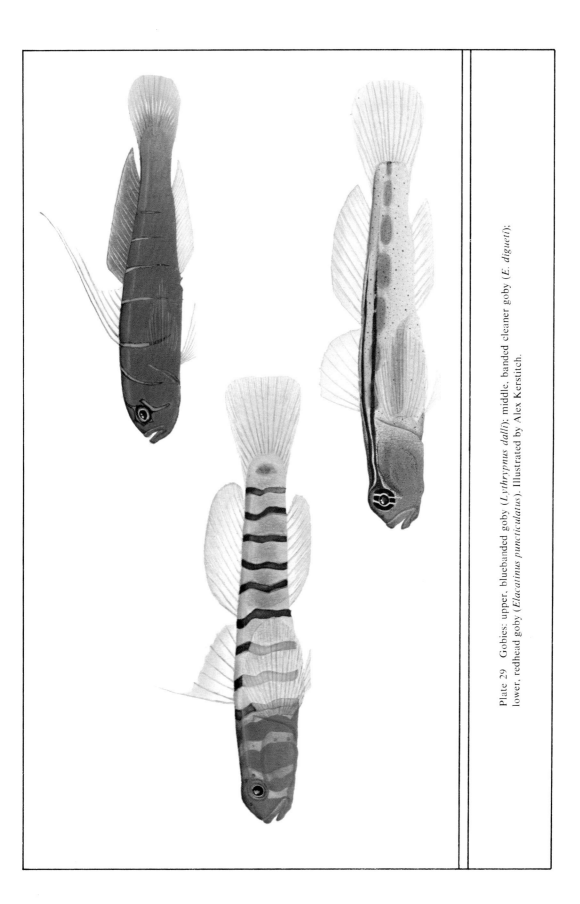

Plate 29  Gobies: upper, bluebanded goby (*Lythrypnus dalli*); middle, banded cleaner goby (*E. digueti*); lower, redhead goby (*Elacatinus puncticulatus*). Illustrated by Alex Kerstitch.

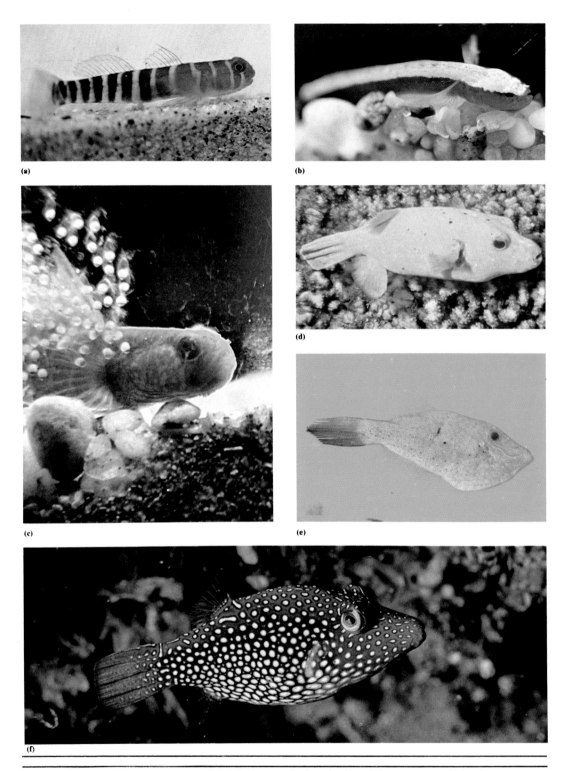

Plate 30 Gobies, puffers, and filefish [all photographs by Alex Kerstitch except (a), which is by L. T. Findley]: a. Widebanded cleaner goby (underscribed species) *Elacatinus* sp.). b. Sandtop goby (*Gobulus hancocki*). c. A male rubble goby (*Chriolepis minutillus*) guarding a spawn of eggs in an aquarium. d. Golden phase of the guineafowl puffer (*Arothron meleagris*). e. Scrawled filefish (*Alutera scripta*). f. Spotted sharpnose puffer (*Canthigaster punctatissima*).

Plate 31   Upper, yellowtail surgeonfish (*Prionurus punctatus*); lower, orangeside triggerfish (*Sufflamen verres*). Illustrated by Alex Kerstitch.

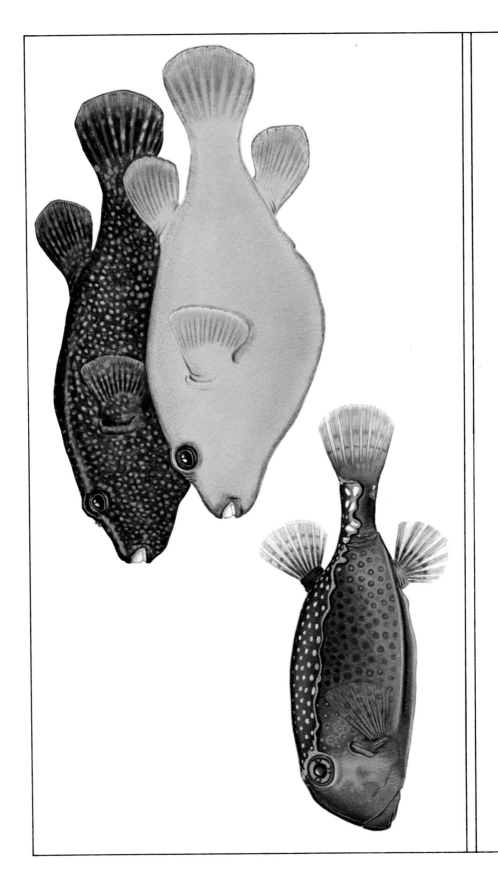

Plate 32 Upper, spotted and golden phases of the guineafowl puffer (*Arothron meleagris*): lower, male Pacific boxfish (*Ostracion meleagris*). Illustrated by Alex Kerstitch.

# PLATES

Plate 16c  Adult Clarion angelfish (*Holacanthus clarionensis*); tropical eastern Pacific.

Plate 16d  Juvenile Clarion angelfish (*Holacanthus clarionensis*); Cabo Pulmo, B.C.S.

Plate 16e  Adult king angelfish (*Holacanthus passer*); Cabo San Lucas.

Plate 16f  Juvenile king angelfish (*Holacanthus passer*); Gulf of California.

Plate 17a  Adult Cortez damselfish (*Eupomacentrus rectifraenum*); San Carlos, Sonora.

Plate 17b  Juvenile Cortez damselfish (*Eupomacentrus rectifraenum*); Bahía San Agustin, Sonora.

Plate 17c  Adult beaubrummel (*Eupomacentrus flavilatus*); Bahía San Carlos, Sonora.

Plate 17d  Juvenile beaubrummel (*Eupomacentrus flavilatus*); Manzanillo, Colima.

Plate 17e  Adult giant damselfish (*Microspathodon dorsalis*); Cabo San Lucas.

Plate 17f  Juvenile giant damselfish (*Microspathodon dorsalis*); Bahía San Carlos, Sonora.

Plate 17g  Juvenile blue-and-yellow chromis (*Chromis* sp.); Bahía San Carlos, Sonora.

Plate 17h  Juvenile silverstripe chromis (*Chromis* sp.); Isla San Pedro Nolasco.

Plate 18  Wounded wrasse (*Halichoeres chierchiae*); Puerto Vallarta, Jalisco. Banded wrasse (*Pseudojulis notospilus*); Mazatlán.

Plate 19  Female and male Cortez rainbow wrasse (*Thalassoma lucasanum*); Cabo San Lucas.

Plate 20  Pacific razorfish (*Hemipteronotus pavoninus*); Cabo San Lucas.

Plate 21a  Male Mexican hogfish (*Bodianus diplotaenia*); Isla San Pedro Nolasco.

Plate 21b  Female Mexican hogfish (*Bodianus diplotaenia*); Steinhart Aquarium, San Francisco, California.

Plate 21c  Male spinster wrasse (*Halichoeres nicholsi*); Guaymas.

Plate 21d  Female spinster wrasse (*Halichoeres nicholsi*); Bahía San Agustin, Sonora.

Plate 21e  Male chameleon wrasse (*Halichoeres dispilus*); Bahía San Carlos, Sonora.

Plate 21f  Male rock wrasse (*Halichoeres semicinctus*); Puerto Peñasco.

Plate 22a  Juvenile wounded wrasse (*Halichoeres chierchiae*); Bahía San Agustin, Sonora.

Plate 22b  Juvenile spinster wrasse (*Halichoeres nicholsi*); Bahía San Agustin, Sonora.

Plate 22c  Adult sunset wrasse (*Thalassoma lutescens*) and Cortez rainbow wrasse (*Thalassoma lucasanum*); Cabo Pulmo.

Plate 22d  Juvenile golden wrasse (*Pseudojulis melanotis*); Isla San Ignacio Farallon.

Plate 22e  Juvenile pearlscale razorfish (*Hemipteronotus taeniourus*); Cabo San Lucas.

Plate 22f  Adult blackspot wrasse (*Decodon melasma*); offshore Sonora.

Plate 23  Bumphead parrotfish (*Scarus perrico*); Bahía San Carlos, Sonora.

Plate 24a  Male bluechin parrotfish (*Scarus ghobban*); tropical eastern Pacific.

Plate 24b  Female bluechin parrotfish (*Scarus ghobban*); Isla Cerralvo.

Plate 24c  Adult giant hawkfish (*Cirrhitus rivulatus*); Isla San Pedro Nolasco.

Plate 24d  Juvenile giant hawkfish (*Cirrhitus rivulatus*); Bahía San Carlos, Sonora.

Plate 24e  Adult coral hawkfish (*Cirrhitichthys oxycephalus*); Cabo San Lucas.

Plate 25a  Male bay blenny (*Hypsoblennius gentilis*); Bahía San Carlos, Sonora.

Plate 25b  Adult Cortez triplefin (*Axoclinus* sp.); Bahía San Agustin, Sonora.

Plate 25c  Male and female flag triplefin (*Enneanectes* sp.); Bahía San Carlos, Sonora.

Plate 25d  Adult margarita blenny (*Malacoctenus margaritae*); Bahía San Agustin, Sonora.

Plate 25e  Male barnaclebill blenny (*Hypsoblennius brevipinnis*); Cabo San Lucas.

Plate 25f  Adult male redside blenny (*Malacoctenus hubbsi*); Guaymas.

Plate 25g  Male mussel blenny (*Hypsoblennius jenkinsi*); Puerto Peñasco.

Plate 25h  Bluespotted jawfish (*Opistognathus* sp.); Isla San Pedro Nolasco.

Plate 26  Panamic fanged blenny (*Ophioblennius steindachneri*); Mazatlán. Male sabertooth blenny (*Plagiotremus azaleus*); Puerto Vallarta, Jalisco. Male lizard triplefin (undescribed genus and species); Isla Angel de la Guarda.

Plate 27 Male browncheek blenny (*Acanthemblemaria crockeri*); Isla Tiburón. Male orangethroat pike blenny (*Chaenopsis alepidota*); Isla Angel de la Guarda.

Plate 28a Male barnacle blenny (*Acathemblemaria macrospilus*); Cabo San Lucas.

Plate 28b Male clubhead blenny (*Acanthemblemaria balanorum*); Cabo San Lucas.

Plate 28c Male browncheek blenny (*Acanthemblemaria crockeri*); Guaymas.

Plate 28d Reefsand blenny (*Ekemblemaria myersi*); Cabo San Lucas.

Plate 28e Plume blenny (*Protemblemaria lucasanum*); Isla San Pedro Nolasco.

Plate 28f Female elusive blenny (*Emblemaria walkeri*); Isla San Pedro Nolasco.

Plate 28g Male angel blenny (*Coralliozetus angelica*); Bahía San Carlos, Sonora.

Plate 28h Male scarletfin blenny (*Coralliozetus micropes*); Guaymas.

Plate 29 Bluebanded goby (*Lythrypnus dalli*); Isla Angel de la Guarda. Redhead goby (*Elacatinus puncticulatus*); Cabo San Lucas. Banded cleaner goby (*Elacatinus digueti*); Bahía San Agustin, Sonora.

Plate 30a Widebanded cleaner goby (undescribed species) (*Elacatinus* sp.); Cabo San Lucas.

Plate 30b Sandtop goby (*Gobulus hancocki*); Bahía San Agustin, Sonora.

Plate 30c Rubble goby (*Chriolepis minutillus*); Isla San Pedro Martir.

Plate 30d Golden phase of the guineafowl puffer (*Arothron meleagris*); Cabo Pulmo.

Plate 30e Scrawled filefish (*Alutera scripta*); Cabo San Lucas.

Plate 30f Spotted sharpnose puffer (*Canthigaster punctatissima*); Bahía San Carlos, Sonora.

Plate 31 Yellowtail surgeonfish (*Prionurus punctatus*); Cabo Pulmo. Orangeside triggerfish (*Sufflamen verres*); Puerto Escondido, Oaxaca.

Plate 32 Male Pacific boxfish (*Ostracion meleagris*); Cabo San Lucas. Guineafowl puffer (*Arothron meleagris*); Zihuatanejo, Guerrero.

# Glossary

**allopatric**  not occurring together within the same geographic region.

**amphipod**  a group of small, usually laterally compressed crustaceans.

**anal fin**  fin on the lower side of the body between the anus and the tail.

**annelid**  segmented coelomate worms; for example, fire worm.

**anterior**  toward the front or head region.

**barbel**  a threadlike or flaplike growth of skin on the lips or chin.

**bars**  any vertical markings along the sides or head.

**benthic**  living in close association with the bottom.

**branchiostegal rays**  bony support of the gill membrane behind the lower jaw and at the lower edges of the gill covers (opercula).

**brood pouch**  a cavity or space on the ventral body surface derived from folds of the abdomen or tail in which the young develop (e.g., as in pipefishes and seahorses).

**canine**  a sharp pointed tooth used for grasping prey.

**carapace**  hard covering encasing the body of trunkfishes.

**carnivore**  an animal whose diet consists predominantly of the flesh of other animals.

**caudal fin**  the tail fin.

**caudal peduncle**  that portion of the trunk between the rear of the anal fin and the caudal fin base.

**ciguatera**  human poisoning caused by eating various tropical shore fishes, usually top carnivores (e.g., moray eels, barracudas, snappers, or jacks), which are the most toxic of these species.

**circumtropical**  around the world in the area of the tropics.

**cirri** (singular, cirrus)  fringelike skin flaps on top of the head or on interspinous membrane (e.g., family Cirrhitidae).

**compressed**  flattened from side to side.

**confluent**  joined together (e.g., dorsal, caudal, and anal fins of moray).

**conspecific**  amember of the same species.

**crepuscular**  active at twilight (dawn or dusk) or in dim light.

**ctenoid scales**  scales that are serrated or have ctenii along their posterior margins.

**cycloid scales**  rounded, thin scales with smooth margins.

**dentary**  bone that forms the anterior part of the lower jaw and usually bears teeth.

**dermal flap**  a flap of skin on the head or body.

**dichromatic**  having two distinct color phases usually depending on maturity or sex.

**dimorphic**  having two different morphological phases (e.g., size, shape, color).

**disjunct distribution**  the geographic distribution of a species characterized by major gaps (i.e., not continuous).

**diurnal**  active during the day.

**dorsal**  pertaining to the upper surface or back.

**dorsal fin**  the fin extending along the upper surface or back.

**ectoparasite**  parasite living on the outer surface of a fish.

**endemic**  restricted to a particular region.

**estero**  a lagoon or "negative" estuary in which the salinity is greater at the head than at the mouth; common along desert coastlines such as the upper Gulf of California, where evaporation exceeds precipitation.

**estuary**  a brackish inlet of the sea fed by a river.

**euryhaline**   tolerance to a wide range of salinities.

**eurythermal**   tolerance to a wide range of temperatures.

**facultative cleaner**   an animal that feeds on ectoparasites of another animal in addition to its regular mode of feeding.

**formalin**   an aqueous solution of formaldehyde used as a preservative.

**gastropod**   mollusks of the class Gastropoda, such as snails, slugs, and limpets.

**gill raker**   bony projections on the gill arch that function to protect the gills and to strain food.

**genital papilla**   a small, fleshy protuberance behind the anus in some fish, often useful in determining sex. It includes the opening of the genital tract.

**gravid**   bearing eggs or young.

**gular**   pertaining to the throat region.

**herbivore**   an animal that eats predominantly plant matter, e.g., algae and diatoms.

**hermaphrodite**   an individual that possesses both male and female sex organs.

**holotype**   the single specimen designated as the "type" by the original author in the description of a new species.

**hypersaline**   having a higher concentration of salts than normal seawater.

**interorbital space**   the area on top of the head between the eyes.

**interradial membrane**   the membrane that separates fin rays.

**isthmus**   a narrow region of the throat between the gill openings.

**jugular**   pertaining to the neck or throat region.

**lanceolate**   shaped like a spear or lance.

**lateral line**   a line of sensory pores along the side of most fishes that generally runs from the back of the head to the caudal fin.

**littoral**   intertidal zone; the region between high and low tide marks.

**livebearer**   an animal that gives birth to live young.

**lunate**   crescent or moonshaped.

**maxilla**   a principal bone of the upper jaw.

**meristic**   pertaining to or involving counts.

**midwater**   in the middle of the water column as opposed to the surface or bottom.

**molar**   a rounded grinding tooth.

**monandric**   protogynous hermaphrodites among which all males are sex-reversed females.

**morphometric**   measurement of body parts.

**mouth breeding**   reproductive systems in which eggs are incubated in the mouth.

**neotenic**   retaining larval or juvenile characteristics in the adult stage.

**nocturnal**   active during the night.

**nuchal**   the region immediately behind the head in the area of the nape.

**obligate cleaner**   an animal that feeds exclusively on the ectoparasites of other animals.

**ocellus**   a pigmented, usually ringed, eyelike spot.

**omnivore**   an animal that feeds on plant and animal matter.

**opercle**   the major bone of the operculum.

**operculum**   the series of bones constituting the gill cover.

**orbit**   the bony cavity of the skull that holds the eye; the eye socket.

**ovoviviparous**   mode of reproduction in which eggs develop and hatch in the uterus.

**palatines**   paired bones on the roof of the mouth that often bear teeth.

**papilla**   any small, soft, rounded protuberance.

**paratype**   one of a group of designated specimens (other than the holotype) from which a new species is described.

**pectoral axil**   posterior (inside) base of the pectoral fin; i.e., the "armpit."

**pectoral fins**   paired, anterior, lateral fins.

**pelagic**   pertaining to the open sea.

**pelvic fins**   paired ventral fins.

**photophore**   a light-producing organ.

**plankton**   microscopic plants and animals suspended in the water column.

**polychaete**   a group of coelomate annelid worms that bear tiny bristles or setae on the lateral extensions of the body (parapodia).

**posterior**   behind or toward the rear.

**premaxilla**   anteriormost paired bone of the upper jaw that usually bears teeth.

**preopercle**   the bone anterior to the opercle and behind the eye that constitutes the forepart of the gill cover.

**protogynous hermaphrodite** a sequential hermaphrodite in which the female sex organs mature before the male sex organs.

**rotenone** a substance from the roots of certain plants, such as derris and cube, used as an ichthyocide for making fish collections.

**sequential hermaphrodite** a hermaphrodite whose sex organs mature at different times; i.e., an organism that functions as only one sex at a time.

**sessile** permanently fixed; immobile.

**sibling species** geographically separated species pairs that are similar morphologically and are assumed to be closely related.

**snout** that part of a fish's head in front of the eyes.

**soft-rays** segmented and often branched rods that support a fin.

**sp.** (plural spp.) abbreviation of species.

**spawn** to deposit eggs or discharge sperm.

**spine** a sharp projecting point; a fin ray that is neither segmented nor branched and usually rigid.

**stenothermal** tolerance to a narrow range of temperatures.

**stripes** narrow horizontal markings along sides or head.

**subdermal** beneath the skin.

**suborbital bone** a usually thin membrane bone lying beneath the eye.

**subspecies** populations of a species that have been geographically isolated from one another and consequently are taxonomically distinctive but not enough to name each of them as a separate species.

**superior mouth** mouth opening directed upward.

**symbiosis** one of several types of association between two organisms (e.g., parasitism, mutualism, or commensalism).

**sympatric** occurring within the same geographic region.

**synchronous hermaphrodite** a hermaphrodite that functions as a male and female at the same time.

**tetrodotoxin** the toxin produced by pufferfishes of the family Tetraodontidae and other animals (e.g., a California newt).

**thoracic** in the chest region.

**truncate** terminating abruptly; cut off.

**trunk** the body apart from the fins and head.

**twin species** see *sibling species*.

**vent** external opening of the alimentary canal; the anus.

**ventral** pertaining to the lower or under surface of an animal.

**vermiculation** a pattern of thin, wavy, wormlike lines.

**viscera** the internal organs of the body.

**vomer** a bone in the center of the palate that often bears teeth.

# General Bibliography

Berdegué-A., J. 1956. *Peces de importancia comercial en la costa nor-occidental de Mexico.* Dir. Gral. de Pesca e Ind. Conexas, Secretaria de Marina, Mexico, D.F. 345 pp.

Böhlke, J. E. and C. G. Chaplin. 1968. *Fishes of the Bahamas and adjacent tropical waters.* Academy of Natural Sciences of Philadelphia. Wynnewood, Pennsylvania: Livingston. 771 pp.

Briggs, J. C. 1974. *Marine zoogeography.* New York: McGraw-Hill. 475 pp.

Brusca, R. C. 1973. *A handbook to the common intertidal invertebrates of the Gulf of California.* Tucson: University of Arizona Press. 427 pp.

Cannon, R. and Sunset Editors. 1966. *The Sea of Cortez.* Menlo Park, California: Lane Magazine and Book Co. 283 pp.

Castro-Aguirre, J. L., J. Arvizu-Martínez, and J. Páez-Barrera. 1970. Contribución al conocimiento de los peces del Golfo de California. *Rev. Soc. Mex. Hist. Nat.* 31:107–181.

Chaplin, C. G. 1972. *Fishwatchers guide to West Atlantic coral reefs.* Wynnewood, Pennsylvania: Livingston. 65 pp.

Chirichigno-F., N. 1969. *Lista sistemática de los peces marinos comunes para Ecuador-Perú-Chile.* Conferencia sobre explotación y conservación de las riquezas maritimas del Pacifico Sur. Chile-Ecuador-Perú. Secretaria General, Lima. 108 pp.

Ehrlich, P. R. 1975. The population biology of coral reef fishes. *Ann. Rev. Ecol. Syst.* 6:211–247.

Ekman, S. 1953. *The zoogeography of the sea.* London: Sidgwick and Jackson. 417 pp.

Fitch, J. E. and R. J. Lavenberg. 1968. *Deep-water fishes of California.* Berkeley: University of California Press. 155 pp.

Fitch, J. E. and R. J. Lavenberg. 1971. *Marine food and game fishes of California.* Berkeley: University of California Press. 179 pp.

Fitch, J. E. and R. J. Lavenberg. 1975. *Tidepool and nearshore fishes of California.* Berkeley: University of California Press. 156 pp.

Gilbert, C. H. and E. C. Starks. 1904. The fishes of Panama Bay. *Mem. Calif. Acad. Sci.* 4. 304 pp.

Goodson, G. 1973. *The many-splendored fishes of Hawaii.* Palos Verdes Estates, California: Marquest Colorguide Books. 91 pp.

Goodson, G. 1976. *The many-splendored fishes of the Atlantic coast including the fishes of the Gulf of Mexico, Florida, Bermuda, the Bahamas, and the Caribbean.* Palos Verdes Estates, California: Marquest Colorguide Books. 204 pp.

Gosline, W. A. 1971. *Functional morphology and classification of teleostean fishes.* Honolulu: University of Hawaii Press. 208 pp.

Gosline, W. A. and V. E. Brock. 1960. *Handbook of Hawaiian fishes.* Honolulu: University of Hawaii Press. 372 pp.

Gotshall, D. W. 1977. *Fishwatchers' guide to the inshore fishes of the Pacific coast.* Monterey, California: Sea Challengers. 108 pp.

Greenwood, P. H., D. E. Rosen, S. H. Weitzman, and G. S. Myers. 1966. Phyletic studies of teleostean fishes, with a provisional classification of living forms. *Bull. Am. Mus. Nat. Hist.,* 131(4):341–455.

Halstead, B. W. 1967. *Poisonous and venomous marine animals of the world.* Vol. 2: Vertebrates. Washington, D.C.: U.S. Government Printing Office. 1070 pp.

Halstead, B. W. 1970. *Poisonous and venomous marine animals of the world.* Vol. 3: Vertebrates continued. Washington, D.C.: U.S. Government Printing Office. 1006 pp.

Hendrickson, J. R. 1974. Study of the marine environment of the northern Gulf of California. Nat. Tech. Info. Serv. Publ. N74-16008. 95 pp.

Herald, E. S. 1961. *Living fishes of the world.* Garden City, New York: Doubleday. 304 pp.

General Bibliography

Herald, E. S. 1972. *Fishes of North America*. New York: Doubleday. 254 pp.

Hildebrand, S. F. 1946. A descriptive catalog of the shore fishes of Peru. *Bull. U.S. Nat. Mus.*, **189**. 530 pp.

Hobson, E. S. 1968. Predatory behavior of some shore fishes in the Gulf of California. *Bur. Sports Fish. and Wildlife, Res. Rep.* **73**. 92 pp.

Hoese, H. D. and R. H. Moore. 1977. *Fishes of the Gulf of Mexico. Texas, Louisiana, and adjacent waters*. College Station: Texas A. & M. University Press. 327 pp.

Hubbs, C. L. and K. F. Lagler. 1947. *Fishes of the Great Lakes region*. Ann Arbor: University of Michigan Press. 186 pp.

Hubbs, C. L. and G. I. Roden. 1964. Oceanography and marine life along the Pacific coast of Middle America. In *Natural Environment and Early Cultures, Handbook of Middle American Indians*. R. Wauchope and R. C. West, Eds. Austin: University of Texas Press. Vol. 1, pp. 143–186.

Jordan, D. S. 1895. The fishes of Sinaloa. *Proc. Calif. Acad. Sci.,* ser. 2, **5**: 377–514.

Jordan, D. S. and B. W. Evermann. 1896–1900. The fishes of North and Middle America. Parts I, II, III, and IV. *Bull. U.S. Natl. Mus.* (47): 1–3313.

Jordan, D. S., B. W. Evermann, and H. W. Clark. 1930. Check-list of the fishes and fish-like vertebrates of North and Middle America, north of the northern boundary of Venezuela and Colombia. *Rep. U.S. Comm. Fish.,* **1928**. Appendix X. 670 pp.

Kato, S., S. Springer, and M. H. Wagner. 1967. Field Guide to eastern Pacific and Hawaiian sharks, *U.S. Fish and Wildlife Circ.* **271**. 47 pp.

Kumada, T. and Y. Hiyama. 1937. *Marine fishes of the Pacific coast of Mexico*. Odawara, Japan: Nisson Fish. Inst. 75 pp.

Lagler, K. F., J. E. Bardach, R. R. Miller, and D. R. M. Passino. 1977. *Ichthyology*. 2nd Ed. New York: Wiley. 506 pp.

Meek, S. E. and S. F. Hildebrand. 1923, 1925, and 1928. The marine fishes of Panama. *Field Mus. Nat. Hist., (Zool.)*, **15**, Parts I-III:1–1045.

Miller, D. J. and R. N. Lea. 1972. Guide to the coastal marine fishes of California. Sacramento: Calif Dept. Fish & Game, *Fish Bull.* **157**. 235 pp. (Reprinted with addendum added 1976, pp. 237–249.)

Nelson, J. S. 1976. *Fishes of the world*. New York: Wiley. 416 pp.

Norman, J. R. 1966. A draft synopsis of the orders. families and genera of recent fishes and fish-like vertebrates. Trustees of the British Museum (Natural History). London: Unwin Bros. 649 pp.

Norman, J. R. and P. H. Greenwood. 1975. *A history of fishes*. 3rd ed. London: Ernest Benn. 467 pp.

Parker, R. H. 1964. Zoogeography and ecology of macroinvertebrates of Gulf of California and continental slope of Western Mexico. In *Marine geology of the Gulf of California*. T. H. van Andel and G. G. Shore, Jr., Eds. *Amer. Assoc. Petrol Geol. Mem.* **3**:331–376.

Ramirez-Hernández, E. and A. Gonzales Pages. 1976. Catalogo de peces marinos Mexicanos. Mexico, D. F.: Secretaría de Industria y Comercio, Instituto Nacional de Pesca. 462 pp.

Randall, J. E. 1968. *Caribbean reef fishes*. Jersey City: T.F.H. 318 pp.

Roden, G. I. 1964. Oceanographic aspects of Gulf of California. In *Marine geology of the Gulf of California*. T. H. van Andel and G. G. Shore, Jr., Eds. *Amer. Assoc. Petrol. Geol., Mem.* **3**:30–58.

Roedel, P. M. 1953. *Common ocean fishes of the California coast*. Sacramento: Calif. Dept. Fish & Game, *Fish Bull.* **91**. 184 pp.

Schultz, L. P. and Collaborators. 1953–1966. Fishes of the Marshall and Marianas Islands. *Bull. U.S. Natl. Mus.* 202. Vol. 1 (1953), 685 pp., Vol. 2 (1960), 438 pp., Vol. 3 (1966), 176 pp.

Steinbeck, J. and E. F. Ricketts. 1941. Sea of Cortez, a leisurely journal of travel and research. New York: Viking. 598 pp.

Strand, S. W. 1977. Community structure among reef fish in the Gulf of California: the use of reef space and interspecific foraging associations. Ph.D. diss., University of California, Davis. 144 pp.

Thomson, D. A. and W. H. Eger. 1966. Guide to the families of the common fishes of the Gulf of California. Bur. Mimeo. & Multil., University of Arizona, Tucson. 53 pp.

Thomson, D. A. and C. E. Lehner. 1976. Resilience of a rocky intertidal fish community in a physically unstable environment. *J. exp. mar. Biol. Ecol.,* **22**:1–29.

Thomson, D. A. and N. McKibbin. 1976. *Gulf of California Fishwatcher's Guide*. Tucson: Golden Puffer Press. 75 pp.

Thomson, D. A., A. R. Mead, and J. F. Schreiber, Jr., Eds. 1969. Environmental impact of brine effluents on Gulf of California. *O.S.W. Res. & Dev. Prog. Rep.,* **387**:1–196.

Walford, L. A. 1937. Marine game fishes of the Pacific coast from Alaska to the Equator. Berkeley: University of California Press. 205 pp. (T.F.H.-Smithsonian reprint, with emendations, 1974.)

Walker, B. W. 1960. The distribution and affinities of the marine fish fauna of the Gulf of California. *Syst. Zool.* **9**(3):123–133.

Walker, B. W. Provisional checklist of the fishes of the Gulf of California. Unpubl. manuscript. University of California, Los Angeles.

Walls, J. G. 1975. *Fishes of the northern Gulf of Mexico*. Jersey City: T.F.H. 432 pp.

# Specific Bibliography

Allen, G. R. 1976. How many sergeant majors? *Marine Aquarist* 7(6):33–41.

Allen, G. R. 1975. *Damselfishes of the South Seas.* Neptune City, New Jersey: T.F.H. 240 pp.

Allen, G. R., D. F. Hoese, J. R. Paxton, J. E. Randall, B. C. Russell, W. A. Starck II, F. H. Talbot, and G. P. Whitley. 1976. Annotated checklist of the fishes of Lord Howe Island. *Rec. Australian Mus.* 30(15):365–454.

Alvarez-Borrego, S., P. Flores-Baez, and L. A. Galindo-Bect. 1975. Hidrología del alto Golfo de California II. Condiciones durante invierno, primavera y verano. *Ciencias Marinas* (Univ. Autón. Baja Calif.) 2(1):21–36.

Alvarez-Borrego, S. and L. A. Galindo-Bect. 1974. Hidrología del alto Golfo de California. I. Condiciones durante otoño. *Ciencias Marinas* (Univ. Autón. Baja Calif.) 1(1):46–64.

Alvarez del Villar, J. 1960. Cincuenta años de ictiologia en Mexico. *Rev. Soc. Mex. Hist. Nat.* 21(1):49–61.

Bailey, R. M., J. E. Fitch, E. S. Herald, E. A. Lachner, C. C. Lindsey, C. R. Robins, and W. B. Scott. 1970. A list of common and scientific names of fishes from the United States and Canada. 3rd ed. *Am. Fish. Soc., Spec. Publ.* (6):1–150.

Baldwin, W. J. 1963. A new chaetodont fish, *Holacanthus limbaughi*, from the eastern Pacific *Contrib. Sci. Los Angeles Co. Mus.* 74. 8 pp.

Barlow, G. W. 1961a. Gobies of the genus *Gillichthys* with comments on the sensory canals as a taxonomic tool. *Copeia* 1961(1):423–437.

Barlow, G. W. 1961b. Intra- and interspecific differences in rate of oxygen consumption in gobiid fishes of the genus *Gillichthys. Biol. Bull.* 121(2):209–229.

Barlow, G. W. 1963. Species structure of the gobiid fish *Gillichthys mirabilis* from coastal sloughs of the eastern Pacific. *Pac. Sci.* 17:47–72.

Barlow, G. W. 1974. Contrasts in social behavior between Central American cichlid fishes and coral-reef surgeon fishes. *Amer. Zool.* 14:9–34.

Beebe, W. 1938. *Zaca venture.* New York: Harcourt, Brace. 308 pp.

Beebe, W. and J. Tee-Van. 1941. Eastern Pacific expeditions of the New York Zoological Society. 28. Fishes from the tropical eastern Pacific. Pt. 3. Rays, mantas and chimaeras. *Zoologica* 26(3):245–280.

Berry, F. H. and W. J. Baldwin. 1966. Triggerfishes (Balistidae) of the eastern Pacific. *Proc. Calif. Acad. Sci.* 34(9):429–474.

Berry, F. H. and L. E. Vogele. 1961. Filefishes (Monacanthidae) of the western North Atlantic. *U.S. Fish Wildl. Serv., Fish. Bull.* 181, 61:61–109.

Birdsong, R. S. 1975. The osteology of *Microgobius signatus* Poey (Pices:Gobiidae), with comments on other gobioid fishes. *Bull. Florida State Mus., Biol. Sci.* 19(3):135–187.

Böhlke, J. E. 1953. A new stathmonotid blenny from the Pacific coast of Mexico. *Zoologica* 38(11):145–149.

Böhlke, J. E. 1955a. The brotulid Fish genus *Petrotyx* from the Great Bahama Bank. *Notulae Naturae* (Acad. Nat. Sci. Phil.) 282. 7 pp.

Böhlke, J. E. 1955b. On the Bahaman fishes of the family Opisthognathidae. *Notulae Naturae* (Acad. Nat. Sci. Phil.), 281. 6 pp.

Böhlke, J. E. 1957a. A review of the blenny genus *Chaenopsis*, and the description of a related new genus from the Bahamas. *Proc. Acad. Nat. Sci. Philadelphia* 109:81–103.

Böhlke, J. E. 1957b. On the occurrence of garden eels in the western Atlantic, with a synopsis of the heterocongrinae. *Proc. Acad. Nat. Sci. Philadelphia* 109:59–79.

Böhlke, J. E. 1960. Comments on serranoid fishes with disjunct lateral lines, with the description of a new one from the Bahamas. *Notulae Naturae* (Acad. Nat. Sci. Phil.) 330. 11 pp.

## Specific Bibliography

Böhlke, J. E. and J. C. Briggs. 1953. The rare cirrhitid fish genus *Oxycirrhites* in American waters. *Calif. Fish & Game* 39(3):375–380.

Böhlke, J. E. and J. E. McCosker. 1973. Two additional west Atlantic gobies (genus *Gobiosoma*) that remove ectoparasites from other fishes. *Copeia* 1973(3):609–610.

Böhlke, J. E. and J. E. Randall. 1968. A key to the shallow-water west Atlantic cardinalfishes (Apogonidae), with descriptions of five new species. *Proc. Acad. Nat. Sci. Philadelphia* 120(4):175–206.

Böhlke, J. E. and C. H. Robins. 1974. Description of a new genus and species of clinid fish from the western Caribbean, with comments on the families of the Blennioidea. *Proc. Acad. Nat. Sci. Philadelphia* 126(1):1–8.

Böhlke, J. E. and C. R. Robins. 1960. A revision of the gobioid fish genus *Coryphopterus*. *Proc. Acad. Nat. Sci. Philadelphia* 112(5):103–128.

Böhlke, J. E. and C. R. Robins, 1962. The taxonomic position of the west Atlantic goby, *Eviota personata*, with descriptions of two new related species. *Proc. Acad. Nat. Sci. Philadelphia* 114(5):175–189.

Böhlke, J. E. and C. R. Robins. 1968. Western Atlantic seven-spined gobies, with descriptions of ten new species and a new genus, and comments on Pacific relatives. *Proc. Acad. Nat. Sci. Philadelphia* 120(3):45–174.

Bolin, R. L. 1944. A review of the marine cottid fishes of California. *Stanford Ichthyol. Bull.* 3(1):1–135.

Bortone, S. A. 1974. *Diplectrum rostrum*, a hermaphroditic new species (Pisces:Serranidae) from the eastern Pacific coast. *Copeia* 1974 (1):61–65.

Bortone, S. A. 1977. Gonad morphology of the hemaphroditic fish *Diplectrum pacificum* (Serranidae). *Copeia* 1977(3):448–453.

Boylan, D. B. and P. J. Scheuer. 1967. Pahutoxin: a fish poison. *Science* 155:52–56.

Breder, C. M., Jr. 1936. Heterosomata to Pediculati from Panama to Lower California. Scientific results of the second oceanographic expedition of the "Pawnee" 1926. *Bull. Bingham Oceano. Coll.* 2(3):1–56.

Briggs, J. C. 1955. A monograph of the clingfishes (order Xenopterygii). *Stanford Ichthyol. Bull.* 6:1–224.

Briggs, J. C. 1960. A new clingfish of the genus *Gobiesox* from the Tres Marias Islands. *Copeia* 1960(3):215–217.

Briggs, J. C. 1961. The East Pacific barrier and the distribution of marine shore fishes. *Evolution* 15:545–554.

Briggs, J. C. 1969. The clingfishes (Gobiesocidae) of Panama. *Copeia* 1969(4):774–778.

Briggs, J. C. and R. R. Miller. 1960. Two new freshwater clingfishes of the genus *Gobiesox* from southern Mexico. *Occ. Pap. Mus. Zool. Univ. Mich.* 616. 15 pp.

Brittan, M. R. 1966. A small collection of shore fishes from the west coast of Costa Rica. *Ichthyologia* 37(3):121–134.

Brock, V. E. 1938. Notes on the ranges of fishes from Lower California and the west coast of Mexico, with a discussion on the use of diving apparatus in making collections. *Copeia* 1938(3):128–131.

Brock, V. E. 1956. Possible production of substances poisonous to fishes by the boxfish *Ostracion lentiginosus* Schneider. *Copeia* 1956(3):195–196.

Brusca, R. C. and D. A. Thomson. 1975. Pulmo Reef: the only "coral reef" in the Gulf of California. *Ciencias Marinas* (Univ. Autón. Baja Calif.) 2(2):37–53.

Burgess, W. E. 1974. Evidence for the evaluation to family status of the angelfishes (Pomacanthidae) previously considered to be a subfamily of the butterflyfish family, Chaetodontidae. *Pac. Sci.* 28(1):57–71.

Bussing, W. A. 1969. *Familias de peces marinas Costarricenses y de aguas contiguas*. Univ. Costa Rica Facultad de Ciencias y Letras, Departamento de Biologia, *Serie Ciencias Naturales* No. 6. 39 pp.

Bussing, W. A. 1972. *Halichoeres aestuaricola*, a replacement name for the tropical eastern Pacific labrid fish, *Iridio bimaculata* Wilson, with a redescription based on new material. *Brenesia* 1:3–9.

Caldwell, D. K. 1962. Western Atlantic fishes of the family Priacanthidae. *Copeia* 1962(2):417–424.

Caporiacco, L. di. 1947. Miscellanea ichthyologica. *Boll. Pesca Piscicolt. Idrobiol. Roma* 23:193–205.

Castro-Aguirre, J. L. and F. de Lachica-Bonilla. 1973. Nuevos registros de peces marinos en la costa del Pacifico Mexicana. *Rev. Soc. Mex. Hist. Nat.* 34:147–181.

Castro-Barrera, T. 1975. Ictioplancton de Bahía Magdalena, Baja California Sur. *Ciencias Marinas* (Univ. Autón. Baja Calif.) 2(2):10–36.

Charney, P. 1976. Oral brooding in the cardinalfishes *Phaeoptyx conklini* and *Apogon maculatus* from the Bahamas. *Copeia* 1976(1):198–200.

Chen, L. C. 1975. The rockfishes, genus *Sebastes* (Scorpaenidae), of the Gulf of California, including three new species, with a discussion of their origin. *Proc. Calif. Acad. Sci.* 40(6):109–141.

Chen, T. R. and A. W. Ebeling. 1971. Chromosomes of the goby fishes in the genus *Gillichthys*. *Copeia* 1971(1):171–174.

Clark, E. 1959. Functional hermaphroditism and self-fertilization in a serranid fish. *Science* 129(3343):215–216.

Clark, E. 1972. The Red Sea's garden of eels. *Natl. Geogr.* **142**(5):724–734.

Clark, H. W. 1936. The Templeton Crocker Expedition of the California Academy of Sciences, 1932. No. 29. New and noteworthy fishes. *Proc. Calif. Acad. Sci.* **21**(29):383–396.

Clemens, H. B. 1957. Fishes collected in the tropical eastern Pacific, 1954. *Calif. Fish & Game* **43**(4):299–307.

Clothier, C. R. 1939. The trigger mechanism of a trigger fish (*Capriscus polylepis*). *Calif. Fish & Game* **25**(3):233–236.

Cohen, D. M. 1964. A review of the ophidioid genus *Oligopus* with the description of a new species from West Africa. *Proc. U.S. Natl. Mus.* **116**(3494):1–22.

Colin, P. L. 1973a. Burrowing behavior of the yellowhead jawfish, *Opistognathus aurifrons. Copeia* **1973**(1):84–90.

Colin, P. L. 1973b. Comparative biology of the gobies of the genus *Gobiosoma*, subgenus *Elacatinus* in the western North Atlantic Ocean. Ph.D. diss., University of Miami, Coral Gables, Florida. 247 pp.

Colin, P. L. 1975. *The neon gobies.* Jersey City: T.F.H. 304 pp.

Congleton, J. L. 1968. Variation in the pink seaperch, *Zalembius rosaceus* (Jordan and Gilbert), and extension of its known range to the Gulf of California. *Calif. Fish & Game* **54**(2):115–122.

Courtenay, W. R., Jr. 1961. Western Atlantic Fishes of the genus *Haemulon* (Pomadasyidae): systematic status and juvenile pigmentation. *Bull. Mar. Sci. Gulf & Carib.* **11**:66–149.

Courtenay, W. R., Jr. 1976. Atlantic fishes of the genus *Rypticus* (Grammistidae). *Proc. Acad. Nat. Sci. Philadelphia.* **119**(6):241–293.

Cowan, G. I. McT. and R. H. Rosenblatt. 1974. *Taenioconger canabus,* a new heterocongrin eel (Pisces: Congridae) from Baja California, with a comparison of a closely related species. *Copeia* **1974**(1):55–60.

Critchlow, K. R. 1972. Resource utilization in some rocky shore fishes in the Gulf of California. Ph.D. diss., University of California, Los Angeles. 133 pp.

Crooke, S. J. 1973. The first occurrence of *Kyphosus analogus* in California. *Calif. Fish & Game* **59**(4):310–311.

Dawson, C. E. 1975. Studies on eastern Pacific sand stargazers (Pisces: Dactyloscopidae). 2. Genus *Dactyloscopus,* with descriptions of new species and subspecies. *Nat. Hist. Mus. Los Angeles Co., Sci. Bull.* **22**:1–16.

Dawson, C. E. 1976. Studies on eastern Pacific sand stargazers. 3. *Dactylagnus* and *Myxodagnus,* with description of a new species and subspecies. *Copeia* **1976**(1):13–43.

Del Campo, R. M. 1939. Nota acerca de una pequeña colección de peces procedentes de Guaymas, Sonora. *An. Inst. Biol. Mexico* **10**(1–2):187–189.

DeRoy, T. A. 1974. Discovering a new species. *Pac. Discovery* (Calif. Acad. Sci.) **27**(3):12–14.

Diener, D. R. 1976. Hermaphroditism in fish: a comparative study of the reproductive biology and endocrinology of the California Labridae. Ph.D. diss., University of California, San Diego.

Diener, D. R. 1977. Protogynous hermaphroditism in the labrid *Decodon melasma. Copeia* **1977**(3):589–591.

Dooley, J. K. 1978. Systematics and biology of the tilefishes (Perciformes: Branchiostegidae and Malacanthidae), with descriptions of two new species. *NOAA Tech. Rep. NMFS Circ.* **411**. 79 pp.

Ebeling, A. W. 1957. The dentition of eastern Pacific mullets, with special reference to adaptation and taxonomy. *Copeia* **1957**(3):173–185.

Ebeling, A. W. 1961. *Mugil galapagensis,* a new mullet from the Galapagos Islands, with notes on a related species and a key to the Mugilidae of the eastern Pacific. *Copeia* **1961**(3):295–305.

Ebert, E. E. and C. H. Turner. 1962. The nesting behavior, eggs and larvae of the bluespot goby. *Calif. Fish & Game* **48**(4):249–252.

Eckert, D. B. 1974. The systematics and biology of the bluebanded goby, *Lythrypnus dalli* (Teleostei: Gobiidae), in southern California. M. A. thesis, Occidental College, Los Angeles, California. 117 pp.

Eger, W. H. 1963. An exotoxin produced by the puffer, *Arothron hispidus,* with notes of the toxicity of other plectognath fishes. M. S. thesis, University of Hawaii, Honolulu. 80 pp.

Eger, W. H. 1971. Ecological and physiological adaptations of intertidal clingfishes (Teleostei: Gobiesocidae) in the northern Gulf of California. Ph.D. diss., University of Arizona, Tucson. 210 pp.

Eschmeyer, W. N. 1965. Western Atlantic scorpionfishes of the genus *Scorpaena,* including four new species. *Bull. Mar. Sci.* **15**(1):84–164.

Eschmeyer, W. N. 1969. A systematic review of the scorpionfishes of the Atlantic Ocean (Pisces: Scorpaenidae). *Occ. Pap. Calif. Acad. Sci.* No. 79. 143 pp.

Eschmeyer, W. N. and J. E. Randall. 1975. The scorpaenid fishes of the Hawaiian Islands, including new species and new records (Pisces: Scorpaenidae). *Proc. Calif. Acad. Sci.* **40**(11):265–334.

Evermann, B. W. and O. P. Jenkins. 1891. Report on a collection of fishes made at Guaymas, Sonora, Mexico, with descriptions of new species. *Proc. U.S. Nat. Mus.* **14**:121–165.

Findley, L. T. An illustrated and annotated checklist of certain species of fishes from the Gulf of California in the California State College at Long Beach ichthyology museum. Unpublished manuscript (1965), California State College, Long Beach.

Findley, L. T. 1975. A new species of goby from Malpelo Island (Teleostei: Gobiidae: *Chriolepis*). *In* The biological investigation of Malpelo Island, Colombia. J. B. Graham, Ed. *Smithsonian Contrib. Zool.* No. 176:94–98.

Findley, L. T. 1976. Aspectos ecologicos de los esteros con manglares en Sonora y su relacion con la explotacion humana. In *Sonora: Antropologia del Desierto.* B. Braniff and R. S. Felger, Eds., Instituto Nacional de Anthropologia e Historia, Mexico, D.F., Colleccion Cientifica No. 27:95–105.

Findley, L. T. (MS). Preliminary notes on the ethnoichthyology of the Seri Indians of Sonora, Mexico. Unpublished manuscript, University of Arizona.

Fisher, R. L., G. A. Rusnak, and F. P. Shepard. 1964. Submarine topography of Gulf of California. *In Marine Geology of the Gulf of California* (T. H. van Andel and G. G. Shor, Jr., Eds.) *Amer. Assoc. Petro. Geol. Memoir 3.*

Follett, W. I., D. Gotshall, and G. Smith. 1960. Northerly occurrences of the scorpid fish *Medialuna californiensis* (Steindachner), with meristic data, life-history notes, and discussion of the fisheries. *Calif. Fish & Game* 46(2):165–175.

Fowler, H. W. 1944. Results of the Fifth George Vanderbilt Expedition (1941). (Bahamas, Caribbean Sea, Panama, Galápagos Archipelago, and Mexican Pacific islands). The Fishes. *Monogr. Acad. Nat. Sci. Philadelphia* No. 6:57–529.

Fraser, T. H. 1972. Comparative osteology of the shallow water cardinal fishes (Perciformes: Apogonidae) with reference to the systematics and evolution of the family. *Ichthyol. Bull.* (Rhodes University) No. 34:1–105.

Fraser-Brunner, A. 1933. A revision of the chaetodont fishes of the subfamily Pomacanthinae. *Proc. Zool. Soc. London* 1933(3):543–599.

Fraser-Brunner, A. 1935. Notes on the plectognath fishes. II. A synopsis of the genera of the family Ostraciontidae. *Ann. Mag. Nat. Hist., Ser.* 10, 16:313–320.

Fraser-Brunner, A. 1940. Notes on the plectognath fishes. IV. Sexual dimorphism in the family Ostraciontidae. *Ann. Mag. Nat. Hist., Ser.* 11, 6:390–392.

Fraser-Brunner, A. 1943. Notes on the plectognath fishes. VIII. The classification of the suborder Tetraodontoidea, with a synopsis of the genera. *Ann. Mag. Nat. Hist. Ser.* 11, 10:1–18.

Freihofer, W. C. 1966. New distributional records of the butterflyfish *Chaetodon falcifer. Stanford Ichthyol. Bull.* 8(3):207.

Fritzsche, R. A. 1976a. A revision of the eastern Pacific Syngnathidae (Pisces: Syngnathiformes). Ph.D. diss., University of California, San Diego. 197 pp.

Fritzsche, R. A. 1976b. A review of the cornetfishes, genus *Fistularia* (Fistulariidae), with a discussion of the intrageneric relationships and zoogeography. *Bull. Mar. Sci.* 26(2):196–204.

Garman, S. 1899. Reports on an exploration off the west coasts of Mexico, Central and South America, and off the Galapagos Islands, in charge of Alexander Agassiz, by the U.S. Fish Commission steamer, "Albatross," during 1891, Lieut. Commander Z. L. Tanner, U.S.N., commanding. *XXVI.* The Fishes. *Mem. Mus. Comp. Zool., Harvard Univ.* 24:1–431 (in two volumes text and plates).

Gates, D. E. and H. W. Frey. 1974. Designated common names of certain marine organisms of California. *Calif. Dept. Fish & Game, Fish Bull.* No. 161:55–90.

Gilbert, C. H. 1890. XII—A preliminary report on the fishes collected by the steamer "Albatross" on the Pacific coast of North America during the year 1889, with descriptions of twelve new genera and ninety-two new species. *Proc. U. S. Natl. Mus.* 13:49–126.

Gilbert, C. H. 1892. Scientific results of explorations by the U.S. Fish Commission steamer "Albatross." XXII. Descriptions of thirty-four new species of fishes collected in 1888 and 1889, principally among the Santa Barbara Islands and in the Gulf of California. *Proc. U.S. Natl. Mus.* 14 (for 1891):539–566.

Gilbert C. R. 1972. Characteristics of the western Atlantic reef-fish fauna. *Quart. Jour. Florida Acad. Sci.* 35(2-3):130–144.

Ginsburg, I. 1937. Review of the seahorses (*Hippocampus*) found on the coasts of the American continents and of Europe. *Proc. U.S. Natl. Mus.* 83(2997):497–594.

Ginsburg, I. 1938a. Two new gobiid fishes of the genus *Gobiosoma* from Lower California. *Stanford Ichthyol. Bull.* 1(2):57–59.

Ginsburg, I. 1938b. Eight new species of gobioid fishes from the American Pacific coast. *Allan Hancock Pac. Exped.* (University of Southern California) 2(7):109–121.

Ginsburg, I. 1939. Twenty-one new American gobies. *J. Wash. Acad. Sci.* 29(2):51–63.

Ginsburg, I. 1947. American species and subspecies of *Bathygobius*, with a demonstration of a suggested modified system of nomenclature. *J. Wash. Acad. Sci.* 37(8):275–284.

Ginsburg, I. 1953. Western Atlantic scorpionfishes. *Smithsonian Misc. Coll.* 121(8):1–103.

Goe, D. R. and B. W. Halstead. 1953. A preliminary report of the toxicity of the Gulf puffer, *Sphoeroides annulatus. Calif. Fish & Game* 39(2):229–232.

Gollub, A. 1974. Tidal activity rhythms in two species of intertidal clingfish (Gobiesocidae) in the northern Gulf of California. M.S. thesis, University of Arizona, Tucson. 57 pp.

Gomon, M. F. 1974. A new eastern Pacific labrid (Pisces), *Decodon melasma,* a geminate species of the western Atlantic *D. puellaris. Proc. Biol. Soc. Wash.* **87**(19):205–216.

Gorman, G. C. and Y. J. Kim. 1977. Genotypic evolution in the face of phenotypic conservativeness: *Abudefduf* (Pomacentridae) from the Atlantic and Pacific sides of Panama, *Copeia* **1977**(4):694–697.

Gosline, W. A. 1958. Central Pacific eels of the genus *Uropterygius,* with descriptions of two new species. *Pac. Sci.* **12**(3):221–228.

Gosline, W. A. 1960. A new Hawaiian percoid fish, *Suttonia lineata,* with a discussion of its relationships and a definition of the family Grammistidae. *Pac. Sci.* **14**(1):28–38.

Gosline, W. A. 1966. The limits of the fish family Serranidae, with notes on other lower percoids. *Proc. Calif. Acad. Sci.* **33**(6):91–112.

Gosline, W. A. 1968. The suborders of perciform fishes. *Proc. U.S. Natl. Hist. Mus.* **124**(3647):1–78.

Gosline, W. A. 1970. A reinterpretation of the teleostean fish order Gobiesociformes. *Proc. Calif. Acad. Sci.* **37**(19):363–382.

Graham, J. B. 1971. Temperature tolerances of some closely related tropical Atlantic and Pacific fish species. *Science* **172**:861–863.

Graham, J. B. 1973. Terrestrial life of the amphibious fish *Mnierpes macrocephalus. Mar. Biol.* **23**:83–91.

Graham, J. B. and R. H. Rosenblatt. 1970. Aerial vision: unique adaptation of an intertidal fish. *Science* **168**:586–588.

Greenfield, D. W. 1965. Systematics and zoogeography of *Myripristis* in the eastern Pacific. *Calif. Fish & Game* **51**(4):229–247.

Greenfield, D. W. 1968. The zoogeography of *Myripristis* (Pisces: Holocentridae). *Syst. Zool.* **17**(1):76–87.

Greenfield, D. W. 1974. A revision of the squirrelfish genus *Myripristis* Cuvier (Pisces: Holocentridae). *Nat. Hist. Mus. Los Angeles Co., Sci. Bull.* **19**. 54 pp.

Greenfield, D. W., D. Hensley, J. W. Wiley, and S. T. Ross. 1970. The Isla Jaltemba coral formation and its zoogeographical significance. *Copeia* **1970**(1):180–181.

Hansen, G. B. 1974. Resource partitioning in two sympatric blennioid fishes (Family Clinidae), *Labrisomus xanti* and *Malacoctenus gigas,* in the northern Gulf of California. M.S. thesis, University of Arizona, Tucson. 70 pp.

Heath, W. G. 1967. Ecological significance of temperature tolerance in Gulf of California shore fishes. *J. Ariz. Acad. Sci.* **4**(3):172–178.

Heller, E. and R. E. Snodgrass. 1903. Papers from the Hopkins Stanford Galápagos Expedition, 1898–1899. 15. New fishes. *Proc. Wash. Acad. Sci.* **5**:189–229.

Helvey, M. 1975. Interspecific discrimination in the territoriality of the Cortez damselfish, *Pomacentrus rectifraenum* Gill. M.S. thesis, University of Arizona, Tucson. 61 pp.

Herald, E. S. 1940. A key to the pipefishes of the Pacific American coasts with descriptions of new genera and species. *Alan Hancock Pac. Exped.* (University of Southern California) **9**(3):51–64.

Herald, E. S. 1953. Family Syngnathidae: pipefishes. In *Fishes of the Marshall and Marianas Islands* (L. P. Schutz and collaborators). *Bull. U.S. Natl. Mus.* 202. **1**:231–278.

Herald, E. S. 1959. From pipefish to seahorse—a study of phylogenetic relationships. *Proc. Calif. Acad. Sci.* **29**(13):465–473.

Herald, E. S. 1970. The garden eels. *Salt Water Aquar.* **6**(4):203–206.

Herre, A. W. 1936. Fishes of the Crane Pacific Expedition. *Fieldiana (Zool.), Field Mus. Nat. Hist. Chicago,* **21**:1–472.

Hiatt, R. W. and D. W. Strasburg. 1960. Ecological relationships of the fish fauna on coral reefs of the Marshall Islands. *Ecol. Monogr.* **30**(1):65–127.

Hildebrand, S. F. and O. Barton. 1949. A collection of fishes from Talara, Peru. *Smithsonian Misc. Coll.* **111**(10):1–36.

Hobson, E. S. 1965a. Diurnal-nocturnal activity of some inshore fishes in the Gulf of California. *Copeia* **1965**(3):291–302.

Hobson, E. S. 1965b. A visit with el barbero. *Underwater Naturalist* **3**:5–10.

Hobson, E. S. 1969a. First California record of the Guadalupe cardinalfish, *Apogon guadalupensis* (Osburn and Nichols). *Calif. Fish & Game* **55**(2):149–151.

Hobson, E. S. 1969b. Possible advantages to the blenny *Runula azalea* in aggregating with the wrasse *Thalassoma lucasanum* in the tropical eastern Pacific. *Copeia* **1969**(1):191–193.

Hobson, E. S. 1969c. Comments on certain recent generalizations regarding cleaning symbiosis in fishes. *Pac. Sci.* **23**(1):35–39.

Hobson, E. S. 1972. The survival of Guadalupe cardinalfish, *Apogon guadalupensis,* at San Clemente Island. *Calif. Fish & Game* **58**(1):68–69.

Hobson, E. S. 1974. Feeding relationships of teleostean fishes on coral reefs in Kona, Hawaii. *Fish. Bull.* **72**(4):915–1031.

Hobson, E. S. 1975. First California record of the

serranid fish *Anthias gordensis* Wade. *Calif. Fish & Game* **61**(2):111–112.

Hobson, E. S. 1976. The rockwrasse, *Halichoeres semicinctus*, as a cleaner-fish. *Calif. Fish & Game* **62**(1):73–78.

Hoese, D. F. 1971. A revision of the eastern Pacific species of the gobiid fish genus *Gobiosoma*, with a discussion of relationships of the genus. Ph.D. diss., University of California, San Diego. 213 pp.

Hoese, D. F. 1976. Variation, synonymy and a redescription of the gobiid fish *Aruma histrio* and a discussion of the related genus *Ophiogobius*. *Copeia* **1976**(2):295–305.

Hoese, D. F. and H. K. Larson (in press). A revision of the eastern Pacific species of the genus *Barbulifer* (Pisces: Gobiidae), with a comment on the tribe Gobiosomini. *Copeia*.

Hong, S. L. 1977. Review of eastern Pacific *Haemulon* with notes on juvenile pigmentation. *Copeia* **1977**(3):493–501.

Hubbs, C. 1952. A contribution to the classification of the blennioid fishes of the family Clinidae, with a partial revision of the eastern Pacific forms. *Stanford Ichthyol. Bull.* **4**(2):41–165.

Hubbs, C. 1953. Revision of the eastern Pacific fishes of the clinid genus *Labrisomus*. *Zoologica* **38**(3):113–136.

Hubbs, C. 1954. Additional records of clinid fishes, with the description of a new species of *Cryptotrema* from the Gulf of California. *Copeia* **1954**(1):17–19.

Hubbs, C. L. 1944. Species of the circumtropical fish genus *Brotula*. *Copeia* **1944**(3):162–178.

Hubbs, C. L. 1945. The record of a fish, *Scorpaena mystes*, from California: a comedy of errors. *Copeia* **1945**(3):129–133.

Hubbs, C. L. 1948. Changes in the fish fauna of western North America correlated with changes in ocean temperature. *J. Mar. Res.* **7**(3):459–482.

Hubbs, C. L. 1960. The marine vertebrates of the outer coast. *Syst. Zool.* **9**(3):134–147.

Hubbs, C. L. 1963. *Chaetodon aya* and related deep-dwelling butterflyfishes: their variations, distributions and synonymy. *Bull. Mar. Sci. Gulf & Caribb.* **13**(1):133–192.

Hubbs, C. L. 1974. Book review of *Marine Zoogeography* by John C. Briggs. New York: McGraw-Hill. *Copeia* **1974**(4):1002–1005.

Hubbs, C. L. and S. D. Hinton. 1963. The giant sea horse returns. *Pac. Disc.* **16**(5):12–15.

Hubbs, C. L. and A. B. Rechnitzer. 1958. A new fish, *Chaetodon falcifer*, from Guadalupe Island, Baja California, with notes on related species. *Proc. Calif. Acad. Sci.* **29**(8):273–313.

Ives, R. L. 1959. Shell dunes of the Sonoran shore.

Jenkins, O. P. and B. W. Evermann. 1889. Description of eighteen new species of fishes from the Gulf of California. *Proc. U.S. Natl. Mus.* **11**:137–158.

Jordan, D. S. 1884. Notes on fishes collected at Guaymas, Mexico, by Mr. H. E. Emeric, with a description of *Gobiosoma histrio*, a new species. *Proc. U.S. Natl. Mus.* **7**:260–261.

Jordan, D. S. 1908. The law of geminate species. *Amer. Nat.* **42**:73–80.

Jordan, D. S. and C. H. Gilbert. 1882a. List of fishes collected at Mazatlán, Mexico, by Charles H. Gilbert. *Bull. U.S. Fish Comm.*, Part 2:105–108.

Jordan, D. S. and C. H. Gilbert. 1882b. List of fishes collected by Lieut. Henry E. Nichols, U.S.N., in the Gulf of California, with descriptions of four new species. *Proc. U.S. Natl. Mus.* **4**(for 1881):273–279.

Jordan, D. S. and C. H. Gilbert. 1882c. Descriptions of thirty-three new species of fishes from Mazatlán, Mexico. *Proc. U.S. Natl. Mus.* **4**(for 1881):338–365.

Jordan, D. S. and C. H. Gilbert. 1883. Catalogue of the fishes collected by Mr. John Xantus at Cape San Lucas, which are now in the United States National Museum, with descriptions of eight new species. *Proc. U.S. Natl. Mus.* **5**(for 1882):353–371.

Jordan, D. S. and E. C. Starks. 1907. Notes on fishes from the island of Santa Catalina, Southern California. *Proc. U.S. Natl. Mus.* **32**(1510):67–77.

Kerstitch, A. N. 1970. Collecting in the Sea of Cortez. *Salt Water Aquarium*, **6**(3):168–176.

Kerstitch, A. N. 1971. Sailfin blenny from Gulf of California. *Salt Water Aquarium* **7**(2):79–81.

Kerstitch, A. N. 1973. Living jewels of the Sea of Cortez. *Dive Magazine* (April) **6**(4):48.

Kerstitch, A. N. 1976. Collecting jawfish with a spear. *Salt Water Aquarium* **10**:34–35.

Kerstitch, A. N. 1977. Butterflies and angels of the Sea of Cortez. *Marine Aquarist*, **7**(9):17–28.

Knaggs, E. H., J. S. Sunada, and R. N. Lea. 1975. Notes on some fishes collected off the outer coast of Baja California. *Calif. Fish & Game* **61**(1):56–59.

Krejsa, R. J. 1960. The eastern tropical Pacific fishes of the genus *Blenniolus*, including a new island endemic. *Copeia* **1960**(4):322–336.

Lavenberg, R. J. and J. E. Fitch. 1966. Annotated list of fishes collected by midwater trawl in the Gulf of California, March-April 1964. *Calif. Fish & Game* **52**(2):92–110.

Leis, J. M. (in press). Systematics and zoogeography of the genus *Diodon* (Pisces: Diodontidae) with comments on egg and larval development. *Fishery Bulletin*.

Lidner, M. J. 1947. The commercial marine fishes, crustaceans and mollusks of the west coast of Mexico. *Trans. Amer. Fish Soc.* **74** (for 1944):71–80.

Lindquist, D. G. 1975. Comparative behavior and ecology of Gulf of California chaenopsid blennies. Ph.D. diss., University of Arizona, Tucson. 147 pp.

Lockley, A. S. 1952. Description of the young of the kyphosid fish, *Hermosilla azurea,* from California. *Copeia* **1952**(1):42.

Losey, G. S. 1968. The comparative behavior of some Pacific fishes of the genus *Hypsoblennius* Gill (Blenniidae). Ph.D. diss., University of California, San Diego. 276 pp.

Losey, G. S. 1972. Predation protection in the poison-fang blenny, *Meiacanthus atrodorsalis,* and its mimics, *Ecsenius bicolor* and *Runula laudandus* (Blenniidae). *Pac. Sci.* **26**:129–139.

Losey, G. S. 1976. The significance of coloration in fishes of the genus *Hypsoblennius* Gill. *Bull. So. Calif. Acad. Sci.* **75**(2):183–198.

McCleneghan, K. 1976. Vertebral counts of some Pacific morays (family Muraenidae). *Copeia* **1976**(1):207–210. Errata in *Copeia* **1976**(4):847.

McCosker, J. E. 1977. The osteology, classification, and relationships of the eel family Ophichthidae. *Proc. Calif. Acad. Sci.* **41**(1):1–123.

McCosker, J. E. and C. E. Dawson. 1975. Biotic passage through the Panama Canal, with particular reference to fishes. *Mar. Biol.* **30**:343–351.

McCosker, J. E. and R. H. Rosenblatt. 1975a. The moray eels (Pisces: Muraenidae) of the Galápagos Islands, with new records and synonymies of extralimital species. *Proc. Calif. Acad. Sci.* **40**(13):417–427.

McCosker, J. E. and R. H. Rosenblatt. 1975b. Fishes collected at Malpelo Island. *In* The biological investigation of Malpelo Island, Colombia. J. D. Graham, Ed. *Smithsonian Contrib. Zool.,* **176**:91–93.

McCosker, J. E., L. R. Taylor, Jr., and R. R. Warner. 1978. Ichthyological studies at Galapagos. *Noticias de Galapagos* (Charles Darwin Foundation, Galapagos Isles) **27**:13–15.

McCourt, R. M. and D. A. Thomson. (MS) Notes on a facultative cleaner, the Panamic sergeant major (*Abudefduf troschelii*), in the tropical eastern Pacific.

McPhail, J. D. 1958. Key to the croakers (Sciaenidae) of the eastern Pacific. *Univ. Brit. Columbia, Inst. Fish., Mus. Contrib.* **2.** 20 pp.

McPhail, J. D. 1961. A review of the tropical eastern Pacific species of *Pareques* (Sciaenidae). *Copeia* **1961**(1):27–32.

Miles, P. S. 1974. Agonistic behavior of some gobiid fishes from the Gulf of California. Ph.D. diss., University of Arizona, Tucson. 158 pp.

Miller, P. J. 1973. The osteology and adaptive features of *Rhyacichthys aspro* (Teleostei: Gobioidei) and the classification of gobioid fishes. *J. Zool. (London)* **171**(3):397–434.

Miller, R. R. 1953. Second specimen of the eel *Gorgasia punctata,* an addition to the known fish fauna of Mexico. *Copeia* **1953**(4):236–237.

Molles, M. C., Jr. 1976. Fish species diversity on model and natural patch reefs: experimental insular biogeography. Ph.D. diss., University of Arizona, Tucson. 176 pp. (in press, *Ecol. Monogr.*).

Montgomery, W. L. 1975. Interspecific associations of sea basses (Serranidae) in the Gulf of California. *Copeia* **1975**(4):785–787.

Montgomery, W. L. 1978. Mechanisms of herbivory in damselfishes (Pomacentridae) from the Gulf of California, Mexico. Ph.D. diss., Arizona State University, Tempe. 91 pp.

Morris, R. A. and D. E. Morris. 1967. A rare hawkfish *Oxycirrhites typus* Bleeker found in Hawaii. *Ichthyologica* **39**(2):71–72.

Morrow, J. E. 1957. Shore and pelagic fishes from Peru, with new records and the description of a new species of *Sphoeroides. Bull. Bingham Oceanog. Coll.* **16**(2):5–55.

Moser, H. G., E. H. Ahlstrom, and E. M. Sandknop. 1977. Guide to the identification of scorpionfish larvae (Family Scorpaenidae) in the eastern Pacific with comparative notes on species of *Sebastes* and *Helicolenus* from other oceans. *NOAA Tech. Rep., NMFS Cir.* **402.** 71 pp.

Myers, G. S. 1935. A new genus of opisthognathid fishes. Reports on the collections obtained by the first Johnson-Smithsonian deep-sea expedition to the Puerto Rican deep. *Smithsonian Misc. Coll.* **91**(23):1–5.

Myers, G. S. 1958. The priacanthid fish genus *Pristigenys. Stanford Ichthyol. Bull.* **7**(3):40–42.

Myers, G. S. and C. B. Wade. 1941. Four new genera and ten new species of eels from the Pacific coast of tropical America, *Allan Hancock Pac. Exped.* (University of Southern California) **9**(4):65–111.

Myers, G. S. and C. B. Wade. 1946. New fishes of the families Dactyloscopidae, Microdesmidae, and Antennariidae from the west coast of Mexico and the Galapagos Islands, with a brief account of the use of rotenone fish poisons in ichthyological collecting. *Allan Hancock Pac. Exped.* (University of Southern California) **9**(6):151–178.

Nelson, E. M. 1955. The morphology of the swim bladder and auditory bulla in the Holocentridae. *Fieldiana (Zool.) Chicago Nat. Hist. Mus.* **37**:121–130.

Nichols, J. T. and R. C. Murphy. 1922. On a collection of marine fishes from Peru. *Bull. Amer. Mus. Nat. Hist.* **46**(9):501–516.

Norris, K. S. 1963. The functions of temperature in the ecology of the percoid fish *Girella nigricans* (Ayres). *Ecol. Monogr.* **33**:23–62.

287

## Specific Bibliography

Norris, K. S. and J. H. Prescott. 1959. Jaw structure and tooth replacement in the opaleye, *Girella nigricans* (Ayres) with notes on other species. *Copeia* **1959**(4):275–283.

Nursall, J. R. 1977. Territoriality in redlip blennies (*Ophioblennius atlanticus*—Pisces: Blenniidae). *J. Zool.* (*Lond.*) **182**:205–223.

Orcés, G. 1959. Peces marinos del Ecuador que se conservan en las colecciones de Quito. *Ciencia y Naturaleza* 2(2):72–91.

Osburn, R. C. and J. T. Nichols. 1916. Shore fishes collected by the "Albatross" expedition in Lower California with descriptions of new species. *Bull. Amer. Mus. Nat. Hist.* **35**(16):139–181.

Pietsch, T. W. and D. B. Grobecker. 1978. The compleat angler: aggressive mimicry in an antennariid anglerfish. *Science* **201**:369–370.

Poll, M. and N. Leleup. 1965. Un poisson aveugle nouveau de la famille des Brotulidae provenant des îles Galapagos. *Bulletin de l'Académie Royale de Belgique* (Classe des Sciences). Ser. 5, 51, **1965**(4):464–474.

Raju, S. N. 1974. Distribution, growth and metamorphosis of leptocephali of the garden eels, *Taenioconger* sp. and *Gorgasia* sp. *Copeia* **1974**(2):494–500.

Ramirez-Granados, R. and M. L. Sevilla. 1963. Lista preliminar de recursos pesqueros de Mexico marinos y de agua dulce. *Nociones sobre Hidrobiologia aplicada a la Pesca, Serie Trab. de Divul.* **5**(42):325–361.

Ramirez-Hernandez, E. 1965. Estudios preliminares sobre los peces marinos de Mexico. *Anales del Instituto Nacional de Investigaciones Biologico-Pesqueras,* **1**:257–292.

Ramirez-Hernandez, E. and J. Arvizu-Martinez. 1965. Investigaciones ictiologicas en las costas de Baja California. I. Lista de peces marinos de Baja California colectados en el periodo 1961–1965. *Anales del Instituto Nacional de Investigaciones Biologico-Pesqueras.* **1**:293–324.

Randall, J. E. 1955. An analysis of the genera of surgeon fishes (family Acanthuridae). *Pac. Sci.* **9**(3):359–367.

Randall, J. E. 1956. A revision of the surgeon fish genus *Acanthurus. Pac. Sci.* **10**(2):159–235.

Randall, J. E. 1958. A review of ciguatera, tropical fish poisoning, with a tentative explanation of its cause. *Bull. Mar. Sci. Gulf & Caribb.* **8**(3):236–267.

Randall, J. E. 1960. A new species of *Acanthurus* from the Caroline Islands, with notes on the systematics of other Indo-Pacific surgeonfishes. *Pac. Sci.* **14**(3):267–279.

Randall, J. E. 1961. A record of the kyphosid fish *Sector ocyurus* (= *azureus*) from the Society Islands. *Copeia* **1961**(3):357–358.

Randall, J. E. 1963a. Review of the hawkfishes (Family Cirrhitidae). *Proc. U.S. Natl. Mus.* **114**:389–451.

Randall, J. E. 1963b. Notes on the systematics of parrotfishes (Scaridae), with emphasis on sexual dichromatism. *Copeia* **1963**(2):225–237.

Randall, J. E. 1964. A revision of the filefish genera *Amanses* and *Cantherhines. Copeia* **1964**(2):331–361.

Randall, J. E. 1965. A review of the razorfish genus *Hemipteronotus* (Labridae) of the Atlantic Ocean. *Copeia* **1965**(4):487–501.

Randall, J. E. 1967. Food habits of reef fishes of the West Indies. *Stud. Trop. Oceanogr.* **5**:665–847.

Randall, J. E. 1968. *Ioglossus helenae,* a new gobiid fish from the West Indies. *Ichthyologica* **39** (3/4, July–December 1967):107–116.

Randall, J. E. 1969. How dangerous is the moray eel? *Austr. Nat. Hist:* 177–182.

Randall, J. E. 1972. The Hawaiian trunkfishes of the genus *Ostracion. Copeia* **1972**(4):756–768.

Randall, J. E. 1974. The effect of fishes on coral reefs. *Proc. Second Int. Coral Reef Sympos.* (Great Barrier Reef Committee Brisbane, October 1974). **1**:159–166.

Randall, J. E. 1976. The endemic shore fishes of the Hawaiian Islands, Lord Howe Island and Easter Island. Colloque Commerson 1973, *O.R.S.T.O.M. Travaux et Documents* No. 47:49–73.

Randall, J. E., K. Aida, T. Hibiya, N. Mitsuura, H. Kamiya, and Y. Hashimoto. 1971. Grammistin, the skin toxin of soapfishes, and its significance in the classification of the Grammistidae. *Publ. Seto Mar. Biol. Lab.* **19**(2–3):157–190.

Randall, J. E. and J. E. Böhlke. 1965. Review of the Atlantic labrid fishes of the genus *Halichoeres. Proc. Acad. Nat. Sci. Philadelphia.* **117**(7):235–259.

Randall, J. E. and D. K. Caldwell. 1966. A review of the sparid fish genus *Calamus,* with descriptions of four new species. *Bull. Los Angeles Co. Mus. Nat. Hist.* **2.** 47 pp.

Randall, J. E. and D. K. Caldwell. 1970. Clarification of the species of the butterflyfish genus *Forcipiger. Copeia* **1970**(4):727–731.

Randall, J. E. and W. D. Hartman. 1968. Sponge-feeding fishes of the West Indies. *Mar. Biol.* **1**(3):216–225.

Randall, J. E. and J. E. McCosker. 1975. The eels of Easter Island with a description of a new moray. *Nat. Hist. Mus. Los Angeles Co. Contrib. Sci.* No. 264. 32 pp.

Reid, E. D. 1940. A new genus and species of pearl fish, Family Carapidae, from off Gorgona Island, Colombia. *Allan Hancock Pac. Exped.* (University of Southern California) 9(2):47–50.

Reynolds, W. W. and L. J. Reynolds. 1977. Observations on food habits of the angelfishes, *Pomacanthus zonipectus* and *Holacanthus passer* in the Gulf of California. *Calif. Fish & Game* 63(2):124–125.

Ricker, K. E. 1959a. Mexican shore and pelagic fishes collected from Acapulco to Cape San Lucas during the 1957 cruise of the "Marijean." *Univ. Brit. Columbia Inst. Fish., Mus. Contrib.* 3. 18 pp.

Ricker, K. E. 1959b. Fishes collected from the Revillagigedo Islands during the 1954–1958 cruises of the "Marijean." *Univ. Brit. Columbia Inst. Fish., Mus. Contrib.* 4. 10 pp.

Robertson, D. R. 1972. Social control of sex reversal in a coral-reef fish. *Science* 177:1007–1009.

Robins, C. R. 1971. Distributional patterns of fishes from coastal and shelf waters of the tropical western Atlantic. In *Symposium on investigations and resources of the Caribbean Sea and adjacent regions.* FAO, Fish. Rep. 71–72, pp. 249–255.

Robins, C. R., C. Phillips, and F. Phillips. 1959. Some aspects of the behavior of the blennioid fish *Chaenopsis ocellata* Poey. *Zoologica* 44(2):77–88.

Robins, C. R. and W. A. Starck, II. 1961. Materials for a revision of *Serranus* and related fish genera. *Proc. Acad. Nat. Sci. Philadelphia* 113(11):259–314.

Roden, G. I. and G. W. Groves. 1959. Recent oceanographic investigations in the Gulf of California. *J. Mar. Res.,* 18:10–35.

Rosen, D. E. 1975. A vicariance model of Caribbean biogeography. *Syst. Zool.* 24(4):431–464.

Rosenblatt, R. H. 1959. A revisionary study of the blennioid fish family Tripterygiidae. Ph.D. diss., University of California, Los Angeles. 376 pp.

Rosenblatt, R. H. 1960. The Atlantic species of the blennioid fish genus *Enneanectes. Proc. Acad. Nat. Sci. Philadelphia* 112(1):1–23.

Rosenblatt, R. H. 1961. A new pearlfish (Family Carapidae) from the Gulf of California. *Proc. Biol. Soc. Wash.* 74:207–212.

Rosenblatt, R. H. 1963a. Some aspects of speciation in marine shore fishes. *Syst. Assoc. Publ. No. 5* (Speciation in the sea):171–180.

Rosenblatt, R. H. 1963b. Differential growth of the ilicium and second dorsal spine of *Antennatus strigatus* (Gill) and its bearing on the validity of *A. reticularis* (Gilbert). *Copeia* 1963(2):462–464.

Rosenblatt, R. H. 1967a. The zoogeographic relationships of the marine shore fishes of tropical America. *Stud. Trop. Oceanogr.* 5:579–592.

Rosenblatt, R. H. 1967b. The osteology of the congrid eel *Gorgasia punctata* and the relationships of the Heterocongrinae. *Pac. Sci.* 21(1):91–97.

Rosenblatt, R. H. 1974. Book review of *Marine Zoogeography* by John C. Briggs. New York: McGraw-Hill. *Science* 186:1028.

Rosenblatt, R. H. and E. S. Hobson. 1969. Parrotfishes (Scaridae) of the eastern Pacific, with a generic rearrangement of the Scarinae. *Copeia* 1969(3):434–453.

Rosenblatt, R. H. and D. F. Hoese. 1968. Sexual dimorphism in the dentition of *Pseudupeneus,* and its bearing on the generic classification of the Mullidae. *Copeia* 1968(1):175–176.

Rosenblatt, R. H. and G. D. Johnson. 1974. Two new species of sea basses of the genus *Diplectrum,* with a key to the Pacific species. *Calif. Fish & Game* 60(4):178–191.

Rosenblatt, R. H., J. E. McCosker, and I. Rubinoff. 1972. Indo-west Pacific fishes from the Gulf of Chiriqui, Panama. *Contrib. Sci. Nat. Hist. Mus. Los Angeles Co.* 234. 18 pp.

Rosenblatt, R. H. and W. L. Montgomery. 1976. *Kryptophaneron harveyi,* a new anomalopid fish from the eastern tropical Pacific, and the evolution of the Anomalopidae. *Copeia* 1976(3):510–515.

Rosenblatt, R. H. and T. D. Parr. 1967. The identity of the blenny *Paraclinus altivelis* (Lockington) and the status of *P. sinus* Hubbs. *Copeia* 1967(3):675–677.

Rosenblatt, R. H. and T. D. Parr. 1969. The Pacific species of the clinid fish genus *Paraclinus. Copeia* 1969(1):1–20.

Rosenblatt, R. H. and J. S. Stephens, Jr. 1978. *Mccoskerichthys sandae,* a new and unusual chaenopsid blenny from the Pacific coast of Panama and Costa Rica. *Contrib. Sci. Nat. Hist. Mus. Los Angeles Co.* 293. 22 pp.

Rosenblatt, R. H. and L. R. Taylor, Jr. 1971. The Pacific species of the clinid fish tribe Starksiini. *Pac. Sci.* 25(3):436–463.

Rosenblatt, R. H. and L. R. Taylor, Jr. 1972. A second record of *Starksia posthon* (Clinidae) with an expanded description. *Copeia* 1972(3):599.

Rosenblatt, R. H. and B. W. Walker. 1963. The marine shore fishes of the Galapagos Islands. *Calif. Acad. Sci., Occ. Papers,* 44:97–106.

Rosenblatt, R. H. and B. J. Zahuranec. 1967. The eastern Pacific groupers of the genus *Mycteroperca;* including a new species. *Calif. Fish & Game* 53(4):228–245.

Rubinoff, R. W. and I. Rubinoff. 1968. Interoceanic colonization of a marine goby through the Panama Canal. *Nature* 217(5127):476–478.

## Specific Bibliography

Rubinoff, R. W. and I. Rubinoff. 1969. Observations on the migration of a marine goby through the Panama Canal. *Copeia* **1969**(2):395–397.

Rubinoff, R. W. and I. Rubinoff. 1971. Geographic and reproductive isolation in Atlantic and Pacific populations of Panamanian *Bathygobius*. *Evolution* **25**:88–97.

Rutter, C. 1904. Notes on fishes from the Gulf of California, with the description of a new genus and species. *Proc. Calif. Acad. Sci.* **3**(8):251–254.

Schultz, L. P. 1942. Notes on some fishes from the Gulf of California with the description of a new genus and species of blennioid fish. *J. Wash. Acad. Sci.* **32**(5):153–156.

Schultz, L. P. 1957. The frogfishes of the family Antennariidae. *Proc. U.S. Natl. Mus.* **107**(3383):47–105.

Schultz, L. P. 1958. Review of the parrotfishes, family Scaridae. *Bull. U.S. Natl. Mus.* No. **214**. 143 pp.

Schultz, L. P. 1966. *Pseudorhegma diagramma,* a new genus and species of grammistid fish, with a key to genera of the family and to the species of the subfamily Pseudogramminae. *Ichthyologica* **38**(4):185–194.

Schultz, L. P. 1969. Taxonomic status of the controversial genera and species of parrotfishes, with descriptive list (family Scariidae). *Smithsonian Contrib. Zool.* No. 17. 49 pp.

Schultz, L. P. and E. D. Reid. 1939. A revision of the soapfishes of the genus *Rypticus. Proc. U.S. Natl. Mus.* **87**(3074):261–270.

Seale, A. 1940. Report on fishes from Allan Hancock Expeditions in the California Academy of Sciences. *Allan Hancock Pac. Exped.* (University of Southern California) **9**(1):1–46.

Shiino, S. M. 1976. List of common names of fishes of the world, those prevailing among English-speaking nations. *Sci. Rept. Shima Marineland* (Mie, Japan). **4**:1–262.

Shipp, R. L. 1974. The pufferfishes (Tetraodontidae) of the Atlantic Ocean. *Publ. Gulf Coast Res. Lab. Mus.* No. **4**. 162 pp.

Smith, C. L. 1961. Synopsis of biological data on groupers (*Epinephelus* and allied genera) of the western North Atlantic. *FAO Fisher. Biol., Synopsis* No. 23. 61 pp.

Smith, C. L. 1965. The patterns of sexuality and the classification of serranid fishes. *Amer. Mus. Nat. Hist. Novitates* No. 2207. 20 pp.

Smith, C. L. 1971. A revision of the American groupers: *Epinephelus* and allied genera. *Bull. Amer. Mus. Nat. Hist.,* **146**(2):67–242.

Smith, C. L. and E. H. Atz. 1969. The sexual

mechanism of the reef bass *Pseudogramma bermudensis* and its implications in the classification of the Pseudogrammidae (Pisces: Perciformes). *Z. Morph. Tiere* **65**:315–326.

Smith, C. L. and J. C. Tyler. 1972. Space resource sharing in a coral reef fish community. *In* Results of the Tektite program: ecology of coral reef fishes. B. B. Collette and S. A. Earle, Eds. *Nat. Hist. Mus. Los Angeles Co., Sci. Bull.* **14**:125–170.

Smith, C. L. and P. H. Young. 1966. Gonad structure and the reproductive cycle of the kelp bass, *Paralabrax clathratus* (Girard), with comments on the relationships of the serranid genus *Paralabrax. Calif. Fish & Game* **52**(4):283–292.

Smith, J. L. B. 1966. Fishes of the sub-family Nasinae with a synopsis of the Prionurinae. *Ichthyol. Bull. Rhodes Univ.* **32**:635–682.

Smith, R. 1886. On *Tetraodon setosus,* a new species allied to *Tetraodon meleagris* Lacép. *Bull. Calif. Acad. Sci.* **2**(6):155–156.

Smith, R. L. and A. C. Paulson. 1974. Food transit times and gut pH in two Pacific parrotfishes. *Copeia* **1974**(3):796–799.

Smith-Vaniz, W. F. and V. G. Springer. 1971. Synopsis of the tribe Salariini, with description of five new genera and three new species (Pisces: Blenniidae). *Smithsonian Contrib. Zool.* No. 73. 72 pp.

Snodgrass, R. E. and E. Heller. 1905. Papers from the Hopkins-Stanford Galápagos Expedition, 1898–1899. 17. Shore fishes of the Revillagigedo, Clipperton, Cocos and Galápagos Islands. *Proc. Wash. Acad. Sci.* **6**:333–427.

Springer, V. G. 1955. The taxonomic status of the fishes of the genus *Stathmonotus,* including a review of the Atlantic species. *Bull. Mar. Sci. Gulf & Caribb.* **5**(1):66–80.

Springer, V. G. 1958. Systematics and zoogeography of the clinid fishes of the subtribe Labrisomini Hubbs. *Inst. Mar. Sci.* (University of Texas), *Publ.* **5**:417–492.

Springer, V. G. 1959b. A new species of *Labrisomus* from the Caribbean Sea, with notes on other fishes of the subtribe Labrisomini. *Copeia* **1959**(4):289–292.

Springer, V. G. 1962. A review of the blenniid fishes of the genus *Ophioblennius* Gill. *Copeia* **1962**(2):426–433.

Springer, V. G. 1967. Revision of the circumtropical shorefish genus *Entomacrodus* (Blenniidae: Salariinae). *Proc. U.S. Natl. Mus.* **122**(3582):1–150.

Springer, V. G. 1968. Osteology and classification of the fishes of the family Blenniidae. *Bull. U.S. Natl. Mus.* No. 284. 85 pp.

Springer, V. G. and M. F. Gomon. 1975. Variation in the western Atlantic clinid fish *Malacoctenus trian-*

*gulatus* with a revised key to the Atlantic species of *Malacoctenus. Smithsonian Contrib. Zool.* **200.** 11 pp.

Springer, V. G. and R. H. Rosenblatt, 1965. A new blennioid fish of the genus *Labrisomus* from Ecuador, with notes on the Caribbean species *L. filamentosus. Copeia* **1965**(1):25–27.

Springer, V. G. and W. F. Smith-Vaniz. 1972. Mimetic relationships involving fishes of the family Blenniidae. *Smithsonian Contrib. Zool.* **112.** 35 pp.

Squires, D. 1959. Results of the *Puritan*-American Museum Natural History Expedition to western Mexico. 7. Corals and coral reefs in the Gulf of California. *Bull. Am. Mus. Natur. Hist.* **118**(7):367–432.

Stephens, J. S., Jr. 1963. A revised classification of the blennioid fishes of the American Family Chaenopsidae. *Univ. Calif. Publ. Zool.* **68.** 165 pp.

Stephens, J. S., Jr., E. S. Hobson, and R. K. Johnson. 1966. Notes on distribution, behavior, and morphological variation in some chaenopsid fishes from the tropical eastern Pacific, with descriptions of two new species, *Acanthemblemaria castroi* and *Coralliozetus springeri. Copeia* **1966**(3):424–438.

Stephens, J. S., Jr., R. K. Johnson, G. S. Key, and J. E. McCosker. 1970. The comparative ecology of three sympatric species of California blennies of the genus *Hypsoblennius* Gill (Teleostomi, Blenniidae). *Ecol. Monogr.* **40**(2):213–233.

Stephens, J. S., Jr. and V. G. Springer. 1973. Clinid fishes of Chile and Peru, with description of a new species, *Myxodes ornatus,* from Chile. *Smithsonian Contrib. Zool.* **159.** 24 pp.

Strasburg, D. W. 1962. Pelagic stages of *Zanclus canescens* from Hawaii. *Copeia* **1962**(4):844–845.

Suarez, S. S. 1975. Reproductive biology of *Ogilbia cayorum,* a viviparous brotulid fish. *Bull. Mar. Sci.* **25**(2):143–173.

Thomson, D. A. 1964. Ostracitoxin: an ichthyotoxic stress secretion of the boxfish, *Ostracion lentiginosus. Science* **146**:244–245.

Thomson, D. A. 1968. Trunkfish toxins. *In Trans. Drugs from the Sea Conf., Mar. Tech. Soc.,* pp. 203–211.

Thomson, D. A. 1969. Toxic stress secretions of the boxfish *Ostracion meleagris* Shaw. *Copeia* **1969**(2):335–352.

Thomson, D. A. and C. A. Flanagan. 1977. Golden Puffer Award. *Assoc. Syst. Coll. Newsletter* **5**(2):17.

Thomson, D. A. and K. A. Muench. 1976. Influence of tides and waves on the spawning behavior of the Gulf of California grunion, *Leuresthes sardina* (Jenkins and Evermann). *Bull. S. Calif. Acad. Sci.*

Todd, E. S. and A. W. Ebeling. 1966. Aerial respiration in the longjaw mudsucker *Gillichthys mirabilis* (Teleostei: Gobiidae). *Biol. Bull.* **130**(2):265–288.

Trott, L. B. 1970. Contributions to the biology of carapid fishes (Paracanthopterygii: Gadiformes). *Univ. Calif. Publ. Zool.* **89.** 60 pp.

Vaillant, L. L. 1894. Sur une collection de poissons recueillie en Basse-California et dans le Golfe par M. Leon Diguet. *Proc. Soc. Philomath. Paris,* Ser. 8, **6**:69–75.

Wade, C. B. 1946a. Two new genera and five new species of apodal fishes from the eastern Pacific. *Allan Hancock Pac. Exped.* (University of Southern California) **9**(7):181–213.

Wade, C. B. 1946b. New fishes in the collections of the Allan Hancock Foundation. *Allan Hancock Pac. Exped.* (University of Southern California) **9**(8):215–237.

Wales, J. H. 1932. Report on two collections of Lower California marine fishes. *Copeia* **1932**(4):163–168.

Walker, B. W., Ed. 1961. The ecology of the Salton Sea, California, in relation to the sportfishery. Sacramento: Calif. Dept. Fish & Game, *Fish Bull.* **113**:1–204.

Walker, B. W. 1966. The origins and affinities of the Galápagos shorefishes. *In* "The Galápagos; proceedings of the symposia of the Galápagos scientific project". R. I. Bowman, Ed. Berkeley: University of California Press. 318 pp.

Warner, R. R. 1975a. The adaptive significance of sequential hermaphroditism in animals. *Amer. Nat.* **109**(965):61–82.

Warner, R. R. 1975b. The reproductive biology of the protogynous hermaphrodite *Pimelometopon pulchrum* (Pisces: Labridae). *Fishery Bull.* **73**:262–283.

Wickler, W. 1964. *Emblemaria pandionis* (Blenniidae) Kampfverhalten. *Encyclopaedia Cinematographica,* E 517/**1963**:1–7.

Wiley, J. W. 1974. Observations on the use of mucus envelopes by the California sheephead, *Pimelometopon pulchrum,* on southern California rock reefs. *Copeia* **1974**(3):789–790.

Wiley, J. W. 1976. Life histories and systematics of the western North American gobies *Lythrypnus dalli* (Gilbert) and *Lythrypnus zebra* (Gilbert). *Trans. San Diego Soc. Nat. Hist.* **18**(10):169–184.

Winterbottom, R. 1971. Movement of the caudal spine of some surgeonfishes (Acanthuridae, Perciformes). *Copeia* **1971**(3):562–566.

Winterbottom, R. 1974. The familial phylogeny of the Tetraodontiformes (Acanthopterygii: Pisces) as evidenced by their comparative myology. *Smithsonian Contrib. Zool.* No. 155. 201 pp.

Woods, L. P. 1965. A new squirrelfish, *Adioryx poco* of the family Holocentridae, from the Bahama Islands. *Notulae Naturae* (Acad. Nat. Sci. Phil.) No. 377. 5 pp.

Woods, L. P. and G. R. Allen (in press). A review of the damselfish genus *Eupomacentrus* from the eastern Pacific with the description of a new species. *Fieldiana* (*Zool.*), *Chicago Nat. Hist. Mus.*

Woods, L. P. and L. P. Schultz. 1966. Family Tetraodontidae. In *Fishes of the Marshall and Marianas Islands* (L. P. Schultz and collaborators). *Bull. U.S. Natl. Mus.* 202, **3:**128–136.

Woods, L. P. and P. M. Sonoda. 1973. Order Berycomorphi (Beryciformes). *In* Fishes of the western North Atlantic. *Sears Found. Mar. Res. Mem. 1,* Part 6:263–396.

# Index

Bold page numbers indicate pages on which illustrations appear.

293

297